Russia's Lost Reformation

Russia's Lost Reformation

Peasants, Millennialism, and Radical Sects
in Southern Russia and Ukraine,
1830–1917

Sergei I. Zhuk

Woodrow Wilson Center Press
Washington, D.C.

The Johns Hopkins University Press
Baltimore and London

Editorial Offices
Woodrow Wilson Center Press
One Woodrow Wilson Plaza
1300 Pennsylvania Avenue, N.W.
Washington, D.C. 20004-3027
Telephone: 202-691-4010
www.wilsoncenter.org

Order from
The Johns Hopkins University Press
Hampden Station
P.O. Box 50370
Baltimore, Maryland 21211
Telephone: 1-800-537-5487
www.press.jhu.edu

9 8 7 6 5 4 3 2 1

Library of Congress Cataloging-in-Publication Data

Zhuk, Sergei I.
    Russia's lost reformation: peasants, millennialism, and radical sects in Southern
Russia and Ukraine, 1830–1917 / Sergei I. Zhuk.
        p. cm.
    Includes bibliographical references and index.
    ISBN 0-8018-7915-9 (hardcover : alk. paper)
    1. Dissenters, Religious—Russia—History—19th century.   2. Heresies,
Christian—Russia—History—19th century.   3. Christian sects—Russia—
History—19th century.   I. Title.
    BX599.Z48 2004
    274.7′081—dc22   2004003026

About the Center

The Center is the living memorial of the United States of America to the nation's twenty-eighth president, Woodrow Wilson. Congress established the Woodrow Wilson Center in 1968 as an international institute for advanced study, "symbolizing and strengthening the fruitful relationship between the world of learning and the world of public affairs." The Center opened in 1970 under its own board of trustees.

In all its activities the Woodrow Wilson Center is a nonprofit, nonpartisan organization, supported financially by annual appropriations from the Congress, and by the contributions of foundations, corporations, and individuals. Conclusions or opinions expressed in Center publications and programs are those of the authors and speakers and do not necessarily reflect the views of the Center staff, fellows, trustees, advisory groups, or any individuals or organizations that provide financial support to the Center.

To my wife Irina and my son Andrei

Contents

x

Figures

Figures

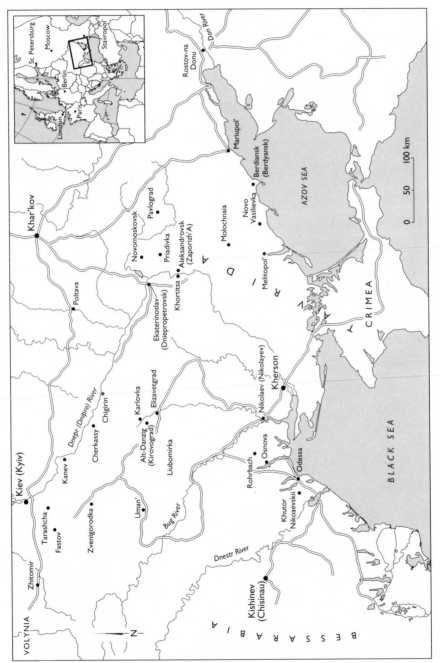

Southern Provinces of the Russian Empire

Preface

Radical theology and religious practices have posed serious problems for established Christianity from its earliest days. In particular, "the pursuit of the Millennium"—anticipation of the Second Advent of Jesus Christ—has provoked unusual social activism and experimentation among Christian radicals who have rejected traditional cultural norms and church hierarchy. During the twelfth and thirteenth centuries, for instance, religious radicalism plagued both versions of Christianity—the Western (Roman) Catholic Church and the Eastern (Greek) Orthodox Church. The activities of the Cathari sect in southern France led to the Albigensian Crusade, which sought to root out this heresy of religious ascetics who rejected the rules and "hypocrisy" of the Church in Rome. The Albigensian heretics expected the coming of a utopian "millennial" heaven on earth that would replace the corrupt and unjust sinful world, which in their view was legitimized by the established church.

One hundred years later, in Orthodox Russia, the same theme of a utopian heaven on earth appeared in the teachings of the heretical Strigol'niki ("shornheads") in Novgorod. Later, in the sixteenth century, Feodosii Kosoi and his radical adherents developed a similar theology and religious practices in Muscovy. Their dissident activities and criticism of the state and church hierarchy led to brutal and bloody persecutions by Russia's Orthodox princes. Despite different historical circumstances and cultural forms, both Western and Russian religious dissenters demonstrated a similar desire to restore the purity of the first Christian communities.

The most radical of these dissenters tried to create conditions for the Millennium in the localities where they lived. They introduced common property and social equality, and those who resisted them were punished. In England, for example, the Lollards, radical followers of the Oxford theologian John Wycliffe, opposed the Roman Church on issues of transubstantiation, secular authority, and extensive landholdings. Itinerant Lollard preachers influenced the leaders of the Wat Tyler Rebellion in 1381, in which English peasants and artisans threatened the English crown itself. The Lollards' teachings also influenced a priest from Bohemia, Jan Huss, who preached the supremacy of the Bible and criticized the corruption of the Roman Church. The excommunication of Huss in 1411 and his execution in 1415 led to the Hussite movement in Bohemia. This movement eventually laid the foundation for the mass religious phenomenon that historians later called the Radical Reformation.

This Radical Reformation led in 1524 to the German Peasant's War and resulted in the first popular communist experiment in European history—the Münster commune of 1534–35. The various descendants of the Radical Reformation, including the Anabaptists and Quakers, influenced various countries of the Christian world in the course of modern history. When the social radicalism of these descendants tapered off in the eighteenth and nineteenth centuries, a new wave of religious radicals returned to the millennial traditions of the Radical Reformation. In the mid–nineteenth century, these traditions spread beyond the Western Christian world and reached as far as non-Christian China, where the Taiping Rebellion attempted to found a heavenly kingdom of social justice and equality under Christian slogans. This "radical reformation" also reached the Orthodox Russian Empire at roughly the same time, when millions of peasant dissidents sought to reform Orthodox Christianity according to the Divine Law of justice and equality. This book is a study of the forgotten Russian and Ukrainian pioneers of that radical evangelical tradition, which led to new social and cultural experimentation in the Russian Empire under the slogans of the Western Radical Reformation.

⌒　⌒

This book began as a story, which I had heard from our neighbors, the Ukrainian evangelicals, in the small town of Vatutino (in the Zvenigorodka district of the Cherkassy region) in Soviet Ukraine during the 1970s. These religious neighbors, who were known as "Stundists" (I did not know the meaning of this word in those days), were very secretive but very kind toward us, the local kids. My friends who played rock and roll in our high school band were hired by these Stundists to play religious hymns and songs for their worship meetings. We used to visit these meetings not because we were religious children but because we loved to hear how our band covered our favorite songs by the Beatles, the Rolling Stones, Led Zeppelin, and Pink Floyd with new religious lyrics in Russian and Ukrainian. This combination of rock music and the religious culture of the local evangelicals stimulated my interest in the story of the Ukrainian Stundists.

Unfortunately, as a Soviet historian, I could not do serious and honest research on the history of the Soviet evangelicals. Therefore, using my knowledge of English (gained mainly from my favorite Anglo-American rock songs), I decided to devote my research to a topic very remote from the problems of "modern ideological struggle": colonial British America before the Revolutionary War. While doing my research on the Pennsylvania Quakers and Mennonites, I discovered that the theology and religious practices of my former evangelical friends from Vatutino were similar to those of these early American religious radicals. Moreover, after the collapse of the Soviet Union, I realized that my Ukrainian students were more interested in their own local Ukrainian history than in the formerly (before 1991) highly fashionable stories of American democracy. That is why I decided to do a comparative study of the radical evangelical traditions in British America and Russian Ukraine. When I moved to the United States in 1997, I began this study as a dissertation for a new (now American) Ph.D. in Russian history at Johns Hopkins University. XVII

By 2001, I had come to concentrate mostly on Russian and Ukrainian religious radicals, and as a result, I devoted my study entirely to a history of my childhood neighbors—the religious people still known as "Stundists" and "Shalaputs" in post-Soviet Ukraine. Therefore, my thanks go to these brave and suffering people who generated my interest in their story. I also express my gratitude to the Beatles, the Rolling Stones, Led Zeppelin, and Pink Floyd, whose music inspired my generation and pushed me in the direction of my "hidden transcripts" of everyday resistance to political and cultural domination in Soviet Ukraine. In 1994, Norman Fiering, director of the John Carter Brown Library at Brown University, and in 1997 my Mennonite friends at Goshen College, suggested that I write about the Ukrainian evangelicals in the context of the social and cultural history of imperial Russia. I offer them many thanks for this wonderful idea. This book is the fulfillment of my promise.

It would have been impossible for me to have done the research for this book without support from various people and organizations. First of all, the Department of History at Johns Hopkins University generously provided funding for four years of my research work, which resulted in my second (now American) dissertation. The Institute for Global Studies in Culture, Power & History at Johns Hopkins University financially supported my research in Russian and Ukrainian archives in 1998. I express my gratitude to Felicity S. Northcott and her colleagues at the Institute for Global Studies, who assisted me in this research. The International Research and Exchange Board provided support for eight months of research in Moscow, Saint Petersburg, Kiev, and Dniepropetrovsk in 1999 and 2000. I am much indebted to the staff of the Russian State Historical Archive in Saint Petersburg, the staff of the Dniepropetrovsk State Historical Museum, which allowed me to use pictures from the museum's collection, the Dniepropetrovsk State Regional Archive, and the Central State Historical Archive of Ukraine in Kiev for directing me to particularly useful material and for their tireless and good-natured assistance. The Kennan Institute for Advanced Russian Studies at the Woodrow Wilson International Center for Scholars awarded me a research fellowship, which enabled me to transform my dissertation into this book. The last, but very important, support for finishing the book came from the American

Council of Learned Societies, which awarded me a Library of Congress Fellowship in International Studies.

Nikolai Nikolaievich Bolkhovitinov and Jeffrey Brooks, the supervisors of my Soviet and American dissertations (respectively, at the Institute of World History in Moscow and at Johns Hopkins University in Baltimore), have always been model teachers, scholars, and guides; I am indebted to them for their interest and support. Both Nikolai Nikolaievich and Jeffrey gave warm encouragement at an early stage of my project and inspired me as imaginative and generous historians and persons. The suggestions and critical comments made by Alexandr Beznosov, Oksana Kudinova (Beznosova), Mikhail Dmitriev, Laura Engelstein, Jack P. Greene, David Goldfrank, Yaroslav Hrytsak, Nikolai Krementsov, Sergei Svetlenko, Daniel Todes, and Michael Zuckerman improved my manuscript. My research assistant Adam Fuss and my colleagues at the Woodrow Wilson Center not only polished the text during discussions but also contributed new ideas for the book. Nicholas Breyfogle, Alfred Rieber, and other participants in two conferences on the "Russian borderlands"— one at the Central European University in Budapest, the other at Ohio State University—read an earlier version of chapter 1 and provided many useful suggestions. My thanks especially go to David Bell, Peter Jelavich, Richard Kagan, Vernon Lidtke, William Rowe, Mary Ryan, Ronald Walters, and Judith Wolkowitz for leading a stimulating discussion of my papers at the History Department's seminars at Johns Hopkins University and for helping me to conceptualize some of my thoughts about popular religion, gender, and identity in world history.

A deep debt of gratitude also goes to the many friends and relatives who provided fellowship, intellectual nourishment, and good cheer, and who made life quite enjoyable in Russia and Ukraine during my research in the years 1997–2001: Nikolai Nikolaievich Bolkhovitinov and Liudmila Antonovna Bolkhovitinova; Svetlana E. Bozhkova and Boris N. Komissarov; Mikhail Dmitriev; Tamara Antonovna Kozintseva, Victor Kozintsev, and Marina Kozintseva; Eduard Svichar, and many others. Also, I express my gratitude to Henry Tom of the Johns Hopkins University Press and to Joseph Brinley and Yamile Kahn of the Woodrow Wilson Center Press for supporting my book   xix and polishing its text to perfection. Without their editing efforts, the book would not exist.

Finally, I wish to acknowledge those who have been the most helpful and supportive, without whom this book would not have been possible: my wife Irina and son Andrei, to whom this book is dedicated.

Throughout this book, the notes use the traditional system of notation for the sources from Russian and Ukrainian archives. The Russian (or Ukrainian) archival document usually is located by the collection, or "archival fund" (in Russian, *fond*); the inventory of this collection (in Russian, *opis'*); the number of the document in the inventory, or "archival case" (in Russian, *delo*); the number of pages, or "archival leaves" (in Russian, *leest*); and the sides of the pages, whether the front or reverse (in Russian, *oborot*) of the archival leaf. Therefore, for example, in the notation for a document, "f. 1234, op. 23 (1867), d. 34, l. 2–2ob." should be read as "archival collection 1234, inventory 23 for 1867, document 34, page 2 front to page 2 reverse side." Sometimes, in official documents, the authors used various registers, which were attached to the main text. In this case, the Russian word *vedomost'* in the notation indicates such a register. Finally, the manuscript collections of Russian libraries sometimes used the word *karton* (sometimes abbreviated "k.") instead of *opis'* (e.g., in such a collection of the Russian State—formerly Lenin—Library, a note for the document would look like this: f. 435, k. 67, d. 6).

Russia's Lost Reformation

Introduction: The Forgotten Pioneers of Radical Evangelicalism in Russia—Historiography, Theory, and Sources

In 1830, a peasant serf from the village Perevoz in the Kirsanov district of Tambov province, Avvakum (or Abakum Ivanovich) Kopylov, established special meetings for "reading and explaining" Holy Scripture in his house. Kopylov taught his neighbors to follow the Gospels as the main principle for life. He rejected the Orthodox Church's institutions, priesthood, sacraments, and rituals as contrary to the New Testament. He noted that all Orthodox Christians lived according to "Adam of the Old Testament" and therefore were the "sinful children of the Old Testament." Man was conceived in sin and born in sin. To be absolved of this sin, a man had to renounce the sinful world and live by fasting and prayer and avoiding women. Sexual intercourse with women was the most serious sin. To achieve salvation, pious Christians had to avoid "carnal" food: meat, fish, and also onions, garlic, potatoes, and alcohol. They had to stop smoking, swearing, and wearing "funny dresses and decorations." Instead of "carnal marriage," he advocated "spiritual love" for his adherents and replaced "spouses betrothed in the Orthodox Church" with "spiritual wives and husbands" (*dukhovnitsa* and *dukhovnik* in Russian). Kopylov stopped having sexual relations with his wife and discovered among his followers his own *dukhovnitsa,* a peasant woman from his village, Tatiana Makarovna Chernosvistova (called Remizova).

Notwithstanding these changes, Kopylov continued to live with his family and support his wife and children until his arrest. Eventually, he refused to work for landlords, refused to perform corvee, and ceased paying quit-rent to his own *barin* (landlord). Because of his industrious and thrifty lifestyle, he had saved enough money to pay for the emancipation of his family from serfdom. But the local priest denounced him as a heretic and religious dissenter, and the police arrested both him and his *dukhovnitsa* Remizova. He died in 1838 in the Kirsanov prison, and Remizova was exiled to Siberia at the beginning of the 1840s. His son, Phillip Kopylov, became his successor and the new leader of his father's followers, who were called the Tambov Postniks ("those who observe fasting").[1]

One of Kopylov's disciples, a peasant from his village, Perfil (Parfenii) Petrovich Katasonov (or Kutasonov), who originally had come to Kopylov's household as his servant at the beginning of the 1830s, quarreled with Kopylov's son Phillip, broke with Phillip's adherents, and founded his own religious sect. Katasonov followed Kopylov's teaching, and his community of "Old Israel" became the successor to the Tambov Postniks, who were called later the Bogomols ("those who pray to God"). Contrary to the conservatism of Phillip Kopylov's community, Katasonov's sect was open to various outside influences and attracted many adherents among the peasants of the central Russian provinces.[2] Kopylov and Katasonov became "pioneers" of the mass peasant religious movement, which combined the old traditions of Russian popular religion with strong evangelical influences. Their followers brought their ideas to the Caucasus, Tavrida, Ukraine, and Bessarabia during their migration to the South in the 1840s and contributed to a movement that sought to reform Russian Orthodoxy.

Eventually, this movement led to the spread of evangelical culture and various radical religious sects among the peasants of the southern frontier in the Russian Empire. These new sects among Russian and Ukrainian peasants that resulted were reminiscent of those in the West three and a half centuries earlier. The overwhelming majority of these sects shared the theology and practices of their Western counterparts. Therefore, it makes sense that these groups should be treated as a part of one international Christian movement, rather than as exotic characters in Russian religious history. This study is about the origins and evolution of these peasant sects and their radical evangelical culture in the southern European provinces of imperial Russia as part of that one movement.

The Lost and Forgotten Story of the Peasants' Radical Religion

The story of the peasants' radical religion was lost and forgotten by those who shared the official ideologies of first imperial Russia and then the Soviet Union because it did not fit the prevailing theories and historiographical mythologies of either political regime. Despite the dissenters' attempts at collaboration with other participants in the oppositional discourse in Russian history, their efforts at cultural dialogue were ignored and misinterpreted by Russian and Soviet historians. Moreover, their Orthodox neighbors, incited by the Orthodox clergy who exploited feelings of "class envy" among the poor peasants, opted against the chance for peaceful dialogue with the peasant evangelicals and unleashed a real cultural war against the religious dissenters. Orthodox priests sanctioned this cultural war and tried to present the dissenters as "cultural aliens" to the Russian Orthodox peasants.

The paradox of this confrontation was that the roots of the peasants' radical religion were in popular Orthodoxy itself. To some extent, the peasant evangelicals tried to be more rigorous and pious Orthodox believers than their less religious and more cynical neighbors. They constructed their religion by appropriating the available and well-known elements of Orthodoxy. But this mass religiosity of the peasants was a threat to the traditional hierarchy of the Orthodox Church because the new zealots challenged the traditional status of the Orthodox clerics. This religiosity showed the clerics' inadequacy and incompetence to work in the new conditions of the post-Emancipation era, especially the colonization of the South. This was the first real crisis for traditional

Orthodoxy, one that was provoked by the evangelicals.[3] That was why the administration of the Orthodox Church recommended that the local clergy portray these new sects as antihumane and politically subversive.

Thus, the officials of the Holy Synod advised missionaries and priests to look for any proof of sexual orgies among the first Russian religious radicals to identify them as criminals who committed crimes against morality. Moreover, in 1884 the Holy Synod officially encouraged them to exaggerate any sign of what could be presented as sexual transgression or collective sex among them.[4] Such attitudes influenced the official historiography as well. After 1884, Russian historians treated all peasant mystic sects as a degenerate, antihumane version of a group known as the Khlysty, which will be described below. The majority of Russian writers, including Soviet historians, followed the same historiographical tradition. They either treated all Russian indigenous religious dissenters as a Khlyst sect or simply ignored them. Such an approach led to a distorted picture of the evangelical awakening in post-Emancipation Russia and encouraged the neglect of the pioneering role of the indigenous Russian sects in the religious upheaval among the peasants.

Orthodox historiography also tried to dismiss the indigenous roots of the peasant evangelicals—who were known as "Stundists"; the word is derived from the German Stunde, meaning "hours"—and portrayed them as "the imitators of German Baptists." Still, for the Russian clergy and local administration, evangelical culture looked like a radical threat to the Orthodox peasant tradition. A fear of the evangelicals' popularity among the Ukrainian and Russian peasants and their connections to revolutionary intellectuals sparked the anti-Stundist campaign in Russia, which resulted in the anti-Stundist legislation of 1894. Radical evangelicalism reached a peak of religious enthusiasm in the movement of Kondrat Maliovannyi in the 1890s, but Russian historiography misinterpreted this movement as one of "psychic epidemics," whereas the Russian administration treated its participants as mentally ill people. Overall, Russian Orthodox historiography treated all evangelical movements among Russian peasants as an abnormality or cultural aberration in Russian religious history. Soviet and post-Soviet historiography have shared this approach.

This hostility is not surprising, because both the Russian imperial and Soviet political regimes tried to destroy evangelical cultures, especially in southern Russia and Ukraine.[5] To some extent, the Soviet administration borrowed the anti-dissident discourses and practices of their predecessors, the Russian imperial bureaucrats.[6] But the paradox was that the Soviet officials and ideologists were fighting their own cultural predecessors, the millennialist peasant dissidents who dreamed of a future society governed by the principles of social justice and equality.[7] At the same time, the peasant evangelical movement contributed to the spread of an oppositional discourse among the rural population of southern Russia and Ukraine and prepared the ground not only for the Bolshevik Revolution but also for mass peasant resistance to the Soviet regime, especially during collectivization.[8]

That is why Soviet politicians and ideologists tried to suppress this oppositional discourse in southern Russia and Ukraine by all possible means. Indeed, they succeeded in erasing the story of the peasants' radical religion from historical memory. In their rejection of the connections between the Russian and Ukrainian religious radicals and the traditions of the Radical Reformation in Western Europe, they went even further than the pre-Revolutionary Orthodox historians of Russian religion. Notwithstanding their criticism and misinterpretation of religious radicals, the Orthodox scholars had to acknowledge the similarity of the peasant evangelical movement in Russia to the Western Reformation. But Soviet historians (at least after 1924) completely denied the fact of the Reformation in Russian history.[9] Thus, the Russian "radical reformation," the mass movement of religious radicals among the rural population of southern Russia and Ukraine, was lost and forgotten in recent historiography.

But the historical memory of the people who live in the regions of southern Russia and Ukraine has kept alive the story of the legendary Stundists and Shalaputs. The people from central and southern Ukraine still call all evangelicals "the Stundists." Despite the mass persecution under the Soviet regime, the evangelical sects of southern Ukraine are still the most numerous and influential religious congregations in the post-Soviet states. Nowadays, after the collapse of the Soviet Union, the existence of millions of evangelicals in the regions of the former Russian southern frontier is remarkable evidence of the

5

vitality of the Russian popular religious reformation, which was lost and forgotten by professional historians.

Background and Origins of Russian Religious Dissent

Starting in the late eighteenth century, a large territory from Bessarabia in the west to the Northern Caucasus in the east, and from Kiev province in the north to Tavrida in the south, was gradually colonized and integrated into the imperial system. This shifting borderland shaped new human characters and created peculiar conditions for new settlers, much as the American frontier shaped new identities an ocean away. Within this frontier region, new and old movements of religious dissent originated and proliferated. By the middle of the nineteenth century, this region had become part of Russia's main imperial territory and lost its frontier status. But its frontier legacy, including the role of religious dissidents, continued to contribute to the distinctive social and cultural character of the region for many years to come.

The Russian administration began colonizing the southern frontier at the end of the eighteenth century by promoting the immigration of Protestant Germans, Mennonites, and other foreign settlers. They were the first representatives of Western Christianity to appear in this region. During the first half of the nineteenth century, Old Believers, Molokans, and Dukhobors[10] joined other non-Orthodox elements in the southern provinces. Although the Old Believers, the much-persecuted traditional apostates from Orthodoxy, constituted the vast majority of religious dissenters elsewhere in the Russian Empire, new religious sects began to settle the southern Russian frontier from the 1830s onward.[11]

By the end of the 1860s, the composition of Russian religious dissent began to change on the southern frontier of the Russian Empire. In the 1890s, the new evangelical sects dominated the countryside of southern Russia.[12] According to the minister of the interior's analysis of the official census of 1897, among more than 2,000,000 Russian religious dissidents, the Old Believers made up 1,050,000 (48.9 percent); the rationalist sectarians (Stundists et al.), 170,000 (7.9 percent); and other sectarians, who did not reveal their sect,

970,000 (44.6 percent).[13] Moreover, the minister confessed that the local administration and especially the Orthodox clergy had underestimated the real numbers of the new sects in their reports to the central authorities because they wished to play down their influence in the Russian countryside, especially in the South. According to the calculations of various scholars, such as the "Constitutional-Democrat" P. Milukov and the "Bolshevik" V. Bonch-Bruevich, by 1917 the Russian Empire had 20 million religious "dissidents," including 6 million non–Old Believers.[14]

During the 1880s and 1890s, according to the governors' reports, in the province of Stavropol' these non–Old Believer "dissidents" (primarily Shalaputs; see just below) made up more than 20 percent of the rural population in some districts. In the province of Kherson, more than three-fourths of the entire rural population belonged to the Stundist sects, and in the province of Kiev entire villages joined the Stundist movement.[15] The new sects gradually replaced the cultural influence of traditional religious dissenters on the frontier.

According to the official census, which did not reveal the "hidden sectarians," the numbers of officially registered dissenters who were not Old Believers grew rapidly from 1897 to 1909. This increase is noteworthy because from 1897 to 1905 the tsarist administration evicted and exiled thousands of new sectarians from the southern provinces to Siberia. Despite mass persecution and eviction, the numbers of religious dissenters continued to grow in the South. The overwhelming majority of these sectarians were members of the new sects, whose names had emerged during the 1830s and the 1860s—the Shalaputs, the Stundists, and others.[16]

The Shalaputs were the largest and most controversial religious group among the post-Emancipation peasantry of the southern Russian frontier. Their name derives from a Russian and Ukrainian word that referred to those who lost their way and took a wrong track in life; they *took Shal'noi put'*—the wrong path to a sinful way of life. The Russian verb *shalit'* means "to sin," "to be naughty." Contemporaries applied this word to the very broad religious movement among peasants linked with the traditional indigenous sects of the Molokans, Khlysty, and Skoptsy in central Russia. Eventually, this movement became the largest and most popular on the southern frontier. It included all

7

those who were disappointed with the formalism of the Russian Orthodox Church. By the 1860s, Shalaput communities made up the majority in the villages of Berdiansk and Melitopol' districts of Tavrida province, and in the Novomoskovsk and Pavlograd districts of Ekaterinoslav province. In Stavropol' province, they occupied whole villages.[17]

In 1897, according to official calculations, no fewer than 615,000 sectarians (more than 30 percent of all Russian religious dissidents, and more than half of the new Russian sectarians) belonged to the Shalaput-Khlyst movement.[18] The overwhelming majority lived or came from the Russian southern provinces. The Shalaput movement absorbed various elements of Russian religious dissent on the southern frontier. During its evolution from the 1860s through the 1890s, it became a mass evangelical movement of pious peasants who attempted to recreate their own version of Christianity in opposition to Russian Orthodoxy.

Another sect of the Russian popular "reformation" was that of the Ukrainian Stundists. From the outset, this sect was related to the religious awakening in the German and Mennonite colonies. In it, the evangelical movement among the German colonists converged with the religious revival among Orthodox peasants and produced a movement that contemporaries referred to as Stundism. Contemporary authors and historians noted this as a remarkable moment in the popular evangelical movement's development in the Russian Empire.[19]

The German-speaking settlers brought Stundism to Russia as a part of the Pietist movement. At the beginning of the eighteenth century, members of the German Pietist movement, followers of Philip Jacob Spener, organized the meetings in their houses for reading and discussion of the Bible during the special hours (*Stunde*) after church ceremonies.

These Pietists from Württemberg, who were called the Stundist Brothers, brought their new religious experience to the German colonies in the Russian province of Kherson in 1817, where the German colony of Rohrbach became a center of Pietist activity. The Pietist minister Johann Bonnekemper was the pastor of the Lutheran community in Rohrbach and a leader of the new Pietist Stundist movement among local Germans. From 1824, his meetings, which

8

were known as "the Stundist meetings," laid a foundation for a broad Pietist movement among the German-speaking settlers of the province.[20] This German Pietist movement converged with religious revivals among the members of the Nazareth sect in the German colonies in Bessarabia during the 1840s and among Mennonites in the provinces of Ekaterinoslav and Tavrida during the 1850s. Along with Western Baptist influences, which were brought by German missionaries to southern Russia during the late 1860s, these evangelical awakenings among the German and Mennonite colonists laid the foundation for the movement among Ukrainian peasants, who were called "the Ukrainian Stundists" by Russian contemporaries.[21]

Beginning with merely a hundred people in the 1830s in the provinces of Tavrida and Bessarabia, the radical peasant religious movement grew to more than 100,000 in the 1870s and to 400,000 by 1883. In the provinces of Kherson and Kiev, these radical sects controlled three-fourths of the provincial territory, and their adherents developed a theology, an ethos, and rituals reminiscent of the Western Protestant Reformation. To some extent, this religious movement intersected with new Western European religious movements, such as German Pietists and Baptists. The overwhelming majority of the new Russian sects from the southern provinces shared the basic fundamental ideas of the Protestant Reformation. Like the Western Protestants, the new sects denied the universal authority of the established church hierarchies (of the Pope or of the Russian Orthodox hierarchy) and affirmed the Reformation principles of justification by faith alone, the priesthood of all believers, and the primacy of the Bible as the source of revealed truth. Russian noblemen and wealthy landowners also took part in this religious movement.

It is noteworthy that in the Russian "reformation" in the nineteenth century, there was neither a "high" or "magisterial reformation" nor indigenous theologians similar to Martin Luther and John Calvin, who represented educated elites in the Western Reformation. Russian intellectuals did not contribute anything significant to the theology and religious practices of popular religious dissent in imperial Russia. The overwhelming majority of the new Russian dissenters were either peasants or representatives of other lower classes. They turned their radical theology and dissent against the established

9

norms of power and society. Therefore, this Russian "reformation" was reminiscent of a popular radical version of Protestantism in Western Europe, which is called the Radical Reformation by historians.

After the German Peasants' War of 1525, the Radical Reformation became an important part of religious dissent in the Western Christian world. The majority of adherents were from impoverished social groups, including peasants, workers, and artisans. From the sixteenth through the nineteenth century, their ideas and practices played an important role in the mass popular religious movements during periods of social crisis throughout Europe. This was a popular version of the Reformation, which developed in opposition to the reforming efforts of educated elites such as Luther and Calvin.

In 1962, George H. Williams published the first comprehensive history of religious radicalism in the sixteenth century. In contrast to the Magisterial Reformation of Luther and Calvin, he referred to the Anabaptist, Spiritualist, and other radical evangelical groups of the European Reformation as the Radical Reformation. Although it has been strongly criticized, his theory is still a productive methodological tool for the interpretation of popular religious radicalism.[22] According to this theory, the exponents of the Radical Reformation

1. Insisted on the separation of their own churches from the national or territorial state.
2. Denounced war and renounced all other forms of coercion except the ban.
3. Sought to spread their version of the Christian life by missions, martyrdom, and philanthropy.
4. Insisted on believers' baptism, on their possession of the gifts of the Spirit, on their prophetic inspiration, and on the divine compassion.
5. Stressed believers' regeneration, their "new beginning in Christ," the power of the Spirit, the quickening of the moral conscience, and, as a result, the deification and reincarnation of Christ in sincere believers.
6. Elaborated "a devout and detailed doctrine of the 'imitatio Christi' or the discipleship of the reborn Christian," including the doctrine of reincarnation.
7. Tried to restore "the inwardly disciplined but externally free 'apostolic' church" as it existed in the age of the New Testament's martyrs.[23]

This theory, which distinguishes radical popular religion from both the ruling church and the traditional and institutionalized forms of dissent, is still helpful for interpreting peasant religious movements, including Russian and Ukrainian sects such as the Shalaputs and Stundists.

The "radical reformation" in Russia's southern provinces developed in three stages. The first, the Shalaput movement, began in the 1830s and 1840s among state peasants from the central Russian provinces of Tambov and Kursk, who settled in the provinces of Bessarabia, Tavrida, and Stavropol'. These peasants brought with them their old Russian traditions of religious dissent, which had developed along Orthodox lines, including the influence of the Khlysty and Skoptsy and also of the Molokans and Dukhobors. Such traditions converged with the Orthodox piety of the local peasants and eventually produced the Shalaput movement. The new sectarians expressed their millennial hopes in the traditional forms and rituals of indigenous religious dissent. Yet the most prominent feature of this stage was a collective religious enthusiasm that united old forms and new experiments in religious practice and theory. At the same time, these peasants developed more modern and rational forms of worship, and they established connections with other similar dissident groups elsewhere in southern Russia. The participants in this movement prepared the ground for the next stage of the popular Russian "reformation."

The second stage began in the 1850s and 1860s. At the end of the 1850s, the religious awakening among the Pietistic Lutheran communities of German colonists began to coincide with a revival of the Radical Reformation's (mainly Anabaptist) traditions among Hutterites and Mennonites in the southern Russian provinces. The Western European Baptist faith, brought by the German missionaries, also influenced German and Mennonite colonists, and the Ukrainian and Russian peasants who worked for them participated in their religious meetings and brought these new ideas to their home villages. In doing so, however, local peasants made these ideas their own, creating a peasant evangelical movement, which was called Ukrainian Stundism by their contemporaries. Gradually, as intense reading and interpretation of Holy Scripture lessened the religious enthusiasm of the new sects, social activism and criticism became the most prominent features of this second stage of Imperial

11

Russia's popular "reformation." Networks slowly emerged that joined the diverse evangelical groups into one Stundist movement and linked them to the educated opposition as well as to the international Protestant community.

The third stage of the Russian popular "reformation" began during the 1890s with the convergence of the first stage's religious enthusiasm and the Anabaptist influences and the social activism of the second stage. Most typical of this stage were the activities of the Maliovantsy (the followers of Kondrat Maliovannyi, the peasant "charismatic" prophet) and other similar sects, called the Stundo-Khlysty by their opponents. This stage saw a symbiosis of the old chiliasm of the Shalaputs with new modern forms of worship. By the beginning of the twentieth century, this Shalaput-Stundist symbiosis colored most radical expressions of Russia's popular "reformation."

The participants in this peasant evangelical movement insisted on reading, comprehending, and interpreting biblical texts in their native language, whether Russian or Ukrainian. In developing more humane and modern notions of childcare, home, work, schooling, and health, they contributed to the formation of human capital for the process of modernization. Also important was an increased respect for human dignity, sexual equality, and critical thinking among children. Notwithstanding their persecutions by the Orthodox Church and tsarist administration, many dissident peasants succeeded in their agricultural and entrepreneurial activities. By the 1880s, the first preachers of Ukrainian Stundism had already demonstrated the power of the Protestant ethic (à la Max Weber) and had become enterprising, prosperous farmers.[24] Therefore, these radical sects can be considered the representatives of a global process of the expansion of the capitalist world system.[25]

At the same time, police persecutions and anti-dissident "pogroms" reinforced the millennial expectations that had existed among the peasant evangelicals since the beginning of their movement. Millenarianism became a distinctive feature of peasant religious dissent in the Russian Empire. The Russian Shalaputs, the Ukrainian radical Stundists, and the Maliovantsy constituted the millenarian religious movement with the belief that "after his Second Coming Christ would establish a messianic kingdom on earth and would reign over it for a thousand years before the Last Judgment." A majority of

Russian peasant dissidents shared this belief and awaited "the end of the world and the coming of a millennial period and an earthly paradise."[26] The most important part of their millenarian theology belonged to the "radical reformation" of Christianity in Russia, which combined elements of Russian Orthodoxy and Western Anabaptism.

Historians of Russian religion have generally denied the existence of a "reformation" in Russian history. Such views suit the old historiographical tradition in which Russia is always distinct from Europe. But the peasant religious awakening in post-Emancipation Russia had so many connections and similarities to the Radical Reformation in Western Europe that it is reasonable to analyze this religious movement as a belated part of the Reformation.[27] The role of radical sects in transforming social relations and in contributing to an alternative culture in the southern part of the Russian Empire has been ignored, neglected, disparaged, or misinterpreted by professional historians.[28] Pre-Revolutionary Russian historians, including such Bolsheviks as Bonch-Bruevich, always stressed the connections between the Western Reformation and radical peasant sects in Russia. Before 1924, the Soviet Communists were interested in collaborating with "revolutionary sectarians," and they supported research on religious radicals, as representatives of "the revolutionary popular Reformation."[29] After 1924, however, Soviet ideologists who were disappointed by the "political apathy" of peasant dissidents and enraged by their resistance to "socialist collectivization" forgot about their earlier idealization of religious radicals. Thereafter, Russian and Ukrainian evangelical sects were mentioned in passing mainly as reactionary and antirevolutionary social groups.

Ukrainian historians, especially M. Drahomanov, T. Zin'kivs'kyi, and M. Hrushevs'kyi, were the first scholars to include the Stundists and other evangelical sects in their study of the social history of the Ukrainian countryside.[30] But recent Ukrainian historians, with the exception of Ukrainian Baptist writers, have been preoccupied with the history of the Ukrainian Orthodox and Uniate (Eastern Catholic) Churches, which they consider a more essential component of Ukrainian national identity. Although American historians have recently acknowledged the abilities of Russian peasants to be innovative and behave rationally, most still present the peasantry of the late Russian Empire as traditional Greek Orthodox Christians holding to the communal organization of village life and defending their "moral economy" against any interference from the outside.[31]

Even American historians of Russian and Ukrainian peasant culture have generally ignored the religious sects. The literature on this subject is very limited.[32] The scholarly neglect of the spread of Protestantism in southern Russia is indicative of a stereotypical view of the Russian peasantry as one-dimensional and backward, and bound to the limits of a traditional village community. In fact, the Ukrainian and southern Russian villages demonstrated a diverse peasant culture that influenced the Orthodox population as well. It is impossible to understand the distinctive social and cultural development of the Ukrainian countryside (at least in its central and southern regions) during Soviet and post-Soviet periods without a history of the Ukrainian evangelical and spiritual sects that contributed to the special enterprising culture, literacy, and awareness of a non-Russian and non-Orthodox national identity among Ukrainian peasants.

Contemporaries who witnessed the beginning of the "radical reformation" in the Russian and Ukrainian countryside reacted immediately to this new peasant culture as an important phenomenon whose influence spread far beyond the radical peasant sects themselves. Such Russian writers as N. Leskov and F. Dostoevsky saw the expansion of Stundism as a threat to the indigenous peasant Orthodox culture and criticized Russian intellectuals who they considered to be blindly infatuated with "Western evangelicalism."[33] Those who sympathized with the religious dissenters, Leo Tolstoy and Populist authors such as Gleb Uspenskii and S. Stepniak-Kravchinskii, presented the radical peasant sects as an expression of the "progressive" innovative spirit of common folk and tried to popularize the sectarians' ideas in their own writings.[34]

Contemporary scholars laid the foundation for the historiography of the Russian radical sects. The first studies in religious historiography were devoted to the sects that came from the "Christ-Faith," the old Russian tradition of popular religious dissent. The participants in these sects called themselves the "People of God" or "Khristy" (from Khristovery, meaning "believers in Christ"). Contemporaries slightly distorted their name as "Khlysty," from the verb "to flagellate," because of rumors that these dissidents practiced self-flagellation. The Khlysty renounced meat, alcohol, tobacco, profanity, and sex. They practiced an ecstatic form of worship: fervid singing of spiritual verse accompanied by swirling dances. The primary focus of this movement was the belief in the personification, or reincarnation, of Christ in all those who sincerely believed in God. They sought to become "the living Christs" and tried to re-create in their society the life of the first Christian communities.[35]

During the eighteenth century, this dissident movement laid the foundation for various Russian sects, including the Khlysty and Skoptsy.[36] Members of these sects practiced severe asceticism and avoided sexual relations, thus devoting their lives completely to the service of God. During their religious meetings, they "felt" the presence of the Holy Spirit in their souls and they communicated the "Divine Will" to each other, producing collective spiritual ecstasy by dancing and singing. Such a religious service was called a "rejoicing," and the religious meeting was known as a "ship." The image of the congregation as a ship derived from the Old Believer tradition and became an important symbol for the entire Christ-Faith movement from the late seventeenth century. The "ships" of the Khlysty were vessels of salvation, piloted by the Holy Spirit, with Jesus at the helm, afloat on the evil waters of the world. The most radical version of the Khlysty was represented by another sect called the Skoptsy ("castrated" in Russian). They extended their renunciation of sex as far as literally possible.[37]

Eventually, the Shalaputs borrowed from the Khlysty tradition and elaborated on it in southern Russia. All historians of this tradition have noted the inclusive, heterogeneous, and radical character of the religious beliefs of the Khlyst peasants who brought this tradition to the new lands in the South.[38] Some of them presented the Shalaput movement on the southern Russian frontier exclusively as a part of the Khlysty tradition.[39] At the same time, such various authors as A. Dorodnitsyn, an Orthodox missionary who worked for many years against the Shalaputs of southern Russia and Ukraine, and the liberal journalist Ia. Abramov, noted the differences between the old Khlyst tradition and the innovative religious practices of the Shalaputs in the South.[40] Even Russian anthropologists and ethnographers, such as Varvara Iasevich-

15

Borodaevskaia, described the Shalaputs as different from the Khlysty. These ethnographers contributed to further confusion on the origin of the Shalaputs. Thus, Iasevich-Borodaevskaia described Grigorii Shevchenko, the famous leader of the Pavlograd Shalaputs in the province of Ekaterinoslav, as the head of the Pryguny ("Jumpers") sect. She also noted that the Khlysty, Pryguny, and Marianovtsy participated in Shalaput meetings for worship as well.[41] Unfortunately, recent historiography has ignored the Shalaput movement in post-Emancipation Russia.

Local priests insisted that severe measures be taken against religious dissidents. The Khlysty and Skoptsy were outlawed, and Orthodox scholars were ready to identify any extremely religious behavior or self-organized religious meetings among peasants with the Skoptsy and Khlysty sects. As a result, the clergy used any sign of castration among peasants or rumors about unusual nightly meetings to accuse the participants of Skopets-Khlyst activities. To make matters more complicated, religious dissenters sometimes actually did borrow various religious practices from the beliefs and rituals of the Skoptsy, Khlysty, Molokans, and Dukhobors. It was difficult for contemporaries to single out the dominant religious theology and practices of these peasant sects. Local priests needed a simple and clear means of classifying religious dissenters.[42]

Therefore, official specialists and statisticians began dividing all religious dissenters into three major groups: (1) the Old Believers; (2) the mystical sects, including the Khlysty, Skoptsy, and Shalaputs; and (3) the rationalist sects, including the Stundists, Baptists, and Adventists. Sometimes Orthodox scholars had serious problems with this classification. When they discovered that some sects failed to fit into these categories, they invented such names as Stundo-Khlyst (e.g., for the Maliovantsy), but most still preferred the official classification. This classification dominated religious studies in late imperial Russia for years, and Soviet and post-Soviet historians have applied it in their studies as well.[43]

The Shalaput movement did not fit this theoretical division because its practitioners incorporated such varied elements as Skopets castration, Khlyst dancing, and worshiping "living Christs," as well as rational elements of the

Protestant sects. At the same time, the Shalaputs variously combined these practices with their own indigenous theology, which was reminiscent of the Radical Reformation. As "sincere seekers of Divine Truth" and the "apostolic church," the Shalaputs followed the Radical Reformation's principles, which included the separation of churches from the national or territorial state, the doctrine of the "imitatio Christi," and the doctrine of the inwardly disciplined but externally free "apostolic" church with a prophetic or inspired vocation.[44]

The Ukrainian Stundists, another large group of radical peasant dissidents, also did not fit the official scheme for a dissident movement in Russian historiography. All historians now agree that Ukrainian Stundism eventually contributed to the development of the broad evangelical movement in Russia and the Soviet Union as well.[45] Yet the history of the Stundist peasants and their theology and religious practices are still unclear and confused. Even at the beginning of the twentieth century, Russian observers of the Stundist movement were not sure about its real origins. The obvious similarities between German and Russian sectarians, who were both referred to as the "Stundists," confused both liberal and conservative authors. At the same time, all observers noted the Shalaput influences and millenarian trends in the theology of Ukrainian peasant dissidents. The more insightful Orthodox scholars of Stundism, such as Arsenii Rozhdestvenskii, Alexei Dorodnitsyn, and Piotr Kozitskii, expressed their uncertainty about the origins of Russian Stundism in their listings of different views regarding various theories on Stundist roots in the Russian empire.[46]

According to these researchers, both liberals and conservatives in pre-Soviet Russian historiography acknowledged the "German roots" of Russian and Ukrainian Stundism. Recent Western scholars have sometimes over-exaggerated these German influences and ignored the Russian cultural background of the evangelical movement in late imperial Russia.[47] Archival materials show how the Russian, Ukrainian, and German cultural elements were combined into one evangelical movement known as Ukrainian Stundism (Khokhlatskaia Shtunda) by contemporaries. The present study will analyze all elements of the evangelical movement among the rural population in southern Russia, attempting to restore the role of the Shalaput movement as a connecting link between the "radical reformation" of Russian Orthodoxy and the Western Protestant Reformation.

Methods and Sources for This Study

The methodology for this study is based on the theories of Max Weber as well as those of Clifford Geertz, Victor Turner, and other anthropologists of radical popular religion. First of all, the main object of this study is the "religious culture." The "semiotic concept of culture" is employed, which treats "culture patterns" as an "organized system of significant symbols."[48] According to Geertz, all human beings are "dependent upon" these symbols, which play the role of "control mechanisms, cultural programs, for ordering [their] behavior." In religious culture, "sacred symbols" generally "function to synthesize a people's ethos—the tone, character, and quality of their life, its moral and aesthetic style and mood—and their world view—the picture they have of the way things in sheer actuality are, their most comprehensive ideas of order."[49]

A former colleague of Geertz, Victor Turner, used the ideas of Arnold van Gennep about the "liminal phase" of "rites of passage" to explain how societies dealt with the problems of cultural changes, such as "changes of place, state, social position and age."[50] Turner followed Norman Cohn's portrayal of the millennial religious movements as a manifestation of the cultural and social protest of uprooted and desperate marginal people. He emphasized the ideas and rituals of the radical religious movements that are related to our analysis of the "radical reformation" in late imperial Russia. All such religious movements arise in times of radical social transition.

Turner's characterization of religious radicals as "liminal people" is applicable to Russian radical dissidents as well.[51] Usually, liminal people come from three categories: (1) those who exist "in the interstices of social structure," (2) those who live "on its margins," and (3) those who occupy "its lowest rungs."[52] The migrant peasants on the southern Russian frontier became such a liminal people that they lost their traditional identity. During their migration, these peasants experienced cultural transitions that resulted in their liminal status. Turner describes two types of liminality. The first type "char-

18

acterizes rituals of status elevation, in which the ritual subject or novice is being conveyed irreversibly from a lower to a higher position in an institutionalized system of such positions." The second type of liminality was created "in cyclical and calendrical ritual, usually of a collective kind, in which, at certain culturally defined points in the seasonal cycle, groups or categories of persons who habitually occupy low status positions in the social structure are positively enjoined to exercise ritual authority over their superiors; and they, in their turn, must accept with good will their ritual degradation." Turner called these "rituals of status reversal."[53] One feature of these rituals was the replacement of masculine authority and roles by women. All the radical religious groups in Russia demonstrated this kind of status reversal.

Max Weber noted that the religious practices of "spiritual humility" described later by Turner as a "ritual of status reversal" played an important role in all the Christian reforming movements—from the early Christians of the first century to the Russian sects of the nineteenth century.[54] The Radical Reformation, like all religious mass movements, demonstrated different forms of two types of liminality (of status elevation and of status reversal). All such upheavals in popular religiosity tend to occur during periods of rapid and unprecedented social change that "themselves have liminal attributes." Religious enthusiasm and intense emotionalism became a part of radical practices. According to Turner, the enthusiastic religions "emphasize humility, patience, and the unimportance of distinctions of status, property, age, sex, and other natural or cultural" differences. The religious enthusiasts stress "mystical union," the brotherhood and sisterhood of all their coreligionists, because they regard this life as a transitional (liminal) phase leading to a higher level of human existence.[55]

Popular radical religion became a part of peasants' resistance (and/or adaptation) to the changing conditions of their life and to the intrusions of the capitalist market in the countryside. James C. Scott argues that any peasant community is driven by what he calls "moral economy" and tries to maintain its "subsistence ethic" and relations with the outside world based on notions of economic justice and reciprocity. According to his theory, a peasant community is organized "around the problem of the minimum income—organized to minimize the risk to which its members were exposed by virtue of its limited techniques and the caprice of nature."[56] To protect their right to subsistence against various threats to peasant community (capitalist market, intrusions of the state, etc.), peasants used various forms of resistance, including "reliance on religious or oppositionist structures of protection and assistance." As Scott notes, radical peasant sects can be seen "as a means by which peasants, having dissociated themselves from dominant religious and social values, choose to give social and symbolic meaning to their personal situation." In this way, he explains peasant millennialism as well: "Where the threat to subsistence routines seems cataclysmic and irresistible, the response appears more often to take on millennial and utopian overtones."[57]

In responding to criticism from the proponents of "the rational peasant's theory" and "political economy of the peasants," Scott elaborates convincing ideas about the everyday resistance of poor people to the rule of elites. He interprets as coexistence the arts of resistance ("hidden transcripts") and the domination ("public transcripts") in the discourse of power in any society.[58] He offers a very useful (for the study of culture) comparison of a transcript "that represents a critique of power spoken behind the back of dominant" with a transcript of the powerful "representing the practices and claims of their rule that cannot be openly avowed." This comparison gives us a new way of understanding everyday resistance to domination in the Russian and Ukrainian countryside. The present study will follow some of Scott's ideas about a dialogue of the "hidden and public transcripts" in telling the story of the radical sects that became a part of the peasants' resistance in imperial Russia.[59]

The primary sources used in this study are archival documents and materials published by the sectarians themselves as well as by their enemies, critics, and sympathetic observers. These include the memoirs and correspondence of peasant dissidents (such as the Shalaput Fedor Lutsenko and the Stundist activist Tymophii Zaiats); a wide variety of periodicals, police reports, and other materials gathered by the Orthodox Church; and special collections of documents related to the sectarians. The overwhelming majority of these materials can be found in the Russian central historical archives in Moscow and Saint Petersburg (the State Archive of the Russian Federation and Russian

State Historical Archive), in the Central State Historical Archive of Ukraine in Kiev, and in the regional archives in Kherson, Odessa, and Dniepropetrovsk.

Chronologically, this study covers the period from the 1830s, when the police first recorded the appearance of the Shalaputs, to the Bolshevik Revolution in 1917. The main emphasis of this book will be on the origins and evolution of the theology and religious practices of radical peasant sects, and their contribution to an alternative religious culture and "the arts of resistance" in the Russian and Ukrainian countryside.

Notes

1 See "Materialy dlia izuchenia sekty shaloputov," *Kavkazskie eparkhial'nye vedomosti* (hereafter *KavEV*), 1873, no. 23, 754–5; 1875, no. 3, 96–100; 1881, no. 13, 455–60; 1882, no. 13, 449–50; and 1891, no. 4, 112–13. Also see Ia. Abramov, "Sekta shalaputov," *Otechestvennye zapiski* (hereafter *OZ*),1882, no. 9, 46–55; A. Dorodnitsyn, "Sekta shalaputov," *Chtenia v obshchestve liubitelei dukhovnogo prosveshchenia* (hereafter *Ch.OLDP*), March 1889, 276–88; and S. D. Bondar', *Sekty khlystov, shelaputov, dukhovnykh khristian, Staryi i Novyi Izrail' i subbotnikov i iudeistvuiushchikh* (Petrograd, 1916), 14, 24–25. See the Soviet historian A. Klibanov on the Katasonovtsy: Klibanov, *Istoria religioznogo sektantstva v Rossii (60-e gody XIX v.–1917 g.)* (Moscow, 1965), 57–62. Compare with a new study of post-Soviet scholar Aleksandr A. Panchenko, *Khristovshchina i skopchestvo: fol'klor i traditsionnaia kul'tura russkikh misticheskikh sekt* (Moscow, 2002), 9, 39, 193–95.

2 *KavEV,* 1875, no. 3, 96.

3 On the crisis of the Orthodox Church in the nineteenth century, see Gregory Freeze, *The Parish Clergy in Nineteenth-Century Russia: Crisis, Reform, Counter-Reform* (Princeton, N.J., 1983).

4 Rossiiskii gosudarstvennyi istoricheskii arkhiv (hereafter RGIA), f. 796, op. 165 (1884–85), d. 1692, 1. 11–12, 13. The official letter from the Holy Synod of July 4, 1884, strongly recommended treating the new sect of Shalaputs as a kind of Khlysty. The authorities applied the word "Khlysty" to a wide variety of Russian mystic sects of the religious enthusiasts who presumably had collective sex during their meetings for worship. See the best analysis of the "Khylst" culture in Aleksandr A. Panchenko, *Khristovshchina i skopchestvo.*

5 On the persecution of Soviet evangelicals, see Walter Sawatsky, *Soviet Evangelicals since World War II* (Scottdale, Pa., 1981).

6 Article 17 of the Soviet Law on Religious Cults of 1929 followed verbatim the law on sectarian meetings issued by the imperial administration in 1910; see Sawatsky, *Soviet Evangelicals,* 36.

7 Alexander Etkind demonstrated how the Bolsheviks tried to collaborate with the radical sects after the Revolution of 1917, and how they began persecution of the dissidents afterward; see Etkind, *Khlyst: Sekty, literatura i revoliutsia* (Moscow, 1998), 631–74.

8 Both Soviet and Western historians noted during the Revolution of 1905 the unusual social radicalism of the peasants from the same localities of southwestern Ukraine where the radical sects were active. See, e.g., Robert Edelman, *Proletarian Peasants: The Revolution of 1905 in Russia's Southwest* (Ithaca, N.Y., 1987), 92. Moreover, Edelman cited the Russian government officials who were "struck by the 'enormous' dispersal of all kinds of periodicals" among the peasants there in the spring of 1905. But the same Russian officials had noted how a spread of evangelical sects contributed to literacy in the Ukrainian countryside. Compare Edelman, *Proletarian Peasants,* 109–10, with Tsentral'nyi derzhavnyi istorychnyi arkhiv Ukrainy, f. 442, op. 855, d. 526, l. 1–9, and d. 109, l. 4.

9 Only Vladimir Bonch-Bruevich and his student Alexandr Klibanov did some serious research work on the problems of the Western Reformation in Russian religious history. See V. Bonch-Bruevich, *Izbrannye proizvedenia* (Moscow, 1959), vol. 1; A. I. Klibanov, *Reformatsionnyie dvizhenia v Rossii v XIV–pervoi polovine XVI vv.* (Moscow, 1960); and Klibanov, *Istoria religioznogo.*

10 The Molokans and Dukhobors were Russian sects of "Spiritualist Christians" who represented the old Russian religious dissident tradition known as God's Belief. Both groups emphasized a spiritual dialogue of Christian believers with God and denied the priesthood as a church institution. These sects established themselves in non-Orthodox congregations after the 1760s. See Klibanov, *Istoria religioznogo,* 55 and 85–121, on Dukhobors, and 122–83, on the Molokans.

11 In the 1830s, when the first Shalaputs appeared among the settlers of the Southern provinces, the Russian administration calculated the numbers of all religious dissidents in the Russian Empire in the hundreds, with an obvious predominance of Old Believers among them (they constituted more than 95 percent of all dissenters). RGIA, f. 1263, op. 1, d. 2966 (1861), l. 87, *vedomost'* 25; d. 3255 (1865), l. 150ob.; d. 3286 (1867), l. 340, 412, 549ob.–551, *vedomost'* 25.

12 *Missionerskoe obozrenie* (hereafter *MO*), February 1898, 330–41.

13 RGIA, f. 1284, op. 241, d. 181 (1901), l. 91–91ob.

14 Pavel Miliukov, *Ocherki po istorii russkoi kul'tury* (Paris, 1931), vol. 2, 157; Vladimir Bonch-Bruevich, "Raskol i sektantstvo v Rossii," in *Izbrannye proizvedenia,* ed. Vladimir Bonch-Bruevich (Moscow, 1959), vol. 1, 175. See a summary of different opinions on dissenters' statistics in Russia in Etkind, *Khlyst,* 32–39.

15 RGIA, f. 821, op. 133, d. 21 (1909–10), especially l. 390ob.–91. See also RGIA, Otchet Khersonskogo gubernatora za 1890 god, 13.

16 RGIA, f. 821, op. 133, d. 21, l. 443–44, 363–67, 379–82. Thus, from 1897 to 1909, the figures of the registered members of the non–Old Belief sects grew in Astrakhan' province from 9,079 to 9,637; in Bessarabia province, from 1,335 to 2,000; in Voronezh province, from 2,981 to 7,259; in the Don Army region, from 3,585 to 3,697; in Ekaterinoslav province, from 202 to 1,463; in Kiev province, from 3,350 to 12,067; in Tavrida province, from 9,607 to 20,238; in Kherson province, from 3,687 to 6,670; and in Kharkov province, from 784 to 4,325. In Stavropol' province, the number decreased from 15,000 to 11,762.

17 On the Shalaputs, see "Sekta shaloputov," *Kievlianin,* no. 98 (1873): 1–3. Also see O. Levitskii, "Shaloputy na granites Poltavskoi i Ekaterinoslavskoi gubernii," *Kievskii telegraf,* no. 41 (1875): 1, 2; no. 42 (1875): 2–3; no. 43 (1875): 2–3; and no. 48 (1875): 4. And see "Zametka iz Ekaterinoslava," *Zaria,* no. 13 (1881): 4. In the Orthodox magazine, the first publication about the Shalaputs appeared in 1873, and such information was published on a regular basis during the 1870s and 1890s, especially in "Materialy dlia izuchenia sekty shaloputov," *KavEV,* 1873, no. 23, 752–63, and in other issues of this journal. See also "Shaloputy," *Ekaterinoslavskie eparkhial'nye vedomosti,* (hereafter *EkEV*), 1877, no. 14, 217; "O shaloputakh sela Vasil'kovki, Pavlogradskogo uezda, Ekaterinoslavskoi gubernii," *EkEV,* 1886, no. 18, 456–63, and other issues of this journal. The most serious interpretations of the Shalaput history were presented in the following: *OZ,* 1882, no. 9, 35–58, and no. 10, 157–93; *Ch.OLDP,* March 1889, 275–301, and June 1889, 646–712; and *Russkii vestnik,* October 1904, 705–39, and November 1904, 126–85.

18 According to the calculations by A. Klibanov, who used the reports of the ober-procurator of the Holy Synod, by 1909 in Russia the dissidents of the Khlyst tradition (*"khristovery"*) made up more than 100,000 people; Klibanov, *Istoria religioznogo,* 83–84.

19 In contrast to the Shalaputs' history, the development of Stundism has been covered in detail by both Russian and Western historians. See these recent dissertations: Heather Coleman, "The Most Dangerous Sect: Baptists in Tsarist and Soviet Russia, 1905–1929" (Ph.D. dissertation, University of Illinois, 1998); and O. V. Beznosova (Kudinova), "Pozdnee protestantskoe sektantstvo Iuga Ukrainy (1850–1905)" (Ph.D. dissertation, Dniepropetrovsk University, 1998).

20 C. Bonnekemper, "Stundism in Russia," *Missionary Review of the World* 17 (March 1894): 203.

21 See A. Rozhdestvenskii, *Iuzhno-russkii shtundizm* (Saint Petersburg, 1889), 42–43, 59–60.

22 See George Huntston Williams, *The Radical Reformation* (Philadelphia, 1962); and Williams, "Rediscovered Dimensions: the Reformation Radicals," in *The Reformation in Historical Thought,* ed. A. G. Dickens and John Tonkin (Cambridge, Mass., 1985), 213–33.

23 Williams, *Radical Reformation,* xxvi–xxx.

24 I use the word "peasants" (in Russian, *krest'iane*) for members of the specific "estate" (in Russian, *soslovie*) in the Russian Empire. The most common features of this estate correspond to the concept of "peasantry" as it was defined by Teodor Shanin. According to him, peasants are "small producers on land who with the help of simple equipment and the labour of their families, produce mainly for their own consumption and for meeting obligations to the holders of political and economic power"; see Shanin, *Russia as a "Developing Society"* (New Haven, Conn., 1986), 82.

25 According to the "modern world-system" theoretical approach proposed by Immanuel Wallerstein in the 1970s, we can view the development of the religious Protestant movement in late imperial Russia as an ideological concomitant to the expansion of the European world system to the East: Immanuel Wallerstein, *The Modern World-System: Capitalist Agriculture and the Origin of the European World-Economy in the 16th Century* (New

York, 1974); Wallerstein, *The Modern World-System: Mercantilism and the Consolidation of the European World-Economy, 1600–1750* (New York, 1980); and Wallerstein, *The Modern World-System: The Second Era of Great Expansion of the Capitalist World-Economy, 1730–1840s* (San Diego, 1989).

26 Norman Cohn, *The Pursuit of the Millennium: Revolutionary Millenarians and Mystical Anarchists of the Middle Ages* (New York, 1970; 1st pr., 1957), 15; Michael J. St. Clair, *Millenarian Movements in Historical Context* (New York, 1992), 7. See the recent studies of millennial movements: Richard A. Landes, *Relics, Apocalypse, and the Deceits of History: Ademar of Chabannes, 989–1034* (Cambridge, Mass., 1995); Michael Barkun, ed., *Millennialism and Violence* (London, 1996); Eugen Weber, *Apocalypses: Prophets, Cults and Millennial Beliefs through the Ages* (Cambridge, Mass., 1999); and Richard A. Landes, ed., *Encyclopedia of Millennialism and Millennial Movements* (New York, 2000). Compare with Michael Baigent, Richard Leigh, and Henry Lincoln, *The Messianic Legacy* (New York, 1986).

27 For a comparative approach to the history of Christianity in Russia, see an article written by a student of Klibanov: Mikhail V. Dmitriev, "Nauchnoe nasledie A. I. Klibanova i perspektivy sravnitel'no-istoricheskogo izucheniia istorii khristianstva v Rossii," *Otechestvennaia istoria*, no. 1 (1997): 77–93. See also a serious criticism of Etkind's work in Aleksandr A. Panchenko, *Khristovshchina i skopchestvo*, 42–43.

28 A recent example of apparent confusion in the portrayal of Russian enthusiastic sects is Etkind, *Khlyst*. He completely ignores the Shalaputs and misrepresents the Maliovantsy.

29 For Bonch-Bruevich's comparison of Russian sects to millenarian movements and the Radical Reformation in Western Europe, see V. Bonch-Bruevich, ed., *Materialy k istorii russkogo sektantstva i staroobriadchestva* (Saint Peterburg, 1910), vol. 4, xxviii, xxxi; and Bonch-Bruevich, "Novyi Izrail,'" *Sovremennyi mir*, 1910, no. 1, 29. His student Alexandr Klibanov, in his study of Russian sects, never mentioned the connections with the Radical Reformation. The best analyses of Soviet attitudes toward the sects after Revolution of 1917 are in Etkind, *Khlyst*, 631–74; Arto Luukkanen, *The Party of Unbelief: The Religious Policy of the Bolshevik Party* (Helsinki, 1994); Coleman, "Most Dangerous Sect."; and William Husband, *"Godless Communists": Atheism and Society in Soviet Russia, 1917–1932* (DeKalb, Ill., 2000).

30 Mykhailo Drahomanov, *Pro Bratstvo Khrestyteliv abo Baptystiv na Ukraini* (Kolomiya, 1892); Trokhym Zin'kivs'kyi, "Shtunda, ukrains'ka ratsionalistychna sekta," in T. Zin'kivs'kyi, *Pisannya Trokhyma Zin'kivs'kogo* (L'viv, 1906), vol. 2, 121–287; Mykhailo Hrushevs'kyi, *Z istorii religiinoi dumky na Ukraini* (L'viv, 1914).

31 Among the most notable American studies about the Post-Emancipation Russian society and peasants, see Jeffrey Brooks, *When Russia Learned to Read: Literacy and Popular Literature, 1861–1917* (Princeton, N.J., 1985); Ben Eklof, *Russian Peasant Schools: Officialdom, Village Culture, and Popular Pedagogy, 1861–1914* (Berkeley, Calif., 1986); Edelman, *Proletarian Peasants;* F. W. Wcislo, *Reforming Rural Russia: State, Local Society, and National Politics, 1855–1914* (Princeton, N.J., 1990), 11–45; Ben Eklof and Stephen Frank, eds., *The World of the Russian Peasant: Post-Emancipation Culture and Society* (Boston, 1990); E. Kingston-Mann, T. Mixter, and J. Burds, eds., *Peasant Economy, Culture, and Politics of European Russia,*

1800–1921 (Princeton, N.J., 1991); and Jeffrey Burds, *Peasant Dreams and Market Politics: Labor Migration and the Russian Village, 1861–1905* (Pittsburgh, 1998).

32 The only studies to date are these Ph.D. dissertations (or M.A. thesis, as noted): on the Stundists, M. Klimenko, "Die Anfaenge des Baptismus in Suederussland nach officiellen Documenten" (University of Erlangen, 1957); on evangelical sects in Russia, Andrew Q. Blane, "The Relations between the Russian Protestant Sects and the State, 1900–1921" (Duke University, 1964); on the Khlyst sect, John Eugene Clay, "Russian Peasant Religion and Its Repression: The Christ-Faith (Khristovshchina) and the Origins of the 'Flagellant' Myth, 1666–1837" (University of Chicago, 1989); on the Molokans in the Trans-Caucasia, Nicholas B. Breyfogle, "Heretics and Colonizers: Religious Dissent and Russian Colonization of Transcaucasia, 1830–1890" (University of Pennsylvania, 1998); on the Russian Baptists after the Revolution of 1905, Coleman, "Most Dangerous Sect"; and on Stundism as a part of a broader evangelical movement (especially of the Baptists) in the Russian Empire, S. Nesdoly, "Evangelical Sectarianism in Russia: A Study of the Stundists, Baptists, Pashkovites, and Evangelical Christians, 1855–1917 (Queens University, 1971), and L. Klippenstein, "Religion and Dissent in the Era of Reform: The Russian Stundobaptists, 1858–1884" (M.A. thesis, University of Minnesota, 1971.

Also see the work done in the Soviet Union, starting with the fundamental study by the Soviet historian Alexander Klibanov, *Istoria religioznogo sektantstva v Rossii (60-e gody XIX v.–1917 g.)* (Moscow, 1965), and including two Ph.D. dissertations on radical sects as a manifestation of class struggle among the Russian and Ukrainian peasantry: Vasilii Sarychev, "Sotsial'no-ekonomicheskie i politicheskie aspekty rasprostranenia baptizma v Rossii (evropeiskaia chast', 1860–e–1917 gg.)" (Iaroslavl' University, 1989), and Oksana Beznosova (Kudinova), "Pozdnee protestantskoe sektantstvo Iuga Ukrainy (1850–1905)" (Dniepropetrovsk University, 1998). The best Soviet and post-Soviet studies on the radical sects in post-Emancipation Russia are Klibanov, *Istoria religioznogo;* V. V. Sarychev, "Sotsial'no-ekonomicheskie i politicheskie aspekty rasprostranenia baptizma v Rossii (evropeiskaia chast', 1860–e–1917 gg.)" (Ph.D. dissertation, Iaroslavl' University, 1989); and Beznosova, "Pozdnee protestantskoe sektantstvo," and Aleksandr A. Panchenko, *Khristovshchina i skopchestvo.* Compare with a recent textbook for the Baptist theological seminary in Odessa: *Istoria baptizma: Sbornik,* pod red. L.Gorodetskogo i dr. [ed. L. Gorodetskii and others] (Odessa, 1996), 312–409. The chapter on Stundism in late imperial Russia is reprinted from Sergei Savinskii's book written for the same seminary: S. N. Savinskii, *Istoria russko-ukrainskogo baptizma: Uchebnoe posobie* (Odessa, 1995). See his recent book, S. N. Savinskii, *Istoria evangel'skikh khristian-baptistov Ukrainy, Rossii, Belarussii (1867–1917).* (Sankt-Petersburg, 1999).

On Russian sects, also see Edmund Heier, *Religious Schism in the Russian Aristocracy 1860–1900: Radstockism and Pashkovism* (The Hague, 1970); Hans Brandenburg, *The Meek and the Mighty: The Emergence of the Evangelical Movement in Russia* (New York, 1977); and Laura Engelstein, *Castration and the Heavenly Kingdom: A Russian Folktale* (Ithaca, N.Y., 1999). Recent studies of the "peasant religion" ignored the radical sects and their influence among Russian peasants: Chris J. Chulos, "Peasant Religion in Post-Emancipation Russia: 25

Voronezh Province, 1880–1917" (Ph.D. dissertation, University of Chicago, 1994); and Vera Shevzov, "Popular Orthodoxy in Late Imperial Russia" (Ph.D. dissertation, Yale University, 1994). See also Chris J. Chulos, *Converging Worlds: Religion and Community in Peasant Russia, 1861–1917* (DeKalb: Northern Illinois Press, 2003).

33 In the 1870s, Dostoevsky wrote about Stundists: "The sect spread with fanatical swiftness, extending to other counties and provinces. The sectarians changed their mode of living and gave up carousing. . . . The (Stundist peasant) started craving for the truth, even sacrificing everything that hitherto had been held sacred by him. In fact, no degree of depravity, no pressure, no kind of humiliation can kill or eradicate in the hearts of our people the thirst for truth, since this thirst is dearest of all to them." The quotation is from F. M. Dostoevsky, *The Diary of a Writer,* trans. B. Brasol (New York, 1954), 62, 63; also see 64, 103–5, 567–69.

34 See Stepniak-Kravchinskii, *The Russian Peasantry: Their Agrarian Condition, Social Life and Religion* (Westport, Conn., 1977; 1st pr., 1888), 341: "This movement is so sprightly and fresh, so full of young reformatory zeal, that it is not easy to determine its precise formulation; but its novelty affords us . . . a precious opportunity . . . for feeling the very palpitation of the popular heart, which seeks in religion a solace for its pains and the satisfaction of its yearnings." Even such authors as I. Aksakov and Vladimir Soloviev, who had little sympathy for Protestantism, stood up to defend these sects when reactionaries unleashed a real "hunting" of Stundists; see Soloviev, "Russkaia ideia," in *O Khristianskom edinstve* (Moscow, 1994), 171ff.

35 As Alexander Klibanov noted, from the end of the seventeenth century, the most popular form of the oppositional religious movement in Russia was the Christ-Faith ("Khristoverie"); Klibanov, *Istoria religioznogo,* 39–56.

36 See also, in English, James H. Billington, *The Icon and the Axe: An Interpretive History of Russian History* (New York, 1966), 176–78; Clay, "Russian Peasant Religion"; and Engelstein, *Castration,* 13–14.

37 Russian Orthodox historiography presented the Khlysty and Skoptsy as largely anti-Orthodox and antihumanist. In 1854, Pavel Mel'nikov, a writer who worked for the Ministry of the Interior, laid the foundation for this interpretation. He used a description of the Khlysty meetings from the secret report of an agent of the bishop of Nizhnii Novgorod. Using this information in his treatise of 1854, which he presented to the administration of the Russian Orthodox Church, Mel'nikov portrayed the Khlysty as bigoted and perverted religious dissidents. Later on, he published articles in Russian periodicals and books about the Khlysty and Skoptsy. His treatise of 1854 became the main source for the first serious study of the Khlysty, which was written by I. Dobrotvorskii, a professor at Kazan' University, in the late 1850s. All others who studied the Khlysty used Dobrotvorskii's book. That is why, later, all Orthodox historians appropriated Mel'nikov's mistakes and misinterpretations. See *OZ,* 1882, no. 10, 168–69; and I. Dobrotvorskii, *Liudi bozh'i: Russkaia sekta tak nazyvaemykh dukhovnykh khristian* (Kazan', 1869). Compare this with the analysis of Clay, "Russian Peasant Religion," 199–200. See also Engelstein,

26

Castration, 69–70. The best summary of the Khlysty historiography in Russia is Aleksandr A. Panchenko, *Khristovshchina i skopchestvo*, 14–43.

38 Dobrotvorskii, *Liudi bozh'i*. He published his first studies of this tradition in *Pravoslavnyi sobesednik* in 1858, parts 1 and 2, and in 1860, part 3. According to K. Kutepov, these essays and the book were the first serious studies of the Khlysty. See K. Kutepov, *Sekta khlystov i skoptsov* (Kazan', 1882), 3–4. The best summary of the Khlysty historiography in English is Clay, "Russian Peasant Religion." See the Russian surveys in: N. Ivanovskii, "Sekta khlystov v ieia istorii i sovremennom sostoianii," *MO*, January 1898, no. 1, 23; and N. Vysotskii, "Kriticheskii obzor mnenij po voprosu o proiskhozhdenii khlystovshchiny," *MO*, 1903, no. 13, 313–25; no. 14, 438–54.

39 From the outset, the Shalaput movement was very broad. It included such diversity that contemporaries and Russian religious historians were confused about its character and evolution, and they presented the Shalaputs either as a mystical sect of the Khlyst type or as a rationalist evangelical group of proto-Baptists. Orthodox missionaries, such as S. Bondar,' and, later, Soviet scholars such as V. Bonch-Bruevich and his student A.Klibanov, included the Shalaputs as part of the "Old Israel" sect of the Khlysty; Bondar', *Sekty khlystov, shelaputov, dukhovnykh khristian, Staryi i Novyi Izrail' i subbotnikov i iudeistvuiushchikh* (Petrograd, 1916), 14–49; Bonch-Bruevich, *Materialy k istorii i izucheniu sovremennogo sektantstva i staroobriadchestva* (Saint Petersburg, 1911), vol., 4, lvi, xl–xli; and Klibanov, *Istoria religioznogo*, 57–62. At the same time, Klibanov never used the word "Shalaputy" and avoided a description of those religious practices, which were different from his concept of "Khlyst tradition." Nevertheless, in the Soviet encyclopedia, Klibanov characterized the Shalaputs as "one among the sects of a sectarian movements of the Khlysty in Russia." He considered them as the Khlyst sect of P. Katasonov (Tambov Postniks), which was later called "Old Israel" in the Orthodox missionary literature. See *Sovetskaia istoricheskaia entsiclopedia*, ed. E. M. Zhukov (Moscow, 1976), vol. 16, 116.

40 Ia. Abramov, "Sekta shalaputov," *OZ*, 1882, no. 9, 35–58; no. 10, 157–93. A.Dorodnitsyn, "Sekta shalaputov," *Ch.OLDP*, March 1889, 275–301, and June 1889, 646–712. Later on, Alexei Dorodnitsyn was ordained as the Orthodox bishop of Sumy. See also the memoirs of another Russian contemporary who confirms Abramov's and Dorodnitsyn's views: Jaakoff Prelooker, *Under the Tsar and Queen Victoria: The Experiences of a Russian Reformer* (London, 1895), 74–95. Prelooker includes the Shalaputs in a chapter about "Rationalist Sects" who were (according to his opinion) the predecessors of the Stundists.

41 V. I. Iasevich-Borodaevskaia, *Bor'ba za veru: Istoriko-bytovye ocherki i obzor zakonodatel'stva po staroobriadchestvu i sektantstvu v ego posledovatel'nom razvitii s prilozheniem statei zakona i vysochaishikh ukazov* (Saint Petersburg, 1912), 218–76; on the Pryguny, see 250–76.

42 Subsequent Soviet and Western historians also needed such a clear classification. That is why they always used pre-Revolutionary classification of Russian religious dissent.

43 See, e.g., the books written by Alexander Klibanov in the 1960s and the psychologist Alexander Etkind in 1998, and the folklorist Alexander Panchenko in 2002:

27

Klibanov, *Istoria religioznogo;* Etkind, *Khlyst,* Panchenko, *Khristovshchina i skopchestvo.* My study also uses this classification, but in a different context.

44 Compare George Williams's concept with the studies of American religious radicals, such as the one by Stephen A. Marini, *Radical Sects in Revolutionary New England* (Cambridge, Mass., 1982).

45 *Sovetskaia istoricheskaia entsiclopedia,* vol. 16, 356.

46 Rozhdestvenskii, *Iuzhno-russkii shtundism,* 12–13; A. Dorodnitsyn, *Yuzhno-Russkii Neobaptism, izvestnyi pod imenem shtundy: Po offitsial'nym dokumentam* (Stavropol, 1903), 117, 122; P. Kozitskii, *Vopros o proiskhozhdenii yuzhno-russkago Shtundizma v nashei literature* (Saint Petersburg, 1908), 3ff. This is a reprint of his articles published in *Missionerskoe obozrenie,* November 1908, 1460–74; December 1908, 1709–30. According to their analysis, it is possible to single out the following points of view in the Russian literature on Stundism: (1) Stundism was primarily a Russian phenomenon and influenced by native Russian sects (Molokans, Shalaputs, and Dukhobors); (2) although Stundism may have foreign (mostly German) origins, its development was dependent on the psychology of the Russian people; (3) Stundism was a product of German propaganda, but other causes, which prepared the ground for it in the Russian countryside, were more important; (4) Stundism was entirely a product of German propaganda and the Germanization of the Ukrainian peasantry; or (5) Stundism was not simply a product of Russian conditions or of the propaganda of German Stundism among the German colonists but was also a direct result of German Baptists' impact on southern Russian society. See *Evangelical Sectarianism in the Russian Empire and the USSR: A Bibliographic Guide.* Compiled and edited by Albert W. Warden, Jr. (Lanham, Md., 1995), 82–100.

47 See the typical studies of this kind: Klimenko, "Die Anfaenge des Baptismus"; Nesdoly, "Evangelical Sectarianism in Russia"; and Brandenburg, *Meek and the Mighty.* See also the popular survey of Russian Baptism (including history of Stundism): G. H. Ellis and L. W. Jones, *The Other Revolution: Russian Evangelical Awakenings* (Abilene, Tex., 1996), 66–70. A slightly different approach to this problem is taken in Coleman, "Most Dangerous Sect." Even the Ukrainian post-Soviet historians, such as Beznosova, overemphasized an influence of the Mennonites for the Ukrainian Stundists. See *Evangelical Sectarianism in the Russian Empire and the USSR: A Bibliographic Guide.* Compiled and edited by Albert W. Warden Jr. (Lanham, Md., 1995), 82–100.

48 Clifford Geertz explains his "symbolic approach" in his research method of the "thick description": "Believing, with Max Weber, that man is an animal suspended in webs of significance he himself has spun, I take culture to be those webs, and the analysis of it to be therefore not an experimental science in search of law but an interpretive one in search of meaning"; quoted from Geertz, *The Interpretation of Cultures* (New York, 1973), 5.

49 Geertz, *Interpretation of Cultures,* 46, 44, 89. This study follows Geertz's definition of religion, which is: "(1) a system of symbols which acts to (2) establish powerful, pervasive, and long-lasted moods and motivations in men by (3) formulating conceptions of a general order of existence and (4) clothing these conceptions with such an aura of factuality that (5) the moods and motivations seem uniquely realistic"; see Geertz, *Interpretation of Cultures,* 90.

28

50 Victor W. Turner, *The Ritual Process: Structure and Anti-Structure* (Chicago, 1969), 94–95.

51 Turner, *Ritual Process,* 110,111–12; Cohn, *Pursuit of the Millennium.*

52 Turner, *Ritual Process,* 125, 128, 129.

53 Turner, *Ritual Process,* 166, 167.

54 Max Weber, *The Sociology of Religion* (London, 1963), 196. He wrote: "Anti-rationality may be manifested in a proud virtuosity of faith, or, when it avoids this danger of arrogant deification of the creature, it may be manifested in an unconditional religious surrender and a spiritual humility that requires, above all else, the death of intellectual pride. This attitude of unconditional trust played a major role in ancient Christianity, particularly in the case of Jesus and Paul and in the struggles against Greek philosophy, and in modern Christianity, particularly in the antipathies to theology on the part of the mystical spiritual sects of the seventeenth century of Western Europe and of the eighteenth and nineteenth centuries in Eastern Europe."

55 Turner, *Ritual Process,* 172–78, 183, 189, 195.

56 E. P. Thompson coined this phrase ("moral economy") as a useful metaphor in 1971. Five years later, James Scott developed a theory of "the moral economy of the peasant" based on Thompson's metaphor. See Thompson, "The Moral Economy of the English Crowd in the Eighteenth Century," *Past and Present,* 1971, no. 50, 76–136; and James C. Scott, *The Moral Economy of the Peasant: Rebellion and Subsistence in Southeast Asia* (New Haven, Conn., 1976), 2, 3, 9.

57 Scott contrasted everyday peasants' resistance to their millennialism (*Moral Economy,* 204, 238, 192): "Compared to everyday forms of resistance that avoid direct symbolic confrontations in the interest of concrete, piecemeal gains, millennial beliefs are all-or-nothing affairs which, once activated, aim at changing the society root and branch. As such they are inherently extra local and depend on a shared collective history, with its anti-establishment symbols and myths." Also see James C. Scott, *Weapons of the Weak: Everyday Forms of Peasant Resistance* (New Haven, Conn., 1985), 333.

58 The main opponent of James Scott was Samuel L. Popkin, who argued that "peasants are continuously striving not merely to protect but to raise their subsistence level through long- and short-term investments, both public and private." See Popkin, *The Rational Peasant: The Political Economy of Rural Society in Vietnam* (Berkeley, Calif., 1979), 4. The best introductions to the Scott–Popkin controversy over the study of Russian peasantry are Edelman, *Proletarian Peasants,* 22-23, and Burds, *Peasant Dreams,* 180–81. I will use two other books by Scott: *Weapons of the Weak,* and *Domination and the Arts of Resistance: Hidden Transcripts* (New Haven, Conn., 1990). Scott defines "the public transcript" as a way of "describing the open interaction between subordinates and those who dominate." He uses the term "hidden transcript" "to characterize discourse that takes place 'offstage,' beyond direct observation by powerholders." According to Scott, the "hidden transcript" "consists of those offstage speeches, gestures, and practices that confirm, contradict, or inflect what appears in the public transcript"; see *Domination and the Arts of Resistance,* 2, 4–5.

59 Quoted from Scott, *Domination and the Arts of Resistance,* xii, xiii.

Chapter One

1 Colonization, Emancipation, and Religious Radicalism

This chapter introduces the main themes of colonization, emancipation, and religious radicalism. Several important topics are covered: frontier and models of colonization; ethnicity and demography on the southern Russian frontier; German colonization; the Ukrainian peasant as a distinctive cultural type; the economic instability and dispossession of the peasants; and the corrupt clergy and conflicts between peasants and priests. The chapter offers conclusions with regard to the economic, social, and cultural causes of the religious awakening on the southern Russian frontier.

The Frontier and Models of Colonization

Territorial expansion and a moving frontier played the same role in the history of the Russian Empire as the Western frontier did in American history.[1] The frontier was "a meeting place for civilization and wilderness," an area in which traditional cultures and institutions collided with new and sometimes opposing forces. From the late eighteenth to the early twentieth centuries, this frontier region of Russia extended over a large territory, from Bessarabia in the west to the Northern Caucasus in the east, and from the province of Kiev in the north to Tavrida in the south.

The Russian southern frontier was a place in which new and old religious dissident movements originated and proliferated in ways similar to those in the United States, where various nontraditional religious sects prospered on that country's frontier. The most numerous sects of post-Emancipation Russia (Shalaputs and Stundists) appeared in this region between the 1860s and 1890s and spread rapidly throughout the Russian Empire. This development likewise fits Frederick Jackson Turner's description of the American frontier.[2] During the colonization of the southern Russian frontier, various groups of foreign colonists, as well Russian and Ukrainian peasants and Cossacks, brought with them different cultural and religious traditions, all of which contributed to the creation of a more diversified and pluralistic society.

Several theories of colonization help explain the frontier society's development. Scholars have argued that any colonial society of the frontier reproduces "certain social and cultural forms" from the first settlers' places of origin. Frontier conditions, however, influence and modify these forms. According to the historical sociology of colonization, the first groups of settlers (so-called charter groups of colonization) establish the main "cultural configurations" for the future development of the colonial society, using the "social forms and values they brought with them."[3] The "charter groups" of settlers create the original matrix of interaction that will affect inhabitants of the frontier for generations to come. The ethos of these groups or their "folkways" ("the normative structure of values, customs and meanings") produce the "initial" sociocultural patterns, the subsequent evolution of which will create the contours of social history on the frontier.[4] In modern history, the three most general patterns of colonization have been the model of military expedition, the model of "moral economy," and the "charismatic" model.

The model of the military expedition can be described as follows. The original military expedition laid a foundation for colonization by "noblemen" and established the manorial system of power in the colonies, based on the labor of slaves and serfs. The expansion and settling of colonies usually began with military operations and the conquest of new territory. The conquerors' main priority in the occupied territory was social control rather than the effective organization of work. As a result, they sought to maintain and enforce the traditional social hierarchies they had brought with them to the new land. These settlers constituted the first social elites in the new provinces who were exempt from hard manual labor. On the southern Russian frontier, the Russian and Ukrainian landlords and Cossacks who used the labor of serfs and peasants are examples of such elites.[5]

The model of moral economy describes how the common people's traditions of "inner colonization" in Europe were linked to a traditional localism. This localism had been based on the power of the community (neighborhood) and family; that is, on a web of personal relations, on "a shared moral universe" of "the norm of reciprocity" and "the right to subsistence." This is now described as a "moral economy."[6] State peasants from the central Russian and Ukrainian provinces who migrated to the new lands tried to restore and maintain traditional social infrastructures and cultural symbols as their means of resisting change. To some extent, foreign colonists also followed this model at the beginning of the colonization of the Russian southern frontier.

Finally, the "charismatic" model pertains to certain religious (ethnoconfessional) groups who tried to restore the "Kingdom of God" and the original Christian community in the colonial environment. These charismatic groups of ascetic Protestants (or other groups with the same religious ethos) followed ethical programs that legitimized many kinds of work, honesty, and promise-keeping in business, trade agreements, and the like. In the southern frontier region of the Russian Empire, the Mennonites, Russian Old Believers, Molokans, and other religious sects with a millennial ideology represented this cultural model.[7]

In the colonial process, the first charter groups of settlers created certain Creole cultures. The local Creoles—persons born and raised in the colonies—followed their local folkways and shaped their new provincial identities through the cultural patterns the first settlers had brought to the provinces. As a result, the new immigrants to the southern Russian frontier adjusted not to a single

35

Russian culture but to a provincial "Creole" culture that had developed there over time.[8]

The new colonial societies in the southern Russian Empire became a seedbed for the proliferation of existing dissident religious groups and for the origin of new sects among new settlers. How did this frontier society create conditions for an evangelical awakening among colonists and peasants? How did the different charter groups of settlers contribute to these conditions? Why and how did local peasants oppose the resident Russian Orthodox clergy? These questions are the subject of this chapter.

Ethnicity and Demography on the Southern Russian Frontier

The southern Russian frontier had long been a multiethnic region. Various social, ethnic, and religious groups were brought to the Black Sea region of southern Russia after the Russian-Turkish wars of 1768–74 and 1787–92. There was a strong demand for hard-working and knowledgeable settlers. To settle the sparsely inhabited steppes of Novorossiia ("New Russia," the name for the colonized territory of southern Ukraine), the Russian government even recruited villages of Old Believers from the central Russian provinces. Moreover, Russian governors offered various privileges to merchants and manufacturers, permitting them to hire free labor in the province of Kherson. During the period from the 1760s to the 1820s, thousands of foreigners—Serbs, Poles, French, Swedes, Jews, Germans, and Danzig Mennonites—settled in southern Ukraine. Each brought to Ukraine their different ways of life and their own religions and cultures.

According to Elena Druzhinina, by 1860 the overwhelming majority of peasants in southern Ukraine were not privately owned serfs. They were either Russian colonists from state military settlements (a third of the entire population in Kherson province), Ukrainian Cossacks, state peasants, Polish small householders (*szlachta*—impoverished Polish nobility), or Jews, who were "enlisted as farmers." In Kherson and Ekaterinoslav provinces, the privately owned serfs represented 31 percent of the entire population, whereas in the typical

36

central Russian provinces of Tula and Smolensk this category of peasants made up 70 percent. In Podolia and Kiev provinces, the figure was 60 percent.[9] The governors of these regions of southern Ukraine reported to the authorities in Saint Petersburg about the heterogeneity of religious belief among local settlers and the dissemination of Judaism, which "became the most popular belief here except for the dominant (Orthodox) religion."[10]

In 1802, Tsar Alexander I officially granted an exemption from serfdom to all foreign colonists. The same year, the tsarist administration sent two groups of religious dissidents, Dukhobors and Molokans, to southern Russia. Although the Dukhobors were exiled to the Caucasus in the 1840s, the Molokans were left behind in Novorossia, where as early as 1809 they started the first open dialogue between Russian religious dissidents and foreign Protestants (Mennonites and Quakers). In addition, during the 1810s and 1820s the Russian government encouraged the migration of Ukrainian Cossacks to the steppe regions of the South.[11]

Ukrainian Cossacks, Russian, Polish and Ukrainian peasants, foreign colonists, and Jews inhabited the central part of southern Russia (Kiev, Volyn', Podolia, Poltava, Kherson, Ekaterinoslav, and Tavrida provinces). Many of these same groups, along with Moldavian peasants (*tsarans*) lived in the province of Bessarabia in the southwestern part of southern Russia. Don, Terek, and Kuban Cossacks, some of whom were descendants of Ukrainian peasants, dominated Stavropol' province and the region of the Don Army in the southeastern part of southern Russia. Besides peasants and European colonists, Russian military settlers, criminals, various runaways, religious dissidents, Roman Catholics, Protestants (Lutherans, Reformed, and Anabaptists), Muslims, and Turkish pagan nomads settled in this region as well.

There is detailed information about the demographic composition of all the southern provinces during the 1850s and 1860s in the official reports of the provincial administration (see the tables for 1861 and 1865–66 in appendix A). Such reports show the extreme diversity of the population in every respect, and the further south one looked, the more diverse the mix of inhabitants became. In contrast to the central provinces of Russia, the majority of the population on the southern frontier region was not ethnically Russian.

Even in the countryside, Ukrainian, Moldavian, Polish and Turkish peasants, and Ukrainian and Russian Cossacks prevailed. Jews and the German colonists (predominantly Calvinists, Lutherans, and Mennonites) made up significant portions of the rural population of the South, and in some districts they made up half of all rural inhabitants.

The entire population of southern European Russia was on the move as settlers arrived in the new lands and participated in the colonization of the territory from Bessarabia to Tavrida and the Northern Caucasus. Constant population movements, a flexible social structure, and a changing social mix typified all these frontier provinces, especially during the post-Emancipation period. As the Tavrida governor noted in 1866, "The state peasants make up (625,360) half of the entire province's population; temporary bound and free peasants comprise 1/17 of this population; and the number of colonists is as much as 888,293 (more than half of all inhabitants)." Besides German colonists and Mennonites, he noted 290 Estonians (Choukhny), 2,395 Jews-Karaites, 10,602 Orthodox (Talmudic) Jews, 107,951 Muslims (Magometans), and 5,000 Gypsies.[12]

During the 1860s, the first sectarian communities appeared in Russian military settlements in the South, such as Zlynka, Glodosy, Novo-Ukrainka, Petro-ostrov, and Piataia rota in the Elisavetgrad district of Kherson province, where the population represented "a mixture of different nationalities" and where it was easy to "find Great Russians, Germans, Jews and many of the Old Believers' sects of various names living together."[13]

According to the governors' reports, the most distinctive demographic feature of the provinces in which the new religious sects originated was the predominance of a free rural population. More than 60 percent of the population of the Russian southern frontier provinces were people who had never experienced serfdom. The demography of southern Russia with its various ethnic groups was also very different from that of typical Russian central provinces such as Moscow, Kursk, and Tver'. The rural population of those typical provinces was more homogeneous socially and ethnically than that of the South. It would not have been rare for a peasant from Tver' or Kursk to meet a Jewish person or a German colonist for the first time only during their migration to the South.

For these typical Russian peasants, this exposure to new cultural influences in the southern frontier proved shocking. The local Russian administration reflected this situation of cultural confusion and disorientation in their demographic analysis during the 1860s and 1890s, a period during which Russian and Ukrainian peasants adjusted to new conditions of life.[14]

In his annual report for 1880, the governor of a typical frontier province, Kherson, emphasized the impact of colonization in his description of the province's population. As he wrote to Tsar Alexander II:

> The main mass of the population consists of the Little Russians, followed by Moldavians, who live chiefly in the western part of the province; the Jews, who dwell in the cities are the next; then the Great Russians, who live chiefly in the eastern part of the province; and finally the Germans, who live mostly in Odessa and Tiraspol' districts. Less numerous are the groups of Bulgarians, Greeko-Bulgarians together with Serbs, and the Greeks, Poles, Armenians, French, Gypsies, and, finally the Italians.[15]

The most important result of colonization was economic growth benefiting the expansion of the non-Orthodox and non-Russian population at the expense of Russian Orthodox peasants. As a rule, all frontier governors noted this phenomenon in their annual reports. In 1890, the Kherson governor described the prevailing mass of inhabitants of his province as Russian Orthodox Christians, who made up 84 percent, whereas the Jews and German colonists made up 8 percent respectively. According to the governor, "Because of Kherson's frontier situation," the ethnic diversity of the province's population presented a "serious inconvenience from the point of view of the unity of the state." Moreover, he noted, "the foreign population of the province owns the bulk of the land, considerably more than belongs to the local Russian people."[16]

The mass dispossession of the peasants after the agrarian reforms of 1861, their geographical mobility and movement to the southern frontier, the foreign colonization of the South, and the utilization of Russian labor by non-Russian colonists created new problems for the tsarist administration in the frontier provinces. The first was a dramatic increase in population. In the province of Kherson, the population increased by 10 percent between 1885 and

1890.[17] The main reason was immigration. According to official statistics, the first and most numerous group of settlers who moved to the southern frontier and eventually became the largest charter group were state peasants from the central Russian provinces. These peasants were more enterprising and less dependent on the community system than Russian serfs. But at the same time, both the serfs and the state peasants from central Russia had never lived in a multiethnic environment. After migrating to the southern frontier, they encountered new cultural groups, particularly Germans and Jews. The German-speaking colonists constituted another charter group of settlers in the colonial South. This group created an additional problem for the local administration—the threat of German economic and cultural domination.

German Colonization: Mennonites, Jews, and the Russian Administration

When Russia expanded its frontiers in the 1760s to the 1780s southward toward the Black Sea, Empress Catherine II decided to organize the colonization and settlement of the new lands by removing the Ukrainian Cossacks from that area. To achieve this, in 1762–63 she began inviting foreign colonists of predominantly German origin to settle southern Ukraine. From the 1760s to the 1780s, the first families of German colonists entered this region and became the most important charter group of settlers there.[18]

By 1850, more than 139,000 of these colonists (among them 20,000 Mennonites from Prussia) had settled in southern Russia. By 1917, 350,000 Germans were spread throughout the Ukrainian provinces of the Russian Empire. By that time, the German population in the Russian Empire exceeded 3.5 million. There were 10,000 settlements scattered throughout fifty-three regions.[19] As a result of the Polish partitions in 1772–95, Russia annexed Ukrainian and Byelorussian lands with considerable Jewish populations. From this time on, Jews began to settle on the Russian frontier as well, but their influence as a charter group was always disparaged and restricted by the Russian administration.[20]

The Russian administration's generally pragmatic attitude toward foreigners can be traced to Peter and Catherine the Great, who both knew the role of religious sects such as Quakers, Mennonites, and Moravians in settling British North America. The first known suggestion of inviting religious sectarians (including Mennonites and Huguenots) to Russia can be found in a document dating from 1729.[21] The logic and rhetoric of this and other documents urging sectarians (mostly of Anabaptist origin) to colonize southern Russia was similar to that used by William Penn and other Quaker propagandists to encourage the colonization of New Jersey and Pennsylvania during the 1670s and 1680s.[22]

In 1762, one of Russia's agents in Germany, Johann Kanitz, in his report to Saint Petersburg, suggested inviting as colonists "those diligent, industrious inhabitants of German lands, who used to work in manufactures, factories and on the land but are now transformed into landless, homeless vagabonds and poverty-stricken beggars." In addition, he noted, "Englishmen in America, peopling the province of Florida, brought to there 800 families last year from Germany, and according to recently published information they had sent the year before more than 5,000 families." Kanitz advised settling Russia with "religious Germans," as the British and French had done in America; and asked: "Are we, Russians, worse than they?" In 1786, Georg von Trappe, the agent of Catherine's favorite, Prince Potemkin, who was commissioned as "a director and curator of Danzig Mennonites," wrote a special letter of invitation to Mennonites to settle in Russia in which he mentioned the Quaker experience in America as an example for Mennonites.[23]

The tsarist administration invited German Protestants, who were aliens to Orthodox culture, with only one purpose: to provide the Russian economy with an exemplary model for development. The period of pragmatic protection of the German colonists soon gave way to efforts to integrate the colonists into the official political structures of the Russian Empire. Russian officials, however, still acknowledged the utility of Germans for Russia. Indeed, sometimes they marveled at the miracles performed by the German colonists in the wilderness of southern Russia:

> The colonists [in Kherson province] are our "Americans," who transform our wild desert into beautiful villages with orchards and gardens; they are our

Colonization, Emancipation, and Religious Radicalism

farmer-capitalists, who enrich themselves every year, cultivate more and more land, determine its value, and raise the price of labor with their growing demand for it. Their stress on the necessity for diligent work and the simplicity of life resembles Stoic principles; and they understand both the social advantage of mutual aid and their obligation to the Russian government.[24]

Russian writers urged administrators and scholars to study the German colonists from the "Russian point of view in the hope that the German achievements and failures would help us to understand the true causes of the disorder and unsettledness of our own peasants, and point simultaneously to the methods to improve their position."[25] The Russian administration used the experience of the German colonists as a model for the colonization of southern Russia (Ukraine) as a contrast to the Ukrainian Cossacks' settlements.

Russian officials especially valued Mennonites among other groups of German-speaking colonists in the South. From the early beginning of the settlement of southern Ukraine, they granted Mennonites various special privileges. Mennonites were considered an exemplary model of industry and diligence not only by local Ukrainians but also by other German settlers:

> The Mennonite colonies in Tavrida region are, so to speak, the large research farm and model of agriculture, where everything is developing and getting better; they apply every innovation to improve the existing order, and during business-like discussions they acknowledge these innovations as useful and successful for implementation. All branches of their economy are equally prosperous—farming, cattle breeding, sheep-breeding, forestry, horticulture, apiculture, and manufactures.[26]

Even later on, when attitudes toward foreigners took a turn for the worse, the local administration emphasized the obvious positive features of the German and Mennonite colonists. Russian officials usually contrasted the industriousness of the Germans with the apathy of local Russian peasants. In 1846, the governor of Tavrida compared Russian peasants with thrifty and enterprising German settlers. He stressed that the Russian peasant has "no independence, he is afraid to count on his own abilities. And his love of work is so unsteady and unstable that it can not bring palpable results."[27] In the official reports, the German colonist was always sober and rational, while the Russian peasant was always drunk and impulsive. The Kherson governor remarked that Russian and Ukrainian peasants were "religious, rather honest and kept the sanctity of family relations," notwithstanding that they were notable "for a credulity [and] propensity to drunkenness and idleness."[28] The governor of Kiev observed the same faults in his report for 1861: "A propensity to drunkenness and idleness, noted among the simple people, prevents their prosperity and results in various crimes."[29]

The first sign of the Russian administration's changing attitude toward German colonists came in 1804. After the establishment of the Ministry of Internal Affairs, all foreign colonies were placed under the rule of its new head, Prince Kochubei, who demanded limitations on the immigration of "all these . . . impoverished, sick, old and useless . . . foreigners." His explanation for these changes confirmed that the Russian practical approach to colonists had not changed; the German settlers still were considered "useful tools" for opening up new lands and implementing new agricultural and industrial "techniques." But the Russian administration showed, however, the first signs of a fear of German dominance in southern Russia:

> When the reproduction of the population and the crowdedness in inner regions of the country will necessitate the resettling of our own subjects, the lands convenient for living in the South will be insufficient. Therefore we ought to invite fewer foreigners here, and perhaps it would be better to settle the southern regions partly with foreigners, who might be exemplary models in agriculture and industry. That is why we need to limit the importation of people from foreign lands and invite them as a last resort, and then only prosperous and well-to-do husbandmen.[30]

Such a requirement was also explicit in the special Rules for the Reception of Foreign Colonists issued on February 20, 1804.

Under Nicholas I, the conservative centralizing trend of Russian policies and the fear of "dangerous Western influences" shown in the Decembrists uprising in 1825 led to still more restrictive attitudes toward foreign colonists.   43

On February 27, 1835, the Russian administration prohibited "the entry of poor, impoverished foreigners" into Russia. In 1837, the Guardianship Committee for Foreign Settlers was automatically merged with the newly formed Ministry of State Property. In 1838, the staff of that committee was limited considerably, its local offices were closed, and the local Russian governors began to play a more significant role in the life of German colonies in provinces.[31]

During the 1830s, these events coincided and to some extent reflected a new turn in official politics expressed in the theory of Official Nationality.[32] For years to come, these tenets provided the main theoretical framework for the official interpretation of Russian national identity. This theory itself was a call for "constructing" and "inventing" a national identity that would exclude non-Orthodox or subversive cultural elements. It was a very important theory, especially for the frontier regions of Russia with their multiethnic, non-Russian, and non-Orthodox populations. In these regions, the Russian Orthodox clergy (especially the local priests) became the first proponents and practitioners (in fact, the first "constructors") of the theory of Official Nationality. They also were the first to discover the threat to Russian national identity posed by the German colonists and peasant sectarians who rejected Orthodox Christianity. The clergy from the frontier provinces started "to sound the alarm" about the necessity for restrictions on the German colonists' activities in southern Ukraine.

During the 1860s and 1870s, the Great Reforms of Alexander II destroyed the special status of German colonists, who were equated by law with the Russian peasantry. Thereafter, the German settlers of southern Russia mixed more openly with the local Ukrainian and Russian population and were legally included in the sociopolitical fabric of Russian life.[33] At the same time, the governors from the southern frontier provinces complained about what they perceived as the beginning of German expansion.[34] Since the 1870s, the local administration had reported on the expansion of Germans in the South as a "German threat." The governor of Kiev province wrote about this threat as well: "By acquiring land (in Russia) Germans enslave or oust the local Russian people, who have to obey their oppressors or leave their homeland and dwellings and look for other means of existence in other provinces as displaced migrants." The governor attributed the spread of sects (especially Stundism) in the South to German influence.[35]

In 1890, the German colonists, who made up more than 3 percent of the rural population owned 12 percent of the "productive" land in Ekaterinoslav province. Each German colonist had at least 15 *desiatin* of the land,[36] whereas each Russian or Ukrainian peasant had only 4 *desiatin*.[37] By the beginning of the twentieth century, according to the local administration, only 3 percent of virgin lands remained in Kherson province as a result of German colonization. More than one-seventh of the territory of this province was concentrated in German hands. At the same time, the number of landless peasants grew by 200,000 in 1892 and remained at the same level for a decade.[38]

The German-speaking charter groups created their own Creole cultures on the southern frontier by the 1860s. They contributed not only to shaping new local identities but also to the economic and cultural modernization of the southern Russian Empire. Their enterprising activities, their patterns of rational behavior, and even their religious practices influenced their Russian and Ukrainian neighbors.

The Mennonites were the most important agents of modernization and religious piety among the German-speaking charter groups in the South. Historically, they were the Anabaptist representatives of the Radical Christian Reformation who brought their religious teachings, their way of life, and finally their famous Protestant ethic to Russia. The classic sociologists of religion emphasized the role of such Anabaptist groups as the Mennonites in creating the "Protestant ethic as a spirit of capitalism."[39] Mennonite colonists became the most active participants in the capitalist transformation of the southern Russian provinces.

It is impossible to imagine the origin of capitalism in the Ukrainian provinces of Russia without taking into account the Mennonites' influence. They created the first efficient agricultural farms in Ukraine that were connected to the capitalist markets of Russia and Europe. Mennonites also organized the first industrial and financial firms in this region. In this way, they influenced the work and business ethics of many thousands of their Ukrainian and Russian neighbors, as well as workers and servants.

45

In 1789, the first group of Mennonites settled in Khortitsa in the Dnieper region of Ekaterinoslav province, and by the beginning of the nineteenth century they had begun settling in Molochnaia in Tavrida province of southern Ukraine. By this time, 2,000 Mennonites lived in the Dnieper region, and by 1850 more than 20,000 Mennonites from Prussia had also settled in southern Ukraine. These groups of Mennonites embodied a particular agricultural way of life, rural ethos, and mentality, and they made important agricultural innovations. During 1830, settlers in the Molochnaia colony organized the Agricultural Society, an organization that revolutionized cultivation of soil in Ukraine and introduced the four-field system in grain harvesting. A year later, the same settlers helped establish of the port of Berdiansk on the Azov Sea coast.[40]

Foreign visitors witnessed the important role of the Mennonites in the modernization of the southern Russian frontier. In May 1819, the famous British Quaker and chemist William Allen and the American Quaker Stephen Grellet visited the Mennonite settlements in Khortitsa. They noted the difference between the Mennonite houses "built of wood, very neatly thatched, and comfortable" and the dirty, small, and dark dwellings of the Ukrainian and Russian peasants. William Allen wrote that the Mennonite households presented "a striking contrast to a Russian cottage, and they [were] all furnished with a commodious barn and granary, and a garden well stocked with fruit trees."

According to the Quakers, the improvements that the Mennonite colonists had made were "delightful." Allen and Grellet marveled at a neat Mennonite house, the path to which was "strewn with lilac blossoms. The rooms also were ornamented with flowers, and every thing bore the marks of neatness and comfort." The Quakers also visited a Mennonite cloth manufactory, where the Mennonites employed "an Englishman to conduct the process of dyeing." Nearby was "a nursery of fruit and forest trees, from whence the colonies in the neighbourhood were supplied." Allen also commented, "the good effects of this wise plan are quite incalculable." According to the Quaker visitors, the Mennonite achievements were beyond praise. In 1867, the British Quakers Isaac Robson and Thomas Harvey visited the same Mennonite settlements in Ukraine, and they were also impressed by their achievements.[41]

The Mennonites from the Khortitsa colonies provided all Ukrainian settlers with their own "German" model of transport wagons. These became so popular among the Ukrainian and Russian peasants that they began to build their own such wagons. The first agricultural machine factories in southern Russia, belonging to the Mennonite families, were Lepp & Wallman, Hildebrandt's Sons and Priess, and Abraham Koop. The Khortitsa Mennonites also established the first watchmaking plant and the first grinding mills. In 1809 the Niebuhr family in Khortitsa introduced rollers in mills, and in 1884 the Thiessen family in Ekaterinoslav introduced steam engines on rollers, also in mills. More than half of all grinding steam mills in Ekaterinoslav province belonged to Mennonites. Because of the Mennonites' economic activities, Ekaterinoslav province produced 10.5 percent of all agricultural machines and equipment in the entire Russian Empire; three-quarters of these machines were manufactured in the Mennonite colony of Khortitsa. According to materials located in the Dniepropetrovsk archive, Mennonites were also pioneers of silkworm breeding in southern Ukraine.[42]

The Mennonites not only brought and invented new instruments and technology but also displayed attitudes and approaches to work that were alien to Russians and Ukrainians. All Russian observers contrasted the economic behavior and ethics of the Mennonites with those of the "Russian settlers." The Mennonites did not waste their time, and they organized their work rationally. They did not drink alcohol, and they maintained healthy family relations. They celebrated twelve fewer church holidays than did Russian or Ukrainian Orthodox peasants. Russian marriage and burial festivities usually lasted ten to fourteen days, with much heavy drinking and eating, whereas the Mennonites allowed only one day for these events. Mennonite farmers tried to finish their work during inclement weather, whereas the Russian peasant usually quit if the weather was unfavorable. Cleanliness, neatness, and rational organization and planning distinguished the Mennonite colonies in Ukraine from the dirty, impoverished, ill-kept Ukrainian and Russian settlements. Honesty, promise keeping, and the absence of theft inside the community were all distinctive components of the Mennonite way of life—in contrast to the everyday cases of cheating and stealing that were typical of villages in southern Ukraine.[43]

In 1848 Cornelis Hildebrand, a young Ukrainian Mennonite, noted in his memoirs that he tried to live honestly by his own labor without wasting time. He cited lyrics from the favorite song of his master, the Mennonite Hamm, which illustrate the Mennonite attitude toward time: "O precious time, you can not waste a moment of your life, because one minute of your life disappears in a blink of eye, and it will never come back; so you have to appreciate every moment of precious time." He likewise censured the "selfishness" and "greed" of those who "accumulated" their capital and land not for productive uses, but for "a wrongful indulgence" of "sinful dreams." At the same time, he praised the thrifty industrious workers in agriculture and in "craftsmanship." Hildebrand described his own version of the Protestant ethic on the southern Russian frontier:

> Craftsmanship nourishes him who pursues it seriously. The true craftsman, however, has to utilize [his] time. There can be no "lying on the bear rug," especially if he wishes to remain independent. There are not many free hours marked on his day calendar. He will get nowhere without callous hands and tiredness in his bones. Not all become rich at all. But no one in the German colonies has starved or really suffered want, for that matter—no one who was healthy and strong and has worked diligently, whether it's on the land or in the shop. The secret of success lies to a large degree in [the] song, "O, precious time!"[44]

The Mennonites likewise praised diligence in their proverbs: "One must build one's home oneself; the years of life pass so quickly that one cannot begin soon enough with the task." Hermann Niebuhr, another Mennonite settler from Dnieper valley, contrasted the behavior of the local Ukrainians with the work ethic of his own family. From the 1840s to the 1860s, the archeological excavations in southern Ukraine generated interest among the local peasants in finding "gold treasure" in the ancient Scythian burial mounds, and some spent their lives in vain digging in those places. Only the Mennonites did not care about the Scythian gold and never visited the excavation cites. They continued to carry out their agricultural work industriously and became rich without digging for hidden wealth. "There was nothing to the buried treasures,"

48

Niebuhr wrote in his memoirs, "Others also found nothing. We worked all the more diligently on the farm and in the mill. We don't have to mention the results. Gold was found, but in a different way."[45]

The members of the Mennonite communities had a direct impact on both agriculture and on the well-being of their workers, who were usually Ukrainian and Russian peasants. As the first charter group, the Mennonites set the main rules for the cultural dialogue with their Russian and Ukrainian neighbors, who settled later in the southern frontier region. After the reforms of the 1860s, thousands of these peasants came to the Mennonite and German households as agricultural workers and had to follow the new work discipline and moral rules of their masters. The Protestant ethic of the German-speaking colonists contributed to the modern organization of agricultural labor on the southern frontier of the Russian Empire.

In 1905, in his famous essay on the Protestant ethic and the spirit of capitalism, Max Weber emphasized the role of evangelical religion (particular Puritanism) in shaping the work discipline of the oncoming capitalist era. "The power of religious asceticism," he wrote, "provided the bourgeois businessman . . . with sober, conscientious, and unusually industrious workmen, who clung to their work as to a life purpose willed by God." Weber was conscious of the importance of work discipline among the labor force as a prerequisite for successful industrial capitalism. The Russian and Ukrainian peasants, who were hired by the Mennonites or other religious German colonists and lived in the German-speaking households, underwent special religious education.

The main objective of this education was to create a new labor discipline among these workers. The Mennonites and other pious colonists tried to inculcate new patterns of obedience in their Russian and Ukrainian workers. The intense religious indoctrination in the German-speaking households influenced these workers. Their Mennonite masters taught them "the virtues of hard work, industry and submission to authority and to behave in the sure knowledge that they were being watched by an all-seeing eye." Moreover, the Mennonites themselves provided to their workers a positive example of such an industrious and sober life. Another important influence for these workers was the Mennonite "sense of community." Russian and Ukrainian peasants who left   49 their families and lost connections with their former communities found in the Mennonite households a substitute for the older social patterns they had left behind. The Mennonites and German Pietists preached new ideas of love and solidarity among all Christians. This preaching also made such ideas attractive to their workers, who were impoverished peasants. As E. P. Thompson noted, the revivalism of the Christian Pietists and their appeal to compensation in the afterlife represented "a chiliasm of the defeated and the hopeless" that tended to attract those who felt themselves uprooted and oppressed.[46]

The Mennonites shaped the mentality of the new agricultural labor force and contributed to increasing human capital on the southern Russian frontier. At the same time, they and their Russian and Ukrainian workers developed what can only be described as an "entrepreneurial ability in acquiring information and adjusting to the disequilibria inherent in the process of modernization."[47]

Rapid social change also provoked envy and hatred, particularly against Jews, and here also the Mennonites had a lesson to impart. During the 1870s and 1880s, the local peasants from Kiev, Kherson, Tavrida, and Ekaterinoslav provinces complained about the "criminal activities of Jews," and a concentration of land "in the hands of the rich German colonists." At the same time, these peasants expressed a "tremendous respect" for "the industrious Mennonists."[48] During the anti-Jewish "pogrom" in Alexandrovsk on May 1, 1881, one Jew fled to the Mennonite colony of Schoenwiese. The local Ukrainian and Russian peasants knew that the Jewish fugitive was hiding in the "German store," but they did not attack the Mennonite house and soon retreated. As David Epp, a Mennonite author, explained: "The Mennonite name could protect any Jewish fugitive, but the Russian house owner could not protect his Jewish tenant."[49] Until the civil war in Ukraine in 1918, local Ukrainian and Russian peasants never attacked Mennonite households. They still respected their peaceful and diligent neighbors, even when the Mennonites tried to protect the Jewish fugitives.[50]

The Jews had posed a serious problem for the Russian administration since the early colonization of the southern frontier. On the one hand, in the 1760s the Russian officials were interested in inviting "all useful foreigners, including the Jews (Yids), for settling the new lands and developing the industry and trade" in the colonial South. On the other hand, in 1790 the Russian administration refused Jews the right to settle in the interior of Russia and directed Jewish settlement to the colonial South.[51] Jewish settlers constituted a distinctive charter group that also influenced the economic and cultural development of the South. Gradually, they learned to avoid the official limitations of their business activities. Sometimes, they adjusted to the strict requirements of the Russian authorities by developing illegal connections with the criminal world. Russian merchants and businessmen considered Jews to be dangerous rivals.

The local Russian administration reflected this attitude of the provincial elites and complained to authorities in Saint Petersburg about the increase in Jewish influence as "the most dangerous demographic trend." In the province of Bessarabia during 1875 alone, the Jewish population grew by 29 percent, while the Russian Orthodox Christian population increased by only 2 percent.[52] In the province of Kherson, from 1885 to 1890, the number of the Jews grew by 22 percent and made up 8 percent of the entire population. According to the governor of Kherson, it was necessary to protect the Russian peasants from exploitation by Jews, who rented land, kept public houses, and sold alcohol. "The Jews," the governor wrote to the tsar, "present a united community, which is moving toward one planned goal—self-enrichment by all possible means at the expense of others."[53]

All governors in the frontier provinces of Russia expressed such misgivings about the Jewish threat, beginning with the 1870 report of the governor of Kiev, who suggested how to prevent a conflict between Ukrainian peasants and the Jews "who exploited them and made them drunkards."[54] The local administration received many complaints from peasants about the criminal activities of Jews in the countryside. In the majority of cases, the authorities accepted these complaints. The police also informed the local administration about the criminal activities of Jewish settlers. The most typical crimes were trade in stolen goods, the unlicensed sale of alcohol, moneylending, and operating gambling dens and brothels.[55]

It is noteworthy that a majority of the peasants' complaints targeted only

Jews or Germans as their main "oppressors" and "bloodsuckers." As the police investigations revealed, there was no mention of Ukrainians and Russians who were active participants in the "Jewish crimes." In fact, every criminal case involved Russian or Ukrainian accomplices of the "Jewish criminals." But local peasants blamed only Jews and Germans. For the Russian and Ukrainian peasants, especially for recent migrants, the "alien others"—Germans and Jews—were the obvious "cultural opponents." Therefore, these "cultural others" became the first victims of the ethnic hatred in the southern provinces. Police documents reflected the local peasants' inclination to blame their Jewish and German neighbors for all their problems.[56]

Nevertheless, Russian and Ukrainian peasants adjusted themselves to the new frontier situation after the first cultural shock and developed new forms of adaptation, including the incorporation and appropriation of new cultural elements. The cultural dialogue between the local peasants, on the one hand, and foreign colonists and Jews, on the other, shaped new identities among the rural population and undermined the dominant preexisting concept of what it meant to be Russian. The Russian administration was anxious to maintain and protect the Russian national identity of the peasantry of the southern frontier in the struggle with the economic and cultural influence of Germans and Jews. Moreover, the provincial administration of the South encountered another ethnic identity among the local peasants, which differed from the stereotype of the Russian Orthodox peasant. Russian officials called those peasants the "Little Russians." The Little Russian (or Ukrainian) peasants made up the most numerous charter group of settlers on the southern frontier. In some provinces, such as Kiev, Poltava, Podolia, and Volynia, they were the first native settlers. During the post-Emancipation period, they took an active part in the colonization of the southern frontier as well (figures 1.1 and 1.2).

The Ukrainian (Little Russian) Peasant as a Distinctive Cultural Type

The Ukrainian historian D. Bagaley notes that for centuries the Dnieper River region of southern Ukraine had been a special free zone without servitude and

Figure 1.1. Peasant and colonist houses in the village of Natalovka, Aleksandrovskii district, Ekaterinoslav province, at the beginning of the twentieth century. The German house is in the middle. Notice the difference between the Ukrainian and German houses. From the collection of the Dniepropetrovsk State Historical Museum, Ukraine.

serfdom. These lands were under the control of Ukrainian warriors, the Zaporizhia Cossacks, who had originally been runaway peasants. These traditions of freedom prevented, in his opinion, the establishment of a stable system of serfdom and servile labor typical in other parts of the Russian Empire.[57] Eventually, in 1775, the Russian administration destroyed the main fortress of the Ukrainian Cossacks, Zaporiz'ka Sich, but at the same time it tried to keep runaways and former Cossacks, who had already settled on the land and cultivated it, in southern Ukraine.[58]

Contemporaries and modern scholars have stressed the differences between the Russian and Ukrainian agricultural systems in that region. Whereas Russian peasants were used to a communal system of ownership in the village, Ukrainian peasants preferred a private family system of households. That was

53

Figure 1.2. The German Mennonite colony in the village of Khortitsa, Dnieper region, Ekaterinoslav province. From the collection of the Dniepropetrovsk State Historical Museum, Ukraine.

why the Ukrainians sometimes settled outside villages in a separate household (*khutor*).

The fundamental characteristic of the Ukrainian village was the absence of collective forms of ownership, labor, and administration. Notwithstanding the prevalence of serfdom in Russia, even bonded Ukrainian peasants retained individual private property and denied all forms of communal agriculture until the Emancipation of 1861. After abolishing serfdom in Russia during the 1860s, Russian authorities forced Ukrainian farmers to adopt an alien communal village social system (the so-called *obshchina*[59] and *krugovaya poruka*[60]), which undermined the Ukrainian peasants' cultural traditions and destroyed their means of resistance to outsiders (their "moral economy") and local politics.[61] As a result of the historical tradition of private property and intensive colonization, southern Ukraine became the only region in imperial Russia

54

where free hired workers rather than serfs did the most of fieldwork during the 1850s.[62]

Immediately before and after the reform of 1861, discontented peasants from the central Russian provinces moved to southern Ukraine in search of food, work, and land. Since the 1850s, thousands of peasant families had found such seasonal migrations from Russian or northern Ukrainian regions to the south necessary for survival.[63] Ukrainian and Russian peasants made up the overwhelming majority of these migrants. Since the beginning of colonization, the Russian administration on the southern frontier had noted the obvious cultural differences between Russians, Ukrainians, and colonists. In 1847, the governor of Ekaterinoslav described the Ukrainians' cultural identity, "distinctive features of which were cleanness and tidiness of home life, puritanism of family morals, a spirit of enterprise, and a love of work." The governor found those features missing among Russian peasants.[64] By the middle of the nineteenth century, an overwhelming majority of the population, not only in the Ukrainian provinces but also in adjacent districts of Russian provinces such as Voronezh and Kursk, was ethnically Ukrainian. This majority consisted of peasants who spoke the Ukrainian language rather than Russian and had different habits and customs. Captain V. Pavlovich, a military officer in charge of the geographical description of Ekaterinoslav province in 1857, described the local Ukrainian peasants as culturally distinct from their Russian neighbors.[65]

Notwithstanding their cultural differences, the Russian and Ukrainian peasants experienced no cultural conflicts between 1861 and 1905. All governors confirmed this in their reports.[66] The common religion established by the charter groups made the accommodation of the newly arrived groups easier. The local administration reflected this accommodation as well as the mutual cultural influences between Russian and Ukrainian peasants.[67]

Nevertheless, all observers, including the tsarist governors, understood the distinctive cultural character of the Ukrainian ethnic type.[68] Sometimes, the governors of the Ukrainian provinces linked these cultural differences to a social transformation of the Ukrainian countryside after the reforms of the 1860s. Thus, in 1902 the governor of Kharkov emphasized how national features of the Ukrainian peasants influenced their economic activity, social

55

organization, and social conflicts in the post-Emancipation Ukrainian village. "The main feature of the Little Russian national character," he wrote to the tsar, "is the predominance of individualistic notions over ideas of public good. In contrast to the Great Russian peasant, the Little Russian is largely an individualist: he is alien to community, cooperative, and family-kin connections; and if the communal land property is the dominant type of peasant landownership in the Little Russian provinces, this fact can be completely explained by the government's regulations providing for a punctual receipt of all the peasants' payments." In his reports, this governor emphasized the existence of "a distinct Little Russian national character," which was "alien to communal landownership."[69]

This Ukrainian identity became especially vivid during the introduction of the communal system of landownership in the Ukrainian countryside. The official documents showed how the agricultural reforms increased the process of the breaking up of the Ukrainian peasants' households and, as a result, the increase in individual small peasants' landholdings. One Russian official noted that the "unrestrained process of breaking up the peasants' property made it difficult for peasants to run their household at a level providing the necessary means for the survival of the family." This led to a search for outside income. The mass dispossession of the Ukrainian peasants resulted in a crisis of identity and their alienation from traditional society. According to Robert Edelman, who studied the participation of "Ukrainian peasant workers" in the Revolution of 1905, these peasants "had become proletarianized."[70]

The Russian administration witnessed a very significant trend among Ukrainian peasants: a growing preference for private landownership and a striving to legitimate this preference by any means, including religion. The agrarian reforms of the 1860s and the dispossession of the Ukrainian peasants led both to their general impoverishment and to conflicts over land. The Ukrainian peasants had become landless "proletarians in the peasant community." This situation also had the effect of raising the Ukrainian peasants' expectations for land allocation on their behalf and psychologically preparing them for future land reform in the Ukrainian village.

56 According to contemporary observers, peasants in the Ukrainian provinces

of Russia expected such land redistribution. A Russian Populist, Vladimir Debagorii-Mokrievich, who was active in Kiev province at the beginning of the 1870s, noted in his memoirs that the local peasants wanted a redistribution of the land "done proportionally according to the number of people of all ranks and estate without any differences." As one Kiev peasant explained to him: "Everything should be distributed equally for everybody: for a peasant, for a 'pan' ["a landowner," in Polish], for a Jew, and for a Gypsy." In 1874, peasants linked their expectations for a repartition of the land to the military reform that was instituted at that time. They thought that the tsar would take everybody into the army—"either pan (a landowner), or Gypsy, or peasant"—and afterwards he would "distribute the land equally to everybody."[71]

The liberal journalist I. Kharlamov quoted a popular Ukrainian proverb to demonstrate the Ukrainians' anticommunal notions: "All communal property belongs to the devil." He maintained that the Ukrainian peasant accepted only one form of community—the family. Hence the famous Ukrainian saying—the "best community is a husband and wife." In their criticism of Russian priests and skepticism about the Russian Orthodox Church, the Ukrainian Orthodox peasants were more radical and stubborn than their Russian counterparts. "Nowhere in central Russia," wrote the same journalist, "would you meet such a vivid, nasty mockery of the Russian priest, such a contemptuous attitude toward him, as here among the 'Little Russians.'" The Ukrainian peasants used to say, "a priest and landowner have the same interests," or "the priest is interested in finding more to eat for himself rather than serving other people." The most radical Ukrainian proverb of the 1860s and 1870s reflected an obvious hatred of the Russian clergy in the Ukrainian countryside: "Beat the priest, but remember to avoid the priest's head since it was consecrated."[72]

Peasants from the Ukrainian provinces were especially frustrated with the lack of changes in church life during the era of reform. They expected more participation from ordinary members of the congregation in church rituals and ceremonies. Ukrainian peasants were fond of singing, but as one reporter noted, their "inner necessity" to sing during the church ceremony was not always satisfied in the Orthodox Church. That was why the religious sects attracted these peasants by the opportunity to sing together, especially "to sing religious

57

song in chorus."[73] The distinct cultural identity of the Ukrainian peasants revealed itself in their perception of religious rituals and the performance of religious services in the Russian Orthodox Church as well. They loved to sing religious songs and psalms, and they knew their melodies and lyrics by heart.

In contrast to the peasants from the central Russian provinces, the Ukrainian peasants developed their aesthetic notions and tastes under different cultural conditions. Historically, the inhabitants of the Ukrainian countryside were more exposed to new cultural influences from Catholic Poles, Jews, German colonists, and Turkish nomads. As a result, the Ukrainians' cultural life was more varied and incorporated all these influences as well. Moreover, the traditions of Cossack freedoms, including the democratic elements of village administration and the important role of laity in the Ukrainian Orthodox Church (before 1654), were still alive in Ukrainian society. As one Orthodox writer noted, the Ukrainian peasant always expressed "a strong distinctive desire to participate in a religious ceremony as an equal of the clergy."[74]

Since the late eighteenth century, the Ukrainian peasants, as the original charter group of the Russian frontier, had been losing their historical freedoms and cultural traditions. In fact, in the Ukrainian countryside, the Russian administration tried to eliminate Cossack freedoms and replace the old Ukrainian traditions with Russian forms and ideas. The reforms of the 1860s generated new hopes among Ukrainian peasants about a restoration of the old liberal traditions of village and church life with an active role for all parishioners. Ukrainians were disappointed, however, because the reforms did not bring any changes to their church life. That was why they tried to find more adequate forms to satisfy their expectations and hopes outside the Russian Orthodox Church.

According to contemporaries, the main reason for the spread of non-Orthodox sects was the fact that sectarian leaders allowed "all peasants to participate not only in singing but in performing religious rituals and preaching." Ukrainian peasants were quoted as saying: "A religious ceremony is better in the Stundist meeting because everybody is singing there, while during our [Orthodox] ritual only a priest and deacon drawl out a melody."[75] They preferred the more democratic and inclusive religious rituals of the new sects.

One Ukrainian peasant who witnessed the sectarians' funeral services noted that the "Stundists have a much better burial service; it is more beautiful than our (Orthodox) ritual."[76]

The language of the service was another serious problem for Ukrainian Orthodox Christians. Many Russian priests realized that Ukrainian peasants did not understand the Old Church Slavonic language and misunderstood the Russian language as well. In the 1880s, in the liberal magazine *Herald of Europe*, Mikhailo Kostomarov, a famous Ukrainian historian, raised the question of conducting religious services in Ukrainian for Ukrainian congregations. The Ukrainian priests complained that the Ukrainian language was forbidden for religious sermons under the threat of defrocking. This ban on the Ukrainian language added to the alienation of the Ukrainian-speaking congregations from the Russian-speaking clergy.[77] Problems of language and the misunderstanding of Orthodox religious ceremonies contributed to cultural confusion in the Ukrainian countryside, and as a result, disoriented Ukrainian peasants tried to create their own religious identity by joining new evangelical sects on the southern Russian frontier (figure 1.3).

Economic Instability and the Dispossession of the Peasants

After the reforms of the 1860s, the peasantry lived through a difficult period of adaptation. Peasant society experienced increased stratification as well as the new territorial mobility. This generated a break in traditional family and communal connections. In search of a better life, impoverished and landless peasants moved to the South and endured en masse the hardships of adapting to and becoming socialized in a new place. The provincial administration was anxious about this and asked the central authorities for assistance.

What alarmed the provincial governors the most was the existence of displaced peasants outside the "village community" and traditional village power structures. In the South, migrant peasants lived without traditional rules, and the provincial administration saw them as peasants without a traditional identity. The governor of Kherson complained in 1887, "Because of the absence of a law about forming new independent village communities from representatives

59

Figure 1.3. Ukrainian peasants in the village of Vasilievka, Novomoskovsk district, Ekaterinoslav province; the estate of Count Nostitz (1885). From the collection of the Dniepropetrovsk State Historical Museum, Ukraine.

of various estates, these people [displaced migrant peasants] do not have rights in a village community, i.e., peasant society, and therefore they have no rights to meetings or decision making regarding their economic activity and the election of the local village administration."[78] The majority of migrant peasants could not join the peasant charter groups in the South and maintain their traditional peasant status. They became agricultural workers in the southern frontier region, losing their traditional identity. Indeed, they underwent a process known as "dislocated identity," something typical for all colonized societies, including southern Russia.[79]

The economic situation was aggravated by the extensiveness of the traditional system of soil cultivation that led to poor harvests. During the 1860s and 1870s, a good yield for winter cereal crops was considered to be six times what was sown, and for spring crops, three and a half times.[80] The Stavropol governor reported to the tsar in 1871: "The harvest yield can not be called sufficient because it was no more then three times what was sown."[81] The Kherson governor wrote Alexander II in his report for 1866: "For a long time, a shortage of workers, the extensiveness of the steppes, and the absence of available capital will result in a poor level of land cultivation in the province. That is why cattle breeding, and especially sheep breeding, are still considered the most profitable spheres of the local economy." The Ekaterinoslav governor noted similar trends: "Processing of wheat and flax, especially processing of flax-seeds for export trade, and breeding of fine-wool sheep make up the main branches of local agriculture."[82] These trends of economic development in the southern frontier required more agricultural workers than traditional peasants, explaining why a majority of the migrant peasants became new agricultural workers.

Those peasants who were lucky enough to maintain their traditional identity in the South had problems of accommodating the new agricultural conditions as well. Since 1871, all the southern provinces of European Russia had suffered periodically from bad harvests. In his report for 1885, the governor of Kherson complained that

> since 1880 Kherson province has had almost two complete crop failures (in 1882 and 1885), one very bad harvest (in 1880), two satisfactory harvests (in 1883 and 1884), and only one good harvest (in 1881). Therefore, notwithstanding the increasing amount of arable land, Kherson province, known as "a granary of the South," now needs foodstuffs almost every year, sometimes for a considerable portion of the population. [The peasants are responsible for these poor results because they tried] to solve their problems by extending the arable land rather than utilizing intensively their existing land.[83]

Many governors tried to encourage peasants to use more modern techniques, but all their efforts were in vain. The peasants did not show any interest in agricultural innovations. Peasants even refused to visit the All-Russian Agricultural Exhibition in Kiev in 1880. The governor urged the local administration to stimulate the peasants' interest in modern agriculture, but officials often found that the local elite also had little interest in disseminating any kind of agricultural knowledge among peasants.[84]

The governors in their official reports to the tsar expressed anxiety about the impoverishment of the post-Emancipation peasantry in the southern provinces.[85] This economic situation was mainly a result of the agrarian reforms of the 1860s, which led to the indebtedness of all groups of peasants (including the state peasants and former serfs).[86] In his special report of 1885, the governor of Tavrida asked the tsar to provide local peasants with a sufficient amount of arable land. He noted that under the agrarian reforms it was necessary to take into consideration each peasant's individual position rather than the interests of the peasant community.[87] Many governors of the southern provinces made the same recommendations and suggestions. In 1900, the governor of Kherson calculated that local peasants needed a minimum of 10 *desiatin* for each household to survive. This governor suggested granting all land as private property to the peasants. Without private land, in his opinion, the peasants had no motivation to work, and as a result they waited constantly for redistribution of communal land.[88]

The institutions of the village community that were foisted on peasants by the central authorities by the Emancipation undermined the traditional work ethic of the southern Russian peasants and generated social conflicts. The communal peasants on the southern frontier lived side by side with prosperous private landowners and foreign colonists. Facing dispossession, these peasants envied their prosperous neighbors. The governor of Kherson noted this dangerous trend among the local peasants. "Holding their land as public property," he wrote, "the communal peasants are dangerous neighbors for private owners, especially small landowners, because in all conflicting situations the former peasants are inclined to solve these conflicts by appealing to their communal law. In general, communal landholding weakens the notion [*chuvstvo*] of property in a peasant society with each new generation."[89]

These negative results of the agrarian reforms in the southern provinces were aggravated by geographical mobility and confusion in social relations among migrant peasants. These uprooted peasants from central Russian and Ukrainian provinces with their "dislocated" identities had problems adjusting

62

to the cultural rules of the charter rural groups in the South. Southern rural society had lost the traditional symbolic code that had been understandable to these "displaced" peasants.

By the end of the nineteenth century, impoverished and culturally disoriented peasants living on the brink of physical survival were ready to react violently against any "cultural alien" who looked threatening—whether a prosperous landowner, a colonist, or a Jew. The governor of Ekaterinoslav reported to the tsar in 1901: "The peasants' landlessness has become a common phenomenon in the province. When there was a landlord's property close to a village, the worsening of social relations did not reach a critical point; but when that property moved from a legitimate heir to either a kulak or a colonist, then the hostility between them and the peasants often became very dangerous."[90] The desperate peasants tried to restore traditional justice in the southern countryside among all rural inhabitants. They considered unequal land distribution the main reason for their sufferings. Eventually, the peasants directed their hostility against anyone who had more land and lived better than they did.[91]

Revolutionary transitions from one phase of social development to another often lead to the dispossession and impoverishment of the masses. Such transitions have always resulted in social and cultural confusion, an identity crisis, and cultural disorientation. The sufferings of the transitional period also tend to provoke religious hopes about compensation in the "afterlife" among the dispossessed classes. This "chiliastic optimism of the oppressed" (according to Karl Mannheim), or "chiliasm of the defeated and hopeless" (according to E. P. Thompson) led to the organization of a religious community that could serve as a substitute for the older social patterns of living destroyed by the revolutionary changes.

The peasants of southern Russia underwent such revolutionary changes. In their disappointment with the social conditions and the Russian Orthodox Church, they turned to dissident religious movements.[92] According to a priest, Ioann Nedzel'nitskii, the Russian Orthodox Church regarded defection as social

63

protest. In Kherson province, the first peasant disturbances after the reform of 1861 occurred in the village of Liubomirka, where the future Stundist movement would originate. The provincial administration sent troops to suppress the peasant riots in Liubomirka in 1862. During debates with such Orthodox missionaries as Nedzel'nitskii, the sectarians always stressed the injustice in land distribution and the clergy's defense of the large landlords' interests. The peasant Stundist from Liubomirka, P. Greeva, publicly expressed his indignation at the local landowner, the nobleman Nikolai Shebeko, a former governor of Bessarabia, who owned 150,000 *desiatin* of land in their village. He told the local priest, M. Kazakevich:

> We [200 householders] don't have even 1,500 *desiatin* per household. I, myself, pay more than 20 rubles a year for two pieces of land [7 *desiatin*]—is this fair? Does this correspond to the Holy Scripture? Because of you [priests], and your bishops, the Divine Word cannot be fulfilled. You [the Orthodox clergy] are the main obstacle to putting Holy Scripture into practice. Because of you, nothing could be done.[93]

In 1880, in another region populated by Stundists, in the Kievan, Tarashcha, and Vasil'kov districts of Kiev province, local peasants resisted a new division of arable land, and the governor sent in troops.[94] The new sects resulted from the social protests of impoverished and frustrated peasants on the Russian southern frontier. As one Orthodox reporter noted, the development of "our rationalist sects represented an opposition to the existing order of the church and new conditions of life."[95]

The Corrupt Clergy and Conflicts between Peasants and Priests

This opposition to "the existing order of the church" generated serious conflicts between the Orthodox clergy and the peasants of the southern provinces. These conflicts undermined the traditional power structures at the parish level and slowed down the process of "social replication" in the countryside of the frontier region. The peasant society of the southern provinces became more

64

diverse and more "culturally alien" than the Russian administration had antic-ipated. Local priests were supposed to play an important role in maintaining the Russian Orthodox Christian character of the Russian peasantry. Yet look-ing for "true religion," local peasants resisted priests they viewed as corrupt, priests who had failed to satisfy their spiritual needs.

The local police reported that the major cause of the spread of non-Orthodox sects on the southern Russian frontier was the alienation of local peasants from the Russian Orthodox Church. Day by day, the peasants became convinced of the corruption of the Russian Orthodox clergy. The more peasants knew about this, the less they respected the local priests. The numerous press reports and rumors of corruption in the clergy also contributed to the peasants' disaffection from the Orthodox Church.

On January 8, 1862, the Third Section of the Imperial Chancellery inves-tigated the case of Leonid, the bishop of the Russian Orthodox Church in Ekaterinoslav. According to the charges, he took bribes of 100 to 500 rubles from candidates for the priesthood to promote them to the position of parish priest. For passing the theology exam with a good grade and obtaining a good position, a candidate also had to pay Leonid. Pilgrims who traveled through Odessa to Jerusalem on pilgrimages complained of "Father Leonid's" bribery and corruption.[96]

The police also noted ambiguous relationships in the bishop's household. Some of the police informants submitted strange information about "some soldier's son" who was staying with him. At the end of his working assign-ment at the bishop's house, when the soldier's son was required to begin his mil-itary service, "His Grace Leonid" exempted him by claiming that he belonged to the ecclesiastical estate. Later on, the bishop "promoted him to a merchant's career and gave him capital of 130,000 rubles."[97] Further investigation pro-duced other evidence of "the Right Reverend Leonid's" scandalous homosexual behavior. In addition, during December 1861, secret police agents collected information that confirmed the pilgrims' complaints.

As it turned out, in his previous place of service in Kostroma, the Reverend Leonid had been caught taking bribes several times. The police reported that he "was sending large sums of money to somebody in the Synod, that is why

65

he still has a strong support there and was promoted safely to Ekaterinoslav as a bishop." Leonid was dismissed from his office because of "extreme cupidity." It is noteworthy that in their response to the police investigation, the ecclesiastical authorities in Saint Petersburg did not even mention homosexuality as a reason for firing him.[98]

The police officers of the Third Section received similar complaints about the "indecent way of life" and "blameworthy actions" of local bishops from the congregations of the southern provinces. Sometimes, as in the case of the complaint against another Right Reverend Leonid, who became the Podolia bishop of the Russian Orthodox Church in 1867, the plaintiffs were afraid of persecution from the parish administration and sent the police their letters anonymously.[99]

An even more scandalous situation was discovered on February 25, 1864, when the police obtained the first evidence of the illegal trade in alcohol organized by Russian Orthodox priests in Kiev province. In the Zvenigorodka district of this province, the priests Semion Binetskii, Fedor Sergovskii, Vasilii Molchanovskii, and many others established taverns for selling spirits to local peasants. Yet it was well known that "the provincial administration did not allow village priests to open taverns." In 1863, the first complaints about the priests' illegal trade reached the minister of the interior. According to Russian law, he insisted in his official correspondence, "It was not allowed to open either pubs or restaurants on church lands." The local priests publicly criticized "the Jewish apostates" for something they themselves had been doing for years, selling alcohol to the peasants.[100]

This behavior of the local priests turned the peasants against the Russian Orthodox clergy. The priests of the southern provinces often used their social position for various swindling schemes. Thus, during the period from October 1886 to April 1887, the Odessa public prosecutor examined the case of the parish priest in the village of Trebusovka, Ol'gopolie district, Victor Moldavskii, who was involved in stealing parish funds, counterfeiting bank checks, forging signatures, and other illegal activities.[101]

The heavy economic obligations imposed on the rural population by the tsarist administration also turned the peasants against the Orthodox clergy.

According to the law of July 20, 1842, in Vitebsk, Mogiliov, Vil'no, Kovno, Kiev, Podolia, and Volyn' provinces, a special plot of communal peasant land of 33 desiatin had been assigned to each church parish. The local peasants had to build houses for the clergy, do all necessary work for the parish, and cultivate 10 desiatin of the parish land every year using their own livestock and agricultural implements. In 1868, monetary duties replaced these "natural obligations" of peasants on behalf of the church parish. A law of April 11, 1872, again confirmed all the peasants' obligations to the Russian Orthodox Church.[102]

On July 26, 1861, the Kanev district marshal of the nobility shared with the governor of Kiev his anxiety about rumors spreading among the Ukrainian peasants. The peasants told stories about knives hidden in Taras Shevchenko's tomb (near Kanev) "for the total extermination of nobles, priests, and all people in fine clothes." The marshal wrote that the main object of the ordinary people's hostility was "all those landowners who demanded from peasants payment for land, all those bureaucrats who enforced the fulfillment of obligations, and those from the Orthodox clergy who had lost the trust of the people because they did not interpret the Christian faith according to the wishes of the peasants themselves."[103]

Ukrainian historians noted the embittered stubbornness of Ukrainian peasants who refused to fulfill obligations on behalf of the priests, especially after 1866, when agrarian reform began in the Ukrainian countryside. That same year, the Tarashcha district police officer reported to the governor of Kiev that local peasants had tried all means to avoid any kind of work on behalf of the Russian Orthodox clergy. When the police asked these peasants why they did not want to fulfill their traditional obligations to the clergy, the dissatisfied *muzhiks* responded that the tsar had liberated them from the landowners' corvee labor. On the basis of this, they concluded that all peasants were exempt from similar obligations to the priests and they stopped performing corvee labor in the parish.[104]

Mikhailo Drahomanov, a Ukrainian intellectual and socialist, recorded a typical peasant song in 1868 in the small town of Korostyshev in Kiev province. The song reflects peasant notions and attitudes toward the local clergy: "Nobody knows how I got married; I became almost bankrupt; I had to pay a priest and his various assistants. I also had to pay extra money for maintenance of the church." Later on, these peasants added new lines to the song: "So you see boys how impoverished our community is because the landowners demanded payments; because we also need to pay a priest and all his assistants; and because our village steward is whispering: 'give me some money as well.'"[105]

The Ministry of the Interior wrote to the Holy Synod's Chancellery about the improper behavior of local priests, whose corruption provoked the peasants' religious dissent. In response to the Synod's constant demands to increase police prosecution of the dissident peasantry, the Ministry of the Interior forwarded a copy of the special report from the Kherson governor of March 15, 1872, to the Synod's Chancellery. The governor informed the minister of the interior that "by his excessive extortions" the Reverend A. Zhukovskii, a priest from the village of Dobrovelichkovka (in the Elisavetgrad district of Kherson province) "stirred up disrespect and distrust not only for himself but also for all Orthodox Christians. Such acts stimulated rumors about the Stund, and all peasants here have sympathy for this sect now."

On February 1, Candlemas Day, after the prime religious service, Zhukovskii announced to his congregation that he had canceled the traditional custom of water consecration. But if someone still needed such water, he should come to his house and buy it. Meeting at the church, which had closed unusually early, the peasants decided to join the Stund rather than accept this priest's deviation from church custom, because "he was always looking out only for his material profits." During Lent, this priest established a new price for confession. On the eve of Lent, the price for confession was 8 kopecks from each person; in the middle of Lent, the required price increased by 15 kopecks; and by the end of Lent, the price reached 20 kopecks—"those who had no money because of their poverty or numerous family were denied their right to confession." During the great Orthodox holidays, Zhukovskii demanded payment for his reading of the Holy Scripture in the peasants' homes, and that was why "all local peasants usually left their houses when they saw the priest arriving in their village."[106] During the post-Emancipation period, the police of southern Russia reported such evidence of the clergy's misbehavior every month to the Ministry of the Interior. Many similar letters can be found in the archival collection of the Holy Synod and the ober-procurator of the Holy Synod.[107]

Since the end of the 1860s, complaints about the misbehavior of priests reached the Kiev governor general's Chancellery every month. But church authorities took no action.[108] It often happened, however, that such complaints reached the police, and police officers investigated the transgressions of the local clergy. On December 12, 1895, the peasants Plato Iurchenko and Nikodim Lazorchuk sent a request on behalf of the "Orthodox inhabitants" of the village of Votyliovka in the Zvenigorodka district of Kiev province to the governor general about replacing their parish priest Nikodim Sementovskii, who encouraged "the development" of religious sects in their parish by his misbehavior. The peasants complained that Sementovskii neglected religious services, his parish, and church school and that he treated his congregation "so rudely that the majority visited other churches and participated in religious services in other parishes." They were enraged at "how the priest cares more about his income than about the needs of his own congregation."

Besides church property, Sementovskii rented land in the village of Kosiakovka (Tarashcha district), which was 10 miles from his parish in Votyliovka. Because of his economic pursuits, he spent all his time outside his parish. That was why peasants from his parish were dying without a confession, their dead relatives were being buried without a church burial service, and priests from other parishes were baptizing their children. It often happened that this priest did not hold church service on Sundays and religious holidays. On the New Year's holiday, for example, he did not perform a liturgy in the church for three days. In their petition, the peasants described how the priest "cruelly mistreated, beat," and humiliated them. They wrote that Sementovskii "swears using indecent expressions; for example, he called Semion Gavryliuk, the village elder on duty, 'an asshole' and 'a moron.'" The priest not only did not care about his church income but also used parish funds for his personal needs. The enraged peasants also submitted a detailed picture of this priest's machinations and speculations with their parish's property. The governor of Kiev province commissioned an investigation of this complaint. Although later, in his report

69

to the governor general, he tried to vindicate the priest and blame the Votyliovka peasants for misrepresenting the case, he reluctantly acknowledged the truth of some critical remarks made by the authors of this "petition" (e.g., about land speculation and the frequent absence of the priest.)[109]

All the governors of the Ukrainian provinces noted that local peasants were dissatisfied with their parish priests. Thus, in his report to the tsar in 1900, the governor of Volynia explained that for the past three years he had received twenty official petitions from local peasants asking for the removal of their priests to other parishes. The reasons for these petitions were the same: "extortions, negligence of the church service, rudeness, depravity, and exploitation." The governor acknowledged the validity of most of these complaints and supported the peasants' claims against the local clergy.[110]

Eventually, even the representatives of the Orthodox clergy felt forced to record a decline in their colleagues' interest in their parishioners' lives. The Ekaterinoslav diocesan journal noted that during the congresses of the Orthodox clergy, no one discussed the every day problems of the common parishioners. "The clergy's material needs and search for material means for satisfying these needs," the correspondent of this journal wrote, "make up the chief subject of the clergy's acts during their congresses."[111]

Orthodox scholars noted that in the Ukrainian provinces, there was a sharp alienation of peasantry from the Orthodox clergy, who stood closer to local noblemen (*pany*) than to the simple folks, whom this clergy often called "rabble" or "slaves" (*bydlo, khlopy*).[112] After losing faith in Orthodoxy, many pious religious peasants joined the non-Orthodox sects. Thus one Stundist peasant described his transition from Orthodox religious piety. He used to visit zealously the Orthodox church, but

> suddenly [he] saw there a great imperfection: the priest himself did bad things, drank alcohol, committed fornication, stole the wife of his neighbor and was glad to cheat a simple man. And I began to think that he had such an important responsibility to pray to God for all people. But I saw that his misdeeds did not correspond to the religious duty assigned him by the church. Therefore I decided to stop paying for all church services and prayers performed by him. It turned out that you usually paid no less than one ruble each Sunday in

the church [and this was a huge sum for a peasant!]. And I sympathized with all simple people who were robbed by such dishonest priests.[113]

The peasants—left without effective help from the secular authority in their struggle against the clergy's misdeeds—resorted to their own means of protest. In 1875, the peasants of Yurkovka (in the Zvenigorodka district, Kiev province) stopped visiting the church to protest against the corruption and rudeness of their parish priest, the Reverend I. Savin, and required his replacement with "a decent person." In 1877, they went to Saint Petersburg and submitted an official complaint about Savin's misbehavior to the emperor. Because of this complaint, in April 1877 the Kiev governor general personally requested that the Kiev diocesan consistory transfer Savin to another parish. Eventually, the ecclesiastical administration gave in and removed Savin.[114]

The most complete list of the peasants' acts of protest against the Orthodox clergy is found among the materials of the Third Section. The police officers from this organization noted that the rise of social turmoil was provoked by misdeeds of the Orthodox priests. An overwhelming majority of these acts took place in villages, which would later become famous for the religious activity of dissident sects. In 1876, the peasants of Petropavlovka parish (in the Elisavetgrad district, Kherson province) refused to visit a church and pay for a religious service "performed by 'Father' Nazarevskii, a former parish priest." He had been removed from this parish for various previous transgressions but had been restored to his position by the diocesan administration. As a result, the Petropavlovka church was almost empty during Nazarevskii's term of service.[115]

The peasants of the village of Krivchany (in the Ushitsy district, Podolia province) complained constantly about the drunkenness, corruption, and negligence of the Reverend I. Beletskii, their parish priest. In 1879, he did not conduct the Easter Sunday liturgy, the religious ceremony that was popular and most loved by local peasants. He arrived only on Sunday afternoon (instead of on Saturday evening), already "dead drunk." The enraged peasants would not let this "depraved and drunk priest" inside the church. They took the church keys, locked the church, and gave the keys to a police officer.[116]

The peasants of the southern provinces demonstrated a high level of consciousness and organization in their struggle against the Orthodox clergy. This struggle helped them to develop new forms of organization and solidarity. At the same time, they developed a new mentality that prepared the way for cultural, religious, and eventually, political opposition. The case of the peasants from the village of Pology (in the Gaisin district, Podolia province) is the best illustration of the new organizational abilities among local peasants.

On April 22, 1887, twenty-five peasants from this village of Pology, including the churchwarden and other parish activists, met the Reverend Piotr Kozitskii, a parish priest, at the church entrance and demanded the church keys. After entering the church, the peasants took the box with the church money, broke its seal, and took 40 rubles from it as a payment to the icon painters who had helped to decorate their church. They then locked the church door, refused to return the keys to the priest, and would not permit him to enter the church. They kept the church door locked in spite of the requests of the diocesan administration to open the church for a religious service. As it turned out, the peasants had asked the priest to give the church money to pay to the icon painters who had just finished painting the church's interior. After Kozitskii proved unwilling to pay the money, the peasants had decided to act. They refused to return the church keys because they "didn't want to have a priest who oppressed his own congregation." The local administration could not recover these keys even after a proper investigation. Therefore, the police changed the lock on the church door and gave Kozitskii new keys.

But on the evening of May 23, 1887, a crowd of seventy-three peasants again stopped Kozitskii in front of the church and prevented the churchwarden from unlocking the church door. At the same time, they told the priest that they would not let him inside the church building. One of the peasants' leaders, the retired soldier Ivan Popliovkin, stood in front of the church entrance, covered the lock with his back, and would not let Kozitskii enter.

As a result, Kozitskii was not able to conduct a religious service over the course of two days during one of the main Orthodox holidays, the Feast of the Holy Trinity. The peasants explained to the police that their acts had been provoked by "the misbehavior of the priest, who was insulting and oppressing them." They announced to the police: "Let it be as God wishes, but we do not want to have Kozitskii as our priest and will not allow him to come to our church." After this incident, according to the suggestion of the peasants' leaders, such as Popliovkin and Varfolomei Kurka, members of the local congregation began to collect money so that their representatives could travel to the town of Kremenets to submit an official complaint about Kozitskii.[117]

At the beginning of June 1887, during his inspection of the Podolia countryside, the governor invited the leaders of the Pology peasants for a special conversation. Having found out that Popliovkin was educated enough and had served in the police before his coming to Pology, the governor threatened to punish him for any future disruption of "Father" Kozitskii's service. After a long break, on Sunday, June 14, Kozitskii conducted a festive liturgy in the Pology church. No one disturbed or interfered with this service. But the church was almost empty during this holiday. A police officer wrote:

Only a churchwarden, a sacristan, a village elder, two peasant policemen, two women with their children and one old peasant were present. All other peasants, their overwhelming majority, went to the village of Teplik for a farmers' market before the beginning of the priest's liturgy. According to the district arbitrator, this absence of peasants in the church was apparently self-explanatory. The main reason was their secret agreement to spend a holiday at the farmer's market rather than participate in Kozitskii's liturgy.

From this time onward, the local peasants ceased to visit the church where Kozitskii had conducted the service. Moreover, they submitted to the governor of Podolia a long list of complaints about their priest. On July 9, 1887, the governor general of Kiev, Podolia, and Volynia asked the bishop of Podolia and Bratslav to do something about Kozitskii, "for preventing an aggravation of the peasants' relations with the local administration."[118] Eventually, the local peasants won, and Kozitskii was dismissed. But as a result of this conflict, many peasants from Pology joined various dissident sects. Later, these local peasants played a significant role in the revolutionary events of 1905–7 in the district of Gaisin.[119]

Colonization, Emancipation, and Religious Radicalism

Many Russian writers have described in detail this process of the peasants' alienation from the corrupt Orthodox clergy in the Russian countryside. The priests' cupidity and corruption led peasants to create their own religious forms, using old traditions and elements of Russian Orthodox Christianity.[120] Like the denunciations of Orthodox clergy in the peasants' complaints, the rumors about the elites' breaking moral obligations or threatening the peasants' moral "rights to subsistence" and "norms of reciprocity" became part of the strategy that James Scott describes as using "weapons of the weak," or "the arts of everyday forms of peasant resistance." The impoverished peasantry reacted negatively to any effort of the local administration to limit their traditional rights, especially their rights concerning worship. The peasants tried to protect their traditions and their right to possess their own sacred objects and sanctuaries. These objects were a part of their symbolic system of group identity.[121]

In June 1894, rumors spread that in one peasant's house in the village of Viazovets (in the Kremenets district, Volynia province) "the Saint Nicholas' icon was marvelously revived [transformed] and began to radiate." Some people even saw Saint Nicholas drop a tear. These rumors generated a mass pilgrimage to this icon. Having been frightened of by these disturbances, the Volynia diocesan administration decided to confiscate the icon. But on September 2, 1894, when the police tried to do this, the peasants resisted and prevented the police from taking the icon. Then, on the night of January 3, 1895, police agents secretly seized the icon and carried it to the police station in the neighboring town of Yampol' Volynskii.

After discovering the loss of the icon, the peasants chased the police, assaulted them, tied them up with ropes, took back the icon, and again beat the police and brought them back to Viazovets. Only the arrival of a squadron of dragoons saved the lives of the unfortunate police. The peasant riots in Viazovets were suppressed only after the arrest of thirty-five local inhabitants. Similar instances of protecting icons and other sacred objects by peasants against the local administration took place in other southern provinces of Russia. In an extreme reaction to the elites' violation of peasants' traditional rights, the religious radicals moved further in rejecting the "cultural hegemony" of the elites in their religious sphere. This reaction led to religious dissent among the peasants, who sought to restore their "moral rights as Christians."[122]

Conclusions: Economic, Social, and Cultural Causes of the Religious Awakening on the Southern Russian Frontier

The region of the southern Ukraine was the most important territory for the rise and dissemination of the evangelical movement on the southern Russian frontier. Economically, this region was dependent on the grain trade from the Black Sea ports. This trade simultaneously utilized and stimulated river transport, the traditional trade of the Ukrainian peasant peddlers (*chumachestvo*),[123] and railway transport. As Patricia Herlihy writes: "Connected whether by chumaky trails, by railroad, or by barge or coastal vessel, the cities of the South Ukraine show clearly the primary characteristic of an integrated market already by the 1860s." From the 1860s to the 1880s, other regions of southern Russia, including Bessarabia and the Northern Caucasus, joined this Black Sea grain trade through a network of traditional and new economic connections. Gradually, an evolving system of transportation of railways and steamboats united the southern Russian frontier into one economic region.[124]

The new transport system of southern Russia stimulated the rapid distribution not only of goods but also of information, drawing the remotest villages and towns into the sphere of communication. Various book distributors became active participants in this process. The most influential among the peasant population were the Bible Society book traders and distributors during the beginning of the post-Emancipation period. Through these book distributors, peasants acquired the text of the New Testament in the Russian vernacular language and began to read it at home.

After the establishment of the Russian Bible Society in 1813, Tsar Alexander I supported the idea of publishing the entire text of the Russian Church Slavonic Bible in 1816; and he eventually permitted the translation of the Church Slavonic Bible into vernacular Russian. The New Testament was published in the Russian vernacular language in 1822, and the Bible Society had plans to publish the Old Testament as well. But further work on the translation

75

was interrupted in 1826, when Nicholas I closed the Bible Society. Only during the period 1860–62, under Tsar Alexander II, were the new revised translations of the New Testament published in vernacular Russian. In 1876, the entire text of Russian Bible (both the Old and New Testaments) was published in vernacular Russian and spread all over imperial Russia. Henceforth, the book peddlers and agents of the Bible Society brought the Bibles to the peasants.[125] The markets in Kherson, Odessa, Ekaterinoslav, and Kiev provinces were notable for peddlers who sold religious literature among local peasants. This explains how Russian Bibles reached peasant households on the southern Russian frontier during the 1860s and 1870s.[126]

The Emancipation sparked spiritual expectations among the peasants. As one of the participants in these events wrote in 1885: "Taking an ordinary peasant from the slavery of bonded serfdom, the reforms radically shook his whole acquired way of life, significantly elevated his human dignity in peasant's own eyes, and therefore woke up certain needs, unknown under bondage."[127] After the reforms of the 1860s, all observers noted "an increasing religiosity among the mass of ordinary people" in the southern provinces. Among the peasants, there was an "extreme religious excitement" that could not express itself within the narrow limits of the Orthodox conservative tradition. The peasants channeled this excitement into the creation of new religious sects.[128]

Many peasants disliked their Orthodox neighbors' way of life. By becoming sectarians, they attempted to escape the Orthodox peasants' sinful life, which involved heavy drinking, violence, fighting, fornication, and so forth. One twenty-seven-year-old Stundist confessed during the police investigation that his joining of a sect was the logical result of his search for a pure and sober life: "My brother beat me up and even wanted to cut my throat; other Orthodox neighbors also sinned a lot, I didn't want to resemble them, therefore, I changed my faith."[129] Honest pious peasants were disgusted by the debauchery and fornication of their neighbors, and by the spread of syphilis and other venereal diseases as "a result of the Orthodox peasants' dissoluteness."[130]

"The peasants' religious ignorance" was considered by some contemporary observers to be one of the main reasons for their religious dissent. During the 1860s, in Kherson province, there was 1 student for every 158 provincial inhabitants. Many villages had no school. According to the governor's report for 1861, in Kherson province there were sixteen schools for state peasants with 433 students and two schools for landowners' peasants with 36 students.[131] In 1871, the governor of Kherson province complained that education was developing slowly. In 1870, there were only 510 people's schools with 22,007 students. "On average," he wrote, "we invest only 133 rubles in each school per year. These schools are still lacking good teachers."[132]

According to calculations published in a provincial church magazine, primary education was available to 90 percent of the children of Jews and non-Orthodox people (Germans and others) in 1873 in Ekaterinoslav province. At the same time, only 17 percent of the Russian Orthodox children had a primary education, including 15 percent of the boys and 2 percent of the girls. Among Germans, the proportion of boys and girls was almost equal.[133] In the town of Glodosy, with population of 3,000, there was no school at all.[134]

In 1871, the governor of Stavropol' reported that the question of schools was "an urgent one for the people, since only through literacy could common folk enter the entirely new world of knowledge and moral truths preached by the Gospel." That was why the governor, on his own initiative, organized among ordinary people the dissemination of the books of the New Testament, which sold more than 2,000 copies in a few months.[135] In 1890, the Kherson governor complained about the lack of schools in his province: "Primary education is not up to the mark in the province: There are relatively few schools, and the majority of school-age children do not go to school at all."[136]

In their effort to promote Orthodoxy, church and State officials emphasized religion in primary schools over the kind of practical learning peasants sought. As early as 1870, the governor of Kiev noted the peasants' unwillingness to send their children to church schools. They did not want to do this because these schools did not give children practical knowledge for their every day needs or the skills necessary "for our rural population." He suggested that the practical side of ordinary people's education would attract peasants' children to school, but meanwhile their parents considered their visits to school to be a waste of time, tearing them away from useful work at home. Eventually, in 1901, he noted with satisfaction that twenty-three "peasants' communities submitted petitions about opening secular schools by the Ministry of the Education in their villages in 1900."[137]

It is noteworthy that these peasants did not mention the church parish schools at all. They preferred practical secular education to religious indoctrination. In this respect, the Orthodox primary school system lagged behind the schools run by local government and by the Ministry of Education. The failure of the church program to disseminate Orthodoxy on the southern frontier was evident to many observers. The majority of peasants did not know their prayers and did not understand the meaning of the Orthodox holidays and customs. All priests were amazed at the persistence of paganism and religious ignorance among the local peasants. They also blamed the formalism, boorishness, lack of manners, and ignorance of their colleagues, the Ukrainian country clergy.[138]

According to an Orthodox magazine in Kherson province, in the village of Valegotsulovka there was only one church with three priests for 15,000 peasants, and in the village of Novgorodka there was one church for 12,000 peasants.[139] In 1890, the governor of Ekaterinoslav reported that the "defection from the Orthodox Church" was mainly the result of a shortage of churches, because there were only 508 for 1,572,000 Orthodox Christians (i.e., one priest for 3,094 parishioners). There were parishes with only one church for 10,000 inhabitants, and villages located as far as 10 miles from the nearest church. Therefore, the governor of Ekaterinoslav asked the tsar to promote the growth of church influence in the Ukrainian countryside. "Satisfying the religious needs of ordinary folks via church visits and church sermons," he concluded his report, "would be a mighty means for preventing their defection and the seducing of them into heresy."[140] According to another Orthodox writer, after the reforms of the 1860s and 1870s, "the national spirit revived," and ordinary people adopted new notions. He further explained that gradually "the common folk identified them [these notions] with religious questions."[141]

All contemporaries noted that the Ukrainian peasants created their sectarian society as a protest against social injustice, and particularly against the injustice of the official church. They noted that the peasants of the Ukrainian provinces "had been known for their independent disposition, their inclination to analyze, and their distrust and terrible stubbornness." According to these writers, such sects as the Stundists ought to be considered "an extreme expression of protest against the present clergy's attitudes toward their flock."[142] The first serious scholar of Stundism in the Ukrainian countryside, A. Ushinskii, confirmed this, noting that the sects were "a lively popular protest against the Orthodox Church and the Orthodox clergy."[143]

Mikhail Kupletskii, an Orthodox priest, likewise acknowledged that the essence and "spirit of the faith" were always important to Ukrainian peasants and other "southern Russian settlers." That was why they expected that religious freedom would follow their Emancipation, and these expectations provoked their natural protest against the conservatism of the Orthodox Church. He wrote:

> Removing the ordinary person from the slavery of serfdom, these reforms shook in a radical manner the habitual way and order of his life. They significantly elevated his human dignity in his own eyes, and simultaneously awakened in him new needs that were almost unknown under the regime of serfdom. The spirit of freedom and personal independence, which was inherent in the Emancipation of 1861 and other reforms, were reflected in the lives of ordinary people. Their natural aspiration to understand and comprehend their own condition under the influence of this spirit generated a desire for education and literacy.[144]

This "aspiration to comprehend" and this "desire for self-education" among the post-Emancipation rural population on the southern Russian frontier resulted from a unique social and cultural situation. The overwhelming majority of this population had never known a system of serfdom; they were former state peasants (more than 60 percent), Cossacks, or military settlers. All these people were literally "on the move." They had been disoriented by their migrations and by the new cultural environment of the multiethnic society. To some extent, they had lost their cultural identity, including their traditional Russian Orthodoxy. In adapting to their new conditions of life, they found themselves in conflict with the "guardians" of the traditional cultural order, the priests of

79

the Russian Orthodox Church. Instead of accepting the traditional cultural order, the peasants in the southern frontier region tried to create their own cultural system. The religious dissidents among these peasants became the real "cultural pioneers" of this new cultural system in the late Russian Empire by providing a new understanding and a new faith.

The southern Russian frontier was a unique social and cultural laboratory in which various patterns of Russian colonization collided with the economic and cultural influences of the Western models of modernization brought by the German colonists, Mennonites, and Jews. Four factors created the favorable conditions for the rise of a new oppositional religious movement: (1) the different stages of colonization and a lack of traditional religious and social institutions; (2) conflicting and asymmetric encounters between different cultures that raised the issue of cultural identity among various charter groups of settlers; (3) the Russian administration's efforts to recreate and maintain the cultural identity of the Russian Orthodox peasant among the migrant peasants and the Ukrainians; and (4) the "chiliasm of the defeated and oppressed" among the dispossessed peasants, particularly those alienated from the Orthodox clergy. The Shalaputs, Stundists, and Maliovantsy became the most numerous representatives of this movement.

The expansion and development of a new society on the southern Russian frontier coincided with the period of the Great Reforms of the 1860s and 1870s that changed the economic and social life of the entire Russian Empire and contributed to rapid economic growth, the building of railroads, the development of a more commercial agrarian economy, and the increased movement of agrarian laborers (figure 1.4). The rise of the evangelical movement was the displaced peasants' peculiar response to these new developments. Eventually, this movement became a part of the new culture in the Russian countryside, which spread from the southern frontier to other Russian provinces and influenced all spheres of life in late imperial Russia. Despite the incorporation of the southern frontier region into the mainland of European Russia after the 1850s, its frontier legacy (e.g., ethnic and religious pluralism) persisted. The region had become a seedbed for all new sects during the eras of late imperial Russia and the Soviet Union.

Figure 1.4. Various agricultural activities
of the peasants in Tavrida and Ekaterinoslav
provinces at the end of the nineteenth and
the beginning of the twentieth centuries.
From the collection of the Dniepropetrovsk
State Historical Museum, Ukraine.

Colonization, Emancipation, and Religious Radicalism

Notes

1 Although, as historians have noted, there are many similarities between American westward expansion and the advance of Russian settlement toward the southeast, the one event cannot explain the other. See Donald W. Treadgold, "Russian Expansion in the Light of Turner's Study of the American Frontier," *Agricultural History* 26 (1952): 147–52. Compare with Frederick Jackson Turner, *The Frontier in American History,* ed. Wilbur R. Jacobs (Tucson, 1986), 1, 37, 38. According to Turner, the frontier region in American history shaped the human personality and created peculiar conditions for new settlers. Although Turner's paradigm has been much criticized and revised since he proposed it in 1893, his discovery of the dynamism of the frontier and its influence on the country largely retains its force. Much has been written about Turner's thesis and Russian frontiers. See Joseph L. Wieczynski, *The Russian Frontier: The Impact of Borderlands upon the Course of Early History* (Charlottesville, Va., 1976); Mark Bassin, "Turner, Solov'ev, and the 'Frontier Hypothesis': The Nationalist Signification of Open Spaces," *Journal of Modern History* 63 (September 1993): 473–511; and a long list of works about Russian frontiers in Thomas M. Barrett, *At the Edge of Empire: The Terek Cossacks and the North Caucasus Frontier, 1700–1860* (Boulder, Colo., 1999), 8–10. See also Boris Mironov with Ben Eklof, *A Social History of Imperial Russia, 1700–1917* (Boulder, Colo., 2000), 29–31; and Nicholas B. Breyfogle, "Heretics and Colonizers: Religious Dissent and Russian Colonization of Transcaucasia, 1830–1890" (Ph.D. dissertation, University of Pennsylvania, 1998), 8–12. Compare with Richard White, *The Middle Ground: Indians, Empires, and Republics in the Great Lakes Region, 1650–1815* (New York, 1991).

2 A mixture of nationalities and religions was a distinctive feature of the moving frontier in the American West. According to Turner, the various sects contributed to shaping the new pluralistic situation on the frontier. See Turner, *Frontier in American History,* 23, 121, 164, 165.

3 As T. H. Breen notes, the first British colonists in North America established the rules for interaction, first by deciding which customs would be carried to the new settlements and then by "determin[ing] the terms under which newcomers would be incorporated into their societies." See his "Creative Adaptations: Peoples and Cultures," *Colonial British America: Essays in the New History of the Early Modern Era,* ed. Jack P. Greene and J. R. Pole (Baltimore, 1984), 204. According to John Porter, the first settlers should be regarded as "charter" groups. In his view, "the first ethnic group to come into a previously unpopulated territory, as the effective possessor, has the most to say. This group becomes the charter group of the society, and among the many privileges and prerogatives that it retains are decisions about what other groups are to be let in and what they will be permitted to do." See his *The Vertical Mosaic: An Analysis of Social Class and Power in Canada* (Toronto, 1965), 60.

4 At the beginning of the twentieth century, Max Weber coined the sociological terms of the "ethos" and William Graham Sumner originated the term "folkways." Weber applied the word "ethos" to a particular set of moral principles generated by a particular type of religion. In his concept of "ethos," Weber included such elements as the "system

of moral values," "style of life," and "orientation of culture." Sumner used the word "folkways" to describe the habitual "usages, manners, customs, mores and morals" that he believed to be practiced more or less unconsciously in every culture. See William Graham Sumner, *Folkways: A Study of the Sociological Importance of Manners, Customs, Mores and Morals* (Boston, 1907), 2, and David Hackett Fischer, *Albion's Seed: Four British Folkways in America* (New York, 1989), 7–11. See also Sergei I. Zhuk, "Leveling of the Extremes: Soviet and Post-Soviet Historiography of Early American History," in *Images of America: Through the European Looking-Glass,* ed. William L. Chew III (Brussels, 1997), 63–78.

5 See Edmund Morgan, "The Labor Problem at Jamestown, 1607–1618," *American Historical Review* 76 (1971): 595–611; and Sergei Zhuk, "Ranniaia Amerika: Sotsiokul'-turnaia preemstvennost' i 'proryv v Utopiiu,'" in *Annual Studies of America 1992* (Moscow, 1993), 16–31.

6 I refer here to James C. Scott, *The Moral Economy of the Peasant: Rebellion and Subsistence in Southeast Asia* (New Haven, Conn., 1976), 166, 167.

7 According to Max Weber, "charisma" was a special ability of the prophetic person to declare and legitimate the break with a traditional normative order. In the Weberian sociology of religion, this "charismatic" person played the role of mediator in the process of the breakthrough from traditional to a more advanced, more rationalized level of religious culture. See Max Weber, *The Sociology of Religion* (London, 1963), xxxiii–xxxiv.

8 See Sergei Zhuk, "Nemetskaia diaspora 18 veka i kolonizatsia Dneprovskogo regiona Ukrainy: Teoreticheskie aspecty sotsiokul'turnoi istorii," in *Voprosy germanskoi istorii,* ed. S. Bobyliova (Dniepropetrovsk, 1995), 16–29.

9 E. I. Druzhinina, *Iuzhnaia Ukraina v period krizisa feodalizma, 1825–1860* (Moscow, 1981), 15, 16,18, 24.

10 The Kherson governor wrote in 1852: "None of the [Russian] provinces has such a multinational population as that of Kherson. There are living permanently [here] Little Russians (Ukrainians), Great Russians, White Russians (Byelorussians), Serbians, Bulgarians, Moldavians, Greeks, Armenians, Germans, Karaites, and Jews." Later he added Poles, Swedes, and Gypsies to this list. See in Druzhinina, *Iuzhnaia Ukraina v period krizisa,* 31, 32.

11 See Druzhinina, *Iuzhnaia Ukraina v period krizisa,* 86, 95–99.

12 Rossiiskii gosudarstvennyi istoricheskii arkhiv (hereafter RGIA), f. 1263, op. 1, d. 3286, l. 520ob. The Ekaterinoslav governor echoed him in 1866: "The peasant landowners and former serfs make up more than 3/4 of the entire population (1,220,176); Greeks and Armenians—1/26; German and Jewish colonists make up almost the same portion of population, while temporarily bound peasants comprise only 1/46"; RGIA, f. 1263, op. 1, d. 3286, l. 407.

13 *Khersonskie eparkhial'nye vedomosti* (hereafter *KherEV*), 1876, no. 14, 182.

14 See "Otchety gubernatorov for 1861–95" in RGIA. See their figures in the tables.

15 RGIA, f. 1263, op. 1, d. 4178, l. 239.

16 RGIA, f. 1263, op. 1, d. 4178, l. 1–2.

17 RGIA, "Otchet Khersonskogo gubernatora za 1890 g.," 1.

18 Extensive research has been done on the history of German colonists in Russia, and

83

it is relatively well covered in the Anglo-American literature: David Rempel, "The Expropriation of the German Colonists in South Russia during the Great War," *Journal of Modern History,* 4 (1932): 49–67; Walter Kolarz, *Russia and Her Colonies* (London, 1952); P. Conrad Keller, *The German Colonies in South Russia, 1804–1904,* 2 vols. (Saskatoon, 1968–72); K. Stumpp, *The Emigration from Germany to Russia in the Years 1763 to 1862* (Lincoln, Neb., 1973); Adam Giesinger, *From Catherine to Khrushchev: The Story of Russia's Germans* (Winnipeg, 1974); and Ingeborg Fleischhauer and Benjamin Pinkus, *The Soviet Germans: Past and Present,* ed. E. Rogovin Frankel (New York, 1986). Richard Wortman's sociocultural study of the Romanov monarchy offers interesting insights on Germans as a negative symbol of foreignness. See Wortman, *Scenarios of Power: Myth and Ceremony in Russian Monarchy—Volume 1: From Peter the Great to the Death of Nicholas I* (Princeton, N.J., 1995), 44, 86–87, 172.

19 I. M. Kulynych and N. V. Kryvets', *Narysy z istorii nimetskikh kolonii v Ukraini* (Kiev, 1995), 5. Fleischhauer and Pinkus offer another kind of calculation, based on the first all-Russian census of 1897: "Of 1,790,489 German-speaking Russian subject of German origin, 1,333,662 lived in 50 regions of European Russia; 407,480 in 10 regions of the kingdom of Poland; 57,502 in the Caucasus; 5,828 in Siberia; and 8,947 in Central Asia ; . . . 1.3 million of Russian Germans (76.62%) belonged to the rural population and 401,960 (23%) to the urban population." In Ukraine, the number of so-called Black Sea Germans grew more than tenfold from 136,000 in 1858 to as many as 660,000 in 1914. See Fleischhauer and Pinkus, *Soviet Germans,* 13, 21.

20 See John T. Alexander, *Catherine the Great: Life and Legend* (New York, 1989), 80, 150, 160; Roger P. Bartlett, *Human Capital: The Settlement of Foreigners in Russia, 1762–1804* (Cambridge, 1804); and Herbert H. Kaplan, *The First Partition of Poland* (New York, 1962). See also studies on Jewish history: Simon Dubnow, *History of the Jews in Russia and Poland, from the Earliest Times until the Present Day,* 3 vols. (Philadelphia, 1916), vol. 1, 259–61, 306–20; John Klier, *Russia Gathers Her Jews: The Origins of the Jewish Question in Russia, 1772–1825* (DeKalb, Ill., 1986); Klier, *Imperial Russia's Jewish Question, 1855–1881* (New York, 1995); Heinz-Dietrich Löwe, *The Tsars and the Jews: Reform, Reaction, and Anti-Semitism in Imperial Russia, 1772–1917* (New York, 1993), 18–28; and A. I. Solzhenitsyn, *Dvesti let vmeste (1795–1995): Part 1* (Moscow, 2001), especially 13–58.

21 Rossiiskii gosudarstvennyi arkhiv drevnikh aktov, Moscow (hereafter RGADA), f. 16, d. 343.

22 The Russian tsar met William Penn and other famous "Public Friends" (including Thomas Story) before the Russian colonization campaign and read the Quaker promotion literature. Compare the texts of Russian archival documents: "Proekt o poselenii v Rossii gugenotov, mennonitov dlia razvitia manufactur i remesla" (1729), "O svobodnom v puske evreiev v Rossiiu" (1762), "Kanits o vyzove inostrannykh kolonistov" (1762), "Proekt o poselenii inostrannykh kolonistov na pomeshchichiikh zemliakh" (1763), in RGADA, f. 16, d. 343, 347, 348, 349, with Quaker materials: *Narratives of Early Pennsylvania, West New Jersey and Delaware, 1630–1707* (New York, 1921), 180, 184; and William Penn, *The Papers of William Penn,* ed. M. Dunn and R. Dunn, 5 vols. (Philadelphia, 1981–86) (here-

84

after *PWP*), vol. 1, 383, 384–85, 410. An appeal to Mennonites to settle in Pennsylvania was published among William Penn's tracts: Penn, "His Travails into Holland and Germany . . . ," in *Works,* 2 vols. (London, 1726), vol. 1, 50–116; *PWP,* vol. 2, 279–80. Regarding the connections of Russian tsar Peter I to the Quakers, see the personal papers of Quaker leaders: Thomas Story, *A Journal of the Life of Thomas Story* (Newcastle upon Tyne, 1747), 123–27, 494–95; and *PWP,* vol. 3, 156–67.

23 Nevertheless, Trappe dissuaded the Prussian Mennonites from following the Quakers' example (to emigrate to America), because the Quakers were persecuted there. He referred specifically to the events of the American War for Independence and to the persecutions of pacifist Quakers by American patriots. Therefore, he strongly urged the Anabaptists to emigrate to Russia. "If the Quakers," wrote Trappe, "had made up their mind to move from America, which became free with the help of France, and decided to settle in France, as happened two years ago so you [i.e., the Mennonites] must take care to choose Russia as your second motherland. Because here [i.e., in Russia] there is much more freedom of religion and more liberty for religious worship than in France, without even mentioning the bliss and prosperity." See in RGADA, f. 16, d. 692, l. 56.

24 *Materialy dlia geographii i statistiki Rosii: Khersonskaia gubernia,* sostavil general'nogo shtaba podpolkovnik A. Schmidt [compiled by A. Schmidt, an officer of the General Headquarters] (Saint Petersburg, 1863), vol. 2, 623.

25 In the 1860s, A. Klaus published a series of articles about Germans in the liberal Russian periodical *Vestnik Evropy* [Herald of Europe] that would be published later as a book. The citation is from his book: Klaus, *Nashi kolonii: Opyty i materialy po istorii i statistike inostrannoi kolonizatsii v Rossii* (Saint Petersburg, 1869), book 1, 3.

26 See "Byt molochanskikh mennonitskikh kolonii (Tavricheskaia goubernia, Melitopol'skii uezd)," *Zhurnal Ministerstva gosudarstvennykh imushchestv,* no. 1, book 2 (1841): 553–62. See also the works of Mennonite historians: James Urry, *None but Saints: Transformation of Mennonite Life in Russia, 1789–1889* (Winnipeg, 1989), p. 50ff. The first serious study of Russian Mennonites with serious attention to their economic life was David Rempel's dissertation, "The Mennonite Colonies in New Russia A Study of Their Settlement and Economic Development from 1789 to 1914" (Ph.D. dissertation, Stanford University, 1933); later, he published more of his findings in various articles. See David Rempel, "The Mennonite Commonwealth in Russia: A Sketch of Its Founding and Endurance, 1789–1919," *Mennonite Quarterly Review* (hereafter *MQR*) 47 (1973): 259–308; 48 (1974): 5-54. On various aspects of Ukrainian Mennonite history, see R. Kreider, "The Anabaptist Conception of the Church in the Russian Mennonite Environment, 1789–1870," *MQR* 25 (1951): 5–16. Also see E. K. Francis, "The Mennonite Commonwealth in Russia, 1789–1914: A Sociological Interpretation," *MQR* 25 (1951): 173–82; and the interesting collection of essays *Mennonites in Russia, 1788–1988: Essays in Honour of Gerhard Lohrenz,* ed. John Friesen (Winnipeg, 1989).

27 RGIA, f. 1281, op. 4, (1846), d. 36, l. 10–10 ob.

28 RGIA, f. 1263, op. 1, d. 2963, l. 799.

29 RGIA, f. 1263, op. 1, d. 2963, l. 497ob. In the province of Bessarabia, the foreign

colonists played the same exemplary role. "Among the non-Russian colonists who have set-tled in Bessarabia," the provincial governor reported to the tsar, "the most prominent are the Bulgarians, Germans, and Swiss. They inhabit large spaces in Akkerman and Bender districts; their pursuits are predominantly agricultural, and their agriculture has achieved a higher level than the agriculture of other localities." See RGIA, f. 1263, op. 1, d. 2963, l. 642–42ob.

30 RGIA, f. 1263, op. 1, d. 2963; *Polnoe sobranie zakonov Rossiiskoi imperii s 1649 goda,* 45 vols. (Saint Petersburg, 1830–75), vol. 1, 20852, 22293, 21163. See, in detail, a descrip-tion of the administration of German colonies in Russian Empire in Klaus, *Nashi kolonii;* A. A. Velitsyn, *Nemtsy v Rossii: Ocherki istoricheskogo razvitia i nastoiashchego polozhenia nemet-skikh kolonii na Iuge i Vostoke Rossii* (Saint Petersburg, 1893); G. G. Pisarevskii, *Iz istorii inos-trannoi kolonizatsii v Rossii v XVIII v. (po neizvestnym arkhivnym dokumentam)* (Moscow, 1909); S. P. Shelukhin, *Nemetskaia kolonizatsia na iuge Rossii* (Odessa, 1915); and Ia. Stach, *Ocherki iz istorii i sovremennoi zhizni iuzhnorusskikh kolonistov* (Moscow, 1916).

31 The new Russian ruler required from all his subjects (including his favorite Ger-mans) German (Prussian) military discipline rather than the liberal innovations of the French Enlightenment. As James Billington wrote: "Under Nicholas I, the imperial pen-dulum swung back from French Enlightenment to German discipline far more decisively than it had done during the brief reigns of Peter III and Paul"; Billington, *The Icon and the Axe: An Interpretive History of Russian History* (New York, 1966), 307. See the Russian laws of 1819, 1835, 1837, and 1838 in *Polnoe sobranie,* vol. 1, 27912, 27954; vol. 2, 7908, 6298.

32 In 1833, Sergei Uvarov, the Russian minister of education, formulated this theory as following: "Our common obligation consists in this: that the education of the people be conducted in the joint spirit of Orthodoxy, Autocracy and Nationality. In the midst of the rapid collapse in Europe of religious and civil institutions, at the time of a general spread of 'destructive ideas,' at the sight of grievous phenomena surrounding us on all sides, it is necessary to establish our fatherland on firm foundations upon which is based the well-being, strength and life of a people. It is necessary to find the principles which form the distinctive character of Russia; it is necessary to gather into one whole the sacred remnants of Russian nationality and to fasten to them the anchor of our salvation." The citation is from W. J. Leatherbarrow and D. C. Offord, eds., *A Documentary History of Russian Thought: From the Enlightenment to Marxism* (Ann Arbor, Mich., 1987), 62–63.

33 As Fleischhauer and Pinkus wrote, "The administrative reform of 1866 annulled the separate administration of the colonies and substituted the general state administra-tion. The Military Reform of 1874 extended general compulsory military service to the colonists as well"; Fleischhauer and Pinkus, *Soviet Germans,* 24.

34 One such complaint read: "Nowadays the provincial population [in Kherson province] grows mostly with new Russian settlers; the German element is the only local element, which is now expanding. Unsatisfied with the land lots assigned by the govern-ment, the German colonists through their industry and spirit of companionship, privileges and loans from the government and because of their accumulated capital, and land inher-itance, have occupied more and more private land and are settling one colony after another,

86

organizing new German districts and ousting more and more the Russians, especially the agriculturalists. Therefore, this German element comprises up to 40 percent of the entire population in some districts (e.g., in that of Odessa)." See RGIA, f. 1263, op. 1, d. 4178, l. 239.

35 RGIA, f. 1263, op. 1, d. 3586, l. 11, 12–15. The governor of Tavrida province expressed the same kind of apprehension: "The German colonization proceeds very successfully, at the expense of the Russian settlements." See RGIA, "Otchet Tavricheskogo gubernatora za 1886 g.," 10.

36 A *desiatina* was an imperial Russian land measure equivalent to 2.7 acres.

37 Cited in D. Brandes, "Istoria uspekha: Nemetskie kolonisty v "Novorossii" i Bessarabii (1787–1914 gg.)," in *Voprosy germanskoi istorii,* ed. S. Bobyliova (Dniepropetrovsk, 1995), 82–83.

38 RGIA, "Otchet Khersonskogo gubernatora za 1892 g.," 1–2; RGIA, "Otchet Khersonskogo gubernatora za 1897," 3, 4–5; RGIA, "Otchet Khersonskogo gubernatora za 1902 g.," 1, 4.

39 Max Weber, *The Protestant Ethic and the Spirit of Capitalism,* trans. Talcott Parsons (New York, 1930); Ernst Troeltsch, *The Social Teaching of the Christian Churches,* 2 vols., trans. Olive Wyon (New York, 1931).

40 I. Vibe, "Kratkoie obozrenie sostoianiia sel'skogo khoziajstva v okruge molochnykh kolonistov," *Zhurnal sel'skogo khoziajstva i ovtsevodstva,* no. 3 (1853): 284–93; Shtakh, *Ocherki,* 152.

41 The citation from *Life of William Allen with Selections from his Correspondence,* 2 vols. (Philadelphia, 1847), vol. 1, 400, 401, 402, 403; see also Owen Gingerich, "Relations between the Russian Mennonites and the Friends during the Nineteenth Century," *MQR* 25 (1951): 283–95; James Urry, "'Servants from Far': Mennonites and the Pan-Evangelical Impulse in Early Nineteenth-Century Russia," *MQR* 61 (1987): 213–27.

42 David H. Epp, "The Emergence of German Industry in the South Russian Colonies," trans. and ed. John B. Toews, *MQR* 55 (1981): 297, 303, 309–16. It is worthwhile to note that the Mennonite settlers from Lancaster County in Pennsylvania invented the "Conestoga wagon" that became a popular wagon for all American colonists who settled the West. The story of the Mennonite wagon in Ukraine was similar. See *Vsia Rossia: Russkaia kniga promyshlennosti, torgovli, sel'skogo khoziaistva i administratsii: Torgovopromyshlennyi kalendar' Rossiiskoi imperii* (Saint Petersburg, 1895), 326; V. Cherniaev, *Sel'skokhoziaistvennoe mashinostroenie: Istorichesko-statisticheskii obzor promyshlennosti Rossii* (Saint Petersburg, 1883), vol. 1, 144; and Dniepropetrovs'kyi derzhavnyi oblasnyi arkhiv (hereafter DDOA), f. 134, d. 144, d. 122, d. 343.

43 The Mennonites constantly complained of Russians' stealing their belongings, instruments etc. See DDOA, f. 134, d. 422, l.5; d. 523; d. 152, l. 4–7; compare with observations of contemporaries: A. I. Umissa, *Sovremennoie polozhenie zemledeliia na iuge Rossii* (Kherson, 1874), 85; A. Bode, *Notizen, gesammelt auf einer Forstreise durch einen Teil des europaischen Russlands* (Osnabruck, 1969), 298; and G. L. Gavel, "Sravnitel'nye ocherki sel'skogo khoziaistva i agrarnogo polozhenia poselian v nekotorykh mestnostiakh Rossii,"

87

Sel'skoie khoziaistvo i lesovodstvo, (October 1874), 321. For Mennonite economic achievements, see James Urry, "Mennonite Economic Development," in *Mennonites in Russia,* 102–20.

44 The citation is from Epp, "Emergence of German Industry," 302–3.

45 Epp, "Emergence of German Industry," 306, 318.

46 *Max Weber: The Interpretation of Social Reality,* ed. J. E. T. Eldridge (London, 1971), 48; E. P. Thompson, *The Making of the English Working Class* (London, 1963), 367–68, 379, 382.

47 Theodore W. Schultz, *Investing in People: The Economics of Population Quality* (Berkeley, Calif., 1981), 23.

48 See RGIA, f. 1263, op. 1, d. 3586, l. 367ob.–68, and also materials of Tsentral'nyi derzhavnyi istorychnyi arkhiv Ukrainy (hereafter TsDIAU), f. 442. But the Mennonites themselves noted in their memoirs that the Ukrainian peasants were hostile to those Ukrainians who followed the Mennonites' examples and tried to use the Mennonite innovations. When, during the 1840s, the Ukrainian peasant Khuma drove his "German" wagon through the village, his neighbors scornfully shouted after him: "There goes the German." See Epp, "Emergence of German Industry," 299.

49 Epp, "Emergence of German Industry," 299, 357.

50 The Revolutionary Army of Nestor Makhno began a campaign of mass terror against the German and Mennonite colonists in the Ukraine. See Alexandr Beznosov, "Kistorii goloda 1921–1923 gg. v nemetskikh i mennonitskikh poseleniakh Iuga Ukrainy," in *Voprosy germanskoi istorii* (Dniepropetrovsk, 1995), 117–26.

51 The citation is from the document of 1762; RGADA, f. 16, d. 347, l. 1–1ob.

52 RGIA, f. 1263, op. 1, d. 3856, l. 409.

53 RGIA, f. 1263, op. 1, d. 3856, l. 10.

54 This governor recommended a plan that would involve Jews in "productive" agricultural and industrious activities. He included such measures as the abolishment of restrictions on Jewish settlement (under the new plan, Jews were supposed to settle anywhere mixing with Russian population); a reformation of the entire system of the Jewish education (Russian language and culture were supposed to be the main components for a curriculum in Jewish schools), an official ban on the Jewish trade in alcohol, and the state promotion of Jewish "productive activities in agriculture and manufacture." RGIA, f. 1263, op. 1, d. 3586, l. 303–8ob.

55 See RGIA, f. 1263, op. 1, d. 3586, l. 367ob.–68, and also materials TsDIAU, f. 442—fund of the office of Kiev, Podolia and Volyn' General-Governor. These documents present a day-by-day description of such crimes. Almost every monthly police report contains facts of crimes committed by Jewish bartenders and merchants.

56 See especially documents from TsDIAU, f. 442.

57 D. Bagaley, *Kolonizatsia Novorossiiskogo kraia i pervye shagi ego na puti kul'tury* (Kiev, 1889), 70. See also Iu. A. Mytsyk, *Kozats'kyi krai: Narysy z istorii Dnipropetrovshchyny, XV–XVIII st.* (Dnipropetrovsk, 1997), 10–53; and Serhii Plokhy, *The Cossaks and Religion in Early Modern Ukraine* (N.Y., 2001).

58 See, in detail, E. I. Druzhinina, *Severnoe Prichernomorie v 1775–1800 g.* (Moscow, 1959), 54–55, 65.

59 This involved the periodic redistribution of farmland according to the number of males in a household and the collective administration of tax and other administrative responsibilities.

60 This entailed the collective legal responsibility of all members of a village community.

61 See Mironov, *Social History of Imperial Russia,* 320.

62 N. M. Druzhinin, *Gosudarstvennye krest'iane i reforma P. D. Kiseleva* (Moscow, 1948), vol. 2, 427; Druzhinina, *Severnoe Prichernomorie,* 52.

63 See N. N. Leshchenko, "Reforma 1861 v Khersonskoi goubernii po ustavnym gramotam," in *Ezhegodnik po agrarnoi istorii Vostochnoi Evropy, 1966* (Tallin, 1971), 425. Details about ethnic groups which settled southern Ukraine, see in V. M. Kabuzan, *Zaselenie Novorossii (Ekaterinoslavskoi i Khersonskoi goubernii) v 18-pervoi polovine 19 veka (1719–1858 gg.)* (Moscow, 1976).

64 RGIA, f. 1281, op. 4, (1848), d. 65, l. 42–43ob.; f. 1263, op. 1, d. 1934, l. 540.

65 "Everything we have read about the character, morals and customs of ordinary Little Russians, who are generally called Khokhols," he wrote, "fits the population of Ekaterinoslav province." He also observed, however, with reference to Little Russians: "There is the same sluggishness, laziness, carelessness, the same stubbornness of character, the same strange, sometime ridiculous, and even absurd habits, the same addiction to alcohol and passion for rivalry as among those from Podolia and Poltava provinces. The good features of this tribe still exist; the Little Russians are reasonably submissive, obedient, not self-interested; and their intellect, although not quick and shrewd, is positive and penetrating. Although the local common folks do not live like rich people, they live in relative prosperity." The citation is from *Materialy dlia geografii i statistiki Rossiii, sobrannye ofitserami General'nogo Shtaba. Ekaterinoslavskaia guberniia,* sostavil Gen. shtaba kapitan V.Pavlovich [compiled by Captain V. Pavlovich, an officer of the General Headquarters] (Saint Petersburg, 1862), 264–65.

66 Thus in 1885 the Kharkov governor wrote: "Although they live close to each other, especially in villages half-settled by Little Russians, half-settled by Great Russians, there has been no evidence of conflicts or rivalry during the past years between people of different languages and customs." He explained that the main reason for these friendly relations between Russian and Ukrainian peasants was "a common religious faith, Russian Orthodox Christianity, which is practiced by each ethnic group with the same zeal." The quotation is from RGIA, f. 1263, op. 1, d. 4543, l. 302ob.–3.

67 The Ekaterinoslav governor also wrote about Ukrainian and Russian peasants becoming good friends in villages where they lived next door to each other. "The indigenous and more numerous population of the province," he reported to the tsar in 1885, "belongs to the Little Russian tribe; but an influx of Great Russian settlers, coming as the landowners' peasants, assisted the convergence of these two branches of Russian nationality, and because

89

of their close coexistence, differences diminished. That is why the local Little Russians have lost the main features of their original ethnic type." The quotation is from RGIA, f. 1263, op. 1, d. 4542, l. 150–50ob.

68 All Russian and Ukrainian intellectuals who studied Russian and Ukrainian folk culture stressed the linguistic and ethnic differences between Russian and Ukrainian peasants. See Iurii Venelin, *Ob istochnike narodnoi poezii voobshche i o iuzhno-russkoi v osobennosti* (Moscow, 1834), and Aleksandr A. Potebnia, *Malorusskaia narodnaia piesnia* (Saint Petersburg, 1877).

69 RGIA, "Otchet Khar'kovskogo gubernatora za 1902 g.," 5–6.

70 Robert Edelman, *Proletarian Peasants: The Revolution of 1905 in Russia's Southwest* (Ithaca, N.Y., 1987), 132. As the Kharkov governor noted, the Ukrainian peasant "who used to consider his land as the only means for his survival could not adjust himself to a nonagricultural job." Russian peasants from the central Russian provinces were used to nonagricultural work and to the community system as well. Therefore, after their migration to the South, they tended to accommodate to the new conditions of the frontier more easily than did Ukrainian peasants from the central Ukrainian provinces. As the Russian official explained, in "this transition to nonagricultural activities the Little Russian peasant lost a competition to the more capable and more enterprising Great Russian." See RGIA, "Otchet Khar'kovskogo gubernatora za 1902 g.," 5–6, see other reports of provincial governors as well. Compare with the studies about migrant peasant workers from the central provinces of Russia. See Timothy Mixter, "Migrant Agricultural Laborers in the Steppe Grainbelt of European Russia, 1830–1913" (Ph.D. dissertation, University of Michigan, 1992); Jonathan Mogul, "In the Shadow of the Factory: Peasant Manufacturing and Russian Industrialization, 1861–1914" (Ph.D. dissertation, University of Michigan, 1996); and Jeffrey Burds, *Peasant Dreams and Market Politics: Labor Migration and the Russian Village, 1861–1905* (Pittsburgh, 1998).

71 Vladimir Debagorii-Mokrievich, *Ot buntarstva k terrorizmu* (Moscow, 1930), book 1, 172.

72 The citation is from I. N. Kharlamov, "Shtundisty," *Russkaia mysl'*, no. 10 (1885): 149–50; and no. 11 (1885): 6. See various publications about this: *KherEV*, 1873, no. 12, 354; *Kievskie eparkhial'nye vedomosti* (hereafter *KEV*), 1873, no. 13, 377; *Slovo*, no. 6 (1880): 97, 102–3; and *Chto podgotovilo pochvu dlia shtundizma?* (Kiev, 1875), 1, 2, 4, 14, 15.

73 *Ekaterinoslavkie eparkhial'nye vedomosti* (hereafter *EkEV*), 1890, no. 3, 91–92.

74 *Trudy Kievskoi dukhovnoi akademii*, no. 5 (1884): 28. The Orthodox historians always emphasized these historical traditions of the Ukrainian laity. This Orthodox periodical published such material every month.

75 *Trudy Kievskoi dukhovnoi akademii*, no. 5 (1884): 28.

76 *KEV*, 1885, no. 15, 717.

77 See a survey of this discussion in "K voprosu o malorusskom slove v tserkovnoi propovedi," *KEV*, 1881, no. 13, 4–6.

78 RGIA, "Otchet Khersonskogo gubernatora za 1887 g.," 6.

79 See an analysis of this phenomenon in Uma Narayan, *Dis-Locating Cultures: Iden-*

tities, Traditions, and Third-World Feminism (New York, 1997).

80 RGIA, f. 1263, op. 1, d. 3286, l. 355; RGIA, f. 1263, d. 3551, l. 143ob. (the data from Khar'kov province are for 1870).

81 RGIA, f. 1268, op. 18, d. 91, l. 2.

82 RGIA, f. 1268, op. 18, d. 91, l. 407.

83 RGIA, f. 1263, op. 1, d. 4543, l. 405, 406.

84 RGIA, f. 1263, op. 1, d. 4193, l. 529–30.

85 As the governor of Kherson wrote: "Because of the need to pay taxes that are disproportionately high compared to their income, some peasants resorted to renting parcels of land at the very high prices set by landowners"; RGIA, f. 1263, op. 1, d. 3551, l. 861ob.–62.

86 See Boris Mironov's book and the American literature about the reforms and Russian peasantry: Fr. W. Wcislo, *Reforming Rural Russia: State, Local Society, and National Politics, 1855–1914* (Princeton, N.J., 1990), 11–45; *Between Tsar and People: Educated Society and the Quest for Public Identity in Late Imperial Russia*, ed. E. W. Clowes, S. D. Kassow, and J. L. West (Princeton, N.J., 1991); *Peasant Economy, Culture, and Politics of European Russia, 1800–1921*, ed. E. Kingston-Mann, T. Mixter, and J. Burds (Princeton, N.J., 1991); and S. P. Frank and M. D. Steinberg, eds., *Cultures in Flux: Lower-Class Values, Practices, and Resistance in Late Imperial Russia* (Princeton, N.J., 1994).

87 RGIA, f. 1263, op. 1, d. 4546, l. 332, 344.

88 RGIA, f. 1263, op. 1, d. 5552, l. 680.

89 RGIA, f. 1263, op. 1, d. 5552, l. 680, 680ob.

90 RGIA, "Otchet Ekaterinosl. Gubernatora za 1901 g.," 5.

91 This hostility led to agrarian riots in the provinces of Poltava and Kharkov in 1902. Impoverished peasants attacked the landowners' estates under slogan "The time has come to kill and rob the *pany*" (noblemen-landlords in Ukrainian). One local peasant—after being caught by the police for stealing grain from the barn of the Vasilets estate in Poltava district on March 28, 1902—told a police officer: "All your efforts to persuade us to stop looting are in vain. We are tired of paying 20 rubles for one *desiatina* of land and cultivating two *desiatin* on behalf of the landowner. We are hungry and we will keep taking grain, but it is a shame to punish people for grain because everybody needs to eat; but peasants work their whole lives for landowners, and they are still hungry and landless. If you had to taste the kind of bread we and our children have to eat, you would go loot an estate too." In the same year, in the province of Kharkov, peasants burst into the merchant Rogovskii's estate and demanded the keys to the barns from the merchant himself. When he refused, the enraged peasants knocked him out and took the keys by force. Responding to the merchant's appeal to respect private property, the peasants shouted in his face: "We ourselves have found our own rights. You are the master of your house today, but tomorrow this house will be at our disposal; in a week we will divide your land, which will be ours, not yours; we will drive you away and leave you only the orchard with a small lot of land; and you will be planting potatoes together with your wife." The quotations are from RGIA, f.1405, op. 521, d. 371, l. 51–51ob., 36ob.–37, 68ob., 20–20ob.

92 An Orthodox missionary explained the role of the economic factor in the spread of sects among peasants. "Our simple peasant," he wrote, "seeks in religion not just the means for salvation of his soul, but rather a moral and even material support in his hard working life, which, as it is well known, is becoming more difficult and unattractive, first of all, because of a land shortage, as a result of its constant redistribution and splitting up among new members of peasant households because of the awful expensiveness of land, and, lastly, because of bad crops. He wanted to find such support both in an adjustment of his own private and family life according to the Gospel ordinances, and in the brotherly mutual assistance prescribed by the same Gospels." The quotation is from *KherEV,* 1883, no. 21, 964.

93 Ioann Nedzel'nitskii, *Shtundizm, prichiny poiavlenia i razbor ucenia ego* (Elisavetgrad, 1893), 32, 31.

94 RGIA, f. 1263, op. 1, d. 4193, l. 548–52ob.

95 *KherEV,* 1883, no. 21, 964.

96 Gosudarstvennyi arkhiv Rossiiskoi Federatsii (hereafter GARF), f. 109, 1 *ekspeditsia,* op. 37, d. 22, l. 2–7, 8–8ob.

97 GARF, f. 109, 1 *ekspeditsia,* op. 37, d. 22, l. 9–10.

98 GARF, f. 109, 1 *ekspeditsia,* op. 37, d. 22, l. 10.

99 GARF, f. 109, 1 *ekspeditsia,* op. 42 (1867), d. 2, l. 1–5.

100 GARF, f. 109, 1 *ekspeditsia,* op. 39, d. 62, l. 3.

101 TsDIAU, f. 419, op. 3, d. 60, 1, l. 216–29.

102 See, in detail, D. P. Poida, *Krest'ianskoe dvizhenie na Pravoberezhnoi Ukraine v poreformennyi period (1866–1900 gg.)* (Dnepropetrovsk, 1960), 79–80.

103 *T. G. Shevchenko v dokumentakh i materialakh* (Kiev, 1950), 279–80.

104 Poida, *Krest'ianskoe dvizhenie na Pravoberezhnoi Ukraine,* 82.

105 M. Drahomanov, *Novi ukrainski pis'ni pro gromadski spravy (1764–1880)* (Geneva, 1880), 119.

106 RGIA, f. 797, op. 41, 2 otd. 3st., d. 63, l. 15–16. According to the minister of the interior's letter, the peasants' hostility against the priest from the village of Liubomirka reached its peak one night when the police watch found this priest with "women prostitutes dancing drunk and naked in a village house." The police hardly stopped the enraged peasants who wanted to cut the priest's hair off and beat him up. See RGIA, f. 797, op. 43, 2 otd., 3st., d. 143, l. 8–9.

107 At the beginning of 1880, the Krements district police officer in Volynia province, wrote to Volynia governor: "The present generation of the local clergy is very pragmatic; it strives not only for the conveniences of life, but also for comfort, for a so-called gentlemen's stylishness. At the expense of their congregation, they build huge houses with painted floors and walls. They also have expensive furniture, a piano; and the priest and his wife are dressed in fine silk clothes. At dinner, the servants bring bottles with foreign labels on them. The priests (together with local Polish landowners) consider the peasants 'cattle' and if they see a striving among their neighbors to raise the intellectual level of these peasants and improve their well being, they will feel very upset." The quotation is

from TsDIAU, f. 442, op. 320 (1880), d. 46, l. 19–20. It is noteworthy that local peasants noted the same details in their complaints. They considered the Orthodox clergy to be "cultural aliens." For the peasants, these priests belonged to the same category of "others" as the noble (Russian, Polish, and Ukrainian) landlords, the Jews, and the German colonists. See such details in GARF, f. 109, 3 *ekspeditsia,* (1873), d. 121, l. 1ob.; TsDIAU, f. 442, op. 320 (1880), d. 46, l. 2ob., 54; TsDIAU, f. 442, op. 321 (1881), d. 70, l. 4.; TsDIAU, f. 442, op. 321 (1881), d. 182, l. 8.

108 A case of the numerous complaints about the alcoholism and corruption of Reverend Iushkevich sent by peasants from the villages of Leskovo and Matveikha in the Lipovetskii district of Kiev province demonstrates the typical approach of the local ecclesiastical administration. This administration ignored these complaints notwithstanding the General Governor's reminders about them. See TsDIAU, f. 442, op. 318 (1879), d. 130, l. 2ob., l. 4.

109 GARF, f. 109, 1 *ekspeditsia,* op. 50 (1875), d. 35. See TsDIAU, f. 442, op. 695 (1896–97), d. 9, l. 7–7ob., 9. In 1883, the Volynia governor wrote the general governor that the Reverend Nitkevich, a priest of Mlinovets parish (in the Kremenets district), led a depraved life, sometimes drank so much alcohol, and "that he was dragged drunk through the street. One day, being dead drunk, he even started swearing in the church of Kremenets town using very rude, indecent language." TsDIAU, f. 442, op. 323 (1883), d. 315, l. 1.

110 RGIA, "Vsepoddaneishii Otchet Volynskogo gubernatora za 1900 g.," 2–3.

111 *EkEV,* 1877, no. 6, 87; *KherEV,* 1876, no. 14, 188. Another Orthodox magazine acknowledged that local priests were abusing the peasants' confidence by asking more money for church services. This magazine proposed to stop "any kind of monetary extortion by the Orthodox clergy" and presented this proposal as the best method in the struggle against religious sects. See *EkEV,* 1891, no. 9, 155. In 1890, the governor of Ekaterinoslav complained to the tsar about the blatant ignorance of the local priests and Orthodox missionaries. He wrote in his report: "Unfortunately, the local clergy is not able to influence the ordinary people because it is dependent financially on the congregation and exists exclusively on gifts and money brought by peasants as payment for religious services." RGIA, f. 1263, op. 2, d. 5556, l. 207–7ob.

112 Gerasim Balaban, one of the outstanding Stundist leaders, was completely disappointed with the Orthodox priests during his spiritual search for a true religion. The local priest systematically ignored Balaban's efforts to talk about the Gospels and to get help in his quest for Divine Truth. Moreover, the priest demanded such a high price for performing Balaban's wedding ceremony that the enraged Balaban decided to be married without the Orthodox wedding ritual. When this priest sent Balaban to an Orthodox monastery for "religious education and correction," Balaban witnessed such depravity and corruption among the monks there that this experience simply intensified his hostility to the Orthodox Church as a religious institution. See *Vera i razum,* no. 20 (1886): 404, 409–10. See also other comments that the idleness and unscrupulousness of the priests reinforced the alienation of the local Ukrainian peasantry from the Orthodox Church. TsDIAU, f. 127, op. 1023 (1895), d. 517, l. 1–1ob., 9–10.

93

113 Otdel rukopidei: Gosudarstvennaia biblioteka Rossii, Moscow (hereafter OR GBR), f. 435, *karton* 46, d. 1, l. 29–30.

114 Poida, *Krest'ianskoe dvizhenie na Pravoberezhnoi Ukraine,* 252–54.

115 GARF, f. 109, 1 *ekspeditsia,* op. 51 (1876), d. 19, l. 1–25. When, on August 23, 1879, one poor peasant from the village of Iskrino (in the Zvenigorodka district) asked the parish priest to perform a burial ritual for his dead child, this priest demanded a large amount of money for this service. When the peasant brought only a part of the requested payment, the angry priest refused categorically to bury the child without payment. Eventually, because the dead child's body started to decompose, the peasant's neighbors buried the child without the priest's assistance. See GARF, f. 109, 3 *ekspeditsia,* op. 54 (1879), d. 60, l. 135–36ob.

116 TsDIAU, f. 442, op. 318 (1879), d. 117, l. 1ob.; TsDIAU, f. 442, op. 320 (1880), d. 44, l. 1ob., 15, 29. A similar story happened in the village of Svinnoe (in the Starokonstantinov district, Volynia region). The local peasants took the church keys from the churchwarden and locked the church building. After an investigation, the police officers confirmed the fairness of the peasants' complaints and insisted that the local corrupt priest should be discharged from the parish of Svinnoe.

117 TsDIAU, f. 442, op. 617 (1887), d. 115, l. 1–2ob.

118 TsDIAU, f. 442, op. 617 (1887), d. 115, l. 3–4ob.

119 See *opis'* for 1905–7 in TsDIAU, f. 442, with documents about peasants riots in the province of Podolia. See also RGIA, "Otchet Volynskogo gubernatora za 1894 g.," 10–11. The peasants' hostility sometimes led them to physically chastise the "corrupted servants of God." See about this in TsDIAU, f. 442, op. 322 (1882), d. 134, l. 1ob. E.g., peasants from the village Potievka (in the Vasil'kovka district, Kiev province) publicly threatened to beat their parish priest, whom they hated for his "extreme extortion of money." On a frosty winter night in 1882, they broke into his house, dragged him out half-dressed, beat him, and "kept him outside in the freezing snow for a long time." A similar story took place in 1886, in the village of Belashki (in the Berdichev district, Kiev province), where local peasants fell upon their parish priest in the village meeting and cruelly beat him "for the misappropriation of the public funds collected by all village's inhabitants." See TsDIAU, f. 442,, op. 616 (1886), d. 33, l. 4. According to information in the local newspaper, during the night of May 19–20, 1889, peasants from the village of Deshki (in the Kanev district, Kiev province) got inside the local priest's house through the window, dragged this priest by his hair from the house, filled his mouth with sand, tied his shirt over his head and beat him unmercifully. The police investigation revealed that the "goal of this act was not a theft, because everything in the priest's house was left intact by peasants." See *Kievlianin,* no. 112 (1889).

120 In 1895, Anton P. Chekhov wrote a wonderful story, "A Murder," about this phenomenon. See in A. P. Chekhov, *Sobranie socinenii v 12-ti tomakh* (Moscow, 1962), vol. 8, 31–59.

121 E. P. Thompson called a strategy of denunciation, rumors, etc., an "anonymous tradition" of resistance among the lower classes. See his "Patrician Society, Plebeian Cul-

ture," *Journal of Social History* 7, no. 4 (1974): 399–401. Compare with Scott, *Moral Economy*, 182, 188–90, 192, 225–38; Scott, *Weapons of the Weak: Everyday Forms of Peasant Resistance* (New Haven, Conn., 1985), 241–352; and Scott, *Domination and the Arts of Resistance: Hidden Transcripts* (New Haven, Conn., 1990), 140–52. Also see the analysis of denunciations strategy among Russian peasants in Burds, *Peasant Dreams,* 186–218.

122 The citation is from RGIA, "Vsepoddaneishii Otchet Volynskogo gubernatora za 1894 g.," 7–8. On more serious cases of the alienation of the laity from the Orthodox hierarchy, see Gregory Freeze, "Subversive Piety: Religion and the Political Crisis in Late Imperial Russia," *Journal of Modern History* 68 (June 1996): 308–50.

123 Peasant peddlers in the Ukrainian villages (*chumaky*) brought salt and spices from the southern provinces to central and northern Ukraine. They established the first trade routes to market places in the South.

124 Patricia Herlihy, "The South Ukraine as an Economic Region in the Nineteenth Century," in *Ukrainian Economic History. Interpretive Essays,* ed. I. S. Koropeckyj (Cambridge, Mass., 1991), 334, 337.

125 I. A. Chistovich, *Istoria perevoda Biblii na russkii iazyk* (Saint Petersburg, 1899), 263, 270.

126 Jeffrey Brooks, *When Russia Learned to Read: Literacy and Popular Literature, 1861–1917* (Princeton, N.J., 1985), 24, 104.

127 *Russkaya mysl'*, no. 10 (1885): 146. Later on, the famous Russian Baptist V. Pavlov noted that "only with the liberation of peasants from bonded serfdom, was there the beginning of an awakening of religious consciousness among Russian people, that expressed itself in a movement, called as Stundism"; *Baptist,* no. 42 (1911): 330.

128 As one Orthodox observer noted, "Such an individualism and personal arbitrariness in religious and public life became more popular among many peasants, especially southern Russians, who had been freedom-loving since times immemorial, and who in their extreme love for freedom, often selected a false and disastrous road of willfulness and arbitrariness." See *KEV,* 1898, nos. 2–3, 65.

129 RGIA, f. 1284, op. 222 (1902 g.), d. 29, l. 42ob.

130 See, in the Kherson governor's report for 1885, RGIA, f. 1263, op. 1, d. 4543, l. 441. See also Ioann Nedzel'nitskii, *Shtundizm, prichiny poiavlenia i razbor ucenia ego* (Elisavetgrad, 1893), 8; and *KherEV,* 1873, no. 12, 354, 356.

131 *KherEV,* 1873, no. 12, 352; RGIA, f. 1263, op. 1, d. 2963, l. 808.

132 RGIA, f. 1263, op. 1, d. 3551, l. 863ob.

133 *EkEV,* 1874, no. 7, 107.

134 *KherEV,* 1876, no. 14, 188.

135 RGIA, f. 1268, op. 18, d. 91, l. 7–7ob.

136 RGIA, "Otchet Khersonskogo gubernatora za 1890 g.," 7–8.

137 RGIA, f. 1263, op. 1, d. 3586, l. 301ob.–302; d. 4193, l. 529–30.

138 Quoted from *Tserkovnyi Vestnik,* 1892, no. 47; Nedzel'nitskii, *Shtundizm,* 16, 17, 20. The observers noted another reason for peasant religious dissent, however. This was "insufficient church singing," a problem that was exacerbated by "the shortage of the

95

churches and the insufficient number of priests in the parishes." As a result of this, according to one observer, instead of "a mood of religious exaltation and praying, the peasants felt an absentmindedness that led to boredom; a feeling of religious necessity was not satisfied, and a peasant left church without feeling the delight and elevation of praying to God." Under these circumstances, the dissatisfied pious Christian would be less attracted to this church, and next time he would visit it with less enthusiasm.

139 *KherEV,* 1890, no. 14–15, 238, 292.

140 RGIA, f. 1263, op. 1, d. 4867, l. 371ob.–72. At the same time, the Orthodox clergy expressed their hostile attitude toward the peasants' independent study of the Bible. The Orthodox press was explicit about this: "Regarding the Gospels, nothing is more dangerous than when the uneducated person takes it into his head to interpret them, and then to consider his interpretation of the Gospels to be a suggestion of the Holy Spirit." See *KherEV,* 1876, no. 14, 187.

141 In fact, all the new sects represented the social protest of people, who showed "a disrespectful and negative attitude toward the dominant religious forms, as well as toward the civil and political establishment." The main reason for this was that the peasants "could not express their aspirations in these forms." *KherEV,* 1883, no. 24, 1144–45.

142 *Chto podgotovilo pochvu,* 1, 2, 14.

143 A. Ushinskii, *O prichinakh poiavlenia ratsionalisticheskikh uchenii shtundy i nekotorykh drugikh podobnykh sekt v sel'skom pravoslavnom naselenii i o merakh protiv rasprostranenia uchenia etikh sekt* (Kiev, 1884), 41.

144 *Pravoslavnoe obozrenie,* no. 8 (1883): 713, 714–15.

Chapter Two

2 The Shalaputs

The pioneers of the Russian "radical reformation" were the Shalaputs, who drew on the old Khlyst traditions of dissent from the Orthodox Church. The Shalaput movement represented the first mass peasant attempt to radically reform Russian Orthodox Christianity. Along with other Christian radicals, such as the early Quakers, Anabaptists, and Methodists, all the Shalaputs (including the Pryguny and Marianovtsy) through all their rituals emphasized the imminence of a divine presence. In their religious enthusiasm, they tried to reach an emotional climax and embody the Holy Spirit. During their "religious rejoicing," they behaved as do those whom anthropologists and psychologists refer to as "spirit-possessed" people. New research on spirit possession and belief in an immediate divine presence provides us with important ideas for understanding the Shalaputs. For instance, anthropologists treat the behavior of spirit-possessed people as a type of sacred theater.[1]

Spirit possession takes place on occasions that anthropologists sometimes call "liminal" thresholds to another kind of experience in which usual conventions and structures break down, "if only for an instant." Spirit possession was a typical element for the radical reformation as well. During a "liminal" occasion, divinely possessed people justified a radical restructuring of spiritual priorities. When God "poured out" His spirit, as prophesy implied, the principal agents of His will were not the established leadership but rather "the humblest and most powerless members of the society." The radical change in personality of the divinely possessed resulted in such divine "gifts" as the power to speak in other tongues, "to heal, to prophesy and to work miracles."[2] This power would lead to different renovations, including the transformation of church and society. Such spirit-possessed Christians see themselves as a divinely chosen elite called to restore Christianity to the simplicity and purity of its earliest years. They reject the institution of marriage and try to live lives of rigorous austerity.

The Beginnings of the Shalaput Movement

According to Orthodox historiography, the Shalaputs were a version of the Tambov Postniks called the Katasonovtsy, or the sect of Katasonov.[3] Orthodox and Soviet historiography has treated all Shalaputs as a version of one dissident group, the Katasonov sect of "Old Israel," and has ignored the other cultural elements that contributed to its varied character. In reality, Katasonov's sect was only a small fragment of the Shalaput movement.[4]

Another version of the Shalaputs' origin is found in archival documents. According to these documents, the police traced the beginning of the new sect back to the 1830s, when the state peasants from the central Russian provinces attempted to reproduce the old forms of Khlyst and Skoptsy dissent in the new environment of the southern frontier in provinces of Tavrida, Bessarabia, and Stavropol'. But because of other cultural influences, including those of the Molokans and foreign colonists, they created new communities of religious dissenters who combined the Skopets as a role model with non-Skopets religious practices. These new practices marked the beginning of a new phase of the Shalaput movement in the mid-1860s. During this phase, the Molokans, Pryguny, and Mennonites contributed to the rationalist elements in the Shalaput movement, while the Khlyst spiritualist tradition influenced and shaped religious enthusiasm among other religious dissenters.

By 1875, the Skopets ideas and practices were replaced with the enthusiastic forms of evangelical traditions of the Molokans and the Mennonites. The Shalaput movement drew mainly on the old traditions of popular Orthodoxy and the Christ-Faith, and the last form of this movement emerged by the end of the 1860s. Contemporaries called this last phase "the Duplii movement," because Pavlo Duplii, a peasant from the province of Ekaterinoslav, was its most prominent representative. During this phase, the peasants expressed millennial eschatological expectations en masse. But at the same time, the new phase of the Shalaput movement stressed the "inner-world" asceticism and other features of rationalization in the behavior of the religious dissidents. Despite the differences and rejection of the cultural dialogue between Shalaputs and the new Stundist sects, the theology and practices of these groups influenced each other, and they shared a common foundation in the Reformation.[5]

Stages of the Shalaput Movement

This section describes the various phases of the Shalaput movement. The periods covered include the Khlyst and Skopets phase, which lasted from 1833 to 1865; the Molokan and Pryguny phase and collaboration with Mennonites, during the years 1861–72; and Duplii's phase, in the provinces of Ekaterinoslav and Poltava, from the 1860s to the 1880s.

The Khlyst and Skopets Phase of the Shalaput Movement, 1833–1865. A puzzling link between the castrated Skoptsy and the Russian radical reformation was apparent from the first police investigations. During the 1840s, the police discovered a sudden spread of the Skoptsy movement from central to southern Russia. In 1843, the police arrested 1,701 castrated peasants, including "two Skopets leaders," in the southern province of Tavrida.[6] Russian law considered these dissenters as "especially harmful and dangerous" and outlawed them together with Khlysty and other sects of the Christ-Faith.[7] The Russian administration, especially officials of the Ministry of State Domains, worried about the influence of the Skoptsy among the state peasants who lived in the southern settlements, and therefore requested a police investigation.

As a result of this investigation, the police discovered new sects of the Shalaputs in the South. The investigation revealed that the most respected activists of the new sects on the southern frontier were the Skoptsy. The first criminal cases of Tavrida and Bessarabia Shalaputs demonstrated that during the 1830s and 1840s the new sect emerged among the state peasants from the provinces of Kursk and Belgorod. These dissidents had castrated leaders, who served as role models for their sect. But the majority of the dissidents were not castrated. Moreover, as it turned out, several leaders of this sect were women from the Ukrainian Cossack communities. Along with the Khlyst form of worship, the new sect introduced the reading and interpretation of Holy Scripture as a pastime among local peasants as early as the 1840s.

The first time the Russian administration mentioned the Shalaputs was in the spring of 1840. Local peasants of the village Mikhailovka (in the Melitiopol' district of Tavrida province) had informed a police officer that a Cossack woman from Poltava (Ukrainian) province, Maria Dakhnova, "laid a foundation for the new sect under a name of Shalaputs, with forty-five members of both sexes."[8] Thus, from the beginning, the Shalaput movement demonstrated both the unusually active (for a patriarchal peasant society) role of peasant women and the involvement of Ukrainian Cossacks in sectarian activities. The presence of female leaders and activists in a religious movement signified a remarkable innovation not only for peasant society but also for traditional religious dissent in Russia.

The peasants told the police that the sectarians did not eat meat or drink alcohol, that married men shunned sexual relationships with their wives, and that young women and men no longer married. They explained that they "had made this commitment because of their illnesses." The neighbors of the sectarians confirmed that they met in a house "for an unknown reason" almost every evening. One peasant woman took a peep through the window and saw that "during such a meeting, women were singing, and young men were whooping and slapping their laps with their hands."[9]

In May 1840, the Melitopol' district officer from the Ministry of State Domains reported on the Shalaput sect to his minister. He explained: "According to the frequent visits to a town of Belgorod by the elders of this sect on the pretext of worshiping the local saint's relics, it could be concluded that their main leader lives in Belgorod."[10] That was why the Ministry of State Domains ordered an investigation of the possible connections between this sect and the Belgorod dissidents. Meanwhile, the investigators discovered three Skoptsy (eunuchs) in Belgorod. One of them, Pavel Zaitsev, was probably "a mentor for the Tavrida Shalaputs."[11] Because the Skopets sect was outlawed in Russia, the minister of state domains gave orders for medical examinations of the sect's members because a sect such "as the castrated Skoptsy could be harmful for people's morality."[12]

The Ministry of the Interior responded to the official request by sending detailed information to the Ministry of State Domains on December 30, 1840. According to police information, the sect had fifty members, all of whom followed "punctually the rites and rituals of the Orthodox Church." The arrested peasants denied their membership in this sect and explained their abstinence from meat and alcohol "by their illnesses or old age, by their parents' example or other reasons." According to their wives, these peasants avoided sexual intercourse. Their secret meetings took place in the evening and on Sundays in the houses of three peasants, Nikolai Bozdyrev, Ivan Shirochkin, and Efrosinia Korneva, where they "did strange singing and dancing, and told each other that marriage was against God's will."[13]

The case of the Mikhailovka Shalaputs was closed for "lack of evidence about their illegal activities." A few weeks later, the supposed leader of these Shalaputs, Shirochkin, returned home. He was examined by a police officer, and it was discovered that he had been castrated. This shocking discovery—and Shirochkin's consequent confession that he had been castrated "by unknown people more than eight years ago, when he, being drunk, was riding from the neighboring village"—changed the entire attitude of the police administration.[14] They decided to reconsider the case.

According to the new evidence, the Shalaput sect was established in the 1830s by Teet Babanin, a peasant from the village Troitskoe (in the Teem district, Kursk province), who came to the district of Melitiopol' looking for a job. Though he was the nephew of the local peasant Fedor Baryshev, Teet "stayed in the house of the Pakhomovs family, Mikhailovka peasants, rather than with his uncle."[15] All the peasants noted that Teet taught Pakhomov's children to read, and "he did not eat meat or drink alcohol, and avoided women." After a long conversation with Baryshev, who criticized his nephew for strange behavior, Teet was induced to marry the daughter of his landlords and come back to Troitskoe. When Baryshev visited that village soon after this in 1833, he saw that "many local peasants there shunned meat, alcohol and women; that was why people called them the Shalaputs." Baryshev later informed the police that "the main mentor of this sect lived in Belgorod, and Teet Babanin organized a branch of this sect in Pakhomov's household in Mikhailovka." Together with female activists, such as Maria Dakhnova, Babanin propagated the ideas of the new sect among migrant Russian and Ukrainian peasants, who settled in Tavrida.[16] According to this evidence, the sect was established in southern Russia in the province of Tavrida as early as 1833.

The Shalaput sect soon spread all over the village of Mikhailovka and included at least fifty-six members. In 1841, the police noted new aspects of the Shalaput movement. The converted peasants began reading the Bible, and their leaders expressed notions close to Protestant ideas. Thus, the Orthodox peasants who joined the Mikhailovka Shalaputs were taught about justification by faith alone, the priesthood of all believers, and the primacy of the Bible as the only source of revealed truth for Christians. Shirochkin's adherents persuaded their neighbors that only their personal faith would win them salvation, and that no "praying and rituals performed by the priest" could substitute for individual relations with God and personal absolution.[17] All these aspects of the Shalaput movement were reminiscent of the Western Reformation.

On December 19, 1841, the Ministry of the Interior reported to the Ministry of the State Domains that the investigation had been canceled because there was nothing suspicious about the Shalaputs. The ministry, however, recommended "strict control over their way of life and their performance of Christian obligations."[18] The head of the Ministry of the State Domains—frightened by rumors about the secretly castrated Skopets among the local peasants—ordered the local official from Tavrida office to inform him about newborn babies among suspected Shalaputs.[19] On April 27, 1842, the Tavrida office sent the ministry information about former Shalaputs who were conceiving new babies, eliminating the reason to fear "secret Skoptsy."[20]

Another case of Shalaput activities characterized more by Khlysty than Skoptsy influences came from the Bessarabia. On September 4, 1841, the Bessarabian office of the Ministry of State Domains reported an unusual sect among the state peasants of the village of Diviziu (in the Akkerman district), whose rituals were reminiscent of the Melitopol' Shalaputs. Staff from this office ordered one settler to monitor the sectarians and inform the police about anything suspicious.[21]

This informer reported that the Diviziu peasant Ivan Kazakov (or Kazachkov), along with his wife Anna and six other married couples, met together on the eve of main holidays and Sundays in the house, where "Ivan Kazakov usually opened the meeting with singing, the others following him." On the night of August 15, the police arrested these peasants during their secret meeting. The peasants attempted both escape and resistance.[22] During the investigation, the police officer discovered that all the arrested peasants "shunned categorically meat food and alcohol." And they explained this as their attempt "to tame the flesh," or "as a result of illness." Everybody denied his or her membership in the sect. Further investigation revealed new details in the case: The peasants used "a tub of water over which they sang, clapped their hands and cited strange verses: 'I'm clapping, whipping, looking for God; Show us yourself,' and during their praying they sat on a floor or just squatted there."[23]

According to the police, their prayers were reminiscent of pagan songs. During their meeting they sang: "Hey our merry spirit, roll in and out, make us joyful." This singing was obviously influenced of the old Khlyst tradition, which was brought by the Diviziu peasants from the province of Kursk. Such religious songs were popular among all sects that belonged to the Christ-Faith movement. The police later discovered similar songs and rituals among the Shalaputs in other southern provinces.

Yet, the district court acknowledged that in their everyday life the defendants "performed the Orthodox Church rituals regularly and always visited church services." Moreover, since 1838 they had participated in all confession and communion ceremonies in the church. What provoked suspicion was not only their conduct but also the words of Ivan Kazakov that "in King David's house the believers were jumping, dancing and clapping their hands." This was a typical argument of the Russian Khlysty in defense of their type of worship, something the police had already known.

In August 1842, the shocking discovery of the castrated peasants attracted police attention to the Diviziu sectarians. One Diviziu peasant, a leader of the local sectarians, Nikolai Sagan, turned out to be a Skopets. The investigation discovered that he had been castrated quite recently.[24] After this, anticipating that something was wrong, the local administration of the Ministry of State Domains ordered an examination of the other defendants. To the horror of the officials, Ivan and Alexei Kazakov and their three peasant neighbors (one eighteen years of age, two twenty) had been castrated as well. Most of the castrated peasants testified that they castrated themselves the same year (1842), presumably during Lent, Easter, or on Whitsunday. Sagan and another peasant confessed, however, that they had castrated themselves more than two years earlier. The castrated peasants explained that they interpreted the words they had heard in the church: "You should have circumcision, brothers, and your flesh will rejoice"—as a justification for castration. Therefore, they "castrated themselves with knives, some did this in the fields, some—at home without anybody's assistance or incitement." According to Sagan's testimony, he had heard about the Skoptsy in church and castrated himself with a scythe in the field.[25]

It turned out that the beginning of castration among the pious settlers in Tavrida and Bessarabia was related to the millennial expectations of the approaching Kingdom of Jesus Christ. During the late 1830s and 1840s, these expectations spread among the various dissident groups, which were derived from the Christ-Faith tradition—the Khlysty, Skoptsy, Molokans, and Dukhobors. The most radical among them, the Skoptsy, insisted on "purification of the body" (castration) as an act of preparation for the Millennium. During the migration of Russian peasants to the South, the Skoptsy activists brought these ideas to local dissidents.

On September 19, 1842, the Bessarabian Office of the State Domains sent a new report about a discovery of sixteen castrated peasants among thirty

106

arrested Shalaputs from Diviziu. The castrated dissidents were the most active members of the sect. As the investigation revealed, one person had performed all the castrations. The police surgeon identified the influence of Skoptsy from the provinces of Kursk and Belgorod.[26] At the same time, the local police and clergy noted the particular manner of worship and a stress on reading and interpreting the Bible, both of which differed from the traditional Russian Skoptsy. It is worth noting that among the majority of illiterate peasants who lived in Diviziu, only the dissidents could read. The Tavrida Shalaputs were also the only literate peasants in their villages. For the police in the 1840s, the distinctive feature of the new sect, in contrast to the predominance of the oral tradition in the Christ-Faith movement, was the culture of reading.[27] Therefore, the local officials called the dissidents Shalaputs rather than Skoptsy.[28]

The Molokan and Pryguny Phase of the Shalaput Movement and Collaboration with Mennonites, 1861–1872. The spread of the "Shalaput Heresy" reflected the stream of Russian colonization into the fertile southern lands of the Northern Black Sea region and Northern Caucasus. In the province of Stavropol', during the 1840s, a strong evangelical movement arose among local Molokan peasants who had previously migrated from the central Russian provinces. Eventually, this movement converged with the "Shalaput Heresy."

The Molokans represented another version of the Christ-Faith tradition. This version of Russian dissent developed theology and rituals that were similar to evangelical traditions. By the middle of the nineteenth century, as contemporary observers noted, the Russian Molokan communities resembled Western evangelical congregations.[29] During their migration to the South, the Molokans brought not only their religious experience as "Spiritual Christians" but also their millennial expectations. To some extent, these expectations coincided with the frustration of rank-and-file Molokans at the rigid hierarchy and power of ministers in their communities. As a result of these factors, religious dissent appeared inside the Molokan communities during their settlement in the South—in the Caucasus and Tavrida. [30]

In 1856, the local police reported to the Third Section of the Imperial

Chancellery that some Molokans with rituals reminiscent of the Tavrida Shalaputs had separated from their old communities and established a new Communal (Obshchaia) sect. Mikhail Popov, a Molokan peasant from the province of Saratov, founded this sect in 1838 among his most pious coreligionists. These Molokans, who had been exiled to the Trans-Caucasian region in 1840, then brought the Communal sect to their new place of settlement (the district of Lenkoran' in Baku province).

The Molokan adherents of this sect (who numbered only 400) considered themselves members of the "Evangelical Church" and called themselves the "Spiritual Christians." Following the Acts of the Apostles, they tried to replace private property with communal property and attempted to restore the communal life of the first Christian communities.[31] In 1844, Mikhail Popov was arrested and exiled from Lenkoran' to Siberia. By the end of the 1850s, his sect disintegrated.[32] But during their migration, the radical Molokans brought the ideas of the Communal sect to the Northern Caucasus as well. In the 1840s and 1850s, these ideas spread among the local peasants and Cossacks who were members of the Molokan and the Katasonov sects.[33]

The sect that was later called the "Caucasian Shalaputs" began in the Northern Caucasus during the 1840s. In 1843, the police arrested Pamfil Popov, a state peasant from the village of Medvedskoe (in Stavropol' province) for anti-Orthodox dissident activities. Popov had established a religious meeting for "reading the Bible and worshiping God" in his house. More than thirty peasants and Cossacks from neighboring settlements visited his meetings and began to "worship their own prophets and prophetesses." In 1850, the police discovered another religious meeting with similar beliefs in the neighboring Cossack settlement of Aleksandrovskaia.

During the 1840s and 1850s, not far from Medvedskoe, two local peasant women, Praskov'ia Larina and Tat'iana Shepeliova, declared themselves to be "the prophetesses of Divine Wisdom." They asked peasants and Cossacks to worship them as representatives of God, and they criticized the Orthodox clergy as "Satan's corrupted servants."[34] As the police discovered, peasants from the province of Tambov, who belonged to the Katasonov sect of Old Israel, settled in two villages in the Medvezhenskii district of the province—in Novomikhailovka and Ladovskaia Balka—and established their branch of this sect there in the late 1840s.[35]

The Caucasian diocesan administration sounded the alarm because of the mass spread of the Shalaput sect among the Russian settlers of the Northern Caucasus. On November 27, 1873, the Reverend German, the bishop of the Caucasus and Ekaterinodar, wrote to the Holy Synod about "a considerable increase of the Khlyst sect known under the local name 'Shalaputs.'" The bishop estimated that their numbers were considerable, "because from ten to twenty peasant families in each village or settlement visited the Shalaput meetings for worship on regular basis."[36]

According to the bishop's data, we can calculate the number who visited Shalaput meetings in twenty-eight villages. Among Russian Cossacks and peasants in the Caucasus, the average number of adult members of households was not less then 5 people. Therefore, no fewer than 50 or 100 peasants and Cossacks participated in the dissident meetings in each village. Overall, from 1,400 to 2,800 peasants and Cossacks visited the meetings every month. In some localities of the Northern Caucasus, Shalaputs made up more than 50 percent of the entire rural population.[37] It is noteworthy that these localities were a part of colonized region, which was sparsely populated with Russian settlers. Due to the spread of the Shalaput movement, some of the frontier Russian villages in the Caucasus were settled entirely by religious dissidents.

The rise of the Shalaput movement in the Northern Caucasus coincided with its revival in the province of Tavrida in 1861. This Shalaput revival was linked to the religious activities of Mennonite and German colonists. On December 12, 1862, a local priest reported to the ecclesiastical authorities of Tavrida that in the farmstead (*khutor*) Ostrikovo of the village Bol'shoi Tokmak in the district of Berdiansk, "a group formed among the state peasants who were meeting during the nights, reading and interpreting the Holy Scripture and Apostles' Epistles; without understanding their true meaning, they distorted the truth and therefore departed from the rites of the Orthodox Church by their incorrect explanation of the Bible." The priest wrote, that those peasants used only the prayer "Our Father which art in Heaven" because they said that Jesus Christ had given only this prayer to the apostles. They did not make a sign of the cross and did not follow the Orthodox calendar of fasting. The dissidents from Ostrikovo communicated with the Germans and Mennonites who lived in the colony close to the villages of Tokmak and participated in their church rituals as early as the 1850s. According to the priest's report, this society, "known as the Shaloputs," had begun to grow in October 1862.[38]

The German colonist J. Klassen from the German colony Liebenau first reported to the local administration about a revival of the Shaluput sect in the district of Berdiansk. Klassen told the local priests that the sectarians often visited German meetings for worship. At the same time, he noted that the Russian dissidents played the guitar and sang psalms during their own meetings, which he had visited at the beginning of December 1862.[39] In a conversation with the priests who visited Shalaput meetings, the peasants explained that they had met exclusively for reading and discussing the Gospels, but they had no need of the priests "because they [the peasants] had learned the Divine Truth by now."[40] The movement of the Shalaputs exhibited new, more Western, features of the Reformation. The Tavrida Shalaputs used the Western editions of the Bible and other religious books for their reading and discussion. What was more unusual, they played the guitar and sang hymns during their religious ceremonies (figure 2.1).

As the governor of Tavrida reported, by 1862 this sect had spread to such German colonies as Rudnerweide, and the dissidents themselves began to throw their icons away and stopped attending Orthodox ceremonies in local churches. The leader of the sect was the state peasant, Damian Vasetskii, "who played the role of the priest [*pop*] among them." When the police arrested him, he confessed that he "maintained friendly relations with the true Christians" from the German and Mennonite colonies. During his arrest, they confiscated a book of the New Testament, printed in London, and a piece of paper with the text of "some prayer to someone called the Shepherd."[41] It turned out that both the book and the prayer had come from the German colony. It is remarkable that Russian dissenters, influenced by Khlyst and Skoptsy traditions, initiated a cultural dialogue with representatives of Western Protestantism and incorporated elements of Western Protestant culture into their theology and rituals.

Figure 2.1. Soviet Ukrainian evangelicals meeting for worship in 1963 in the same localities where the Tavrida Shalaputs had collaborated with the Mennonite Brethren 100 years earlier. Notice the central position of the guitar among the Soviet evangelicals, who continued the traditions of their predecessors. From the collection of the Dniepropetrovsk State Historical Museum, Ukraine.

The bishop of Tavrida wrote to the Holy Synod on April 9, 1863, that the Shalaputs still met nightly in their houses, sang psalms, and sometimes visited Mennonites and participated in their services. The church authorities worried particularly that these "literate" dissidents had become friendly with the Mennonites and Molokans. As one church official observed, "They began to read the books of the New Testament, which they bought in the market, and they visited each other in their houses, bringing these books with them." The promoters of the Shalaput sect in Ostrikovo were the most literate people there. The majority of Ostrikovo Shalaputs had been taught how to read in their dissident community by Mennonites and Skoptsy.[42]

During the Shalaput revival in Tavrida, Skopets activists reestablished their connections with their coreligionists from the central Russian provinces.[43] In

November 1864, the bishop of Tavrida himself emphasized in his report that the Skoptsy sect had appeared, as was evident in the local police report, in the same locality (the villages of Ostrikovo, Ocheretianoe, and others), where "the Shaloput sect had appeared two years ago under the influence of the German colonists, who lived near these villages."[44] The Melitopol' and Berdiansk Shalaputs, who were friendly both with the Belgorod Skoptsy and Tavrida Mennonites, considered themselves "true Evangelicals" who "followed closely the principles of the Gospels." In telegrams sent to the Holy Synod on August 12 and 15, 1865, forty-three Skoptsy and Shalaputs from the district of Berdiansk emphasized this fact and complained of unjust persecutions.[45]

Meanwhile, in March 1867, the bishop of Tavrida reported further on "the Skopets sect with a touch of Mennonitism." According to the testimony of the German colonist Klassen from Liebenau, local peasants often visited the colonists Jacob Reiner and Jacob Gibert in the German mill, where they (fifty people together, including the castrated peasants) met for worship, played the guitar, sang the psalms, and read the Gospels. "The colonist Jacob Reiner," Klassen testified, "gave a book of the Gospels to Damian Vasetskii; and the German teacher from Liebenau colony, Grigorii Vilam, taught the Gospels to Ivan Vasetskii."[46]

According to the local priest, the main initiator of the Skopets dissent was "the Mennonite colonist Jacob Reiner, who interpreted the Gospels, and rejected the icons, sacraments and rituals of the Orthodox Church." Reiner, the priest wrote, "established specially warm relations with the Ostrikovo peasants under the pretext of helping them."[47] As we can see, a revival of the Shalaput movement in Tavrida during the 1860s turned out to be a result of the unique combination of Mennonite influences and old Skoptsy traditions.

The sect expanded despite various official measures. The bishop of Tavrida reported on October 31, 1863, that there were 516 male and 542 female sectarians in one Tokmak parish.[48] Among 5,000 parishioners, the Shalaputs accounted for more than 20 percent of the Orthodox population! They made up 10 to 15 percent of the entire district peasant population. The real numbers of the participants in this religious movement were larger than those suggested in the official investigation. Yet even the police data were impressive.[49] In fact, according to the police and Orthodox clergy, almost a fifth of the rural population in the provinces of Tavrida and Stavropol' belonged to the Shalaput sect during the 1860s.

Given systematic police persecution, the Skoptsy leaders began to disappear from the Shalaput movement after 1875. In the Shalaput communities during the 1870s and 1880s, the ideal of the physically mutilated castrated prophet-Skopets was gradually replaced by a more modern image of a religious leader who offered salvation through the inner-worldly and active asceticism. Instead of physical mutilation and complete withdrawal from the problems of this world, the new Shalaput prophets advocated adjustment to life in this world as the sole means of serving God. At the same time, the Shalaputs continued their enthusiastic meetings, following the old traditions of Russian dissent.

The evangelical culture of reading and exposure to the influences of the radical Molokans and Mennonites contributed to the creation of new religious ideals and new religious practices. These gradually replaced the Skopets ideal of castration among the Shalaputs. Moreover, during the 1860s and 1870s, the Shalaputs elaborated more efficient and sophisticated forms of worship, which allowed them to "sublimate" their sexual energy in collective religious ecstasy. More rationalized and abstract evangelical ideals, coupled with more impressive religious enthusiasm, created a new cultural atmosphere in the Shalaput communities. This left no place for the irrational act of castration. The evolution of religious practices among the Shalaputs moved in the direction of religious enthusiasm, which was typical for all European Christian radicals, such as the first Anabaptists, early Quakers, Methodists, and Shakers.

During 1865 and 1866, the governor of Tavrida reported new influences in the Shalaput movement. One was related to a radical sect among the Molokans of the Berdiansk district of Tavrida province called the Pryguny (Jumpers), or the "followers of the Holy Spirit and Apostle Agreement."[50] According to police reports, "the first appearance of the 'Prygunki' [Pryguny] heresy—a belief in a 'descending of the Holy Spirit on a Christian during prayer'" was discovered in 1833 before the use of the name of Shalaputs in the villages of Tavrida. Contemporaries called them the Jumpers because these

113

radical Molokans jumped and danced during their meetings "under the influence of the Holy Spirit."

According to participants, the jumps demonstrated how "the Holy Spirit filled and moved the Christian soul." As one eyewitness wrote, the Pryguny "acted during their ceremonies like intoxicated people." "Under their religious ecstasy," he noted, "they climb on the walls, window sills, and then they jump over the benches and tables and pray to God shouting something weird and strange, and afterwards they interpret their shouts as Divine Revelation."[51]

These groups were part of the millennial movement among the radical Molokans. Under the leadership of Luki'an Sokolov, Terentii Belogurov, and Fedor Bulgakov, they went to Tavrida and the Caucasus during the years 1836–47 and waited for the coming of the Kingdom of Jesus Christ. In the 1840s, the radical Molokans, who settled in the Trans-Caucasian province of Erivan' (in Armenia) and hoped to find the New Jerusalem there, joined the Luka (Luk'ian) Sokolov group, whom the police called "Pryguny" or the "Zion sect." In 1853, Sokolov's adherents, who anticipated the oncoming Advent of Jesus Christ, began their "enthusiastic meeting," which was characterized by scenes of emotional ecstasy and by constant singing and dancing, which attracted not only Molokans but also their pious Orthodox neighbors. After 1854, Sokolov's successor, Maksim Rudomiotkin (Komar'), a peasant from the province of Tambov who had settled in Trans-Caucasia and had connections with members of the Communal sect, became the new leader of the "Jumping Molokans." During the 1840s and 1850s, the Molokan Pryguny became the first Russian radical sect that attempted to establish connections with other millennial groups in the southern provinces.

Like other dissident networks forming throughout the region, the Caucasian and Tavrida Pryguny established close connections with one other and maintained an active correspondence with those who had been exiled to Siberia. They also contacted Shalaput groups in the South. The police discovered in 1864 that Trifon Lisov, a forty-nine-year-old Molokan peasant from Novovasilievka, had become a new Pryguny leader in Tavrida. He communicated both with Maksim Rudomiotkin's radical Molokans from the Caucasus and with the Skopets leaders from Tavrida. Along with Rudomiotkin, Lisov presented himself as a successor to Luk'ian Sokolov, the legendary founder of the radical Molokans. Lisov expanded Pryguny activities to other Molokan settlements in Tavrida and invited Orthodox peasants to the Pryguny meetings. Lisov introduced more democratic forms of worship and replaced the rigid hierarchy of ministers in the Molokan community. Moreover, his sect elevated the role of women, and the "prophetesses" performed various religious ceremonies among the local Pryguny.[52]

Rudomiotkin, Lisov, and other radical Molokans corresponded with their coreligionists in the provinces of Stavropol', Bessarabia, Ekaterinoslav, Tavrida, and Kherson. At the same time, other prophets from the Old Israel sect of Katasonov corresponded with their adherents in these same provinces. As the police discovered, the same congregations sometimes read epistles written by different prophets. The Skoptsy, Katasonov, and radical Molokans sent their letters to the same localities and sometimes to the same people, whom they considered "sincere Christian believers."[53] By doing this, they established an information network, maintained close relations, and spread literacy among the dissidents.

By the 1880s, the Shalaput peasants who had saved some money tried to escape police control in countryside by moving to the cities. In the Ukrainian provinces of the Russian Empire, the peasant dissidents began to settle in the cities as early as the 1860s. During the next twenty years, this spread of the dissident movement to the cities resulted in new urban influences in the religious movements in southern Ukraine. Gradually, these influences contributed to a loss of traditional forms of peasant identity among religious radicals. Eventually, all major Ukrainian cities attracted peasant dissidents, including Shalaputs and Stundists. They were convenient places for exchanging ideas among various groups, and new religious practices came to the Shalaput movement through dissidents who moved to the cities.

Nikolaev, a port city on the Black Sea with well-known Khlyst and Old Believer communities, became another center of the Shalaput movement in southern Russia. Among the different sects of Nikolaev, the "Marianovtsy," led by the soldier's widow Marianna, was the most famous. In 1864, Marianna (or Mariamna) Stepanovna Timofeieva declared herself a Divine prophetess, began

115

living like a nun, preached throughout all the southern provinces of Russia, and eventually became a new legendary figure of the Shalaput movement. Each religious holiday, she made a pilgrimage to Kiev and its famous monasteries. During her travels, she met with other leaders of the radical sects and borrowed their ideas and rituals for her own group.

Marianna became not only a prophetess for her adherents but also "God's Mother," who simultaneously embodied the Holy Ghost and symbolized Divine Wisdom. According to contemporary accounts, she knew secrets of medical healing and helped many sick peasants recover. "Saint Marianna" also organized a system of mutual assistance among impoverished peasants, which helped them to survive during times of bad harvest and drought. She attracted other peasant women to her sect, where the most active and talented among them eventually became the leading prophetesses.[54] The Shalaputs were the first religious dissidents among the peasants of imperial Russia who elevated the position of women in their communities. As we can see, some Shalaput groups such as the Marianovtsy had female leaders who replaced the traditionally male leadership in old Russian sects.

On September 5, 1865, a police officer reported that he had discovered 153 members of the Marianovtsy sect in five villages of the Dneprovskii district (of Tavrida province). They called themselves the "Church of the Apostle Agreement" and behaved like Shalaputs: They did not drink alcohol or eat meat and avoided sexual relations. When a police officer asked about this, they explained that they wanted to be monks and nuns and planned to devote their lives to God.[55] The theology and rituals of the Marianovtsy combined elements of Molokan and Khlyst beliefs with the evangelicalism of German and Mennonite colonists. During the 1890s, the Marianovtsy participated in the activities of other Shalaput sects. Eventually, they joined these sects, and by 1900 the Marianovtsy ceased to exist as an independent congregation.

Despite the criminal charges and persecutions, the Shalaput movement grew and spread to the provinces of Kherson and Ekaterinoslav during the 1860s and the 1870s. Because of its rapid growth and influence, the Russian administration included a special section in the table of religious dissenters, titled "the Shalaputs" from 1865 onward. Sometimes, following the recommendation of Orthodox clergy, the provincial governors united the Shalaputs with other "mystical sects," such as the Khlysty and Skoptsy, in their reports.[56] The mass defection of the peasants from Orthodoxy in the southern frontier provinces worried the Russian government. The Ministry of the Interior even established a special department to investigate cases of religious dissent among Orthodox citizens. The police and officials of the Ministry of the Interior regularly informed the hierarchy of Orthodox Church about such dissent. The growth of the Shalaput movement had become the main concern of the Russian administration.[57]

In its second phase, the Shalaput movement spread over the southern provinces and absorbed various dissident groups ranging from the Katasonov sect to the radical Molokans. During the 1860s and 1880s, this movement became more inclusive and open to the new religious practices and theology. As a result, by the middle 1870s, new, more modern, and more Western elements had replaced the Skoptsy tradition in the Shalaput movement. Along with quasi-Protestant elements from the Molokans and the Mennonites, the traditional millennial motives and enthusiastic religious practices shaped and distinguished the Shalaput sects from other religious dissidents, such as the Old Believers and Stundists.

Duplii's Phase in Ekaterinoslav and Poltava Provinces, 1860s–1880s. Contemporaries usually identified the third phase of the Shalaput movement with the Duplii sect and called them the Shalaputs-Duplii, because Pavlo (or Petro) Duplii was the most prominent and famous figure among the religious dissenters in the province of Ekaterinoslav. Duplii was an overzealous Orthodox peasant from the village of Priadivka who looked for support from the clergy for his zeal. Having become disappointed by the indifference of the local clergy, he began meetings for worship in his house. Eventually these meetings became the center of a new religious movement among the Ekaterinoslav peasantry.

At the outset, in contrast to previous phases of the Shalaput movements, the Duplii adherents distanced themselves both from the mystic extremities of the Khlysty and from the Protestant rationalism of the Stundists and

Mennonites. They stressed the traditionalism of Russian Orthodoxy in their preaching and rituals. Yet, by the 1890s, the Shalaputs-Duplii had developed the same millennial theology and enthusiastic religious practices as other Shalaput groups. Though they had begun as a popular Orthodox movement, they eventually followed the same direction and contributed to the chiliastic atmosphere of radical religious dissent among the rural population in late imperial Russia.

The predecessors of the Duplii-Shalaputs in Ekaterinoslav were religious dissidents, similar to the Tavrida and Kherson Shalaputs. After the discovery of Skoptsy and Khlysty activity in Tavrida and Kherson during the 1840s, the Ekaterinoslav police decided to strengthen their control over local peasants. In 1847, to their surprise, the police discovered a sect in the district of Pavlograd whose activities were reminiscent of the Tavrida Shalaputs. The leader was a state peasant named Sergiy Tsyba, who traveled and preached in the southern provinces. The police discovered that in 1847 Tsyba had established a special meeting for worship in his house. "Father Sergiy," "the prophet of God," as he called himself, prayed like a spirit-possessed preacher. During nightly sessions, he fell to the floor as if dying and afterward imitated his own resurrection "under the influence of God." The local peasants called him "Saint Sergiy" because they believed that he could heal wounds, cure diseases, and predict the future. He taught his neighbors to avoid alcohol, meat, tobacco, and sex and to live peacefully. He asked his male adherents not to shave their beards.

As for the Russian Orthodox clergy, Tsyba saw no need for them to serve as intermediaries between Christians and God. In his struggle with "Demons" and "the Evil Spirit," he practiced exorcism. The peasants considered him a "messenger of God," and he told them about his communication with angels and the Christian saints. After his arrest, his followers told the police that they could not imagine life without him, because he was both Jesus Christ and the Mother of God for them.[58] Such sects as Tsyba's were predecessors of the mass Shalaput movement in Ekaterinoslav. Here we see the belief in Christ's re-incarnation among the Ekaterinoslav peasants as early as 1847, a trend that persisted in later developments of the Shalaput movement.

The first Russian publication mentioning the Shalaputs appeared in August

1873. It located the beginning of this "sectarian" movement among Ukrainian Cossacks from Poltava. According to this article, a local Cossack, Elisei Monachinskii, had traveled as an agricultural worker in 1858 to Tavrida and brought the ideas of the Tavrida dissidents to the Poltava countryside. He established a sect of 90 local Cossacks, who were called Shalaputs by their neighbors. By 1863, this Shalaput sect spread from Poltava to Ekaterinoslav.[59]

Local peasants initially called this version of the Shalaput movement in Ekaterinoslav the sect of Bosonogie ("the barefoot"). In April 1867, a priest from the village of Spasskoe reported on the Bosonoguie sect established by Nikita Ignatenko, a state peasant (i.e., who was not a serf) from the same village. Ignatenko had been already imprisoned for "dissident religious views" in 1861. But after he promised to be a "loyal member of the Russian Orthodox Church," he was released from jail and returned to Spasskoe. He invited local peasants to visit his house to read and discuss the Bible. Because of his piety, sobriety, and wisdom, he was popular with his neighbors. The local clergy called Ignatenko and his followers *bosonoguie* because Ignatenko usually walked barefoot even in the snow during the coldest winter weather (figure 2.2). According to the priest, this habit of walking barefoot was the main reason why the local peasants called Ignatenko "their own saint, Father Nikita." Using Orthodox religious books, Ignatenko taught his coreligionists that he was one of the Holy Men. He told them that God protected him from jail; therefore, though arrested twice, he was eventually released. "Soon all people would die," he used to say, "only angels and I would be left and brought to heaven."[60]

Under pressure from the Orthodox clergy, the Novomoskovsk district police conducted an investigation but found no dissident sect in Spasskoe. In responding to the requests of the Holy Synod and the Ministry of the Interior, the governor of Ekaterinoslav reported to the minister of the interior on October 18, 1867, that the main reason for concern about the Bosonoguie sect was its "unusual piety, sobriety and charity," which had attracted the attention of its neighbors. The governor also noted that they were literate.

In his report, the governor stated that these suspicious Bosonoguie dissidents distributed the Orthodox Christian literature they had been given in monasteries free of charge. During religious holidays, they permitted "the

Figure 2.2. The Old Father Rossoloda at the end of nineteenth century in Nikopol', Ekaterinoslav province; a typical image of the followers of the Duplii—*bosonoguie*. From the collection of the Dniepropetrovsk State Historical Museum, Ukraine.

meetings of those who shared their notions" in their houses, where they read religious books "explaining what they read, and then they sang the psalms." The governor nevertheless wrote that "nothing wrong was found in their lifestyle and conduct." Indeed, Platon, the bishop of Ekaterinoslav and Taganrog, met Duplii and characterized him afterward as "a harmless and pious Orthodox Christian." On November 27, 1867, the bishop wrote a special report confirming "his Russian Orthodox faith" to the Holy Synod. Nevertheless, the local police and clergy insisted on banning religious meetings in private houses.[61] The activities of these peasants from the Novomoskovsk district later laid a foundation for the Duplii sect, in which the monastic ideal of Orthodoxy was supplemented with evangelical practices.

According to another investigation undertaken during the period 1869–73, the founders of the Novomoskovsk Shalaputs came from the Poltava Cossacks. The beginning of this sect in the Novomoskovsk district was related to the activities of Ivan Oleinik (Oleinikov), a lower-middle-class inhabitant (*meshchanin*) of the town Konstantinograd (in Poltava province) who settled in the village of Pereshchepino (in the Novomoskovsk district) in 1861. The first adherent of Oleinik was a local state peasant, Klimentii Malasai (Klim Malasol). During the 1860s, Oleinik and Malasai made frequent pilgrimages to the consecrated places of the Orthodox Church (monasteries, shrines, etc.). After their return to Pereshchepino, they organized a special meeting for local peasants, where they read the Bible and "other religious books." The peasants donated food and nonalcoholic beverages to these meetings, where they had "common dinners and prayers at one large table."[62]

The activities of Oleinik, Malasai, and Bosonoguie contributed to the establishment of the first monastic communities formed by peasant dissidents in the district of Novomoskovsk and Pavlograd. The Shalaput activists tried to live like the Orthodox monks on the outskirts of their villages.[63] Such peasant monastic communities contributed to the diversity of religious practices in the province of Ekaterinoslav. They laid the foundation for the creation of additional Shalaput congregations, such as Grigorii Shevchenko's sect, the history of which was recorded in detail by Orthodox scholars.

By 1879, a retired soldier, Shevchenko, a former peasant from the village of Alexandropol', returned to his native village and together with his brother Tymophii established in his house a sect "hostile to the Orthodox Church." This sect became another center of the Shalaput movement in Ekaterinoslav, and it established connections not only with peasants but also with residents of such cities as Ekaterinoslav and Alexandrovsk. By 1889, at least 268 peasants of the Pavlograd district had publicly acknowledged that they belonged to Shevchenko's sect. Even the Orthodox clergy noted that the majority of peasants in such villages as Alexandropol' supported Shevchenko's sect.[64]

In response to the Orthodox clergy's request, the police began its investigation in Ekaterinoslav. They seized books and other religious objects from Shalaput households. It turned out, however, that the Orthodox publishing houses had printed all these books, and all the religious objects were Orthodox as well. The provincial administration had difficulty distinguishing religious Orthodox peasants from sectarians. On November 4, 1880, during the trial of the Ekaterinoslav Shalaputs, the Odessa court vindicated the Novomoskovsk peasants, "not finding any serious evidence of their religious dissent." The nature of the Ekaterinoslav Shalaputs confused both the prosecutor and jury. The overwhelming majority of these dissidents behaved like their most popular leader, Duplii. They strictly observed all the rituals and rules of the Orthodox Church. Overall, the theology and religious practices of the Duplii-Shalaputs were so close to Russian Orthodoxy that the prosecutor considered them to be "overly pious Christians."[65]

During the 1880s and 1890s, roughly 400 peasants in the province of Ekaterinoslav registered as Shalaputs, but the number of those who still considered themselves Orthodox was considerable. Even the local police could not provide the exact figures of the Shalaputs to the governor. The entire population (more than 500 peasants) of such a large village as Priadivka, for example, shared the ideas of Duplii. Local officials even called some of the villages in the Novomoskovsk and Pavlograd districts "the Shalaput settlements."[66]

The Shalaputs as the Radical Reformers of Orthodox Christianity

This section describes the various aspects of the Shalaputs as the radical reformers of Orthodox Christianity. The topics covered include Shalaput religious practices as a combination of Christ-Faith, Russian Orthodox, Sabbatarian, and evangelical elements; spirit possession and divine reincarnation in anticipation of the Millennium; and the stages in the evolution of Shalaput religious practices.

Shalaput Religious Practices as a Combination of Christ-Faith, Russian Orthodox, Sabbatarian, and Evangelical Elements. The Shalaputs were typical religious enthusiasts who, in Victor Turner's terminology, tried to escape their cultural and social marginality (liminality) by creating a new "sacred theater" in which they incorporated all available symbols and traditions. In their close communities, they became simultaneously the performers and the audience of the sacred drama of the first Christians. This sacred drama they repeated during each meeting for worship.

The documents of the Orthodox missionaries from the provinces of Tavrida, Ekaterinoslav, and Stavropol' contain various descriptions of Shalaput theology that demonstrate the radical, charismatic character of the Shalaput reformation, especially their theory of reincarnation. From the beginning, the Shalaputs incorporated ideas and forms from different traditions into their theology and religious practices. By the 1860s, the most prevailing influences on Shalaput theology came from the Russian Khlyst and Skopets traditions.

It is possible to single out the most prominent elements of the Shalaput theology and religious practices.[67] According to the Shalaputs, before his baptism, Jesus Christ was a normal human being. When John the Baptist baptized Jesus Christ, the Holy Spirit descended on Him and He became God. During His Ascension into Heaven, the Holy Spirit (or the Spirit of Christ) left Him, moved into another "worthy" person and transformed him into a Christ. With the death of this Christ, the Spirit of Christ moved to another person and so on.

This chain of incarnation of Jesus Christ continued with each new generation. The same happened with the Apostles and prophets, whose spirits descended on "worthy" people as well. Each new Christ appears with a group of elected prophets. During meetings for worship, anyone who could demonstrate possession by the Holy Spirit and an unusual ability to prophesy joined the group of elected prophets. These prophets predicted the future by laying their hands on the heads of one another. A special hierarchy was established among them. During this ceremony of the laying on of hands, those who stopped pronouncing prophesies earlier took the lower positions in the Shalaput hierarchy and accepted their inferior status among the prophets. Those who continued to prophesy gained a superior status. Among these persistent prophets, the one who during this ceremony demonstrated his spiritual power of prophesy by silencing all others would be called the new Christ.

During the police investigation in Tavrida in the period 1862–67, the committee of inquiry discovered the main tenets of the "Skopets sect of Shalaputs," which were shared by the state peasants in the district of Berdiansk. It was the first police record of the Shalaputs' creed.[68] This text revealed that at the beginning of its development, the Shalaputs' theology contained notions reminiscent of traditional Khlyst and Skopets ideas. The document followed precisely the famous Khlyst documents published by such Orthodox scholars as I. M. Dobrotvorskii and Pavel Mel'nikov.[69] Other elements also fit what is known about the imagery of Skoptsy from the province of Kursk. According to police evidence, the Tavrida Shalaputs interpreted the image of the beast from the Book of Revelation as a description of what Emperor "Nikolai Pavlovich" had done in persecuting "Godly people—Skoptsy." They explained the rule of Emperor "Alexander Nikolaievich" as the eve of the Messiah's coming, when a new tsar would arrive and the end of the world would come.[70] If we compare this document with the famous descriptions of "God's People" by Dobrotvorskii and other materials on the Khlysty and Skoptsy, the influence of the Khlyst and Skopets traditions among the Shalaputs becomes obvious.

It is significant that an emphasis on "spiritual celibacy" noted among the first documents of the Shalaputs was not just a pure Russian Khlyst and Skopets invention. All radical popular movements in Christian history incorporated notions of spiritual possession and celibacy, and they insisted that Christ's Second Coming was at hand. All religious radicals (both in Europe and America) who experienced a spiritual awakening held that it was possible for the regenerate person to live in a spiritualized state in which sexuality was transcended. Some of these radicals also professed to have achieved a state of physical perfection through spiritual discipline that would make them immortal.[71] The radical Shalaputs and the Maliovantsy shared these ideas of the European Radical Reformation as well.

The Shalaputs changed their theology and religious practices by incorporating elements from other religious traditions. After the 1860s, these dissidents from the Russian southern provinces moved far from the old Khlyst and Skopets traditions in developing various forms of religious enthusiasm and radical organization. During the late 1860s and the 1870s, all Shalaput communities used elements of Orthodox rituals and liturgy. Such Orthodox scholars as A. Dorodnitsyn noted that during their meetings for worship, Shalaputs conducted their religious ceremonies according to the canons of the Russian Orthodox Church but without the institution of the priesthood. All observers wrote about the strange combination of Orthodox hymns in Church Slavonic and Khlyst religious songs in vernacular Russian during Shalaput meetings. To some extent, Shalaput religious ceremonies looked like a popular version (with a strong democratic element) of Orthodox rituals.[72] Police reports give us an opportunity to compare various religious practices in different Shalaput communities at this time.

One of the Tavrida Shalaputs, Pavel Kobets, a twenty-two-year-old peasant, told the police the story of his conversion. A neighbor invited him to a Shalaput meeting during Easter week of 1864. With his friends, he went to the village of Timoshevka and visited the meeting in Stepan Robotiagov's house. Andrey Lesniak (Sofienko), a peasant from the village of Bol'shoi Tokmak, led this meeting and invited newly arrived Kobets to join their group. Sofienko began the meeting with a ritual of conversion to bring newly arrived peasants such as Kobets to the new faith. He asked each peasant one question: "Do you want to live as a monk or a nun without sin?" If the peasant gave an affirmative answer to this question, he could stay in the house and join the meeting. Those who did not answer or hesitated in answering left the building. Sofienko began to pray and sing Orthodox hymns in Slavonic, and everyone joined him. After singing and reading the Bible, Sofienko asked Kobets and the other newly converted peasants to keep the information about the meetings secret. The new converts pledged to be loyal to Sofienko and their new coreligionists by taking a solemn vow of secrecy.

The most important part of the meeting was devoted to the solemn dance and collective singing of the religious songs. During the round dance, which was similar to the traditional Slavonic folk dance (*khorovod*), the Shalaputs spoke "different languages" and made various prophesies when "the Holy Spirit   125 descended" on them. The meeting concluded with a collective supper and prayer. This type of Shalaput meeting for worship became typical for all other Shalaput communities on the southern frontier. From the 1860s on, the ability to speak in tongues and prophesy were the main elements of all Shalaput communities in the South.[73]

Along with the traditions of "God's people," the radical Molokans contributed to the new Shalaput theology and rituals as well. By 1864, the Molokan dissident sect of "Pryguny" (Jumpers) became the most important part of the Shalaput movement. A police officer described this sect's creed in detail.[74] This document reveals another important influence on the Shalaputs and Pryguny: the ideas of "Sabbatarians" among the Molokan sect, who followed Hebrew traditions of the Old Testament. After 1864, new Molokan and Sabbatarian influences gradually replaced the old traditions of Skoptsy in the Shalaput movement. A return to the Hebraic origins of the Christian faith and an emphasis on the Jewish roots of Christian theology was a prominent feature of the European Reformation as well.[75] From medieval times on, Russian religious radicals shared the same interest in the Hebrew religious background of the first Christian communities described in the Acts of the Apostles. Pryguny and other Shalaput groups introduced Sabbatarian theology and practices into the Russian radical reformation and elaborated rituals based on the Old Testament, which became an important component of the popular Russian Sabbatarian movement up to the twentieth century.

All Shalaput groups stressed the direct influence of the Holy Ghost on religious "enthusiasts." For example, the peasant woman Marianna, a leader of the Marianovtsy, demonstrated publicly how the Holy Spirit descended on her and made her "Christ reincarnate." This sect was important not only because of its size but also because its founder was one of the first female "Christs" among religious radicals. The theology and rituals of the Marianovtsy combined elements of Molokan and Khlyst beliefs with the evangelicalism of the new religious movement of German and Mennonite colonists, the neighbors of the Ukrainian dissidents. Besides the various descriptions of this sect's activities, the most graphic portrayals of the dissidents came from peasants who participated in their rituals.

126

Efrosinia Pindik, a woman from the village of Krasnianka in Tavrida, was invited to visit a Marianovtsy meeting in March 1883. This meeting was organized in a neighboring village Kostogryzovo in the famous Molokan area by the prophet Iakov Ad'iutantov (Dvorianskii) and the prophetess Akilina, both of whom were peasants from the village of Vonopansk (in the Dmitrov district, Riazan' province). When Efrosinia arrived at the meeting, all the dissidents, who were dressed in long white shirts, sang a song with this lyric: "I, poor girl, will go to God's ship to feel the Holy Spirit and pray to God and work hard in His name; and our God, our Creator will look at us and be moved by our pious conduct; and the Holy Spirit will be like a bread for us." While singing this song together, all the men danced in a circle, and all the women sat along the walls of the meetinghouse. After this dance, the men and women began another dance together, while forming figures of the cross with their bodies, whirling and singing: "As angels would sing, we go crosswise." During this spinning around, everyone was holding a white handkerchief in one hand, and thumping his or her chest with the other hand with a "terrible noisy whooping." When the dissidents finished dancing, they prostrated themselves on their handkerchiefs in front of their leader Ad'iutantov, who stood with a metal cross in his hand and prayed loudly.

After his prayer, Ad'iutantov took everybody by the hand and prayed to God for forgiveness their sins. His adherents remained prostrate on their handkerchiefs with their arms folded crosswise. This procedure of absolution continued until the men and women separated. Then Ad'iutantov supervised confessions and prayers among men who sat in one room, and the prophetess Akilina did the same among women in another room. At the end of the meeting, the men and women met together in one large room and had a "common supper" at one large table. When the dissidents were leaving the meetinghouse, one of the peasants who had invited Efrosinia to this meeting reminded her that she had been baptized many years ago in the Orthodox Church "just by water" to be an Orthodox believer, but now the dissidents baptized her "by the Holy Spirit" to be "a real Christian." And he concluded: "You are my sister in the Holy Spirit; but I gave you birth as a spiritual person."[76]

This testimony corresponds to other descriptions of the Shalaputs' religious practices collected by the local clergy and police. As we can see, the main framework of the liturgy for all the Shalaput groups (including the Pryguny and Marianovtsy) was an elaboration of the Russian tradition of the "Christ-Faith," which was common among such old Russian dissidents as the Khlysty, Skoptsy, and Molokans. By changing from their peasant dress into white robes before the meeting, the dissidents symbolically rejected their "sinful peasant lives" and prepared themselves to receive the Holy Ghost. In their Khlyst ecstatic dances, they formed figures of the cross as a symbol of the Christian church, which united all believers. By elevating the role of women in the religious community, they emphasized the divine character of their church in which all social and gender distinctions disappeared. This symbolism resembled that of the early English Quakers, Methodists, and Shakers. The Shalaputs used their collective dinners as a symbolic reminder of the Last Supper. All Shalaput communities practiced evangelical ceremonies of communion, similar to the Anabaptist rituals. Thus, Russian dissidents demonstrated the religious enthusiasm of the ecstatic (mostly millennialist) sects with elements of evangelical religious practices.

The Shalaput "Christs," prophets, and apostles had "spiritual wives," but they had no sexual relations with them, following the New Testament principle, "They that have wives be as though they had none" (I Corinthians 7:29).[77] The Shalaput prophets performed the ritual of water baptism for those who came of age and could understand the Gospels. At the beginning of their meetings, all Shalaputs kissed each other and bowed to the prophets and apostles. The first part of a Shalaput meeting was usually devoted to reading and explaining the Bible. Then, after they had changed and put on white clothes, the Shalaputs began the next ritual—prayer and prophesy. During the intensive, ecstatic praying, they sang religious songs and danced "under the influence of the Holy Spirit." The peak of the meeting was a state of spiritual ecstasy, during which the Shalaputs tried to feel the descent of the Holy Spirit. They prayed in a trance while someone in a state of frenzy spoke "with unknown tongues." The prophets tried to interpret this, following the New Testament rule: "Greater is he that prophesieth than he that speaketh with tongues, except he interpret, that the church may receive edifying" (I Corinthians 14:5).

The Shalaput diet (abstinence from meat, spices, alcohol, and tobacco) and their severe system of fasting contributed to their emotional enthusiasm and ecstatic praying. They practiced two kinds of fasts. The first, the lowest fast, included only abstinence from meat. They followed Saint Paul's teaching: "If meat make my brother to offend, I will eat no flesh while the world standeth, lest I make my brother to offend" (I Corinthians 8:13). The highest fast included an abstinence from all food during a period of one to seven days. In some communities, the Shalaputs practiced ten- and forty-day fasts. The Shalaput Christs, apostles, and prophets were supposed to practice the last kind of fast. Sometimes only a ten-day fast was required of the newly converted.

After such fasting, the novices were admitted to the second part of the meeting, which included praying and the admission of the new members. During the ecstatic praying and prophesying, the new Shalaputs took the solemn oath to be loyal to this community and joined the general praying. The last part of the meeting was devoted to a collective dinner and a discussion of practical questions of everyday life. During the dinner, the Shalaputs discussed problems of organization, mutual assistance, the education of children, and the collection of money for community needs.[78] The main theological and organizational elements described here demonstrate the combination of the old Orthodox and Khlysty traditions, especially in the theology and ritual of the reincarnation of Christ. At the same time, the Shalaputs elaborated these traditions and developed new, more democratic, and rational moments in their organization and rituals.

Spirit Possession and Divine Reincarnation in Anticipation of the Millennium. All Shalaput meetings emphasized the mystic nature of Divine reincarnation during their praying. Ecstatic moments of spirit possession became the central component of their liturgy. As the police reported, Shalaput activists ("prophets" or "apostles") had serious problems with their mental health; they often behaved as "God's fools" or simply madmen. All police descriptions of the Shalaput communities noted the central role of the ecstatic counterpoint, possession by the Holy Spirit.

A typical report about Shalaputs from the village of Dobrin'kaia provides a good illustration of this phenomenon. In December 1886, the police discovered that peasants from different villages in the Pavlograd district had organized a meeting for worship in the house of Maria and Iakov Lebed' in the village of Dobrin'kaia. They arrested the leaders. All six were literate ("self-educated") peasants who "knew almost all texts from the Holy Scripture by heart."[79] According to these peasants [later described as Shalaputs by the Holy Synod], "doing good deeds," helping other people, regular fasting, and following literally all the principles of Jesus Christ could result in the descent of the Holy Spirit on "worthy, sinless" people. In such people, God could become incarnate. The dissidents called such people "saints." God usually selected women as "saints" or "prophetesses." All Christians had to follow the prophesies of such women. Maria Lebed' played the role of the main prophetess in the meeting of Dobrin'kaia dissidents. Everybody called her "Mother of God."

During the meeting, all Maria's coreligionists would make a circle and pray, and then she would take the center of this circle and lead the ceremony. After a long prayer, everyone would begin to sing, dance, and jump, and behave as if possessed by the Holy Spirit. When this ecstatic praying reached its peak, Maria would suddenly fall to the floor, saying that she was dying. Then everyone would kneel, kiss her, cry, and pray about her resurrection. A few minutes later, she would rise up as a resurrected person and cry three times: "Christ is resurrected!" After praying, she would sit down at a table and announce that she "gave birth to the Savior of the world, and produced the Light and the Truth." This kind of "sacred performance" took place regularly until the police intervened. After a medical examination, Maria was diagnosed as mentally ill, and she was sent to the Ekaterinoslav mental asylum in December 1886. Only her husband's persistent requests saved her and secured her release the following year. It is worth noting that the Ekaterinoslav physicians could not find any serious mental illness. But during the 1880s, it became a common practice in the struggle against spirit-possessed Shalaputs for the local clergy and police to send dissidents to mental institutions.

Filimon Syrokvasha, a male Shalaput activist from the village of Shul'-govka, was noted among local peasants for his spirit possession and "visions." He told his neighbors how he saw "visions" and heard "voices." The Holy

Spirit sent him "angels" and persuaded him to join the local Shalaput community. During the police investigation, Filimon told the police that before he made a decision to join the Shalaputs, he had seen the huge silver letter "B" (in Russian, capital "B" stands for "Bog"—"God") in the sky and heard the loud voice from the sky, saying: "I will burn all your land!" He tried to read the Gospels and not to think about this vision. But suddenly the wind started to blow in his house, the entire building began to ring, and the voice from the sky shouted, "Pray, Filimon, pray!"

After this experience, Filimon decided to fast and avoid sexual relations with his wife. And again the voice asked him to read the Bible and to pray. While praying on Friday, he lost consciousness, and for three days he stood with the open Bible in his hands. Then, on Sunday, he was finally resurrected "like Jesus Christ with a new regenerated soul." His first words after his resurrection were: "Fear God because our Lord wants to punish us!" Filimon began to prophecy afterward, and he became the most enthusiastic prophet among the Shul'govka Shalaputs. During the meetings for worship, he would imitate his spiritual death, falling to the floor, and then, after the ecstatic praying of his coreligionists, suddenly rising up from the dead. In August 1886, after his arrest, the police doctors diagnosed him as suffering from "mania religiosa" and sent him to a mental hospital.[80]

In the cases of Maria Lebed' and Filimon Syrokvasha, the legitimation of "charismatic" authority depended on the traditional ecstatic practices of "God's People," namely, the ability to rise from the dead and reincarnate God in oneself. The leader of the Shalaput community had to publicly conduct the ceremonies of resurrection and reincarnation to the satisfaction of his or her coreligionists. Their approval meant acceptance of the actor as their leader. To some extent, such a ceremony had the function of elections in other religious communities. Only the most capable and talented actors of the sacred theatre of spirit possession could prove their "charisma" in ceremonies of resurrection and reincarnation. After such demonstrations, dissidents supported or rejected their aspiring leaders. "Charismatic" leaders practiced such performances when their position was threatened.[81]

The best-documented case of such a scenario in the Shalaput historiography is that of Grigorii Shevchenko's community. Shevchenko, the head of the Shalaputs from the village of Alexandropol', performed the "sacred theatre" of resurrection for his coreligionists whenever his authority was challenged.[82] All Shalaputs worshiped Shevchenko as Jesus Christ; called him "Lord" or "Ravii," bowed to him, and kissed his hands and legs. He wore long braided hair. He usually appeared before the Shalaputs in a special wagon as an Old Testament prophet, dressed in a long robe, with a carved rod, accompanied by his wife Aksinia, "the Mother of God." In this manner, he reaffirmed his authority.

During Shalaput meetings, Shevchenko always led the "sacred performance" of spirit possession. He always spoke in unknown tongues while praying, was the first to interpret the tongues, and was the most creative and innovative prophet in the meeting. His relatives were the main audience and the main actors of his sacred theater. According to his sister-in-law, the drama of the Holy Spirit possession usually began at midnight in the Shevchenko household. He awoke and began to shake terribly. Afterward, he ran around the house, moving his hands and loudly inhaling. Then he came back to the house, making circles while he was running and hid in the remotest room. The family awoke and waited for him. After a long time, he appeared before his relatives and cried: "Peace for you, brothers. Now the world has changed!" Everybody greeted him, "Our Lord!" as the resurrected Christ, and kissed his hands and legs.

Shevchenko faced a particularly serious challenge after his arrest in 1884, when his followers tried to find the new leaders among their coreligionists. That year, after his release from jail, he announced to his "brothers and sisters" from the neighboring villages that he would begin a long fast. While fasting, he fell asleep for three days, and afterward he awoke and told his coreligionists that the Holy Spirit moved in his body. After this experience, he presented himself as the incarnation of God to representatives of all Shalaput communities in the province of Ekaterinoslav.[83]

As we can see, all Shalaput communities, including those of Pryguny and Marianovtsy, participated in similar "sacred performances" accompanied by fits, trances, and visions among their members. According to scholars of religious enthusiasm, emotional excesses have always accompanied radical religious awakenings—from the first Christian communities to the Radical Reformation of the sixteenth century, from the British Methodist revival to the Great Awakenings in British North America, including the appearance of the Shakers and Mormons.[84]

Examples from Germany, Britain, and early North America clearly show that the Shalaputs had much in common with Western religious radicals. Religious radicals of the sixteenth-century German Reformation, along with the Ranters and early Quakers of the English Puritan Revolution in the seventeenth century, demonstrated similar forms of behavior. Those were also considered to be spirit possession by contemporaries. During the 1680s, a group of religious enthusiasts from Long Island in the British colony of New York became noted for their rituals of spirit possession. The local colonist Thomas Case, who was a leader of these "Singing Quakers," conducted very long meetings for worship, "which last for many days in succession."

During these meetings, "some were singing and making odd noises" and "either moving about in a dancing quaking manner" or "lying like dogs, hogs and cows." Once Case asserted that he "was come to perfection and could sin no more than Christ." He declared himself to be "God, but afterward qualified it and said he was of God." According to their contemporaries, Case's adherents "claimed to have the gift of languages, and Case, on certain occasions, pretended to raise the dead, condemned marriage, and said it was of the devil, perverting that text of Scripture, 'The children of the resurrection neither marry nor are given in marriage.'"[85]

In 1684, Increase Mather, a Congregationalist theologian in Boston, devoted one chapter of his *Essay for the Recording of Illustrious Providences* to the dangerous phenomenon of "the Singing and Dancing Quakers" who "are really possessed with Infernal Spirits." He described them as "bewitched People" and accused them of murder and "witchery." Mather described how all the new converts after joining the sect began "to dance, and sing, and to speak of extraordinary raptures of joy; and to cry out upon all others as Devils, who were not of their Religion."[86] According to him, from 1682 to 1683, the "Singing Quakers" penetrated into Puritan colonies and brought with them "freedom of sin," sexual perversions, and adultery.

Overall, Mather's picture of such activities is similar to descriptions of "Spirit Possessed fanatics" by their opponents, as the Anabaptists in Germany in 1525, the Ranters and early Quakers in mid-seventeenth-century England, the American Shakers in the 1780s, or the Khlyst and Shalaput sects of late imperial Russia. As typical religious enthusiasts, the Puritan women, who joined "Case's Crew," imagined that they would embody Christ and the Divine Spirit in themselves. These acts of Divine Incarnation became important parts of the early stages of all radical Christian sects. The Singing Quakers attempted to "embody" Jesus Christ, and Mather used these "acts" as proof of the sect's connection to the Devil. "One Mary Ross falling into their company," he wrote,

> was quickly possessed with the Devil, playing such Frentick and Diabolical tricks, as the like has seldom been known or heard of. For she made her self naked, burning all her Clothes, and with infinite Blasphemy said that she was Christ, and gave names to her Apostles, calling [her follower] by the name of Peter, another by the name of Thomas, declaring that she would be dead for 3 days, and then rise again; and accordingly seemed to die; and while she was pretendedly dead, her Apostle [Peter] gave out, that they should see glorious things after her Resurrection. But that which she than did, was, she commanded Apostle Peter to sacrifice a Dog. The man and two women Quakers danced naked together, having nothing but their shirts on.[87]

During the eighteenth century, the English Methodists experienced similar cases of "Spirit possession" and ecstatic hysterical praying. During their praying, the Methodists jumped and danced, demonstrating the presence of the Holy Ghost. In 1747, a Moravian missionary left a description of a meeting in Manchester, where everybody was "shouting Hurra, weeping for their sins, punching each other in the ribs, laughing, flinging stones and dirt, dealing boxes on the ear; in short a mixture of the extremes of Good and Evil."[88] Sometimes during their ecstatic praying, the English radicals tore their dresses and looked like "devilish creatures."

Another "enthusiastic group" from England, the Shakers, who in 1774 migrated to America, demonstrated the main stages and practices of the "Spiritual enthusiasm," which was a part of the most radical trend in the Reformation. According to one description in 1769, the first Shakers in Manchester began their meetings with prayer and singing "until the moving of the spirit comes upon them," and they were "trembling, shaking, and screeching in the most dreadful manner," simultaneously moving their heads from side to side. Then they were whirling, shouting their prophecies, "singing and dancing" all night long.[89]

Another description of Shakers came from an observer who witnessed a meeting in America in 1780. It resembles the portrayal of the Russian Shalaputs in 1864. The American Shakers also behaved like Russian Pryguny or Mennonite Jumpers:

> One will stand with his arms extended, acting over odd postures, which they call signs; another will be dancing, and sometimes hopping on one leg about the floor; another will fall to turning around; . . . another will be talking with somebody; . . . some groaning most dismally; some trembling extremely; . . . others swinging their arms, with all vigour, as though they were turning a wheel . . . [Their leader Ann Lee] would often communicate to a whole assembly by singing. Some were singing without words, and some with an unknown tongue or mutter, and some with a mixture of English [while leaping and whirling all the time].[90]

The Shakers in America and the Shalaputs in Russia professed spirit possession and used intensive whirling dancing and singing to reach a condition of trance in which they could unite their souls with the Holy Ghost and experience various forms of spiritual transformation. These forms included speaking "the unknown language," having visions, vomiting, trembling, and so forth.

One description of the Shakers' meeting in 1783 in Massachusetts demonstrated the same elements that characterized the Shalaput meetings in southern Russia during the 1860s. The Shakers at the settlement of Harvard began their meeting with long ecstatic praying, which reached a peak when some women began dancing and whirling around as fast as they could. All the Shakers cried "Ho, ho or Love, love," and clapped loudly. Then they "were shaking and trembling, others singing in whining canting tones words out of the Psalms, but not in rhyme, and others were speaking what they called the unknown tongue. [At] other times the whole assembly would shout as with one voice and with one accord." This description is similar to the portrayal Shalaput meetings in Grigorii Shevchenko's community in the province of Ekaterinoslav, and of Shalaput "rejoicing" in the province of Stavropol'. When the praying reached its peak, the Shakers "ran with great violence" from room to room at the farm where the meeting took place. Some of them whirled for a long time; a few of them grew dizzy and vomited. They explained their vomiting as "putting off the old man and his deeds."[91]

These examples of the religious radicals' experiments with Spirit possession are meant to show that this was a feature of the Radical Reformation and continued to exist in post-Reformation Europe and in the North American colonies. Along with the Singing Quakers on Long Island, the English Methodists in Manchester, and the Shakers in the State of New York, the Shalaputs in the provinces of Tavrida and Ekaterinoslav represented the "enthusiastic stage" of the Radical Reformation. The theological basis for this stage was formulated by Saint Paul, when he wrote: "My speech and my preaching was not with enticing words of man's wisdom, but in demonstration of the Spirit and of power. The things of God knoweth no man, but the Spirit of God" (1 Corinthians 2:4, 11). Thus, from the early beginning of Christianity, the Pentecostal trend of the first Christian communities legitimized possession by the Holy Spirit. Those possessed by the spirit were considered to be close to God: "He that is spiritual judgeth all things, yet he himself is judged of no man" (1 Corinthians 2:15).

This spiritual trend of original Christianity was emphasized again during the Radical Reformation in sixteenth-century Western Europe, and afterward it became an element of European popular religion. In the Russian radical reformation of the nineteenth century, Shalaput groups radicalized the "spiritualist trend" of original Christianity to an extreme. According to Clarke Garrett, the religious radicals had three common features. The first was the continuing manifestation of God's presence among believers in "gifts" of miracle working, ecstatic song and dance, and possession by the Holy Spirit. The second was the deification of leaders and the compulsory confession of sins to such leaders. The third was "mandatory, permanent celibacy."[92]

The Stages in the Evolution of Shalaput Religious Practices. In late 1876, a police officer's conversation with Pavlo Duplii, who was considered by the local priests the head of the Novomoskovsk Shalaputs, revealed that Duplii had tried to distance himself from all sects, including the Stundists and Shalaputs. It is noteworthy that all participants in the Shalaput movement (including Duplii himself) denied the name of Shalaputs, which was coined by the Orthodox clergy and police. Nevertheless, Duplii's denial of his connection to the mainstream of the Shalaput movement is remarkable evidence of the diversity of the movement.

Thus, in contrast to his own group, Duplii described the Shalaputs as a sect hostile to Orthodoxy. At the same time, he provided interesting information about the structures and subdivisions of the Shalaput movement in southern Russia. According to him, the Shalaput movement had five phases. The first was an extension of Orthodox piety and religiosity during which the dissidents behaved as pious Orthodox peasants, who participated in services in their parish churches. They spent their free time praying, reading the lives of the Holy Men, and discussing the Gospels.

During the second phase, the dissidents still visited their Orthodox church, but simultaneously they introduced new rituals of their own, which they performed during their own meetings for worship. At this phase, the Shalaputs began dividing themselves into two groups: the elect "consecrated" prophets and those other Christians, who "had not yet been reborn." In the third phase, the Shalaputs still called themselves Orthodox, but they rebaptized themselves as members of a new "spiritual Christian community" and introduced their own rituals and ceremonies, including the new ritual of the Eucharist. During the fourth phase, the Shalaputs openly broke their connections to the Orthodox Church and followed only the rules of their own community. They "even tried to provoke their own persecutions by the local clergy and police," because they "wanted to be martyrs" for the "restoration" of the primitive Christian faith. During this phase, the Shalaputs rejected sexual relations and marriage and "devoted all their life to God." Finally, in the fifth phase, the Shalaputs prepared themselves for the coming Kingdom of God and castrated themselves.

Duplii singled out the basic moments in the evolution of this movement, including the development of his group, which he contrasted to the radical Shalaputs who rejected the marriage and castrated themselves. He identified this extreme version of the Shalaputs with a sect from Nikolaev, and he described the Marianovtsy and the Soukhotin groups in detail. According to his testimony, a "captain" Soukhotin from Nikolaev with his two prophetesses, called "Mothers of God," had been visiting Shalaput communities all over southern Russia for three years (since 1873) and had sanctioned the transition. At the same time, he made allusions to the Stavropol' Shalaputs and Pryguny as the representatives of the fifth phase of the Shalaput movement as well.[93]

Duplii's typology of the Shalaput movement corresponds to the evidence of the police and Orthodox Church. Overall, Duplii presented an evolution of popular Orthodoxy, which sociologically fit into the well-known descriptions of the "spiritual trends of revival" in the Western Christian tradition from the Reformation to the recent "charismatic" sects. Only the phenomenon of castration seems to be largely a local innovation.[94] According to his typology, Duplii was only at the first phase of what he described as a development of the Shalaput movement. But this development took the course of the "radical reformation" of popular Russian Orthodoxy. As the Radical Reformation in Western and Central Europe began in the sixteenth century within old Roman Catholic traditions but led to new radical anti-Catholic denominations, so too the Shalaput movement drew on old Russian Orthodox traditions but led to the birth of new dissident sects that challenged the Orthodox Church establishment.[95]

What Duplii missed in his typology was the Anabaptist influences of the Mennonite settlers on radical Shalaputs. By the 1870s, the convergence of popular Orthodox dissent with Anabaptism transformed the Shalaput movement in southern Ukraine, and Shalaput activists joined the new evangelical sects of the Ukrainian Stundists. After the Revolution of 1905, the peasant dissidents in the localities of Duplii's influence were mainly Stundists rather than Shalaputs. Beginning as members of the Orthodox Church, Duplii and others in the Shalaput movement laid the foundation for a Great Religious Awakening among the peasants of the Russian Empire. Thus, the Shalaputs served as a cultural link between old Russian dissident traditions and the evangelical movement of post-Emancipation Russia.

The Shalaputs drew on the different traditions of popular Orthodoxy and developed as a popular religious movement to reform the hierarchical and formalistic Orthodox Church. All serious Orthodox scholars noted how the Shalaputs appropriated and applied traditional forms of Orthodox theology and liturgy in their rituals and ceremonies.[96] Amid the colonization of the southern frontier, the Shalaput movement started from the central Russian provinces in the 1830s as an extension of old dissident movements such as the Khlysty and Skoptsy. During the 1850s and 1860s, the Shalaputs borrowed from the Molokan movement and even from the Mennonites. But their main inspiration came from the traditions of God's Belief. These traditions were already a foundation for the popular reformation of Russian Orthodoxy among peasants in the central Russian provinces.

As a further elaboration of these traditions, the entire Shalaput movement, which influenced from 5 to 20 percent of the rural population in the provinces of Tavrida, Stavropol', Bessarabia, Kherson, Poltava, and Ekaterinoslav, became a popular radical reformation of Russian Orthodoxy from the 1860s to the 1890s. In the 1850s and 1860s, during their migration to the southern frontier, Shalaput activists created the infrastructure for a dissident movement through their travels, written correspondence, pilgrimages, and exchange of news. They also established patterns of behavior for their successors, such as the Stundists and Maliovantsy. The spirit possession and the religious ecstasy of the Shalaputs became an integral part of radical Stundism. At the same time, the persecution of the Shalaputs by the Orthodox clergy laid a foundation for future anti-dissident practices and discourses.

Besides the Russian Molokans and German-speaking Mennonites, the Shalaputs became the first pioneers of the Protestant ethic on the southern frontier. Although they had begun as Orthodox Pietists, the Shalaputs nevertheless created their own patterns of rational behavior, avoiding alcohol and concentrating on thoroughly carrying out everyday plans. Following the monastic ideal, they demonstrated their own version of an inner-worldly asceticism, which was reminiscent of the Protestant religious ethos. The Shalaputs

139

Figure 2.3. Parfenii Petrovich Katasonov, a leader of the Old Israel sect, a part of the Shalaput movement of the nineteenth century. From *Materialy k istorii i izuchenia russkogo sektantstva i staroobriadchestva, Vypusk 4: Novyi Israil'*, ed. Vladimir Bonch-Bruevich (Saint Petersburg, 1911), between pp. LVI and LVII.

promoted the role of women in the life of their communities and made them leaders of their movement. They elaborated on the ideas of the Radical Reformation and applied them to Orthodox traditions. They combined different cultural traditions and created a new cultural identity among the rural population of the southern frontier. They introduced and elaborated on a new principle of kinship—Christian spirituality and a search for Divine Truth, instead of ethnic, regional, or denominational criteria in identity formation. By their activities and through their pilgrimages and travels, the Shalaputs integrated various "charismatic" sects of the southern frontier into one cultural framework and set the stage for subsequent religious dissident movements.

140

Chapter Two

Figure 2.4. The successors of Katasonov, leaders of the "Israel" sect of the twentieth century: Vasilii Fedorovich Mokshin (on the left) and "Mama" Irina Ustinovna, *dukhovnitsa* of Mokshin (on the right). Note the dual leadership of this sect. From *Materialy k istorii i izuchenia russkogo sektantstva i staroobriadchestva, Vypusk 4: Novyi Israil'*, ed. Vladimir Bonch-Bruevich (Saint Petersburg, 1911), between pp. LXIV and LXV.

The Shalaput sect began the popular evangelical awakening among Russian and Ukrainian peasants in post-Emancipation Russia. The Shalaputs later converged with the Stundist movement and contributed to the intensive cultural formation and social transformation of the population of the southern Russian frontier. Recent historians have treated the Shalaputs and Stundists as different religious moments. Contemporaries, however, emphasized the links and influences between them.[97] The Shalaputs were the first to provide cultural links between the old traditional Russian sects and new evangelical groups among the Western colonists and the Russian and the Ukrainian settlers on the southern Russian frontier (figures 2.3, 2.4, and 2.5).

141

Figure 2.5. Members of the New Israel sect, successors of the Shalaputs, exiled to the Transcaucasia at the beginning of the twentieth century. From *Materialy k istorii i izuchenia russkogo sektantstva i staroobriadchestva, Vypusk 4: Novyi Israil'*, ed. Vladimir Bonch-Bruevich (Saint Petersburg, 1911), between pp. LXXII and LXIII.

Notes

1 The actions of the Shalaputs can be interpreted as a ritual performance based on their distinctive conception of the sacred or as an act of communication "intended for an audience whose shared values and expectations enable it to interpret the behavior in culturally normative terms." From this perspective, the strange ritual dances, jumps, singing, and speaking in tongues of the Shalaputs were a part of "spectacular body language" or, according to Clarke Garrett, they were elements of "sacred theatre"—"sacred," Garrett wrote, "because all of them presupposed the descent of divinity into humans as a fulfillment of the biblical scenario of personal salvation and universal regeneration; theatre because they entailed a cultural interaction between 'performers' and 'audience'"; see Clarke Garrett, *Spirit Possession and Popular Religion: From the Camisards to the Shakers* (Baltimore, 1987), 3, 5. The new research on performance and ritual gives us an opportunity to see religious radicals as performers and actors and helps us to understand their rituals as a performance of "a Divine drama," which included every member of the dissident communities. Moreover, as Joanna E. Ziegler notes, "This new performance-oriented perspective offers a more accessible and humanizing view" of these religious radicals, as well as of their often incomprehensible activities. The best example of the new research is *Performance and Transformation: New Approaches to Late Medieval Spirituality*, ed. Mary A. Suydam and Joanna E. Ziegler (New York, 1999); the citation is from xiii.

Chapter Two

2 On this, see Ronald Knox, *Enthusiasm: A Chapter in the History of Religion* (Oxford, 1950), 21–49; *Perspectives on Charismatic Renewal,* ed. Edward D. O'Connor (Notre Dame, Ind., 1975), 115–18. The citation is from Garrett, *Spirit Possession,* 8–9. On popular psychological notions of groups such as the Shalaputs as hysterics coping with unresolved psychological and psychosexual conflicts, see Cristina Mazzoni, *Saint Hysteria: Neurosis, Mysticism, and Gender in European Culture* (Ithaca, N.Y., 1996).

3 *Kavkazskie eparkhial'nye vedomosti* (hereafter *KavEV*), 1873, no. 23, 754–55; 1875, no. 3, 96–100; 1881, no. 13, 455–60; 1882, no. 13, 449–50; 1891, no. 4, 112–13. Also see Ia. Abramov, "Sekta shalaputov," *Otechestvennye zapiski* (hereafter *OZ*), 1882, no. 9, 46–55; and A. Dorodnitsyn, "Sekta shalaputov," *Chtenia v obshchestve liubitelei dukhovnogo prosveshchenia,* March 1889, 276–88. Soviet historians followed this tradition as well. On the Katasonovtsy, see A. Klibanov, *Istoria religioznogo sektantstva v Rossii (60-e gody XIX v—1917 g.)* (Moscow, 1965), 57–62.

4 *KavEV,* 1875, no. 3, 96; *Ekaterinoslavskie eparkhial'nye vedomosti* (hereafter *EkEV*), 1884, no. 10, 185–202. Orthodox historiography begins the story of the Shalaputs with the migration of peasant members of the "Old Israel" sect from the province of Tambov to the Northern Caucasus at the end of the 1840s. The Katasonovtsy had established their sect in the village of Ladovskaia Balka (in the province of Stavropol') by 1850. According to the official version of the Orthodox Church, the local priest, Trophim Orlov, called them "Shalaputy" in a police report. He coined this name during the police investigation in 1850, because he was so confused by their rituals and theology that he could not find an appropriate name for them. During the 1850s and 1860s, this sect spread from the Northern Caucasus to other provinces of the southern frontier. This interpretation of the Shalaputs' origins became part of Russian historiography, and even serious criticism by other Orthodox authors could not change it. On this, see A. Dorodnitsyn, "Shelaputskaia obshchina," *Russkii vestnik,* October 1904, 705–39; and *Russkii vestnik,* November 1904, 126–85.

5 In this discussion of the Russian Radical Reformation, I try to avoid the contrasting definitions of class struggle by Alexander Klibanov. E.g., Klibanov portrayed the original Molokan movement as the democratic one, and he contrasted it with the bourgeois-church movement of the Stundo-Baptists. See Klibanov, *Istoria religioznogo,* 183. It was the typical approach of Soviet historiography, whereby each conclusion was based on oppositional dichotomies.

6 Nikolai Nadezhdin, *Issledovanie o skopcheskoi eresi* (Saint Petersburg, 1845), 324, 334. According to Nadezhdin, more than 400 Skoptsy lived in Tavrida by 1843.

7 See a discussion about Russian legislation against Skoptsy during the period 1806–48 in Laura Engelstein, *Castration and the Heavenly Kingdom: A Russian Folktale* (Ithaca, N.Y., 1999), 48–51. But she ignores connections of the Skoptsy with other dissenters such as the Shalaputs.

8 Rossiiskii gosudarstvennyi istoricheskii arkhiv (hereafter RGIA), f. 786, op. 121, d. 929, l. 1–4. On May 20, 1840, the Ministry of Justice transferred a report of Tavrida governor to the Holy Synod. See in RGIA, f. 797, op. 10, d. 26637, l. 2. The Ukrainian form of Maria's surname was Dakhno, which was Russified as Dakhnova in this report.

143

9 RGIA, f. 797, op. 10, d. 26637, l. 2ob. An officer reported to the police administration that "the present meaning, the aim of this sect, and the origin of the name of Shalaputs are still a mystery."

10 RGIA, f. 381, op. 1, d. 23087, l. 2, 3–4.

11 RGIA, f. 381, op. 1, d. 23087, l. 14–16. The district court of Belgorod had already considered a case about Zaitsev, who was suspected of seducing "the peasant Bredikhin and four more peasants to join a Sabbatarian sect (subbotniki)."

12 RGIA, f. 381, op. 1, d. 23087, l. 4–5.

13 RGIA, f. 381, op. 1, d. 23087, l. 13–13ob.

14 RGIA, f. 381, op. 1, d. 23087, l. 29ob.

15 RGIA, f. 381, op. 1, d. 23087, l. 34–35.

16 RGIA, f. 381, op. 1, d. 23087, l. 35ob.

17 RGIA, f. 381, op. 1, d. 23087, l. 36–36 ob.

18 RGIA, f. 381, op. 1, d. 23087, l. 41–44ob.

19 RGIA, f. 381, op. 1, d. 23087, l. 48. The minister was suspicious about those peasants, who by "cutting their sinews and genitals made themselves incapable to conceive." According to the official definition of the Skoptsy sect, it was the main distinctive feature of the sect.

20 RGIA, f. 381, op. 1, d. 23087, l. 51–52.

21 RGIA, f. 381, op. 1, d. 23136, l. 2–2ob., 3.

22 RGIA, f. 381, op. 1, d. 23136, l. 6–7.

23 RGIA, f. 381, op. 1, d. 23136, l. 9–12ob.; this is "Pleshchu, khleshchu, Boga ishchu; iavis' nam naruzhu" in Russian. It was reminiscent of the Khlyst singing. Compare with the songs of the "God's People" in I. Dobrotvorskii, *Liudi bozh'i: Russkaia sekta tak nazyvaemykh dukhovnykh khristian* (Kazan', 1869), 101–200.

24 RGIA, f. 381, op. 1, d. 23136, l. 13.

25 RGIA, f. 381, op. 1, d. 23136, l. 14–14ob. Ivan Kazakov was apparently emaciated and he lost a lot of blood after castration.

26 RGIA, f. 381, op. 1, d. 23136, l. 18–18ob.

27 RGIA, f. 381, op. 1, d. 23136, l. 11ob.–12. Compare with Engelstein's notes on literacy among the Skoptsy in her *Castration,* 112–13, 151–54.

28 Despite the severe police repressions, the sect still existed in Bessarabia. Even on September 30, 1857, fifteen years later, the archbishop of Kishinev reported to the Holy Synod about a new discovery of "the dissident sect under a name of Shalaputs" in a village Vasilievka (near Diviziu) in August 1857; RGIA, f. 796, op. 138, d. 1764, l. 1.

29 *Life of William Allen with Selections from his Correspondence,* 2 vols. (Philadelphia, 1847), vol. 1, 389–99; Jacob P. Bekker, *Origin of the Mennonite Brethren Church: Previously Unpublished Manuscript by One of the Eighteen Founders,* trans. D. E. Pauls and A. E. Janzen (Hillsboro, Kan., 1973), 97; L. G. Deich, *Za polveka* (Moscow, 1926), 128; Jaakoff Prelooker, *Under the Tsar and Queen Victoria: The Experiences of a Russian Reformer* (London, 1895), 74–95.

30 On the Molokans' migration to the Caucasus, see Nicholas B. Breyfogle, "Heretics

and Colonizers: Religious Dissent and Russian Colonization of Transcaucasia, 1830–1890" (Ph.D. dissertation, University of Pennsylvania, 1998)," 79–145.

31 Gosudarstvennyi arkhiv Rossiiskoi Federatsii (hereafter GARF), f. 109, op. 31, d. 36, pt. 10, l. 2–l.6, l. 15ob.–16.

32 On this sect, see, in detail, Klibanov, *Istoriia religioznogo,* 135–44.

33 GARF, f. 109, op. 31, d. 36, pt. 10, l. 2–6, 15ob.–16.

34 *Stavropol'skie eparkhial'nye vedomosti* (hereafter *SEV*), 1900, no. 21, 1213–29. After 1850, local peasants and Cossacks began to read and discuss various religious books in public. They stopped visiting the Orthodox church and stopped paying tithes to the Orthodox clergy. GARF, f. 109, op. 31, d. 36, part 3, l. 1–1ob., 4–5. On March 16, 1856, the head of the gendarme division in Tiflis reported to his superiors that in February 1856 his colleague, the police officer M. Grabia-Gorskii, had submitted to him a book, approved for publication by the Moscow Theological Academy. This book was titled *The Human Heart Is either the Divine Temple or Satan's Dwelling.* The police officer explained that this book generated a "peculiar heresy" among local peasants. This heresy, he noted, "was absurd in its essence, harmful for people's morality and dangerous for the government." According to his investigation, the adherents of this new teaching "that was even lacking a name, rejected everything established by the Orthodox Church and the laws; they did not accept the Divine churches, holy icons and any authority; they did not celebrate the Orthodox holidays; they denied confession, the Holy Eucharist, the sanctity of marriage and kinship; they acknowledged only their Spiritual faith and brotherhood, and asserted that nothing existed beyond the human being." The quotations are from GARF, f. 109, op. 31, d. 36, part 3, l. 8–9, 15–17. It is noteworthy that in 1861, the Holy Synod rejected the information about the heretical character of the book under the investigation. Nothing wrong was discovered in that book. Perhaps, some of its pictures were not properly done for such an edition, but that was its only shortcoming.

35 The first Orthodox observers in the Northern Caucasus again applied the name of Shalaputs, which had already been used in the 1840s in Tavrida and Bessarabia. Thus local clergy and police appropriated this name in the Northern Caucasus in the 1860s. See *KavEV,* 1873, no. 23, 753–62; 1874, no. 24, 796–800; 1875, and no. 3, 95–100. Also see *SEV,* 1900, no. 21, 1219–22. In 1857, Katasonov sent his representative, a "prophet Gabriel" from the province of Tambov, to Ladovskaia Balka. According to the Orthodox Church's investigation, this was the beginning of the expansion of the Khlyst sect to the Caucasus and the first attempt of the Katasonov Postniks (Bogomols) to establish their Khlyst "ship" (congregation) in the province of Stavropol'.

36 RGIA, f. 796, op. 154, d. 582, l. 1b–l.2. He noted that this sect had appeared for the first time around 1857 in the villages of Novomikhailovka and Ladovskaia Balka. By 1872, the adherents of the Shalaputs were active in seven villages of the Stavropol' province, fourteen settlements of the Kuban' Cossack region, and seven settlements of the Terek Cossack region.

37 RGIA, f. 796, op. 154, d. 582, l. 2. The local diocesan periodical published detailed descriptions of the Shalaputs' rites and customs with the lyrics of their religious hymns

and songs in every issue during the period 1873–79. See *Kavkazskie eparkhial'nye vedomosti* for 1873–79.

38 RGIA, f. 796, op. 143, d. 602, l. 1–1ob.

39 RGIA, f. 796, op. 143, d. 602, l. 2–2ob.

40 RGIA, f. 796, op. 143, d. 602, l. 3.

41 RGIA, f. 796, op. 143, d. 602, l. 5–5ob

42 RGIA, f. 796, op. 143, d. 602, l. 10–12ob.

43 In 1864, the peasant Parfion or (Parphenii) Babanin (a close relative of Teet Babanin, a founder of the first Shalaput group in Tavrida in 1833) added to the Shalaput sect in Ostrikovo "a strong Skoptsy influence" and expanded this sect to the villages of Ocheretianoe and Bol'shoi Tokmak in the Berdiansk district. In all, there were five Skoptsy and thirty noncastrated members. The prevalence of the Skoptsy was noted also among the peasants of Mikhailovskoe, Timoshevka, and other villages in the Melitopol' district. The citation is RGIA, f. 796, op. 143, d. 602, l. 27–27ob. Both the Shalaputs and the Skoptsy "considered one Akulina Ivanovna from a town of Belgorod in the province of Kursk as their tsarina Divine."

44 RGIA, f. 796, op. 143, d. 602, l. 28.

45 RGIA, f. 796, op. 143, d. 602, l. 30. The majority of these Skoptsy came from the Shalaput families connected to the Mennonite colonies.

46 RGIA, f. 796, op. 143, d. 602, l. 35–36.

47 RGIA, f. 796, op. 143, d. 602, l. 37.

48 RGIA, f. 796, op. 143, d. 602, l. 23–23ob.

49 Abramov gave the same proportion of Shalaputs (5–15 percent) among the settlers in the Northern Caucasus in the early 1880s. See Abramov, "Sekta shalaputov," 40. The arrested peasants were the heads of the richest and most prosperous peasant households in both districts. The local officials were afraid to lose the most diligent portion of the rural population because of these arrests. Eventually, they intervened and the police released the majority of the arrested peasants. The citation is GARF, f. 109, 1 *ekspeditsia,* op. 40, part 2, d. 21, l. 39–39ob., 41, 42–42ob., 52–52ob., 67ob.

50 GARF, f. 109, 1 *ekspeditsia,* op. 40, d. 21, part 2, l. 4–4ob. See a description of the 'Pryguny" origins in Klibanov, *Istoria religioznogo,* 131–34.

51 S. Maksimov, "Za Kavkazom, " *OZ,* 1867, no. 6, 493.

52 GARF, f. 109, 1 *ekspeditsia,* op. 40, d. 21, part 2, l. 5–5ob.

53 Early in the 1870s, Rudomiotkin and Lisov were popular figures among "the Molokans-Pryguny" and among other radical sects on the southern frontier. During the 1880s, the Pryguny became the integral part of the Shalaput movement, and such figures as Sokolov, Rudomiotkin, and Lisov, along with Katasonov, became their legendary prophets, who contributed to their theology and rituals. On this, see Klibanov, *Istoria religioznogo,* 130–35. In the 1880s, Rudomiotkin settled in the province of Ekaterinoslav (in the district of Rostov) and became a member of the local Shalaput community. See *EkEV,* 1893, no. 17, 427–41; no. 18, 459–77; and no. 19, 491–504.

54 Tsentral'nyi derzhavnyi istorychnyi arkhiv Ukrainy (hereafter TsDIAU), f. 356,

op. 1, d. 60, l. 1–3. The first official complaint about the Marianovtsy's activities was recorded in a report of the governor of Tavrida in 1866. See RGIA, f. 1263, op. 1 (1867), d. 3286, l. 550–50ob.

55 According to this report, the Marianovtsy had connections with another Shalaput group in the city of Nikolaev. The Nikolaev sect had no less than 300 members and was led by a retired official, a captain Soukhotin. The local police considered Soukhotin and his Nikolaev coreligionists, such as the sailor Vasilii Sidorenko, the main dissident leaders who inspired the widow Marianna and her "Shalaput sect." According to the police investigation, Soukhotin generated the ideas for the Marianovtsy who still considered their "Nikolaev brothers" their "religious mentors"; GARF, f. 109, 1 ekspeditsia, op. 40, part 2, d. 21, l. 68ob.–69. Later on, the Soukhotin group would influence even the Ekaterinoslav Shalaputs.

56 The governor of Tavrida submitted the first report with a special section about the Shalaputs in 1865. See RGIA, f. 1263, op. 1, d. 3257, vedomost' 25.

57 RGIA, f. 797, op. 51, 2 otd. 3 st., d. 81, l. 2, 7–7ob.,10, 12–12ob.

58 N. Varadinov, Istoria ministerstva vnutrennikh del (Saint Petersburg, 1863), vol. 8, 598–99. See also V. Iasevich-Borodaevskaia, Bor'ba za veru: Istoriko-bytovye ocherki i obzor zakonodatel'stva po staroobriadchestvu i sektantstvu v ego posledovatel'nom razvitii s prilozheniem statei zakona i vysochaishikh ukazov (Saint Petersburg, 1912), 219–20. She started her essay about the Shalaputs with Sergei Tsyba's story.

59 The first publication about Shalaputs from the settlement of Portnianskie Khutora (in the Mirgorod district, Poltava province) was an article in a Kiev newspaper. See T., "Sekta shaloputov," Kievlianin, no. 98 (1873): 1–3. See other local periodicals: Nedelia, no. 31 (1873): 1128–30; Orest Levitskii, "Shaloputy na granitse Poltavskoi i Ekaterinoslavskoi gub," Kievskii telegraf, no. 41 (1875): 1, 2; no. 42 (1875): 2–3; no. 43 (1875): 2–3; no. 48 (1875): 4; and Zaria, no. 13 (1881).

60 RGIA, f. 797, op. 37, d. 107, l. 1–1ob.

61 RGIA, f. 797, op. 37, d. 107, l. 4–7ob. During the 1860s, many pious peasants, after visits to the Orthodox monasteries, tried to establish their own patterns of Orthodoxy and organized meetings for worship in their houses. E.g., in 1866 the peasant Nechai organized a group analogous to Duplii's sect in the village of Blagodatnoe in the district of Mariupol'. See EkEV, 1886, no. 23, 593–99. By 1875, the village of Shul'govka (with thirteen families and seventy-five members of the sect) had become a new center of the Shalaputs in the Novomoskovsk district. It is noteworthy that the local priests who complained about the increase of the Shalaputs in their parishes were not able to give their exact numbers. The most active and intelligent peasants joined the new movement, and it was hard to tell the Shalaputs from the pious and sober Orthodox peasants; RGIA, f. 796, op. 165 (1884–85), d. 1692, l. 1–1ob.

62 RGIA, f. 796, op. 156, d. 455, l. 2ob.–4. The Oleinik's activities were related to the first Shalaputs of the towns of Svinarnoe and Portnianskie Khutora in the province of Poltava. See also RGIA, f. 796, op. 150, d. 449, l. 1–4ob. Another state peasant from the village Lychkovo (in the Novomoskovsk district), Ivan Bosoi ["barefoot" in Russian]   147

had become the most famous activist of the Shalaput movement by 1873; RGIA, f. 796, op. 165 (1884–85), d. 1692, l. 17, 18ob.–19.

63 *EkEV,* 1886, no. 18, 453–63.

64 Dorodnitsyn, "Shelaputskaia obshchina," 708–10. He devoted this essay to a story of Grigorii Shevchenko's group.

65 RGIA, f. 796, op. 165 (1884–85), d. 1692, l. 19–26.

66 See a summary of the reports of the local police officers from the Novomoskovsk and Pavlograd districts in RGIA, "Otchet Ekaterinoslavskogo gubernatora za 1883 god," 25; and "Otchet Ekaterinoslavskogo gubernatora za 1890 god," 371ob., 405–5ob.

67 What follows is based on material from diocesan publications and archival documents, especially on Duplii's testimony and the records of Grigorii Shevchenko's case. See especially: *EkEV,* 1890, no. 8, 226–28.

68 GARF, f. 109, 1 *ekspeditsiia,* op. 40, part 2, d. 21, l. 23–25. According to this creed, (1) Shalaputs believed in the "God Father, God Son, and Holy Spirit." (2) They considered castration to be "purification from the filth by the Divine seal, without which nobody could get into the Heavenly Kingdom"; according to them, the Savior Himself, Apostles, and Prophets were Skoptsy. (3) They worshiped one Akulina Ivanovna from Belgorod as "the Heavenly Tsarina." (4) They were obliged to keep in secret the sect's tenets, rituals and their membership in it. That was why the new converts took an oath that "under the investigation and at the court they would say nothing about Skoptsy." (5) They considered prayers with singing and dancing to exhaustion to be "the business pleasing to God." (6) Meat and alcoholic beverages were forbidden among them. (7) Some of them did not use the sign of the cross; and they called the Orthodox Church "the mighty city Babylon of fornication," referring to chapter 18 of the Book of Revelation. (8) They did not respect the Orthodox clergy, and they rejected the right of priests to give them absolution. (9) They did not accept the water Baptism from the priests as true ritual. (10) They did not accept the sacrament of Christ's body and blood, because for them these elements were "just bread and wine." (11) They rejected marriage and considered "carnal intercourse with a wife as fornication." (12) The adherents of this teaching considered Emperor Peter I as the second Christ because "he was a Skopets and similar to the Savior, and he had 12 disciples-Skoptsy who preached about the Skoptsy sect." They worshiped Empress Elisaveta Petrovna and Emperors Pavel Petrovich and Alexander I as "saints who assisted the Skoptsy sect."

69 On the theology of "God's People" and their Skopets idealization, see Dobrotvorskii, *Liudi bozhii,* 66–100, 101ff.

70 GARF, f. 109, 1 *ekspeditsiia,* op. 40, part 2, d. 21, l. 26ob.

71 See George H. Williams's and Norman Cohn's descriptions of such religious practices: Williams, *The Radical Reformation* (Philadelphia, 1962), and "Rediscovered Dimensions: the Reformation Radicals," in *The Reformation in Historical Thought,* ed. A. G. Dickens and John Tonkin (Cambridge, Mass., 1985), 213–33; and Cohn, *The Pursuit of the Millennium: Revolutionary Millenarians and Mystical Anarchists of the Middle Ages* (New York, 1970; 1st pr., 1957), 15. Compare with Keith Thomas, *Religion and the Decline of Magic* (New York, 1971) and Garrett, *Spirit Possession,* 179. Recent studies also treat the religious rad-

icals' theology and practices. See, e.g., *The Culture of English Puritanism, 1560–1700*, ed. C. Durston and J. Eales (New York, 1996); and *The World of the Rural Dissenters, 1520–1725*, ed. M. Spufford (Cambridge, Mass., 1995).

72 About Orthodox rituals and Slavonic usage, see Dorodnitsyn, "Sekta shalaputov," 294–97, 652. Compare with *OZ*, October 1882, 164–65, 189.

73 Kobets testified to this under pressure from his relatives. Yet he did not accuse his coreligionists, whom he regarded as true Christians. According to him, the majority of local peasants (including all his friends) sympathized with the Shalaputs. See: GARF, f. 109, 1 *ekspeditsiia*, op. 40, d. 21, part 2, l. 40–41. Compare with GARF, f. 109, 1 *ekspeditsiia*, op. 40, d. 21, part 2, l. 54ob. and various descriptions of Shalaput meetings in the local Orthodox newspapers.

74 The creed included "(1) a complete belief in various acts of the Holy Spirit; (2) non-admittance of sinful people to the meetings; (3) a public repentance in front of the whole meeting or the elected person; (4) a celebration not only of New Testament holidays, but Old Testament biblical holidays as well; following the old Jewish tradition, they kept observance of three such days—September 1, Day of Labor (or Pipes), September 10, Day of Purification, and September 15, a celebration of the Feast of Tabernacles; they celebrate both the Old Testament and New Testament holidays according to the lunar calendar rather then the general Christian one"; GARF, f. 109, 1 *ekspeditsiia*, op. 40, d. 21, part 2, l. 6–8ob.

75 Sergei Zhuk, "'La tradition hebraique': les Puritans, les Calvinistes hollandaise et le debut de l'ambivalence des Juifs dans l'Amerique britannique coloniale," *Les Chretiens et les Juifs dans les societes de rites grec et latin. Approche comparative. Textes reunis M. Dmitriev, D. Tollet et E. Teiro* (Paris: Honore Champion, 2003), 123–164. See Salo W. Baron, "John Calvin and the Jews," in *Essential Papers on Judaism and Christianity in Conflict: From Late Antiquity to the Reformation*, ed. J. Cohen (New York, 1991), 380–400; Armas K. E. Holmio, *The Lutheran Reformation and the Jews: the Birth of Protestant Jewish Missions* (Hancock, Mich., 1949); Peter Toon, *Puritans, the Millennium, and the Future of Israel: Puritan Eschatology 1600 to 1660* (Cambridge, 1979); Richard H. Popkin, "Jewish Messianism and Christian Millenarianism," in *Culture and Politics from Puritanism to the Enlightenment*, ed. P. Zagorin, (Berkeley, Calif., 1980), 70–71; Egal Feldman, *Dual Destinies: The Jewish Encounter with Protestant America* (Chicago, 1990), 5–6; and David S. Katz, *Philo-Semitism and the Readmission of the Jews to England, 1603–1655* (Oxford, 1982).

76 RGIA, f. 796, op. 164, d. 1326, l. 13ob.–16ob.

77 Such Shalaput groups as the Pryguny acknowledged only those marriages that originated under the Divine Spirit "when all members put their hands on the heads of newlyweds." See GARF, f. 109, 1 *ekspeditsiia*, op. 40, d. 21, part 2, l. 8–9ob.

78 This scenario is presented in available publications and archival documents. See issues of *KavEV* for the 1870s and 1900s and *EkEV* for 1880s and 1890s. One of the best descriptions of the Northern Caucasian Shalaput's theology was published in *Missionerskoe obozrenie* (hereafter *MO*), September 1898, 1278–89.

79 What follows is based on the report of the Ekaterinoslav bishop of March 23, 1887.

(Dobrin'kaia is located in the Pavlograd district of Ekaterinoslav province.) The source is RGIA, f. 796, op. 168, d. 1394, l. 1–7ob.

80 TsDIAU, f. 419, op. 1 (1886–87), d. 1396A, l. 33–35ob; for his visions in detail, see l. 36–37.

81 Such sects as the Marianovtsy and Maliovantsy also used the "sacred theater" of resurrection whenever their leaders' authority was challenged. For the Maliovantsy, see chapter 5.

82 Alexandropol' was a large village in the Pavlograd district of Ekaterinoslav province. In September 1880, the Ekaterinoslav diocesan administration submitted a special report to the local police about Shevchenko and his sect. The Ekaterinoslav clergy requested their arrest, responding to "rumors about collective sex and other sexual transgressions" among the Shevchenko adherents. But the Odessa district court closed the case in January 1884, because it did not find any evidence to support the accusation. The disappointed local clergy requested new arrests. These resulted in new trials and new acquittals of Shevchenko during the 1880s. But eventually, in 1892, he was exiled to Caucasus as the leader of the anti-Orthodox movement. See RGIA, f. 796, op. 165 (1884–85), d. 1692; op. 168 (1887), d. 1368; TsDIAU, f. 419, op. 1 (1886–87), d. 1396A; and also these publications: *EkEV,* 1890, no. 8, 205–16; no. 9, 237–45; no. 10, 293–95.

83 According to police reports, at the end of 1884 Grigorii Shevchenko performed his last act of resurrection. Shevchenko complained about the attempts of his followers to find the 'new saints and prophets" for their community. Therefore, he decided to legitimize his "prophetic" position by staging the act of his resurrection. He had announced this "sacred performance" among other Shalaput communities and invited them to Alexandropol' to participate in this ritual. On Sunday, when many guests arrived at his house, they found him asleep on the floor, covered by a coat. The Shalaputs began their liturgy, singing their songs and praying about "Christ's resurrection." When their ecstatic praying reached a peak, Shevchenko appeared from the coat and cried: "Live with peace; I arose from the dead"; RGIA, f. 796, op. 165 (1884–85), d. 1692, l. 19ob., 20–22.

84 Much has been written on religious enthusiasm and spirit possession in Christian history. See, e.g., Garrett, *Spirit Possession,* and new studies: Stephen J. Stein, *The Shaker Experience in America: A History of the United Society of Believers* (New Haven, Conn., 1992), 66; David Hempton, *The Religion of the People: Methodism and Popular Religion c. 1750–1900* (London, 1996), and Ann Taves, *Fits, Trances, and Visions: Experiencing Religion and Expalining Experience from Wesley to James* (Princeton, N.J., 1999).

85 On Thomas Case's activities, see James Riker Jr., *The Annals of Newtown, in Queens County, New York: Containing Its History from Its First Settlement* (New York, 1852), 92–95, 96, 97–98. See also Jessica Kross, *The Evolution of an American Town: Newtown, New York 1642-1775* (Philadelphia, 1983), 114–15; Arthur J. Worrall, *Quakers in the Colonial Northeast* (Hanover, N.H., 1980), 64–67; and *Quaker Crosscurrents: Three Hundred Years of Friends in the New York Yearly Meetings,* ed. Hugh Barbour, C. Dendmore, et al. (Syracuse, 1995), 12–13.

Chapter Two

86 Increase Mather, *An Essay for the Recording of Illustrious Providences: Wherein An Account Is Given of Many Remarkable and Very Memorable Events, Which Have Happened in This Last Age* (Boston, 1684), 341–42.

87 Mather, *Essay for the Recording of Illustrious Providences*, 346–47. For a comparison of such "enthusiastic" scenes, see also Thomas, *Religion and the Decline of Magic*, 127, 149, 153; Christopher Hill, *The World Turned Upside Down: Radical Ideas during the English Revolution* (New York, 1972), 186–207; William G. Bittle, *James Nayler, 1618-1660: The Quaker Indicted by Parliament* (Richmond, Ind., 1986), 35 ff.; and Phyllis Mack, *Visionary Women: Ecstatic Prophesy in Seventeenth-Century England* (Berkeley, Calif., 1992).

88 Garrett, *Spirit Possession*, 154.

89 The citation is from the *Virginia Gazette,* November 9, 1769, 1.

90 Valentine Rathbun, *Some Brief Hints of a Religious Scheme* (Boston, 1782), 7. For a comparison with similar behavior among early Quakers, see Kenneth Carroll, "Singing in the Spirit of Early Quakerism," *Quaker History* 73 (1984): 1–13.

91 William Plumer to Lydia Coombs, June 17, 1782, and February 19, 1783; Plumer Papers, Library of Congress. Garrett, *Spirit Possession.*, 181, 191. Compare with the descriptions of the Shalaput rituals in *Ekaterinoslavskie* and *Stavropol'skie eparkhial'nye vedomosti.*

92 Garrett, *Spirit Possession,* 153.

93 Dniepropetrovs'kyi derzhavnyi oblasnyi arkhiv, f. 11, op. 1, d. 61/62, l. 5–6.

94 William G. McLoughlin, *Revivals, Awakenings, and Reform: An Essay on Religion and Social Change in America, 1607–1977* (Chicago, 1978). See his concept of "awakenings as revitalizations of culture" on 1–23.

95 As John Clay once noted, dissenters who continued the Khlyst religious practices "drew both from the cult and traditions of the official church and from popular culture to create their own form of Orthodoxy." My study of the Shalaputs supports his conception as well. The citation is from John Eugene Clay, "Russian Peasant Religion and Its Repression: The Christ-Faith (Khristovshchina) and the Origins of the 'Flagellant' Myth, 1666–1837" (Ph.D. dissertation, University of Chicago, 1989), 4.

96 See, e.g., Dorodnitsyn, "Shelaputskaia obshchina," 719–20.

97 Summing up the reasons for the peasants' defection from the Orthodox Church in southern Russia, one Orthodox scholar wrote in 1886 that Stundism "originated because the lawful and most usual religious needs of the people were not satisfied in the way the people had expected." He noted that all sectarian forms were "linked by the spirit of rejection." According to him, this spirit "produced the open or secret (but common in essence) Shalaputs," who represented "a transitional stage in their transformation from Russian Orthodoxy to Baptism and Stundism." It did not necessarily mean that eventually "every Shalaput becomes a Stundist; but each convinced Stundist, before he has reached this state, has had to live through the moment of the Shalaputs' doubting and rejecting." Another scholar noted the same psychological process. According to him, the uncontrolled feeling of disappointment with reality, "developing on the native ground of the Orthodox Church," produced the Shalaput phenomenon. In those cases where non-Russian representatives of

non-Orthodox propaganda "satisfied this feeling of disappointment," they produced Stundist sects. And he put it, the Shalaput movement should be considered a "transitional stage leading to Stundism." See *Trudy Kievskoj dukhovnoi akademii,* no. 10 (1886): 281; no. 11 (1886): 529; and *Vera i razum,* no. 20 (1887): 456. Compare with Jaakoff Prelooker, *Under the Tsar and Queen Victoria: The Experiences of a Russian Reformer* (London, 1895), 78–82.

Chapter Two

Chapter Three

3 The Stundists

The Stundists were the second largest group of religious radicals in the southern provinces of the late Russian Empire. This chapter describes the various important aspects of their development: the evangelical awakening among German and Mennonite colonists; the Mennonite-Shalaput revival and the beginning of Ukrainian Stundism; the formation of first Stundist communities in the province of Kherson, during the period 1862–68; the spread of Ukrainian Stundism and the beginning of the Stundo-Baptist movement in the 1870s and 1880s; and the radical reformation among the Ukrainian Stundists.

The Evangelical Awakening among German and Mennonite Colonists

Stundism was a part of the Pietist movement among the German colonists who settled in the province of Kherson in 1817. This movement converged with the radical revivalism among the Mennonites and became the foundation for a broad evangelical movement in imperial Russia known as "Ukrainian

Stundism." The Mennonites played the most important role in this movement.[1] Mennonite settlers brought the traditions of the Western European Radical Reformation to Russia as representatives of its Anabaptist wing. They insisted on believers' Baptism and on the separation of their church from the state, and they denounced war or any other kind of violence. New Mennonite settlers, who arrived from Prussia after 1818, brought more millennial and ecumenical ideas and rituals, which had been influenced by Prussian Pietism. In 1819, Elder Franz Goertz's group settled in Molochnaia in the colony of Rudnerweide. The Mennonites who had settled earlier in Ukraine were struck by the very enthusiastic and emotional rituals of the new Prussian Mennonite settlers.

The new colonists shared the millennial expectations of the Lutheran Pietists. As one old settler recalled, when they started talking, "we quickly came around to the [oncoming] 'Thousand Year Reign [of Christ]' and how at that time the spears would be made into scythes and the swords into plowshares and that this millennium would soon be instituted." The same millennial impulse appeared in 1821, when a small group of thirty Old Flemish Mennonites from Prussia, led by Peter Wedel, founded the village of Alexanderwohl. The Pietist settlers prepared themselves for "the arrival of the Kingdom of Jesus Christ." Some of them burned their clothes and abandoned their property. Their prayers became more emotional, and they were so "overwhelmed with the Holy Spirit" that they cried and shook "tremendously" while worshiping.[2] As a result of these Pietist influences, in 1821 the Mennonite communities split into the "conservers," who tried to protect the exclusiveness of the old Mennonite traditions, and the "progressives," who supported Pietist ideas.[3]

The Mennonites, in experiencing the religious revival, renounced their property and demonstrated in public that they were ready for the arrival of the Millennium. They humiliated themselves and sold all their belongings. It was noteworthy that the "revivalists" underwent spirit possession during their meetings and began to spread their prophesies among their neighbors. After one meeting of enthusiasts, one of their leaders explained that the Holy Spirit "had shown him that the world would perish that very same summer, [and] he spoke powerfully from the Holy Scripture through which many people were filled with fear and terror." During the 1820s, religious enthusiasm, influenced by "Prussian Pietism," took over all the Mennonite settlements of Molochnaia. The leaders of the Pietist revival "carried out ostentatious displays of devotion to God."[4] Besides denunciations of property and social differences, a strong ecumenical and proselytizing trend became part of this religious awakening among the Mennonite settlers. Many colonists who were influenced by the revival became ready for new radical ideas and practices, which would come to the Mennonites during the 1840s and 1850s.

In the 1840s, a new religious revival began among the Lutheran Germans who lived in the colonies of Sarata, Borodino, and Leipzig in Bessarabia. The center of this revival was the Sect of Nazareth. The leaders of this sect, Lindle and Johan Strolle, criticized the moral "decadence" of the colonists and admonished them to prepare for the Advent of Jesus Christ, which they promised would happen in 1843. When the police evicted Lindle from Russia, Strolle continued the religious practices of the sect. Borrowing from Prussian Pietism, he introduced the special hours (*Stunden*) for private prayer in his house after the official religious service in the Lutheran church. During the "silent" praying, Strolle's adherents waited for the descent of the Holy Spirit, experienced spirit possession, trembled, and recounted prophecies. During the years 1843–46, some of them sold their property and planned to go to Jerusalem to meet the Messiah. Eventually, the most active participants in this sect separated from the Lutheran community, moved to the provinces of Kherson and Tavrida, and settled in the German colonies there.[5] These Lutheran-separatists influenced the neighboring Molochnaia Mennonites, who had begun to experience a religious revival by that time.

The new leader of the Lutheran separatists, who had settled in Tavrida in 1845, was Edward Wüst. In his preaching he denounced property and invited German-speaking settlers of all social ranks and religious denominations to visit his meetings. The revivalist Mennonites joined his meetings during the 1850s. In 1858, Wüst preached to the German colonists that "worthiness here does not reside in being Separatists, or Lutherans, or Reformers, or Mennonites, but only in Christ and His brethren." The ecumenical ideas and the motives of social criticism, which were obvious in his preaching, attracted poor colonists from Lutheran, Calvinist, Anabaptist, and even Roman Catholic communities. Radical Mennonites interpreted Wüst's sermons as a prophesy of the coming Millennium. They considered him and other Pietist preachers from the eighteenth century on as the successors of Menno Simons, who had then predicted the Advent of Jesus Christ. As one Mennonite radical wrote later, "In His grace, [God] gave us Menno and Wüst, Spener and Tersteegen, Zinzendorf and Spurgeon, among many other greater or lesser characters of church history as teachers of righteousness." As they anticipated the approaching Millennium, the Mennonite revivalists became more "exuberant" in their enthusiastic behavior. One witness noted: "Eventually their meetings were little more than a time of entertainment; they played and danced until they were soaked with sweat."[6]

Pietist influences and Wüst's preaching contributed to a religious revival among the Lutheran settlers in the colony of Rohrbach in the province of Kherson during the 1850s. The local colonists resumed regular meetings in their homes after church services to read and discuss the Bible. These German Pietists, called Stundists by their conservative neighbors, preferred the name of "God's Friends." By the beginning of the 1860s, their meetings attracted German-speaking Lutherans, Calvinists, and Roman Catholics. The God's Friends in Rohrbach separated from the conservative Lutheran congregation in 1858, but officially the Russian administration still considered them members of the Lutheran Church. The Rohrbach Stundists' practice of free discussion of the Bible and spiritual prayers became popular among the German-speaking colonists in the southern provinces. In 1867, the new minister of the German Stundists in Rohrbach, Carl Bonnekemper—who was a son of Johann Bonnekemper, the first leader of the German Pietism in the province of Kherson—resumed the activities of the Brotherhood of God's Friends. He attracted even local Orthodox peasants.[7]

These Pietist influences reached the radical Mennonites in the province of Ekaterinoslav as well. During 1851 and 1852, revivalists from the Mennonite colonies in Khortitsa established their separate meeting at the house of their leader, Jacob Janzen, in the settlement of Schoenwiese. These enthusiastic Mennonites called themselves "true Christians," in contrast to the old Mennonite elite, whom they treated as traitors to "Christian truth." The radicals from the neighboring settlements of Kronsweide and Einlage joined this movement of "true Christians." On January 25, 1855, Janzen and nineteen of his adherents submitted their petition to the Khortitsa Mennonite administration about their intention to withdraw from the Mennonite community.

By 1860, the conservative Mennonites called the participants of this revival the Jumpers (*Hüpfers*). As in the case of the Russian Pryguny, the origin of this name was connected to the effect of the Holy Spirit descending on the believers during prayer. Under the influence of the spirit, the enthusiastic Mennonites began to jump and sing. The leader of these enthusiasts recalled later that during the summer meeting of 1860 some of his coreligionists "had become excessive in their conception and expression of free grace. Their praise of the grace of God was so zealous and enthusiastic that they shouted for joy, jumped and leaped, which in turn elicited approving responses from others, shouting 'Hallelujah! Victory! Glory! Amen! May the lord grant it!'" The leaders of the Mennonite radicals from Molochnaia, Heinrich Hübert and Jacob Bekker, united all the Mennonite "Jumpers" from the neighboring settlements in another separate congregation and began rebaptizing the revivalists in "the true Christian faith." On January 6, 1860, the Molochnaia radicals stated their intent to withdraw from the old "corrupt Mennonite church" and establish the "Mennonite Brethren Church."[8]

In 1861, the Mennonite Jumpers organized new meetings for worship in all the settlements of Khortitsa. Their leaders, Heinrich Neufeld, Abram Unger, and Gerhard Willer, began the rebaptizing rituals. All old Mennonite theology and ceremonies were denounced. Eventually, they joined the new "Mennonite Brethren Church." The first public rebaptizing of the Mennonite Brethren, in April 1862 near the colony of Liebenau in the Molochnaia district (of Tavrida province), resulted in local Mennonites committing acts of violence against the dissidents. In responding to the colonists' complaints about the illegal activities of Mennonite revivalists, in 1862 the police discovered that religious dissent had spread among many foreign settlers in the South. As a result of the radical Mennonites' activities, eleven German colonists had converted to the "Anabaptist sect" of the Mennonite Jumpers and established a separate

159

congregation. The police identified the main leaders of the Anabaptist sect as Mennonite revivalists from the provinces of Ekaterinoslav and Tavrida.[9]

It is noteworthy that this Mennonite awakening began before German Baptist ideas reached southern Russia and that it developed its own theology and religious practices without the influence of the German Baptists.[10] The Baptist faith first appeared in the Polish and Latvian territories of the Russian Empire in 1858 and 1859, under the influence of the German Baptist mission church in Tilsit, East Prussia. According to police documents, the first German Baptist, Johan Brandmann, settled in 1857 in the city of Grobin and was arrested in 1860 for spreading Baptist ideas among Latvian peasants in the province of Courland. The police discovered that beginning in 1859, German Baptist ministers performed Baptist rituals for their coreligionists, the German-speaking inhabitants of the city of Libava. But there was no German Baptist influence in southern Russia until the end of the 1860s. Johann Oncken, who brought the Baptist faith from England to Germany in the 1830s and was considered the founding father of the German Baptist mission, visited the German colonies in the Ukrainian provinces of Russia only in 1869. Even the leaders of the Mennonite Brethren denied any connections to the German Baptists before 1868.[11]

These facts make it easier to argue that the religious awakening of the Mennonite Jumpers and the subsequent evangelical revival among Ukrainian and Russian peasants began without direct Baptist influence. The evangelical revival of the 1840s and 1850s spread all over German and Mennonite colonies in the southern Russian Empire and involved thousands of colonists and their Russian and Ukrainian workers. This revival not only prepared the ground for the subsequent Ukrainian Stundist movement but also shaped the main directions and practices of the Ukrainian evangelicals.

The Mennonite-Shalaput Revival and the Beginning of Ukrainian Stundism

The movement of the Mennonite Jumpers in the 1850s and their obvious ecumenical Pietist attitudes attracted other religious radicals from neighboring

German, Jewish, Russian, and Ukrainian villages. In 1860, German Lutherans and Russian Molokans became active participants in Mennonite Brethren "revivalist" meetings. The radical Molokans, who established the separate movement of Pryguny, discovered the similarities in the Mennonite Brethren's rituals, and they invited the "enthusiastic" Mennonites to visit their Russian meetings in 1860. It was the beginning of a collaboration between German-speaking and Russian-speaking dissidents in southern Russia. After the Molokans' visits to the Mennonite meetings, the Mennonite Jumpers even borrowed from the Russian religious radicals the new ritual of the so-called sister kiss. As Jacob Bekker, the Mennonite minister who became the leader of a separatist Mennonite church, later recalled:

> At farewells these brethren and sisters [Molokans] kissed each other. This manner of greeting was unusual for our Mennonite sisters, and being aware that these bearded men would also expect to kiss them farewell, some of our sisters sneaked away from the assembly. Two of the Mennonite brethren admonished the sisters who had left, saying that by doing so they had embarrassed the visiting Molokan brethren whose farewell kisses were given sincerely.[12]

Through the radical Molokans, the Mennonite Jumpers established close connections to other Shalaput groups among the local peasants as well. The radical Mennonites and Russian Shalaputs influenced each other, especially during the new Shalaput revival in Tavrida after 1861. The Russian Pryguny and other Shalaputs invited the Mennonite ministers to preach for the local Russian and Ukrainian dissidents and borrowed some rituals from the Mennonite Jumpers as well.[13]

Near the Lutheran colony of Liebenau, local Ukrainian peasants organized their own meeting for worship in 1861 and invited the Mennonites to preach to them. One Ukrainian servant girl worked for "Brother [Heinrich] Hübert," learned German, and helped the Mennonite radicals deliver their sermons to local peasants. According to Bekker's memoirs, she was the first Ukrainian to take part in the evangelical revival among the Mennonite Brethren. By the end of 1861, she and the German teacher from Liebenau, who was influenced by Wüst's preaching, were propagating evangelical ideas among Ukrainian

161

peasants. Bekker described this as the beginning of "a great religious revival among the Russians."[14]

The Tavrida Shalaputs joined local Ukrainian Orthodox peasants in this movement in 1861. The local Orthodox clergy and the police noted these connections between "revivalist" Mennonites and Russian dissidents as early as 1861. The memoirs of the "revivalist" Mennonites not only confirm the existence of such connections, but they also stress how Skoptsy leaders of the Tavrida Shalaputs contributed to the evangelical awakening among Orthodox peasants from neighboring villages. Bekker wrote of "two messengers" [Shalaputs] who arrived in the villages near Liebenau in 1861:

> They taught the same doctrines as the German Quakers, but in addition, forbade the Russian believers to eat meat, saying that if they refrained from eating meat, their urge for fleshly indulgences would gradually diminish. One of them, a eunuch from Great Tokmak, hiding from the authorities, fellowshipped [sic] with the brethren of the Russian settlement referred to above. When it became known through some women that their husbands were avoiding the marriage bed, the Russian priesthood and the civil authorities became suspicious of the visitors from Old Russia and presumed that there must be a number of eunuchs among them. They investigated and discovered several. These men were arrested and put into prison in Berdiansk, a city on the Sea of Azov.[15]

After the complaints of the Mennonite ministers and Orthodox priests, the local administration of the colonies and the police arrested, flogged, and exiled to Siberia the most active Mennonite and Orthodox "revivalists." Despite the threat of legal persecution for proselytizing among the Orthodox peasants, the Mennonite Brethren tried to help and provided a shelter for all new converts, both Lutheran and Orthodox, who were punished by the police. By 1865, even some Jews from the Jewish colony of Kamianka were participating in the evangelical revivals of the Mennonite Jumpers.[16] In the period 1861–65, during the police persecution of the Shalaputs and Mennonite Jumpers, the German-, Russian-, and Ukrainian-speaking dissidents in the provinces of Tavrida and Kherson began identifying themselves as evangelical Christians rather than by

162

nationality or ethnicity. The persecutions also contributed to the creation of a martyrs' myth and to spreading religious dissent among the relatives and neighbors of the persecuted colonists and peasants.[17] It was the beginning of evangelical solidarity among all persecuted Christians in southern Ukraine.

The activities of Russian Skoptsy and Shalaputs, in the same localities where German Stundism had started earlier, also attracted the attention of the Russian police during their separate investigation of the Tavrida Shalaput revival in 1862. It was discovered that not only Shalaputs but also Orthodox peasants and workers who lived in the Mennonite households were involved in the new religious revivals in the southern provinces. The police accused the leaders of the "Mennonite Brethren" ["the Anabaptist sect," in the police records] of proselytizing among local Orthodox Christians.[18]

The police detectives were confused at first about how to treat the Mennonite dissidents. They called them Anabaptists and Jumpers, but they still considered them part of the Mennonite congregation. What they could not understand was the nature of the relations between the Mennonite radicals and Russian dissidents, such as the Molokans and Shalaputs. According to the Orthodox clergy's accusations, the Mennonites were guilty of spreading "the Shalaput Heresy" and of promoting castration among the Russian peasants.[19] Eventually, the police adopted the name of Mennonite Brethren for the new dissidents and stopped accusing them of castration. Indeed, they noted the disappearance of castration among those Shalaputs and Orthodox peasants who became involved in the "revivalist" meetings in the German colonies. The police and local clergy later considered those Ukrainian peasants who behaved similarly to the Mennonite revivalists as part of an Anabaptist sect.

As we can see, the convergence of the Shalaput and Mennonite revivals with the Pietist religious practices in the German colonies during the period 1861–65 resulted in both ecumenical and proselytizing activities among the rural population in the provinces of Tavrida, Ekaterinoslav, and Kherson. At the same time, these activities laid the foundation for a new stage of the Russian popular reformation. By the 1870s, contemporaries had begun calling this new movement the "German-Ukrainian Stunda."

The First Stundist Communities:
The Province of Kherson, 1862–1868

The first community of Ukrainian evangelical peasants, which was called the "Society of the Stundists" [Obshchestvo Shtundistov] by its contemporaries, appeared as early as 1862 in the village of Osnova.[20] In January 1865, the Reverend Ilia Kiriakov, the priest in charge of the Odessa district, complained to the archbishop of Kherson that some of the peasants from Osnova met each night to read the Bible and sing "very strange religious hymns." At the same time, he admitted his confusion because the same peasants were the most religious Orthodox believers and the most active participants in all the Orthodox ceremonies.[21] Kiriakov ordered V. Stoikov, the local priest from the parish of the villages of Osnova and Riasnopol', to investigate the nature of the peasants' meetings. In response to the priest's request, in February 1865, the village administration reported to the Orthodox parish that the peasants from Osnova had been meeting for four years in the house of Mikhail Ratushny, a former village elder [*starosta*], to read the Bible and pray. According to this report, the peasants did not visit "the German churches," and "the German pastors" did not preach to them in Osnova.[22]

In October 1865, analogous meetings for reading the Bible were held in the neighboring villages of Ignatovka and Riasnopol'. The local police were disappointed with the activities of the local Orthodox clergy, because they realized that the dissident religious movement was spreading among the peasants all over the districts of Odessa and Anan'iev. On March 14, 1866, a police officer from Osnova reported to his superiors in Kherson:

> A sect of twenty people gathered in the village of Osnova. They meet at night and sing psalms from Russian and *German* books. The village Osnova is near the German colony Rohrbach; as a result of constant contact with local colonists, and of working for them, those peasants, who were simple enough and ignorant enough, learned practical German, adopted the customs of colonists, and eventually, under the impact of *Reformed Germans* (Stundists), were converted to the German faith. In Osnova the sect was established by Ratushny Mikhail, who had long worked for the Rohrbach colonists; he was the first 'old brother' (founder) in Osnova.

The police officer, however, could not find any evidence of a German presence at the peasant meetings. The peasants read only books printed by the Russian Orthodox publishing houses. By 1867, however, the new dissident movement among the peasants became increasingly anti-Orthodox and appeared to some contemporaries as the Russian Protestant Reformation. On February 16, 1867, the same officer reported again to the Kherson governor about the sect, which "is indeed offensive," because it has "a schismatic character similar to the Reformation":

> [This] sect has now included 15 members from Ignatovka, five families [25 peasants] from Riasnopol', and 14 families [70 peasants] from Osnova. They meet in homes, read books in Church Slavonic, which they interpret for themselves, sometimes under the leadership of other Reformed schismatics from Rohrbach. As a result, the peasants who have adhered to the schism have developed a stubborn attitude. They no longer attend the Orthodox Church, or venerate the icons, or observe the customs of the Orthodox faith.

The policeman finished by urging an investigation of the Germans—the "main seducers into schism."[23]

The police investigation revealed not only Lutheran influences but also connections between the Osnova peasants and the Mennonite-Shalaput revival in the southern provinces. Mikhail Ratushny's first "teacher" was an old Ukrainian peasant, Onishchenko, from the village of Osnova. During the 1850s, Onishchenko visited various Orthodox monasteries and the Pietist meetings of the German colonists. He knew about the Mennonite revivals and the Shalaput groups in the provinces of Kherson and Tavrida. According to observers, Onishchenko behaved as a typical Shalaput: He did not drink alcohol, kept long fasts, avoided sex, lived separately from his wife, made regular pilgrimages to the Orthodox monasteries, and preached that the Holy Spirit could descend on true Christian believers.

By 1870, when he was seventy years old, Onishchenko stopped visiting the Orthodox church and established connections with the local German ministers. Still, he insisted on the mystical enthusiastic moments in the religious rituals, which could help unite the human soul and the Holy Spirit.   165

Onishchenko brought Shalaput influences to Osnova Stundism as well. At the beginning, Ratushny followed the advice of his teacher, Onishchenko, by visiting his home and asking him for instructions. As Onishchenko explained to Arsenii Rozhdestvenskii, "God gave me the Divine Light, and then God gave to Mikhailo [Ratushny] reason [the ability to analyze]." According to Onishchenko, the Light was more important than reason and analytical talent; therefore, he explained that he inspired Ratushny and his group in Osnova, as the Divine Light inspired the human mind.[24]

When he began his search for "Divine Truth" in the late 1850s, Ratushny himself visited Orthodox monasteries and met Shalaputs during his pilgrimages. As Ratushny later told one journalist, he had no intention of establishing a new sect. When he was a village elder in 1862, he participated in one village meeting where, by chance, the peasants asked the local priest questions about religion. The priest was unable to answer these questions during the meeting. After this meeting, Ratushny, who had visited many Orthodox and Mennonite religious communities, decided to help the peasants with their questions. He invited them to his house and tried to explain to them the meaning of various passages from the Gospels. They began meeting every week to read Holy Scripture and "answer questions about religion."[25] During all those meetings, he used only Orthodox books that he had brought back from his pilgrimages to Orthodox sanctuaries. Orthodox observers initially viewed his dissent as traditionally Russian. Only in 1867 did they begin to emphasize German influences in their reports about the Osnova dissidents.[26]

This emphasis on Germans was a result of the new Pietist revival among the German colonists in Rohrbach under the influence of the Reverend Carl Bonnekemper, the newly arrived pastor. As Bonnekemper explained in 1869 to P. Kotsebu, the governor of Kherson province, Ratushny and other members of his group, who were frustrated with the local Orthodox clergy, had turned to him and the German Pietists for help.[27] In a private conversation with Alexander Ushinskii, the first Orthodox scholar of Ukrainian Stundism, Bonnekemper denied his role in the beginning of Stundism in Osnova. He told Ushinskii that he "never seduced any Russian into Protestantism." "On the contrary," he continued,

I always recommended that the Orthodox peasants who asked me for advice hold firmly to their Orthodox faith and follow all the Orthodox rituals and rules. I just advised them to overcome their flagrant ignorance. I suggested that they follow the example of the German Stundists and begin educating themselves for only one reason. It would help them to read God's Word and understand the religious service in the Church.[28]

Bonnekemper confessed how surprised he was that the meeting for worship in Osnova had been organized even before his arrival in the province of Kherson. He wrote later about the independent character of Ukrainian Stundism in Osnova:

> My father kindled at Rohrbach in 1824 the holy Pentecostal fire. About forty years after, Michael Ratushny himself set Rohrbach aglow, set Passiko on fire, and kindled it through Passiko in Russia.[29] [*Note:* The village of Osnova belonged to the landlord Passek; therefore, Bonnekemper used the family name of Passek as the name of the village.]

In 1867, another Stundist group emerged among the Russian rural population in the district of Anan'iev, independently from the sect in Osnova. On June 14, 1867, the local police officer reported to the governor of Kherson that Adam Voisorovskii, a Polish inhabitant of Anan'iev (a district town), had established the "sect of Shtundovye" at the farmstead of Nikolaevskii near the village of Akmechetka. Fifteen members of this sect met every night to read and discuss the Bible. A police officer reported that they rejected the Orthodox icons and all other symbols and rituals of Orthodoxy.[30] It turned out that this group had close connections to the Shalaputs and radical Molokans. The police discovered that Lev Popov, the main leader of this sect, a retired soldier who taught local peasant children, had visited other Russian dissident groups and used their experience in his teaching of the children. Another leader of the sect, Daniil Kondratskii, corresponded intensively with the Tavrida Molokans. The police confiscated a box of letters from Kondratskii. The radical Molokan leaders, some of them prominent figures among the Tavrida Shalaputs, had written all these letters. In them, Kondratskii, Molokans, and the Shalaputs discussed problems of spiritual baptism and new forms of rituals.[31]

It is apparent that the Stundists from Anan'iev district had closer ties with the Molokans and Shalaputs than with Protestant sects. The police discovered that the new Stundist group from the farmstead Nikolaevskii had no relations with the Pietist Germans. Only later did the Nikolaevskii's Stundists establish close connections to other analogous groups from the province of Kherson. In addition to the Shalaput connections, Nikolaevskii's Stundists demonstrated another new phenomenon in Stundism: the involvement of the Polish Roman Catholics in the evangelical movement in southern Russia. The main leaders of the Nikolaevskii's Stundists were the Polish Roman Catholics from the town of Anan'iev: Adam Voisorovskii and Daniil Kondratskii. In 1867, the Nikolaevskii's Stundists not only began employing non-Orthodox religious practices in their farmstead but also influenced peasants from neighboring villages. By the end of the year, in the districts of Odessa and Anan'iev, the police estimated that there were no fewer than 300 peasants in groups similar to the Stundists in Osnova and Nikolaevskii.

In 1867, a new center of Ukrainian Stundism was discovered in the villages of Karlovka and Liubomirka in the Elisavetgrad district. In contrast to the case of the Osnova Stundists, where the local clergy attracted the police's attention to new dissent, in the Elisavetgrad district it was the local police who reported to the Orthodox clergy about the new sect. At first, a priest from Liubomirka did not consider the religious peasants who met in the house of Ivan Riaboshapka "dissenters." Riaboshapka, a local peasant, was influenced by conversations with Martin Hübner, a German colonist from the neighboring colony of Old Danzig. Hübner, who had connections with both the Lutheran Pietists and Mennonite Hüpfers, taught Ivan Riaboshapka to read Russian and helped him understand biblical texts. After these lessons, Riaboshapka invited his neighbors to read and discuss the Bible in his house. According to Rozhdestvenskii, he started these meetings early in the 1860s, and by 1867 he had a community of twenty followers, who called themselves "Anabaptists."[32]

Riaboshapka was the first Stundist leader to preach among his Orthodox neighbors and criticize the Orthodox Church in public. As a result, he and his adherents were arrested several times during 1867 and 1868. Moreover, his enthusiasm and sincerity also attracted local Jews. The first documented case of the conversion to evangelical Christianity ("Stundism") of a Russian Jew was connected to Riaboshapka's proselytizing activities as well. In December 1869, Riaboshapka persuaded Srul' (Israel) Zimmerman, a sixteen-year-old Jewish boy from the town of Krivoi Rog (or Krivoe Ozero) in the Balta district, to leave "Judaism and to join evangelical Christianity." Later on, Zimmerman converted to the German Baptist faith and settled with German colonists.[33] Afterward, in the 1870s and 1880s, along with Ukrainian peasants and German colonists, Jewish inhabitants from local towns became regular visitors at the Stundist meetings for worship in the Ukrainian countryside.[34]

The activities of Ratushny and Riaboshapka led to the growth of the Stundist movement in the province of Kherson. According to the Kherson governor's report, by 1870 the number of Ukrainian Stundists had grown to 547 peasants in those districts.[35] The local priest from Liubomirka complained in 1872 that "one-sixth of the entire parish was contaminated by Stundism." He commented later that although only 45 peasant families were Stundist activists among 150 households of the village, the number of "Stundist sympathizers" was considerably higher. He wrote the Kherson bishop that he could consider only 3 families from these 150 households "true Orthodox Christians."[36] In his official report to the Ministry of the Interior, he noted the rapid growth of the Kherson Stundists (in 1875, there were 1,546 "Stundist peasants").[37]

The public activities of the Liubomirka Stundists and Riaboshapka's anti-Orthodox preaching attracted the attention of the press. The first publications about this movement during 1867 and 1868 appeared in an Odessa newspaper, and through them the reading public learned of "Little Russian [Ukrainian] Stundism."[38] Subsequently, all official documents and publications used this word. In 1872 and 1873, the local periodicals of the Russian Orthodox Church began regular coverage of the movement and employed the word "Stundism" to describe all peasant evangelical sects. By the end of 1890s, this word gradually replaced the word "Shalaput" in police and Orthodox documents. Sometimes, the word "Stundist" was mistakenly applied to all non-Orthodox sects, including the Khlysty. Only the new revival of the spiritualist mystical trend in Ukrainian Stundism during the Maliovantsy movement in the 1890s

revealed how broad and inclusive the usage of this word had become. This was indeed appropriate, because in its early beginning in the late 1850s, the evangelical movement had incorporated different religious elements and cultural influences from Mennonites, Pietist Lutherans, Molokans, and Shalaputs.

These influences shaped the character of the initial phase of Ukrainian Stundism and contributed to the varied religious practices of the Ukrainian dissident communities. By 1868, the most numerous and influential were the Stundist communities in the villages of Osnova and Liubomirka. Their

Figure 3.2. Mikhail Ratushny (1830–1915), a founder of Ukrainian Stundism. From *Istoria evangel'skikh khristian-baptistov* (Moscow, 1989), picture 7, between pp. 128 and 129.

founders, Ivan Riaboshapka and Mikhail Ratushny, were the first indigenous leaders of Ukrainian Stundism (figures 3.1 and 3.2). From 1862 to 1868, in the first stage of Ukrainian Stundism, all peasant participants in this movement were still officially members of Orthodox Church. Their Stundist activities existed alongside their traditional Orthodox Church practices. They still married, baptized their children, and buried their relatives according to Orthodox rules. A new stage of Ukrainian Stundism began during the 1870s with the mass separation of Stundist communities of the former Orthodox peasants from the Russian Orthodox Church.

The Spread of Ukrainian Stundism and the Beginning
of the Stundo-Baptist Movement, 1870s–1880s

In the late 1860s, peasants from the provinces of Kiev, Tavrida, Bessarabia, Chernigov, and Ekaterinoslav visited the meetings of Ukrainian Stundists in the province of Kherson. A group of migrant peasants from Kiev province was the most numerous and active at these meetings. The landless and poor peasants and landholders from this province went to Kherson province at least once a year during the 1860s as agricultural workers in the German and Mennonite colonies. Kiev peasants became active participants in the evangelical movement in Kherson province. Two of the most prominent figures among the early propagandists of Stundism in the Odessa and Kherson districts were Gerasim Balaban and Lazar' Shura, migrant peasants from the Chigirin district and the close friends of Mikhail Ratushny. Through their connections and travels, the ideas of Ukrainian Stundism reached Kiev province in 1868.

Pavel Tsybul'skii and Iosif Tyshkevich, two Polish small landholders, organized the first Stundist meeting for reading and discussing the Gospels during the winter of 1868 in the village of Plosskoe in the Tarashcha district. Their promotion of evangelical ideas and criticism of Orthodoxy attracted the attention of both the clergy and the police in 1869. Tsybul'skii and Tyshkevich were arrested the following year, but this did not stop the spread of Stundism. In 1870 Gerasim Balaban, a Stundist activist from Ratushny's community, was arrested and exiled from the province of Kherson to his native village of Chaplinka in the Tarashcha district. After his return, he continued his Stundist propaganda and involved Ivan Liasotskii, the village clerk, in his activities. When the police arrested Balaban in 1871, they discovered that he had already left the established community of his followers in Chaplinka with sixty peasants who participated regularly in Stundist meetings. After local Stundists arranged for Balaban's escape from the village prison in January 1872, he fled to the province of Kherson. Ivan Liasotskii, together with Iakov Koval'chuk and Kliment Tereshchuk, continued to spread Stundist propaganda in the Tarashcha district.[39]

In December 1872, the police arrested Balaban and 8 of his followers. After his arrest, no fewer than 200 peasants from the villages of Plosskoe, Popovka, Kuchkovka, Chaplinka, and Kosiakovka in the Tarashcha district joined the Stundist movement. In January 1873, the Stundists in Osnova received a letter from the Tarashcha Stundists, who asked Ratushny to submit a special petition to the tsar about releasing Balaban and his coreligionists from jail. From five of the villages mentioned above, 112 peasants considered their evangelical communities to have separated from the Orthodox Church. These 112 Stundist activists called themselves "Brothers united according to the Holy Gospels," and they expressed their wish to converge with "their Brothers" in the province of Kherson in "the Holy Apostolic Church."[40] Even the Orthodox clergy from the province of Kiev, who tried to underestimate the numbers of religious dissenters, reported to the Holy Synod that 237 peasants had joined the Stundist sect by 1874.[41] According to the governor of Kiev's report, the number of Stundists in the province increased from 450 in 1875 to 1,175 by 1877.[42] (See appendix A.)

During the 1870s, Stundism reached not only Kiev but also other southern provinces of Russia. The new movement became institutionalized, as Ukrainian Stundist peasants tried to establish their own communities, separate from the Orthodox Church. The Kherson Stundists had separated from the Orthodox Church by 1869, and the Kiev Stundists officially separated by 1874.[43] In doing so, they were influenced by the German Baptists. In 1869, Baptist ministers began preaching in the German colonies of Kherson and Tavrida, and some Ukrainian Stundist leaders joined the Baptist movement. On June 11, 1869, together with thirty German colonists, Efim Tsymbal, a Stundist peasant from the village of Karlovka (near Liubomirka) was baptized by the Baptist minister. This date is considered to be the beginning of the Baptist movement among Ukrainian peasants. Later that year, Tsymbal baptized Ivan Riaboshapka, and in 1871 Ivan Riaboshapka baptized Mikhail Ratushny together with his forty-eight adherents from Osnova.[44] After this the baptized leaders followed their German coreligionists and introduced elements of Baptist theology and ritual and a new hierarchy into the Ukrainian Stundist communities. Tsymbal, Riaboshapka, and other baptized leaders became the first ministers [*presvitery*] of the Ukrainian Baptists. Not all the Stundist peasants acknowledged these Baptist innovations and the establishment of a new "priest-hood," however.

During the years 1869–71, Ukrainian Stundism divided in two parts: (1) the Stundo-Baptist faith, which was more conservative in theology and religious practices and tried to reproduce the institutions of the German Baptist con-gregations in the Ukrainian countryside; and (2) the more radical "New" or "Young" Stundism, which resisted the institutionalization and formalization of the movement and followed the traditions of the Shalaput Reformation with its stress on the unmediated spiritual communication of believers with God. From their early beginning, these two trends in the Russian popular Refor-mation appeared among the first Stundist communities of Ukrainian peasants, and they contributed to the confusing character of the Stundist stage of the Russian Reformation. In fact, Shalaput traditions survived the German and Mennonite influences, and thus they persisted in the religious practices of all Russian and Ukrainian evangelicals.[45]

The first Stundist communities in the Odessa district were divided because of Baptist influences. After his Baptist conversion in 1871, Ratushny intro-duced the Osnova Stundist community to Baptist rules and rituals, including the institution of the minister (*presviter*). Half of the Osnova Stundists sup-ported the Baptist innovations, but the radical adherents of Gerasim Balaban opposed Ratushny's conservative followers and did not acknowledge the author-ity of the Baptist ministers. When the angry Ratushny asked those partici-pants in the meeting who shared his ideas to raise their hands, only half of his coreligionists did so. Those who did not raise their hands joined Balaban. These radicals insisted that every Christian believer "who felt the presence of the Holy Spirit in his soul" could preach in the meeting for worship, not only the experienced minister who had been ordained by "the old German Baptist Brother." Balaban rejected all formal Baptist rituals. He told the Baptist sup-porters: "The religious ceremonies are a theatrical performance" ["*Obriady—eto teatry*"]. According to him, the religious meeting existed for an emanation of sincere spontaneous feelings, for the "true inspiration" of the believer's heart, and for joining all Christians in one "enthusiastic prayer" of the "pure soul." The true faith, he insisted, did not need formal rituals, ceremonies, or ministers.[46]

The first Ukrainian Stundists in Osnova largely shared Shalaput notions of spontaneous prophesizing and enthusiastic praying. Radical Stundists criticized the social and church hierarchy. They tried to eliminate social injustice and corruption, and to prepare themselves for the approaching Kingdom of God. The same division took place among Stundists in Kiev province. A minority of Stundists from the Tarashcha district followed Ivan Liasotskii and his new Baptist rules and ceremonies, and the majority followed Gerasim Balaban and his antiauthoritarian principles. The radicals made up a majority among evangelicals of Kiev province from the outset. According to the first reports from the Tarashcha district in 1874, the members of the radical branch of Ukrainian Stundism from the village of Chaplinka made up the overwhelming majority—202 of 237 detected Stundists of Tarashcha.[47] Even in 1881, the radical "Chaplinka" Stundists were more numerous than their conservative coreligionists. Orthodox authors estimated that in 1881 there were 1,086 radicals among the 1,677 Stundists in the province of Kiev.[48]

It is noteworthy that the first Orthodox observers commended the conservative Stundists from Kosiakovka, who used traditional Lutheran and Mennonite rituals, for their loyalty and obeisance to the authorities, while at the same time criticizing the radicals from Chaplinka, who rejected all familiar religious rituals. Thus, Alexander Ushinskii, an Orthodox observer, who studied the new peasant sects in the provinces of Kiev and Kherson and visited Stundist centers there in 1875 and 1881, noted that Stundism from Chaplinka originated from the Lutheran and Reformed tradition but became more radical than "traditional Protestantism." According to Ushinskii's description, these Ukrainian radicals were similar to "Russian Molokans, Dukhobors and the so-called 'spiritual Christians' [Shalaputs], who rejected all religious sacraments and ceremonies on the ground that the Christian religion was supposed to be an inner spiritual faith." Ushinskii was indignant at the Chaplinka radicals, who "denied any written rule for their organization," because any person "who could read the Russian translation of Holy Scripture was a preacher and minister to them."[49]

The radicalism of the Chaplinka Stundists was obvious from the outset. These dissenters, in rejecting the symbolic connections of the Orthodox Church, were both consistent and revolutionary. After the new arrest of Balaban, their leader, and eleven Stundist activists, dissident peasants from Chaplinka, organized an anti-Orthodox demonstration in November 1872. They took all the Orthodox icons from their houses and dragged "these useless idols" along the dirty road in the autumn rain up to the parish church building, where they left them. The next day, when the village police tried to arrest the Stundist leaders for this "public demonstration," the dissident peasants resisted, beat the representatives of the local administration, and released their activists. Following this scandal, the district police intervened and arrested the perpetrators.[50] Such clashes in the 1870s and 1880s contributed to the image of the new Ukrainian evangelicals as religious rebels.

By the end of the 1870s, younger and more radical leaders succeeded Balaban. These leaders, such as Iakov Koval' from Chaplinka, rejected any human authority except the Holy Spirit. Koval's followers called themselves "evangelical (or spiritual) Christians." They considered everyone who experienced the influence of the Holy Spirit in his or her soul to be their preacher. According to them, such "spirited" prophets were "the bearers of Divine Wisdom." During their meetings, the spirit-possessed prophets considered themselves representatives of God. Ushinskii, who recorded the main ideas of Iakov Koval' in 1881, presented their beliefs as a kind of "Molokan religion," which denied all exterior forms of religion and instead affirmed an inner spiritual one.[51] Some of these "spiritual Christians," in their millennial search for social justice, brought their notions of Divine Truth to their Orthodox neighbors and tried to persuade them to follow the Holy Spirit. The most radical "spiritual Christians" sometimes participated in peasant riots and other antistate activities during the 1870s and 1890s.

Thus, the social criticism and political activism of radical Stundism became significant factors in this stage of the evangelical movement in Russia. Such social radicalism was a distinctive feature of the radical reformation in general among the rural population of the southern provinces. The social activism of the radicals, the millennial expectations of impoverished peasants, the religious practices of the Shalaputs, and the international character of the evangelical movement in southern Russia shaped all the character of the Russian popular "reformation" and attracted all those who were disoriented, oppressed, or mistreated: impoverished Ukrainian peasants, peasant women, Polish Roman Catholic landholders, Jews, and others who had lost their traditional social and cultural "bases" in the Ukrainian countryside.

By the beginning of the 1890s, thousands of peasants from the Ukrainian provinces (the overwhelming majority were ethnically Ukrainian) joined this reformation. Beginning with only twenty members in 1862, the Stundist sect among the Ukrainian peasants grew to thousands and spread over southern and central Ukraine in the 1870s. During the 1880s, Stundism reached the provinces of Tavrida, Ekaterinoslav, Poltava, Kharkov, Chernigov, Volynia, and Podolia (there were 2,956 dissidents in the province of Kherson in 1886, 2,006 in the province of Kiev in 1884, and 300 in the province of Ekaterinoslav). Overall, in 1885 the members of the Ukrainian Stundist meetings, who were registered by the local police, numbered more than 7,000 people.[52]

By 1889, the Kiev administration alone counted more than 3,500 Stundists, and by 1892 there were 4,897 (predominantly Ukrainian) Stundists within its boundaries. The Stundists themselves estimated their figures at between 10,000 and 200,000 in 1882–83.[53] These figures are apparently exaggerated. The local administration and police in their secret annual reports usually presented far smaller numbers of local religious sects and dissenters. On the basis of calculations of these annual reports and their appendices, the number of Stundists had grown from 200 in 1872 to 5,002 in 1890 in Kiev province, from 20 in 1862 to 4,648 in 1890 in Kherson province, and from 300 in 1888 to 1,000 in 1897 in Ekaterinoslav province. What these figures do not reveal is that Stundist influence was much greater than the numbers suggest. In fact, the Stundists dominated some villages, in which they made up more than 2 percent of the local population, influencing no less than one-third of the population there.[54]

In his report to the tsar, the Kherson governor noted in 1890 that the Stundist sect controlled the rural population "on three-fourths of the entire territory of the province."[55] In 1890, Stundists lived in 167 localities in the province. The Kherson governor also noted their increasing organizational skills. "The huge number of Stundist leaders (one for every 29 adult members)," the governor wrote, "indicated the larger inner strength of this growing sect."[56] By 1895, there were nearly 7,000 Stundists in the province of Kherson, according to official calculations.[57] The governor of Kiev also noted the growth of Stundism and criticized the Orthodox clergy's underestimation of the numbers of dissidents among Ukrainian peasants. By 1895, there were more than 6,000 Stundists in the province of Kiev.[58] Along with the Shalaputs, Stundism had become, during the 1890s, the most numerous evangelical movement among the rural population of southern Russia. According to the present author's calculations, in the main provinces of the southern Russian Empire—in Kiev, Podolia, Volynia, Kherson, Tavrida, Ekaterinoslav, Kharkov, Bessarabia, Stavropol', and Astrakhan'—between 1891 and 1895 the police registered no fewer than 20,000 Stundist activists.[59] (Also see the official figures in appendixes A, B, and C.)

The Radical Reformation among the Ukrainian Stundists

The Ukrainian Stundists drew first on Anabaptist theology and the Pietist religious practices of Western Protestantism, and then, during the 1870s, on the German Baptists. Under the influence of the latter, the movement divided into radical and conservative fractions. The conservatives became an integral part of the all-Russian Baptist movement after 1882. The radicals preserved their ties with the enthusiastic and millennial traditions of the Shalaputs and developed their own theology and religious practices, distinct from the Stundo-Baptist movement.

The Guidance of the Holy Ghost and the Rejection of Church Institutions in Early Stundism. At the outset, the Ukrainian Stundists emphasized the Holy Spirit as the chief inspiration for all Christians. They insisted on improvisation as the basis for all religious experience and rejected all traditional religious rituals. Like the Shalaputs, they stressed the direct communication of believers with God without any human intermediary or church. They also shared with the Shalaputs the idea of the oncoming Millennium of Jesus Christ.[60]

178   The influence of Lutheran Pietists and Mennonite Brethren also con-

tributed to the theology and rituals of Ukrainian Stundism. The first description of the Stundist creed and theology was recorded in 1870 in the village of Liubomirka. This document, which showed obvious Anabaptist influence,[61] rejected the sacraments, church discipline, ministers, and the notion of hierarchy. The Stundists believed that the worship of icons made by men was equal to idolatry.[62]

All Stundists (including the radicals and Baptists) also rejected the written tradition of the Orthodox Church. Like the first Christians of the New Testament, they followed Holy Scripture and the revelations of the Holy Spirit. As Ivan Riaboshapka, one of the leaders of the Kherson Stundists, explained in a conversation with a local priest in 1875: "We simply believe in the Holy Gospels, read the Word of God, and follow the Divine teaching every moment of our lives."[63] They told the Orthodox missionaries: "Only the Holy Spirit inspires us; if we read God's words we do not need the guidance of Orthodox priests. We have the Divine temple in our hearts. Why do we need to go to the Orthodox church?"[64] Another Stundist peasant explained that Stundists did not need the Sacred written tradition of the Orthodox Church (*predanie*) because they were taught and instructed by the Holy Ghost: "Why do Christians have to follow some written traditions? We do not need written recommendations of the Orthodox Church because we are sure that the Holy Spirit dwells in us and that our faith is the only true belief."[65]

These statements coincide with "the rules of the creed for the newly converted Russian Brotherhood" discovered by Kievan police during January 1873. According to this document, the members of the Russian Christian Brotherhood emphasized that their belief in God derived from "only the Divine revelation of the Holy Scripture and the Holy Ghost." "The creed" noted that "the true Christian believer is not one who follows strictly all the rules and rituals, but rather one who is reborn in the Holy Spirit and who repents." All Stundists shared this antiformalist trend in both theology and religious practice.[66] The emphasis on the revelations of the Holy Spirit and rejection of church institutions were the defining elements of early Stundist theology in the 1860s. The radical Ukrainian Stundists drew on these elements in their religious practices as well.

179

The Institutionalization of the Stundo-Baptist Movement and the Taming of the Radicals. The institutionalization of the Stundo-Baptist movement gradually brought the new religious rituals and forms to the Stundist communities after the 1870s. The first descriptions of Stundo-Baptist meetings in the province of Kherson demonstrated the gradual infiltration of Baptist ritualistic forms (including the church sacraments and rituals that the Stundists had earlier rejected). At the same time, the Stundo-Baptists combined Baptist rituals with Orthodox images (e.g., the sacrament of the Eucharist with a symbol of the crucifixion). The Stundo-Baptists usually selected the most spacious peasant house for their meetings, which were held on Sundays and holidays.

At the center of the meetinghouse was a large table, which was covered with a clean decorated tablecloth, with a crucifix in the middle and a candle on each side. The elder played the role of the minister (*presviter* in Russian). He wore a special long black robe over his usual dress. This formalization of dress and ritual gradually replaced the uncontrolled spontaneity and emotionalism of the early Stundist meetings. Now the minister controlled the religious enthusiasm of his coreligionists. The hierarchy of seats at the table during a standard Baptist meeting also maintained a strict emotional discipline among participants. The minister usually sat on one side of the table, and all others sat on the opposite side, with the elders and teachers in front.

The *presviter* directed the meeting. He began singing the psalms, and participants joined in. After the singing, he usually read the Gospels and explained the text. Then the elder read from the Epistles of the Apostles and led a discussion. At the end of the meeting, the minister took a chalice with red wine and passed it to the congregation. Sometimes the elder also handed out pieces of white bread and said the words from the Gospels: "Take, eat; this is Christ's body." After passing the cup of wine, the elder would say: "Drink ye all of it; for this is Christ's blood of the New Testament, which was shed for many for the remission of sins."[67]

Such a scenario was common for all Stundo-Baptist communities also during the 1880s and 1890s. With new Baptist influences, the sacred theater of the meeting became more formalized and structured. The new hierarchy of elders and teachers in the formerly loose Stundist communities came to resemble the

German Baptist congregations of the southern Ukraine, with strict discipline and no improvisation during the worship service. By the end of the 1880s, all the Stundo-Baptist congregations of southern Russia used the same selections of readings for religious ceremonies.[68] By 1900, the most important rituals of the Stundo-Baptists—Baptism, Communion, weddings, and funerals—had been formalized and become similar to those of other Baptist groups in southern Russia.[69]

After the 1880s, to use Max Weber's terminology, the evangelical movement among the Ukrainian peasants was transformed by the "routinization of charisma" among the Stundist leaders and the "institutionalization" of the Stundist congregations. In addition, Baptist rituals and discipline supplanted Stundist radicalism in Stundo-Baptist congregations. The German Baptist faith played the same role among the Ukrainian peasant radicals as Methodism and the Salvation Army did among British farmers and workers.[70] The intensive Baptist indoctrination with the evangelical themes of humility, self-sacrifice, and the "renunciation of self" tamed the peasant radicals psychologically, while the new church hierarchy and strict moral discipline controlled them in their congregations. The establishment of the All-Russian Baptist Union in 1884 brought new uniformity and hierarchy among Baptist congregations in southern Russia. The conservative Baptist orientation in politics and their hierarchical organization had become evident by the beginning of the twentieth century. By this time, all radical elements with their ideas of social justice had been purged from the major Baptist congregations of the Russian Empire. The Ukrainian Stundo-Baptists showed a similar political conservatism. Many of the Ukrainian evangelical communities petitioned the Russian government about their loyalty and distanced themselves from Stundism.[71]

The Radicalism of the "Chaplinka Creed": Religious Practices of "Radical Stundists." After 1870 in some Stundist communities, Baptist rituals and forms replaced the "spiritual" Shalaput elements. But a majority of the radical Stundists resisted Baptist practices, and in the 1870s and 1880s they developed their own theology and religious practices, which became the Stundist version of the Russian radical reformation. The first records of the radical

181

Stundist creed appeared in the 1880s in a community of dissident peasants from the village of Chaplinka (in Kiev province). It was later called "the Chaplinka creed." By comparing the ideas of the Stundist radicals from Chaplinka with those of other Stundists, we can single out the basic elements of radical Stundist theology. Iakov Koval', a leader of the Chaplinka Stundists and probably the author of their creed, described his faith in these words, "Our creed came from Holy Scripture, from spiritual illumination, from the testimony of Jesus Christ, from the spirit of prophecy, the light of which enlightens every human being who is coming into this world."[72]

Koval' believed that those who professed such a faith did not need the institutions and images of the Orthodox Church, which had betrayed original Christianity and become a "ritualized organization of Pharisees." Thus, the radical Stundists rejected all Orthodox symbols and sacraments, including the veneration of Orthodox saints, icons, and the Holy Cross. They also rejected the Orthodox calendar of fasts, which they considered the means by which priests controlled the peasants. They tried to rely on common sense and logical arguments to justify their position. One told a journalist: "Sometimes to control cattle we do not give them enough corn. The same is true of the system of fasting. The Orthodox priests invented this system to rule and control the ordinary man."[73]

The basic elements of the radical Stundist worldview were social criticism, rejection of violence, pacifism, and the restoration of evangelical principles. According to these peasant dissidents, humankind had reached the peak of corruption and dissolution. God gave man bread and other important things for his life, but by trading these things, man was selling his conscience, faith, and even other human beings for money. Therefore, God had become angry with humankind and enslaved people. Nowadays humankind is living in a second Egyptian slavery, created by new Egyptians—that is, the powerful wealthy people who rule the world. These Egyptians exploit ordinary poor people and expropriate their work. This is why misery is everywhere. There is bloodshed in wars, violence, robberies, rape, theft, cheating, and swindling in everyday life. Because of human misdeeds, God has imposed His punishments on the people of the Earth. God has punished people who have forgotten the faith with wars, diseases, and so on.[74]

It is noteworthy that all radical Stundists—from the Chaplinka dissidents to the Maliovantsy—emphasized the images and ideas of the Book of Exodus. For peasant dissidents, the familiar biblical images of Moses, Egyptian slavery, and Canaan became a call for a literal exodus—"an escape from oppression and a journey to the promised land." Like all European religious radicals, the Ukrainian Stundists followed the "paradigm of the Exodus" in their interpretation of reality and explanation of their mission in this world. As Michael Walzer has explained this paradigm, "Wherever people know the Bible, and experience oppression, the Exodus has sustained their spirits and (sometimes) inspired their resistance."[75]

The Stundists tried to restore the Christian faith and "the search after God" in their communities as a way to freedom from "the new Egyptian slavery." To do this, they wanted to cleanse their life of sin. As the arrested Stundist peasants explained to the criminal court in 1876: "We do nothing wrong and commit no crime. We just try to eradicate the habit of drinking alcohol and other vices from our peasant life. Therefore, we meet every holiday for common prayer because the Savior said: 'For where two or three are gathered together in my name, there am I in the midst of them.' We just read and explain the Gospels. We are not Stundists, we are Anabaptists."[76] Thus, the first Stundists used not only images and notions from the Holy Scriptures but also ideas of the Protestant Radical Reformation[77] (i.e., the name of the Anabaptists, the principle of "imitatio Christi") to legitimate their religious experience. The goal of their religious experience was the salvation of the human race. Radical Stundists such as the Chaplinka dissidents tried to restore social justice and evangelical principles in their peasant communities. In contrast, the Stundo-Baptists sought to reach this goal within their congregation by conducting their rituals and maintaining strict moral discipline among their coreligionists. The radicals took a more millennial approach to the problem of human salvation than the conservatives, and they connected their moral rebirth to the urgent problems of the outside world as well.[78]

The radicals interpreted the reincarnation of Christ as God using human flesh for future human salvation. In their theology, they shared some ideas with the Shalaputs, who believed that Christ was reincarnated in each true believer.

According to the Chaplinka Stundists, one of the reasons for the reincarnation of Jesus Christ was to restore the significance of human flesh as a "a temple of God, a dwelling of the Holy Ghost, the blessing of love of Our Father in Heaven." The true believer in Christ would be a reborn person when Christ was born in his or her heart. This rebirth of Christ in the true believer's heart would "produce the deep awareness of this believer's sinfulness and his or her resolution to leave the world of vice and follow the Divine Law. " This rebirth of the sinner into a virtuous Christian was the real Christian Baptism.[79] Therefore, the radical Stundists rejected the ritual of water Baptism and emphasized "Spiritual Baptism" and the descent of the Holy Spirit on the reborn Christian. One Stundist told a journalist: "Water Baptism is just an exterior sign, it has no power. It is necessary to be baptized by 'the water of life' [the Holy Spirit], which Christ offered the Samaritan at the water well, rather than by dead water."[80]

In their religious practices, the religious radicals challenged the hierarchy of wealth, privilege, and of government ranks. According to the Stundists, the main goal of each true Christian after his or her spiritual Baptism was spiritual union with Jesus Christ. This union would be achieved by Spiritual Communion and the enthusiastic praying and singing rather than by eating and drinking the symbols of Christ's body and blood. The radical Stundists emphasized ecstatic prayer, which they contrasted with the rituals of the Stundo-Baptists. The first observers of Ukrainian Stundism noted the intensive religious enthusiasm during their meetings for worship. It was common among the first Stundists from the province of Kherson that "after praying all the dissidents began to cry and shout."[81] In a Stundist meeting in the village of Riasnopol' in 1873, during the praying local peasants sang, shouted, danced, "tore their hair, punched themselves with their fists in the breast, fell on the floor, and rolled over the floor, crying 'Christ, give us, give us, Christ, save us!'"[82]

One example of the descent of the Holy Spirit was recorded in 1883 in a community of fifty members in the small settlement of Malovodianaia. During the ecstatic prayer, the two women, a mother and daughter who played the role of local prophetesses, demonstrated the descent of the Holy Spirit. At first, their bodies began to tremble. Then they fell on the floor and made strange sounds, which were considered to be signs of the presence of the Holy Spirit. Sometimes while praying, they began speaking and singing in a trance, shouting strange words. In such moments, they embodied the Divine Spirit, and all the attention of the meeting was concentrated on them. Other Stundists tried to decipher the phrases of their prophetesses as revelations from God himself.[83] This and other cases of spirit possession and intensive religious enthusiasm among the Ukrainian Stundists proved the continuing existence of Shalaput traditions among these radical evangelicals. As we can see, the Shalaputs' ecstatic religious practices became an integral part of the Stundist movement as well.

In their radical rejection of the sinful world and emphasis on the rebirth of the Christian soul, some dissidents came to the conclusion—which they shared with the radical Shalaputs as well—that reborn Christians would eventually embody God and personify Him. In 1900, Alexei Iurchenko, a peasant from the town of Korsun' in Kiev province, became a popular figure among those Ukrainian Stundo-Baptists who were exiled to the Caucasus. He taught that every man was "a Divine creature" created by God in His image and endowed by God with a Divine soul. Therefore, the virtuous man, who followed "the Divine rules" and avoided "sinful ways of life," would "certainly become God himself." Iurchenko called himself and his followers "God's children."

Iurchenko based his ideas on the text of the Bible and the Gospels. At the same time, he tried to correct the text of Holy Scripture and remove mistakes, which had been supposedly made during translations. His main goal was to restore the humanistic ideal of Jesus Christ in the Bible.[84] The new popularity of old Shalaput ideas among persecuted Stundist activists in 1900 demonstrated the persistence and importance of the religious practices of the Russian radical reformation's first phase for the development of the evangelical movement in the Russian Empire. Even some Stundo-Baptists in the Ukrainian provinces in the early twentieth century demonstrated religious practices reminiscent of radical Stundist theology.[85]

In some evangelical congregations in the provinces of Kiev and Volynia, the trends of radical Stundism revived again during the years 1902–3. To some extent, this revival of religious radicalism was a reflection of the social radicalization of landless, impoverished peasants who participated in the many uprisings and disorders that preceded the Revolution of 1905. The most famous peasant uprisings took place in the provinces of Kharkov and Poltava in March and April 1902. The radical ideas of the peasant movement infiltrated the evangelical movement among local peasants as well.[86]

In the village of Pekarshchina in Volynia province, one Stundist peasant, Nikita Bondar', split with a group of his adherents from the local Baptist congregation "because of the Baptist hierarchy of ministers." As a result, Bondar's followers withdrew their children from the German Baptist school and began to teach them themselves. According to the report of the governor general, the Stundists from Pekarshchina restored the religious practices of the radical Stundists. Bondar' and his coreligionists rejected the hierarchy of ministers and all rituals except those described in the Gospels. "They have no elders or

Figure 3.3. Stundo-Baptist peasants in Kiev province (1902). Note the books, the citations from the Gospels, and the portraits of the Russian emperor's family on the wall. From Varvara I. Iasevich-Borodaevskaia, *Sektantstvo v Kievskoi gubernii: Baptisty i Maliovnatsy* (Saint Petersburg, 1902), picture I, between pp. 6 and 7.

juniors," the governor general wrote, "they have no teachers or subordinates. They have only brothers and sisters who are equal and can perform religious ceremonies, when they are ready to do so."[87] Such social radicalism was always present among those Stundists who had rejected the "formalism" of the German Baptists.

As we have seen, the Russian Baptist movement began in the 1860s with the radical religious practices of the Ukrainian Stundists (figures 3.3, 3.4, and 3.5). But after the 1880s, conservatives prevailed in the evangelical movement in southern Russia and tried to purge radical elements. The Stundist radical reformation became a struggle not only against the Orthodox Church in the

Figure 3.4. A typical family of Stundo-Baptist peasants in Kiev province (1901). From Varvara I. Iasevich-Borodaevskaia, *Sektantstvo v Kievskoi gubernii: Baptisty i Maliovnatsy* (Saint Petersburg, 1902), picture II, between pp. 12 and 13.

Figure 3.5. *Top:* Tymofii Artemovych Zaits (1836–1907), a Stundist peasant activist and the author of a famous Stundist memoir. *Bottom:* An example of Zaits's handwriting from his manuscript, which was published by Vladimir Bonch-Bruevich in 1910; note the Ukrainian language. From *Materialy kistorii i izuchenia russkogo sektantstva i staroobriadchestva, Vypusk 3: Shtundisty—Postniki: Svobodnye khristiane: Dukhovnye Skoptsy: Staroobriadtsy,* ed. Vladimir Bonch-Bruevich (Saint Petersburg, 1910), picture between pp. 7 and 8.

Ukrainian countryside but also against the conservative Baptist hierarchy and church discipline in Stundo-Baptist congregations. Until Soviet times, this conflict between "spiritualist" (radical) and "ritualistic" (conservative) elements shaped the evangelical movement in Ukraine.

Notes

1 On the Mennonites' influences, see, in detail, Sergei Zhuk, "Russia's Lost Reformation: Peasants and Radical Religious Sects in Southern Russia and Ukraine, 1830–1905" (Ph.D. dissertation, Johns Hopkins University, 2002), chap. 2.

2 One of these Pietist Mennonites "burnt all her vainglorious clothes and was filled with

terror and fright. She came to . . . worship service after which she approached her brother Bernhard Rempel and they hugged each others hand and wept bitterly"; see in *The Golden Years: The Mennonite Kleine Gemeinde in Russia (1812–1849)*, ed. Delbert F. Plett (Steinbach, Manitoba, 1985), 173, 175, 176, 185.

3 The "conserver" group of Jacob Warkentin became known as the Lichtenau Church, or Die Grosse Gemeinde, in 1824. Their more ecumenical opponents (with Bernhard Fast as their leader) gravitated to the more radical churches of Ohrloff, Rudnerweide, and Alexanderwohl in the Molochnaia district of Tavrida. Through the adherents of Bernard Fast, the ecumenical and Pietistic influences reached the Mennonites in Molochnaia and later in Khortitsa as well. The oldest ecumenical influences came from the Moravian Brethrens at Herrnhut, who kept the Molochnaia Mennonites informed about their ecumenical missionary activities among the pagans, Muslims, and Jews. The "conservers" opposed this and any other connections with non-Mennonite missionaries; see John Friesen, "Mennonite Churches and Religious Developments in Russia 1789–1850," in *Mennonites in Russia, 1788–1988: Essays in Honour of Gerhard Lohrenz*, ed. John Friesen (Winnipeg, 1989), 43–74, especially, 62–64.

4 The citation is from Plett, *Golden Years*, 182, 183, 184. "One of them presented lengthy prayers which he had composed in advance and frequently he lay (poorly clad) for lengthy periods in the streets and ditches at home as well in other villages. In so doing he prayed very loudly and whimpered. When [the revivalists] were unable to cry during their prayers for a meal they would leave the table without eating. They ate poor food and in addition they often went hungry." One of the radical revivalists actually died from cold and hunger.

5 A. Rozhdestvenskii, *Iuzhno-russkii shtundism* (Saint Petersburg, 1889), 42, 43.

6 Peter M. Friesen, *The Mennonite Brotherhood in Russia (1789–1910)*, trans. J. B.Towes and A. Friesen (Fresno, Calif., 1978; 1st pr. in German in Russia, 1911), 223, 225, 326. Some of the Mennonites became the preachers for Wüst. As Friesen wrote: "In the fall of 1858 at a conference in connection with a mission festival in Rosenfeld (in Wüst's parish), these 'joyous brethren,' with a certain Kappes, a former school teacher in the Mariupol colonies, at their head, left the church amidst singing and shouts of joy. Kappes was endowed with an excellent memory, was a gifted speaker, possessed a rich imagination and wit, and was a good singer. He became the ugliest caricature of Wüst and his worst rod of correction." Jacob P. Bekker, *Origin of the Mennonite Brethren Church*, trans. D. E. Pauls and A. E. Janzen (Hillsboro, Kans., 1973), 22–30; the citation is on 26.

7 Rossiiskii gosudarstvennyi istoricheskii arkhiv (hereafter RGIA), f. 796, op. 149, d. 448, l. 2ob.–3ob., 8ob.; f. 821, op. 5, d. 991, l. 1–6ob.; Rozhdestvenskii, *Iuzhno-russkii shtundism*, 59–60.

8 Bekker, *Origin*, 85. As Bekker wrote: "Some of the Mennonite Brethren were infected with this over-exaggerated demonstration of joy, which finally, in 1865, reached proportions that led to a division, making the work in the church more difficult." For their services these enthusiasts even used various musical instruments such as flute, drum, etc. See also documents from the Dorodnitsyn collection: Episkop Alexii [Dorodnitsyn], *Materialy dlia*

istorii religiozno-ratsionalisticheskogo dvizhenia na iuge Rossii vo vtoroi polovine XIX–go veka (Kazan', 1908), 6–9.

9 Alexii, *Materialy*, 43–45. The police investigation revealed that by 1865 followers of the new sect had appeared in all Mennonite colonies in the Khortitsa district (in Ekaterinoslav province) and in the Molochnaia district, in the German colonies such as Liebenau (all in Tavrida), and Neue-Danzig in the province of Kherson, in the Swedish colonies of Slangendorff and (Kherson), and in the Jewish colonies of Kamianka and Izluchistaia in the province of Ekaterinoslav and of Dobraia in the province of Kherson.

10 Rozhdestvenskii, *Iuzhno-russkii shtundism*, 44; Alexii, *Materialy*, 14–39, 44–45.

11 Gosudarstvennyi arkhiv Rossiiskoi Federatsii (hereafter GARF), f. 109, III otd., 1-ia *ekspeditsia*, op. 33 (1860), d. 267, l. 1–6; *Kievskaia starina*, no. 10 (1884): 311. On Oncken, see H. Luckey, *Johann Gerhard Oncken und die Anfaenge des deutschen Baptismus* (Kassel, 1958). Compare with Alexii, *Materialy*, 497; A. Klibanov, *Istoria religioznogo sektantstva v Rossii (60-e gody XIX v.–1917 g.)* (Moscow, 1965), 204; and Heather Coleman, "The Most Dangerous Sect: Baptists in Tsarist and Soviet Russia, 1905–1929" (Ph.D. dissertation, University of Illinois, 1998), 18. As Bekker noted (in *Origin*, 182), "The Old Colony Mennonite Brethren invited [in 1868] Baptist Elder Oncken of Hamburg, Germany, to ordain Abr. Unger of the Old Colony as elder. Because they succeeded doing this service among us, they now proceeded on the presumption that all was accomplished under the Baptist umbrella, and hence were entitled to make known that the Mennonite Brethren Church is a product of their work. This writer declares this assumption to be false."

12 And he continued, "Our brethren said that to rejoice with them in the Gospel so that our hearts melted together through prayer fellowship and then to slip away for the farewell, was embarrassingly humiliating! . . . [Afterward,] when we received further visits from the Molokans, our women did not withdraw timidly for the welcoming salutation, but reasoned that 'if I can greet these bearded men with a kiss, why not also our own brethren?' Since some sisters interpreted Romans 16:16, 'Salute one another with an holy kiss,' as commending mixed kissing, they also began to greet our brethren with a kiss under the guise of innocence and humility. Other sisters who did not understood Romans 16:16 to mean mixed kissing, rather than applying wisdom to reason, also allowed themselves to be drawn into this practice." The quotation is from Bekker, *Origin*, 97–98.

13 On this, see RGIA, f. 796, op. 143, d. 602.

14 "Two of our brethren could preach quite fluently in Russian and Brother Huebert of Liebenau, teaching minister of the Mennonite Brethren congregation, had employed a Russian servant-girl for a number of years who spoke German fluently. She was converted in the Huebert home. When among newly revived Russians, she would pray in Russian; when among Germans, in German. This Russian servant-girl exerted a great influence upon the Russians who visited our services. At times Brother Huebert had a roomful of Russian peasants (Khokhollen). They prayed freely. If seats had been provided for them, there would not have been enough room to accommodate all of them"; see in Bekker, *Origin*, 99.

15 He wrote that "[they] had received news of the revival among the Russians [in the

villages near Liebenau in 1861], arrived from Old Russia and claimed to be prophets"; Bekker, *Origin,* 100.

16 On the participation of the Lutherans, Russian "settlers," and Jewish colonists in the "Anabaptist meetings of Hüpfers" (Mennonite Jumpers), see Alexii, *Materialy,* 15, 45. On the Mennonite Brethren hiding their Lutheran and Ukrainian coreligionists from the local police, see Bekker, *Origin,* 101.

17 Jacob Bekker wrote about this in his memoirs: "Inquires were made regarding the beginning and origin of the revival. It was discovered that the revival had its origin as a result of the witness by the Russian servant-girl who was employed in the Hübert home. Because she had no parents, her uncle justified in adopting the role of father. He blooded her back by flogging her and then hired her out in the village of Gnadenheim, where there was no trace of the Brethren. Her uncle believed that if she were removed from the Hübert home and placed in a village free from "heresy," she would forsake her "mistaken" beliefs. But he was mistaken in considering her belief a delusion. Her faith became stronger and more firmly grounded because of her beatings. She did not stop praying while in the service of her new employers. Her new hosts overheard her pray earnestly in secret. They eavesdropped several times and heard that she was also praying for them, her employers. Her mistress became curious and questioned her. The result was that her master and mistress were both saved. The conversions spread and reached her brother, who operated a liquor tavern. He was converted and discontinued his business. Through this the conversions spread in the village [in 1862]"; Bekker, *Origin,* 100–101.

18 The investigation revealed that by 1862 the Khortitsa revivalists, Abram (Abraham) Unger, Gerhard Willer, and Peter Berg had converted at least thirteen migrant Ukrainian peasants who were employed as agricultural workers in Khortitsa. The police also reported on the active role of two young Ukrainian peasant girls, Ekaterina Lukasheva and Tat'iana Orishkova, in the Mennonite revival in Khortitsa district. In October 1863, Willer baptized and converted into "the evangelical faith" the peasant boy Matvei Serbushenko (Sabulenko) from the village of Volosskoe. In April 1864, he did the same to Andrei Pedasenko from the town of Alexandrovsk in the province of Ekaterinoslav. According to the Russian laws, proselytizing among the Orthodox subjects by representatives of non-Orthodox religions was considered a crime. Therefore, the police arrested the leaders of the Mennonite revivalists and began a new investigation in 1864–65. See Rozhdestvenskii, *Iuzhno-russkii shtundism,* 44; and Alexii, *Materialy,* 21, 40, 41, 45. Peter Frese, Willer's coreligionist, rebaptized Iakov Sarana, another Ekaterinoslav peasant, during the same time.

19 As Jacob Bekker noted in his memoirs, in 1865, "Brother Heinrich Hübert, minister of the congregation [in Rudnerweide], was arrested on the charge that he had baptized a Russian girl and also that he had taught the doctrine of emasculation among the Russians." See in Bekker, *Origin,* 172–73. The Mennonite leaders were acquitted in the court, because the investigation did not discover castration among the Mennonite Brethren. See also archival materials in RGIA, f. 796, op. 143, d. 602.

20 This village was located in the district of Odessa in Kherson province (near the German colony of Rohrbach). According to the documents, "The founder of the Society of

Stundists, sometimes called the New Brotherhood, a peasant Mikhail Ratushny began the spreading his teaching from 1862, when he was the elder [*starosta*] of the village of Osnova"; RGIA, f. 796, op. 149, d. 448, l. 31.

21 RGIA, f. 796, op. 149, d. 448, l. 1. This is the file of the first documents on the Ukrainian Stundists in the archival collection of the Holy Synod, the original of which had been used by the first serious scholars of Stundism, such as Arsenii Rozhdestvenskii and Alexii Dorodnitsyn. See also Rozhdestvenskii, *Iuzhno-russkii shtundizm,* 56–57.

22 The Rev. V. Stoikov, the local priest, a Greek, could not speak Russian or Ukrainian fluently. Therefore, he had difficulties conversing with the religious peasants. After his arrival in Osnova, he ordered the local peasants to stop reading the Bible in their homes and to instead visit his house on Sundays and ask questions about Holy Scripture. The source here is Rozhdestvenskii, *Iuzhno-russkii shtundizm,* 57.

23 He wrote, "The (Orthodox) priest here was a Greek, he could not speak Russian well and thus was unable to talk them round. The group is said to have formed in the year 1862." The source here is Alexii, *Materialy,* 47, 48; compare with Hans Brandenburg, *The Meek and the Mighty: The Emergence of the Evangelical Movement in Russia* (New York, 1977), 68, 69.

24 Rozhdestvenskii, *Iuzhno-russkii shtundizm,* 52.

25 *Vestnik Evropy,* no. 7 (1881): 304.

26 RGIA, f. 796, op. 149, d. 448, l. 31–32.

27 Bonnekemper told Kotsebu: "The majority of Russian peasants wanted to read and understand the New Testament. They asked the Orthodox priests for instructions and help. But not receiving assistance from the Russian clergy the religious peasants turned to the representatives of non-Orthodox churches"; RGIA, f. 796, op. 149, d. 448, l. 9; f. 821, op. 5, d. 991, l. 2–2ob.

28 Alexander Ushinskii, *Verouchenie malorusskikh shtundistov* (Kiev, 1883), 130.

29 C. Bonnekemper, "Stundism in Russia," *Missionary Review of the World* 17 (March 1894): 203, 204. At the same time, he rejected all accusations that Stundists were "socialists and nihilists." Bonnekemper tried to prove that Stundist beliefs contradicted the very principles of Russian anarchy and "Nihilism." Instead, it expressed the typical religiosity of the Russian peasantry. He wrote: "Some local Russian noblemen and land proprietors claimed that in Rohrbach exists a secret conspiracy purposing nothing less than the subversion of Church, State, and society. This they are working, as so-called Stundists, under the cloak of extreme religiousness."

30 Rozhdestvenskii, *Iuzhno-russkii shtundizm,* 69; Alexii, *Materialy,* 52–54.

31 RGIA, f. 796, op. 149, d. 448, l. 38–38ob.

32 Another participant in the evangelical movement in southern Ukraine described the spread of Stundism to other localities of Kherson province as follows: "During the 1860s Ivan Riaboshapka bought a Russian New Testament in the market place of Liubomirka near the city of Elizabethgrad. Through much reading and meditation he came to understand the way of salvation, as did many of his fellow-farmers. A sixteen-year-old Russian boy by the name of Grigorii Kushnerenko from the market place Poltavka (Bashtanka),

began to study God's Word about this same time. He was gripped so deeply by what he read that he challenged his priest not only to show the Word of God to the people on his head, but to read it so that they might find the way of redemption there." See "Johann Wieler (1839–1889) Among Russian Evangelicals: A New Source of Mennonites and Evangelicalism in Imperial Russia," trans. and ed. L. Klippenstein, *Journal of Mennonite Studies* 5 (1987): 46, 47. The Russian Orthodox Church tried to discredit foreign information about Russian Stundists. See also "Zagranichnaya pechat' o russkikh shtundistakh," *Missionerskoe obozrenie,* January 1896, 89–92.

33 *Kievskaia starina,* no. 11 (1884): 502. In his report to the Kherson governor in 1870, the police officer from Elizavetgrad noted that the local court turned down a complaint of Zimmerman's parents about the Riaboshapka's proselytizing activities. See Alexii, *Materialy,* 100.

34 On the popularity of Stundism among the Jews, see *Pravoslavnoe obozrenie,* no. 4 (1876): 810.

35 RGIA, f. 1263, op. 1, d. 3551 (1871), *vedomost'* B, l. 874ob.–875. As a result of the Riaboshapka activities, in 1870 the most numerous were the Stundists in Elisavetgrad district—224 peasants. Compare this with the police report in Alexii, *Materialy,* 123.

36 *Khersonskie eparkhial'nye vedomosti* (hereafter *KherEV*), 1873, no. 1, 17, 18.

37 Alexii, *Materialy,* 264. Klibanov used figures of Stundists from Rozhdestvenskii's and Dorodnitsyn's books, but he ignored the archival materials. Moreover, in the case of Kiev Stundists, he confused the data and misrepresented the numbers. As other Soviet historians, Klibanov did not differentiate between the Stundists and Baptists. Therefore, he shared Dorodnitsyn's ideas and calculations of all evangelicals as Baptists. See Klibanov, *Istoria religioznogo,* 192.

38 The first publications about the Ukrainian Stundists are "Iz Novorosii," *Odesskii vestnik,* no. 273 (1867), and A. Znachko-Yavorskii, "Sekta shtundovykh," *Odesskii vestnik,* no. 35 (1868). The local Orthodox periodicals published the first articles about this in *Kievskie eparkhial'nye vedomosti* (hereafter *KEV*), 1872, no. 7, 147–52; 1873, no. 1, 16–18.

39 RGIA, f. 796, op. 155, d. 680, l. 1–1ob.; Rozhdestvenskii, *Iuzhno-russkii shtundizm,* 75–77, 79–84; RGIA, f. 797, op. 42, 2 otd., 3 stol, d. 40 (1872), l. 1–2. Later on, the police arrested fifty-six of the most active Stundists, followers of Balaban. See RGIA, f. 797, op. 43, 2 otd., 3 stol, d. 43 (1873), l. 1–1ob.

40 Alexii, *Materialy,* 165–66. Klibanov mistakenly wrote that the authors of this letter "called themselves the Baptists." There is no such word in this document. See Klibanov, *Istoria religioznogo,* 192.

41 Tsentral'nyi derzhavnyi istorychnyi arkhiv Ukrainy (hereafter TsDIAU), f. 442, op. 53, d. 357, l. 29. See the report of the Orthodox clergy in RGIA, f. 797, op. 90 (1875), d. 38, l. 3.

42 TsDIAU, f. 442, op. 55, d. 447, l. 67; RGIA, f. 1263, op. 1, d. 4193, l. 567ob. The Orthodox missionary in the province of Kiev gives slightly different figures for these years: 565 Stundists in 1875 and 944—in 1877; see *KEV,* 1882, no. 16, 294.

43 Rozhdestvenskii, *Iuzhno-russkii shtundizm,* 98.

44 Rozhdestvenskii, *Iuzhno-russkii shtundizm,* 101, 102, 103. See the detailed description of the institutionalization of Stundism and its transformation in the Baptist faith in Rozhdestvenskii, *Iuzhno-russkii shtundizm,* 99–150ff. All Soviet historians, from Klibanov to Sarychev, and all the Western historians, from Klimenko to Coleman based their analysis of the first Russian Baptists on Rozhdestvenslii's description.

45 Emel'ianov, "Ratsionalizm na iuge Rossii," *Otechestvennye zapiski* (hereafter *OZ*), 1878, no. 5, 206–30; K. Starynkevich, "Religioznoe dvizhenie na Iuge Rossii," *Slovo,* no. 8 (1880): 124; E. R., "Russkie ratsionalisty," *Vestnik Evropy,* no. 7 (1881), 301, 308.

46 Rozhdestvenskii, *Iuzhno-russkii shtundizm,* 105, 106.

47 RGIA, f. 797, op. 90 (1875), d. 38, l. 3. According to Alexander Ushinskii, in 1875 there were 243 dissidents in Chaplinka, and they still made a majority among 561 Stundists of the province of Kiev. See Ushinskii, *O prichinakh poiavlenia ratsionalisticheskikh uchenii shtundy* (Kiev, 1884), 23.

48 Ushinskii, *O prichinakh poiavlenia,* 27. In 1879, there were 360 Stundists in Chaplinka and 270 in Kosiakovka; see in *KEV,* 1880, no. 18–19, 12.

49 Alexander Ushinskii, *Verouchenie malorusskikh shtundistov* (Kiev, 1883), iv, v. All observers agreed with Ushinskii that the radical Stundists rejected any authority except the Bible.

50 *KEV,* 1880, nos. 18–19, 11–15; *Delo,* no. 1 (1883): 215–16.

51 Ushinskii, *Verouchenie,* 16, 63; *OZ,* 1878, 212–13, 225. See an interpretation of Koval's dissent as a predecessor of Pentecostal movement in Russia in Klibanov, *Istoria religioznogo,* 217.

52 Rozhdestvenskii, *Iuzhno-russkii shtundizm,* 145, 147. According to the official report of the Kiev governor, there were 3,085 Stundists in the province in 1885. In the province of Kherson, the local governor counted 3,049 Stundists in 1885. In Volynia, the police registered from 36 to 65 Stundists. In the province of Ekaterinoslav, by 1890 the police registered 267 Stundists. Before this, 260 Stundists had returned to the Orthodox Church. Therefore, between 1885 and 1890, we can calculate 527 officially registered Stundists in the province of Ekaterinoslav. Between 1885 and 1890, the Kharkov police registered 240 Stundists among the local peasants. See RGIA, f. 1263, op. 1, d. 4546, l.836; d. 4543, l. 424ob.; RGIA, "Otchet Volynskogo gubernatora za 1885 god," 8; "Otchet Volynskogo gubernatora za 1889 god," 7; "Otchet Ekaterinoslavskogo gubernatora za 1890 god," l. 371ob.; and "Otchet Kharkovskogo gubernatora za 1890 god," l. 607.

53 Russian journalists from a popular Moscow newspaper calculated in 1884 that there were 24,700 Stundists in Kiev province, 9,000 in Kherson province, 7,500 in Bessarabia province, 4,000 in Ekaterinoslav province, and 1,000 in Tavrida province; *Moskovskie vedomosti,* no. 326 (1884). Compare with: *KEV,* 1885, no. 19, 902.

54 See Rozhdestvenskii, *Iuzhno-russkii shtundizm,* 134, 135, 136, 145, 147. All other scholars base their studies on the calculations of Arsenii Rozhdestvenskii. Compare with Klibanov, *Istoria religioznogo,* 208ff. My calculations are based on data from the following: TsDIAU, f. 442, op. 52, d. 433, l. 35, 36ob., 61–62; f. 127, op. 690, d. 43, l. 5ob.; f. 442, op. 53, d. 357, l. 14, 29; f. 442, op. 55, d. 447, l. 67–67ob.; and f. 442, op. 623, d. 364,

l. 36ob., 37. And also see RGIA, "Obzor Ekaterinoslavskoi goubernii za 1881 god," 8, 23, 24; "Obzor Ekaterinoslavskoi goubernii za 1882 god," 8, 21, 22; "Obzor Ekaterinoslavskoi goubernii za 1883 god," 8, 25, 26; "Obzor Ekaterinoslavskoi goubernii za 1884 god," 7, 24; and "Obzor Ekaterinoslavskoi goubernii za 1889 god," 27, 56, 57.

55 RGIA, "Otchet Khersonskogo gubernatora za 1890 god," 13. In the Russian original, the governor literally complained of "the spread" of Stundism influence. He wrote in Russian: "Raion rasprostranenia shtundizma okhvatyvaet okolo 3/4 obshchei ploshchadi gubernii."

56 RGIA, "Otchet Khersonskogo gubernatora za 1890 god," 14. The majority of the Kherson Stundists were concentrated in Elizavetgrad district—64 places, including 20 towns and cities, 42 villages, and 105 rural settlements. The number of Stundists who had officially separated from the Orthodox Church totaled 4,648 people (including 2,169 children under the age of twenty-one years). The police discovered that 83 leaders ruled the Stundist communities of the province. Among these leaders, 30 were called the ministers (*presvitery*), who performed the religious ceremonies, "including the baptism of the children, the weddings, the communion and burial rituals."

57 RGIA, f. 1263, op. 1, d. 4182, l. 431–4.

58 RGIA, f. 1263, op. 1, d. 4868, l. 138ob. According to his report, in 1890 the Stundist movement in the province of Kiev had increased by 131 members and included 5,002 activists. The governor noted an expansion of Stundism in 18 new localities of the province as well. The Orthodox clergy reported the figure of 4,681 Stundists the same year, i.e., 320 people less than the police detected. According to the report of the governor general of the South Western Region (which included the provinces of Kiev, Podolia, and Volynia), by 1893 in the province of Kiev alone there were between 5,500 and 6,000 Stundists in 200 localities. See RGIA, f. 1276, op. 17, d. 189 (1911), l. 88.

59 See the provincial governors' reports and Klibanov, *Istoria religioznogo*, 208–9. We can assume that the number of participants in the Stundist meetings was larger than that reported by the police.

60 See about the first Stundist religious practices in Rozhdestvenskii, *Iuzhno-russkii shtundizm,* 169–73.

61 The creed contained eight rules: (1) Do not drink alcohol, do not encroach on anybody's property; but help each other by all means. (2) Do not acknowledge other religious books except the Gospels; do not follow the fasts and the orders of the Orthodox Church. (3) Visits to the Orthodox Church are not obligatory because the Gospels said when two or three believers met under the name of Jesus Christ there would be God's church. ("For where two or three are gathered together in my name, there am I in the midst of them"; Matthew 18:20.) (4) Repentance for committed sins should be done in private, inside the soul of believer in the name of God, rather than in public before another human being, the priest. (5) It is not necessary to have icons or other religious images; but they can be used as decorations for the house. (6) Baptism should be done according to Our Savior's, example, after the purification from all sins. Therefore, the ritual of baptism ought to be performed over grown-up people, who are able to comprehend the significance of confession.

Moreover, Holy Scripture did not mention the baptism of infants or the existence of godfathers and godmothers. Hence, infant babies should not be baptized at all. (7) It is obligatory to participate in the meeting for worship at least once in two weeks. (8) It is not allowed to celebrate holidays that were not mentioned in the Holy Scripture. See Rozhdestvenskii, *Iuzhno-russkii shtundizm,* 173–74.

62 See, e.g., Alexii, *Materialy,* 535–37.

63 *KherEV,* 1875, no. 19, 557.

64 *KherEV,* 1875, no. 19, 559; Rozhdestvenskii, *Iuzhno-russkii shtundizm,* 179.

65 *KherEV,* 1886, no. 6, 265.

66 RGIA, f. 797, op. 43, 2 otd., 3 st., d. 43, l. 2. The text of the document (l. 2–6) is close to a theology of the Kosiakovka Stundists, who were described by A. Ushinskii.

67 *KherEV,* 1876, no. 14, 185–86. The Orthodox author noted that the Stundist peasants developed a new culture of literacy and reading. After their meeting, the Stundists usually came home and spent all the holiday reading and discussing religious books. See also *KherEV,* 1881, no. 5, 148. It is noteworthy that the Orthodox authors compared Stundist practices with Calvinism. But according to these authors, the Stundists "rejected even more religious forms and rituals than the Calvinists did."

68 Arsenii Rozhdestvenskii described this process based on material about the Kiev and Kherson Stundists. See Rozhdestvenskii, *Iuzhno-russkii shtundizm,* 243–61. See also a good description of the transitory stage in religious practices of the peasant dissidents in the village of Sholokhovo (in Ekaterinoslav province), who moved from inspirational Stundism to the formalized Baptist faith by 1886, in *Ekaterinoslavkie eparkhial'nye vedomosti,* 1886, no. 11, 288–303.

69 See, e.g., the description of the Baptist creed of the dissident congregation in the village of Bashmachka in Ekaterinoslav province in 1897 by Alexii, *Materialy,* 538–42. The theology and religious practices of the first Russian Baptists are well studied in the German- and English-speaking historiography. So we do not need to analyze them here.

70 Elie Halevy argued that during the years "in which the demons of revolution dominated the continent—between 1789 and 1815—England was spared the revolution toward which the contradictions in her polity and economy might otherwise have led her, through the stabilizing influence of evangelical religion, particularly of Methodism." See his *The Birth of Methodism in England,* trans. and ed. Bernard Semmel (Chicago, 1971), vs. different scholars who had criticized Halevy's hypothesis. Nevertheless, his thesis continued to be persuasive and maintained its grip on the imagination of historians who began to fill in the evidence. See also Pamela J. Walker, "'I Live But Not Yet I For Christ Liveth In Me' Men and Masculinity in the Salvation Army, 1865–90," in *Manful Assertions: Masculinities in Britain since 1800,* ed. Michael Roper and John Tosh (London, 1991), 92–112.

71 Their petitions of 1903 demonstrate the mass transformation of Stundist theology into Stundo-Baptist theology all over southern Russia. A typical petition of the dissident peasants from Pavlograd district in the province of Ekaterinoslav is a good illustration of this transformation. "We are sectarians," these peasants wrote to the minister of internal affairs on August 20, 1903: "And according to our faith we belong to the community of

Christians of the Evangelical creed, who accept water baptism only at mature age. We derive all truth about achieving eternal life from God's word—from the Bible, which commands us to live peacefully with other people and to obey the tsar and all his administration. Trying to live virtuously and love everybody as best as we can, we are still loyal sons of Russia: we obey all the secular authorities, we pray for them. We pay taxes, serve in the army, and overall, we obey all the Russian laws that establish the state order and property relations among subjects of the Russian state." This petition described in detail the religious practices of the Stundo-Baptists, their stable church rituals, strict religious discipline, and respect for religious and secular hierarchy, which prevented any radical and antistate activities. These petitioners tried to show that the Ukrainian evangelicals had "no political ideas for which the Russian police could persecute them as dangerous to the state." See RGIA, f. 1284, op. 222 (1903), d. 142, l. 1–2; the text of their creed is on l. 7–8. In his letter to the minister of internal affairs, the bishop of Ekaterinoslav noted many other petitions of this kind from other evangelical congregations, and assumed that "this was a part of the centralized campaign, initiated from one center." He called these Stundo-Baptists "ritualistic Stundists in contrast to spiritualist Stundists who rejected all rituals." See RGIA, f. 1284, op. 222 (1903), d. 142, l. 9, 10. Compare with other petitions. 1903 was the peak year for these petitions. See a petition from the Stundists from the province of Kiev: RGIA, f. 1284, op. 222, d. 167, l. 1–2ob., 3–4; and others: d. 63, 67, 69, 71, 74, 77, 83, 85, 86, 88, 92, 93, 94, 97. For 1903, the Department of the General Cases of the Ministry of the Internal Affairs registered more than forty analogous petitions.

72 Ushinskii, *Verouchenie,* 179. According to the Chaplinka Stundists, to save the human race true Christians had to restore true faith in God. This true faith was the belief in the "law of the Spirit," following the inspiration of the Holy Ghost. That was why they called themselves "spiritual Christians." The main source of their inspiration was the Holy Spirit. They made their own church with their coreligionists without rituals and religious ceremonies. According to their creed, the members of the radical Stundist congregation were "united exclusively by Love and by fruits of the Divine Grace" and they followed literally the principles of Holy Scripture. The Chaplinka Stundists considered themselves to be under the invisible rule of the Holy Ghost. Their head was Jesus Christ Who through "His incarnation and works" attracted them to Him and "made them the participants in His body [His Church]." See Ushinskii, *Verouchenie,* 184, 189–90.

73 *OZ,* 1878, no. 5, 208.

74 *Nedelia,* no. 2 (1877): 54; Rozhdestvenskii, *Iuzhno-russkii shtundizm,* 189. As the New Testament said: "There is none that understandeth, there is none that seeketh after God. They are all gone out of the way, they are together become unprofitable: there is none that doeth good, no, not one" (Romans 3:11–12).

75 Michael Walzer, *Exodus and Revolution* (New York, 1985), 6, 4. Walzer studied this paradigm as "the idea of a deliverance from suffering and oppression: this-worldly redemption, liberation, revolution, [because] revolution has often been imagined as an enactment of the Exodus and the Exodus has often been imagined as a program for revolution" (p. ix). See also classic works about the Exodus and political culture: Lincoln Steffens, *Moses in Red:*

197

The *Revolt of Israel as a Typical Revolution* (Philadelphia, 1926); Ernst Bloch, *Atheism in Christianity: The Religion of the Exodus and the Kingdom* (New York, 1972); and J. Severino Croatto, *Exodus: A Hermeneutics of Freedom* (Maryknoll, N.Y., 1981).

76 A. Gorzhalchinskii, "Shtunda i shtundizm," *KherEV,* 1876, no. 14, 181.

77 As Mennonite Brethren, the radical Stundists literally followed the words from the Gospel of Saint Matthew about the expulsion of the nonrecalcitrant members (Matthew 18:15–18).

78 Ushinskii, *Verouchenie,* 184, 189–90.

79 Ushinskii, *Verouchenie,* 208–9. Some of the Stundists shared the notion that Jesus Christ literally dwelled in the body of each re-born person. One Stundist peasant explained to the Orthodox missionary that every true believer was "a temple, where Christ was living"; p. 210. Rozhdestvenskii, *Iuzhno-russkii shtundizm,* 196.

80 *OZ,* 1978, no. 5, 228, 229.

81 *KEV,* 1872, no. 7, 150–51. Such meeting usually began with reading the Bible, then the Stundists sang the psalms, and after the singing an ecstatic praying began, when all the dissidents knelt down and then suddenly everybody cried as in hysteria.

82 This village was located in the Odessa district of Kherson province; Rozhdestvenskii, *Iuzhno-russkii shtundizm,* 247–48. The police report of January 22, 1873, about this enthusiastic meeting of the Riasnopol' Stundists was published by A. Dorodnitsyn in his documentary collection; see Alexii, *Materialy,* 169. The liberal journalist noted the same demonstration of "intense" religious enthusiasm at the beginning of Ukrainian Stundism. See in I. Kharlamov, "Shtundisty," *Russkaia mysl',* no. 11 (1885): 3, 5.

83 This settlement was located in Alexandria district, the province of Kherson; *KherEV,* 1884, no. 11, 352–53. For some reason, Rozhdestvenskii, who mentioned this case, ignored the entire story of the Stundist prophetesses; see Rozhdestvenskii, *Iuzhno-russkii shtundizm,* 249. Other serious Orthodox scholars also wrote about the religious enthusiasm of radical Stundists; see V. A. Mavritskii, "Sthundisty," *Pravoslavnoe obozrenie,* no. 2 (1881): 360, 375. Mavritskii also gives a good description of Stundist religious practices.

84 GARF, f. 102, op. 226 (1898), d. 12, p. 4, l. 12, 15.

85 Police records from the province of Volynia provide us with an interesting description of such popular theology. The police investigation in February 1903 discovered that the main activist of the Volynia Stundists was Mikhail Onishchuk, a peasant from the village of Suiemtsy. As a typical peasant theologian, Onishchuk described in detail his faith and his religious ideas. In responding to the police officer's questions, he explained that he considered himself a Baptist and his faith—an evangelical one: "I am not an Orthodox Christian. But I do not deny the Orthodox Church as one among other Christian churches. I do not visit the Orthodox Church; I do not carry the cross and do not worship the icons. Though I do not follow the fasts established by the Orthodox Church, I do follow my own spiritual fast, when my soul is ready for it. When I am fasting I do not eat or drink and I just pray to God. My prayer is inside my heart, and in my prayer I ask God for everything that I need. Among the religious sacraments I accept baptism at a mature age, the wedding, the communion, and the confession. One of our brothers, who is gifted by the Holy

Ghost, can perform these sacraments and rituals. Such a brother is noted according to his deeds and selected by other brothers. He is not supposed to be envious, greedy for money, predatory or have hatred in his soul, and overall he must live according to the Gospels." See RGIA, f. 1284, op. 222, d. 29, l. 40–40ob. From this description, we can see how the legacy of radical Stundism still influenced the Baptist congregations, even in 1903.

86 See chapter 7 on the social activism of Stundist peasants. On peasant disorders in the provinces of Kharkov and Poltava, see the documents of the police and the local administration: RGIA, "Otchet Khar'kovskogo gubernatora za 1902 g.," l. 3–5; and RGIA, f. 1405, op. 521, d. 371, l. 1–8ff.

87 RGIA, f. 1284, op. 222, d. 29, l. 95.

4 Peasant Theologians and the Protestant Ethic

The ethic of rational economic behavior, of a work ethic and discipline, was an important element of new capitalist cultures everywhere. According to the Weberian sociology of religion, the religious ethos of the Reformation contributed to the modernization of Europe, and the various Christian sects practicing an "inner-worldly asceticism," including English Puritans and German Anabaptists, became "agents of the capitalist spirit" in Western Europe. In Russia, various dissident groups had a similar religious ethos. Some of these groups, beginning with the Old Believers and Skoptsy, participated to a degree in the modernization of the Russian Empire.[1] In post-Emancipation Russia, two dissident groups demonstrated behavior that was close to Weber's models of the Protestant ethic in popular religion. These were the Shalaputs and Stundists.

The Shalaputs

As early as the 1860s, Shalaput communities began creating new cultural patterns distinct from Russian Orthodox peasant culture. The Reverend M.

Samoilov, the priest of a parish church in the province of Ekaterinoslav, noted that at first "the Shalaputs looked like very pious and religious Orthodox peasants." He described their dress as always very clean and neat. In contrast to their Orthodox neighbors, Shalaput houses were very clean and rationally organized; there were many icons, candles, and icon-lamps in their rooms. This priest was struck by the fact that all Shalaputs were literate and had many religious books, which they read every day at the family table. Other local priests reported similar information. The local administration emphasized the Shalaputs' diligence and industrious character. Both the police and clergy noted the well-being of Shalaput communities, the productivity of their farming, and the efficiency of their households.

Notwithstanding complaints about the Shalaputs' dissident activities, all observers (including the Orthodox clergy) acknowledged that Shalaput peasants had a higher level of literacy and knowledge of the Bible, better agricultural productivity, and stronger cooperation with their coreligionists than their Orthodox neighbors. The Shalaput activists who followed the principles of inner-worldly asceticism in their everyday life tended to be more prosperous than Orthodox peasants. The industrious Shalaputs were generally friendly, affectionate, and cordial. They were ready to help their neighbors, and instead of conflict in interpersonal relations, they sought peaceful and friendly relations with their Orthodox neighbors, offering to help anyone in need.[2]

However, rumors of sexual transgressions among the Shalaputs began spreading, and the ecclesiastical administration of Kherson province tried to punish and exile them. But this was not a unanimous position. Some local priests presented the Shalaputs as "harmless pious peasants" who visited the village church and regularly participated in church rituals. Moreover, when under the pressure of the ecclesiastical administration, local peasants tried to evict the Shalaputs from the village of Shirokoe, the Kherson provincial administration did not approve this decision "because all the dissident peasants were noted as the most industrious and efficient farmers of the province" and they "did not commit any crimes against society." The governor highly praised the conduct of these religious people and wrote that "nothing wrong was found in their lifestyle and conduct." Therefore, Kherson's secular powers vindicated the dissident peasants who disobeyed the local clergy.[3]

The first Shalaput activists in the Ukrainian and Russian countryside usually were among the most zealous Orthodox peasants who tried to restore "the pure spirit" of the early church. The predecessors of the Ekaterinoslav Shalaputs, members of the sect Bosonoguie (meaning *barefoot*), began their search for the Orthodox truth with long pilgrimages to monasteries. The founding father of the Shalaput movement in the district of Pavlograd was Piotr Dovgopostolyi, a peasant from the village of Vasil'kovka. Beginning in 1859, he made regular yearly pilgrimages to various monasteries. He brought new religious literature to his village and taught his neighbors to "live like Orthodox monks." His followers and neighbors, the Vasil'kovka peasants Ivan Ges' and Il'ia Bazarnyi, even left their families and settled in caves near the village as hermits. By 1867, they had established a meeting for worship in Vasil'kovka.[4]

Their followers continued to visit holy Orthodox places. Some of them followed the example of the Bosonoguie from the Novomoskovsk district, who represented another version of the same sect. They walked barefoot (even in the winter), collected money for their community in neighboring villages, and carried a stepladder with them. The Vasil'kovka Shalaputs explained to the peasants that this stepladder was for "God who sometimes came downstairs to communicate with Christians." The Orthodox author who described this noted that Shalaputs looked and behaved as "God's fools" (*iurodivyie*).[5] According to Russian Orthodox tradition, "God's fools" were imbecile persons believed to possess the divine gift of prophesy. All leaders of the Shalaput movement demonstrated this kind of behavior. These "God's fools" represented a Russian version of inner-worldly asceticism, with elements of mysticism, that was typical for the "God's people" tradition of religious dissent.

In some parishes in the Pavlograd and Novomoskovsk districts, the overwhelming majority of the activists in the Orthodox Church behaved like the Shalaputs. What struck the first observers were the improvements in the lifestyle of these pious peasants. They had become more sober, religious, and industrious. After an analysis of the local clergy's reports in 1875, the bishop of Ekaterinoslav and Taganrog wrote a quite positive description of the new sect:

205

The Shaloputs [sic] are apparently the most pious people who visit the church, follow the fasts strictly, [and] prepare themselves for Communion; they confess and take communion. They are fond of reading religious ("soul-saving") books and making pilgrimages to various consecrated places. They keep their dwellings clean and tidy; they decorate their houses with icons, icon-lamps, and various religious paintings; they do not like idle talk, especially swearing and profanity, and they always try to withdraw from the society where they notice noise and swearing. They do not visit taverns and do not drink alcohol and do not smoke tobacco; they live together in a special accord, calling each other brother or sister; they are distinguished from other rural inhabitants by their compassion and charity for poor people. Because of the Shaloputs' religiosity and piety, some of the local priests call them progressive people.[6]

As the bishop noted, all newly converted peasants were taught to read and write, using Shalaput books. Because of this "literacy campaign," the Shaloputs attracted "the most zealous and loyal peasants, who surpassed their fellow villagers in religious knowledge and intellect."[7]

The case of Petro (Pavlo) Duplii (Chekhlatyi) in the province of Ekaterinoslav is the best illustration of the confusing nature of the Shalaput movement. Duplii, its most influential leader, was a peasant from the village of Priadivka in the Novomoskovsk district.[8] Police documents and the descriptions of ethnographers and journalists reveal his heterogeneous background and controversial role. Platon, the bishop of Ekaterinoslav and Taganrog, met Duplii and characterized him afterward as "a harmless and pious Orthodox Christian." On November 27, 1867, the bishop wrote a special report confirming "the Russian Orthodox faith" of Duplii to the Holy Synod.[9] In the early 1870s, the governor of Poltava reported to the minister of the interior on the spread of the Shalaput movement among the rural population of his province. According to his information, Duplii was its most famous leader. On December 14, 1876, responding to the Poltava governor's reports, the Ministry of the Interior requested from the Ekaterinoslav governor a special investigation into Duplii's "personality and dissident activities." The district police of Novomoskovsk organized an investigation and reported its results on March 1, 1877.[10]

206   The police officer gave a sympathetic description of Duplii. He described

him as a "hale and hearty" peasant of seventy years. All peasants apparently respected Duplii as a wise and reasonable man. He was considered to be one of the most industrious "agriculturalists" in his village, succeeding in both farm work and beekeeping. Peasants referred to him respectfully and lovingly as "our old man." Following his religious principles based on the Gospels, Duplii stopped farming and began to live the life of an ascetic monk. He gave all his property to peasants who were poor and hungry, and he tried to help anyone who suffered physically or spiritually. His preaching and the example he set influenced the Priadivka peasants, who eventually stopped "drinking alcohol" and abandoned their "former existence of idleness" for the new "diligent and productive" lives of successful farmers. According to the police, because of Duplii's influence, the population of Priadivka became the wealthiest in the Novomoskovsk district. At the same time, all observers noted the changes in Priadivka's appearance. Now this village appeared gloomy and very different from a typical Ukrainian village. Young people no longer sang and danced in the evening but spent all their time reading the Gospels and praying.[11]

The police report noted the unusual religious piety of Duplii, who visited all the church services and made regular pilgrimages to the Kiev and Solovetskii monasteries. Moreover, Duplii sent his brother, who became a monk of the Orthodox Church, to a Kharkov monastery. Despite Duplii's obvious religiosity, the local priest, M. Zhitetskii, noted for his corruption, characterized Duplii as the worst enemy of Orthodoxy. But the police officer vindicated Duplii and cited Zhitetskii's cupidity and inefficiency as the main reasons for the peasants' defection from the Orthodox Church. As the police officer wrote, Duplii "has a mania to embody the monk's life, [while] living in this world." As he and later V. Iasevich-Borodaevskaia noted, Duplii all his life wanted to be an Orthodox monk, and he followed monastic rules "every day of his life."

Duplii had grown up in a typical poor family of state Ukrainian peasants. He was half-illiterate; that is, he was able to read the printed text in Russian but could not write. From early childhood, he was attracted to religious books and church rituals. But having become disappointed with the formality of religious services in his village church, he began to travel as a pilgrim to various

Russian Orthodox holy places, monasteries, and cloisters, "seeking Divine truth." The priest from Priadivka tried to persuade him to stop his travels and stay with his father. But his father, who was always intoxicated, could not serve a positive model for his religious son. Duplii did not want to stay home and thus continued visiting monasteries. Enraged by Duplii's stubbornness, his drunkard father almost beat him to death. Duplii suffered such cruel beatings each time he came back from his travels. As a result, he decided to devote all his life to God and live in an Orthodox monastery. Once, during his regular pilgrimage, he decided to stay in the Kiev-Pecherskii monastery, but the local monk Job (called by peasants "the holy hermit Iona") persuaded him to return to his village and live in this world. The monk explained to him that to live as a monk among sinning people in the world and thus serve as an example of righteousness was more difficult and important than a sinless existence in the isolated monastery. When Duplii showed the letter from this monk to the police officer, he noted that "real Christian work for a sincere believer was to remain a righteous man and serve God by overcoming all temptations and difficulties of this sinful world."[12]

Duplii articulated notions reminiscent of what Max Weber defined as "inner worldly ascetic Protestantism."[13] Duplii taught his young adherents: "Remember, you do not need to flee from this world, you must overcome it and resist its temptations and strengthen your spirit in the struggle with this world's sins." As had thousands of religious radicals before him, Duplii insisted on a struggle for the transformation of the sinful world, living among sinners rather than in a secluded monastery. It is noteworthy that he and his followers lived by the principle that had become the way of life for many Protestants all over the world. At the end of the seventeenth century, another reformer of this religious tradition, William Penn, the British Quaker and founder of Pennsylvania, defined this principle in his advice to his coreligionists. In his famous treatise "No Cross No Crown," he urged against the "withdrawal" of Christians from "this world" into closed religious communities: "The Christian Convent and Monastery are within, where the Soul is encloistered from Sin. True Godliness does not turn Men out of the World, but enables them to live better in it, and excites their endeavors to mend it."[14] Thus, this uneducated

Ukrainian peasant, the leader of the Priadivka Shalaputs, together with an English aristocrat, expressed what Weber calls the important moral aspect of modernization—the inner-worldly asceticism of Protestant Christianity.[15]

Duplii emphasized the humility and self-abasement of the sincere Christian believer who should be humble and ready to serve other people. Sometimes his self-abasement took extreme forms, and he looked and behaved as "God's fool" in his shabby and worn dress, while making jokes and humorously critical comments on his own life. According to Duplii, the best remedy for pride was self-humiliation and the self-limitation of human desires. "Imitatio Christi," following Jesus Christ's example in everyday life, was the best way to salvation. Like Christ, the Duplii-Shalaputs tried to help other people and sometimes devoted all their property to the service of others. Like the typical ethical prophets described by Weber, the Ekaterinoslav Shalaputs tried to show their neighbors the importance of self-denial and self-sacrifice for the Christian ethic. Accordingly, they insisted on strict rules for dress and rigorous fasting. They kept a "comprehensive fast" for ten days and sometimes avoided any kind of food at all. The followers of Duplii picked special healing herbs on the steppes and made from them a beverage to drink while fasting. Local peasants called this beverage "the Shalaput herbs."[16]

All observers noted the radical asceticism of Duplii and his followers. These dissidents combined it with millenarianism and expectations of the oncoming end of the world. They preached about the coming of the Antichrist and his prophets. Like other Shalaputs, they exhausted themselves with extensive praying on their knees while reading the Gospels and by their comprehensive fasting to prepare their souls for the Holy Spirit. In their self-humiliation, they exaggerated the traditional emphasis of the Orthodox Church on human suffering. According to Duplii, those who suffered in this world and denied all wealth were ready to enter the Kingdom of God. Until the end of his life, he helped other people by all possible means. He taught that Christians should "be great by their meekness, and rich in their poverty." For him, "the beginning of human pride was a defection from God."[17]

In his preaching and religious practices, Duplii emphasized what was obvious in other Shalaput criminal cases—the Shalaputs' Orthodox roots. Like other Shalaput leaders, Duplii first attempted to reform his Orthodox parish church. He tried "to make Holy Scripture intelligible to ordinary" Ukrainian peasants who could not understand either Church Slavonic or Russian. He organized a special meeting for reading and explaining the Bible in his house. He also tried to make religion freely available, without special taxation or exploitation. That was why he organized his neighbors in their struggle against the decision of the local clergy to introduce new taxes to finance the building of a new parish church. At the same time, he tried to help monasteries and cloisters that had financial problems. Several times, the Shalaputs of Duplii's group organized a collection among their coreligionists to help such monasteries. And, finally, frustrated with the formalism of the Orthodox Church, Duplii tried to compensate "for the lack of warmth and spirituality" by creating his own Christian community, which could help peasants to survive and prepare for the coming Kingdom of God.[18] Like other Shalaputs, Duplii's group demonstrated strong Orthodox elements and a certain mysticism in its ethical program. In its extreme forms, the Shalaput religious ethos emphasized the spiritual and mystical side of religious morality distinct from rationalist Protestant behavior.

The Stundists

In contrast to the Shalaputs, the Ukrainian Stundists developed a religious ethos similar to what Weber described as the "Protestant ethic." Their first leaders exemplified the new religious ethos in the Ukrainian countryside. They also demonstrated the stages in developing a charisma of ethical prophecy with the subsequent routinization and institutionalization of the charismatic religious movement, which led to its transformation into a new religious congregation. All the leaders of dissenting movements in the southern Russian provinces gradually underwent what Weber described as a "historical evolution" from "ethical prophets of a sect" to "theologians of an institutionalized church."[19]

Ivan G. Riaboshapka, a peasant from the village of Liubomirka, was one of Ukrainian Stundism's founders. In 1857, Riaboshapka settled in Liubomirka and began working as a shepherd on the local estate. As a young shepherd, he visited the local blacksmith's shop and became the smith's apprentice. During his apprenticeship he drank heavily, associated with loose women, and participated in fistfights. He eventually became a qualified smith, and he was invited to the local mill, where Martin Hübner, a German colonist from the colony of Old Danzig, was a steward. By 1862, this German had taught Riaboshapka to read Russian, particularly the Bible. Riaboshapka conversed with German colonists who spoke both Ukrainian and Russian, and their lifestyle impressed him so much that he stopped drinking and other sinful behavior.

After the Emancipation in 1863–64, Riaboshapka went to Bessarabia to earn money as a smith. He desperately needed money because he had recently gotten married. By industry and thrift, he saved and brought some money to Liubomirka in 1867. He started to preach his new faith the same year and called his adherents "Anabaptists." Together with the local German colonists, he began spreading evangelical ideas among the local peasants. By 1880, he had become the most influential promoter of Stundism (his friends called him "the bishop of the Russian Brotherhood") and traveled throughout all the southern provinces, visiting new evangelical congregations.[20] He stopped smoking and drinking, and he soon became prosperous.

By 1886, Riaboshapka owned a large house, two smith shops, and two barns, one threshing-machine, four horses, three cows, and four heads of cattle. In addition to his own allotment of land, he rented another one. Before his exile to the Caucasus in 1893, he had become one of the richest peasants in the district.[21] In 1881, an Orthodox author portrayed him as a city dweller rather than a peasant. A mixture of Ukrainian and European fashion was evident in his dress. Meanwhile, he insisted that all changes in his appearance and conduct were the result of his own "spiritual revival" under the influence of reading the Bible. In his conversation with journalists, he emphasized that it was not the German colonists who had influenced him religiously. Only a serious reading of the Bible had changed his mind. When an Orthodox priest asked him about German financial support, he showed him his hands and said: "These are the source of my income. I am the mill engineer, and now I am building a mill for a landlord."[22] In his preaching, he always emphasized a thrifty and industrious life as a token of the Divine grace for true believers. Thus he identified the religious ethos of the Ukrainian evangelicals with their material success and prosperity. All Orthodox critics noted that the Stundists became the wealthiest and most prosperous peasants in the Ukrainian villages where they lived.[23]

The Shalaput and Stundist movements attracted the most active, educated, and ambitious peasants, including the migrants to the cities, ex-soldiers and tramps. A common feature of "the peasant theologians" of the Ukrainian countryside was that many of them began their career as displaced peasants and lived as vagrants traveling from place to place, as had the founding fathers of Ukrainian Stundism.[24] Iakov Koval', a leader of the radical Stundists from Chaplinka also went through period of vagrancy before he settled as a shepherd in his village. He was famous among his neighbors for his ability to persuade people. Through his connections with other peasant Shalaputs, he brought to Stundism a strong "spiritualist" trend. When he joined the local Stundist community, he became the most popular leader among the Chaplinka dissidents. He was also known for his antiritualism. To protest against the Orthodox establishment, he cut the eyes from his icon of Saint Nicholas and put the icon with holes as a scarecrow in his orchard. Thereby, Koval' symbolically rejected the images of the ruling church and behaved like the leader of "iconoclasts" who had rebelled against both the Orthodox Church in the Byzantine Empire and the Roman Catholic Church in Western Europe. Such leaders as Koval' connected the Shalaput phase of this peasant religious dissent with the Stundist one.[25]

The peasants with displaced identities were more likely to become the activists of religious dissent. For many of them, the Protestantism of the new sects also meant social mobility. According to A. D. Ushinskii, by 1884 in the province of Kiev there were three categories of Stundists: (1) the "pioneers," who were persecuted by the police, and who considered their religious activities as their career; (2) the curious and inquisitive, who wished to study religion and understand Holy Scripture; and (3) the discontented, who tried to improve their lives and who used their dissident communities as a means for gaining emotional and material comfort.[26]

The modernization of Russian society, including that of the Russian army, contributed to the spread of new ideas and new cultural forms among peasants. This experience laid the foundation for an oppositional discourse among the rural population as well. Ushinskii and other Orthodox observers noted the role of retired soldiers, who returned to their villages and became dissident activists after finishing their military service. Literacy and exposure to the new cultural influences in the Russian army (after the military reforms of the 1870s) contributed to the formation of a new outlook and mentality among peasants who became soldiers. They combined a critical approach to the problems of their daily lives as retired soldiers with their new interests, including reading the Bible and newspapers.[27]

By the 1890s, the most prominent and intelligent leaders among the peasant dissenters (both Shalaputs and Stundists) were the retired soldiers. In 1893, the Holy Synod of the Russian Orthodox Church began a special investigation of the role of retired soldiers in the spread of Stundism. According to the data from this investigation, more than one third of all Stundist activists were soldiers who returned to their villages after their military service in the newly reformed army.[28] During the 1890s, more than 20 percent of the Shalaput and Stundist leaders in the Ukrainian provinces were former soldiers of the Russian army.[29]

From the very beginning of Ukrainian Stundism, even the Orthodox press described the new peasant dissidents in positive terms. Orthodox journalists contrasted the "good morality," "sobriety," and diligence of the Stundist peasants with "the prevalent alcoholism all over the countryside." Conservative Russian intellectuals understood that the literacy and industry of Stundists were elements of social, economic, and cultural progress. During the first decades of Stundism, they still thought about the incorporation of Stundists into the mainstream of Orthodoxy as the most religious peasants.[30] One Orthodox author noted that the success of Stundism and its attractiveness to local peasants resulted from the Stundist requirement for a "virtuous, honest, sober and industrious life."[31] Even opponents of the evangelical movement had to acknowledge in 1880 that peasant Stundism was "a considerable step forward compared with the ignorant and superstitious mass of our peasantry."[32] It is

213

noteworthy that the initiative in persecuting the Stundists was taken by the Orthodox clergy rather than by the police. At the outset, the clergy had hopes about the return of the dissidents to the church. Some of the Orthodox priests even praised the revival of religious piety among the local peasants. But when they realized that the Stundist peasants were persisting in their dissent and did not want to repent, they turned to the police for criminal persecution.

The local administration and police praised the morality and virtuous lifestyle of the Stundist peasants at the outset. In January 1875, the prosecutor from the Odessa district sent a special report to the Ministry of Justice in which he defended Stundist peasants and accused the local Orthodox clergy of ignorance regarding their religious needs. He noted that "the best, the most intelligent and industrious peasants were joining the Stundist movement."[33] The governor of Kherson province also cited positive features of the movement and explained this as a natural reaction of the "intelligent part of peasantry" to the corruption and ignorance of the Orthodox priests.[34] No reports of crime can be found in the province of Kiev in localities with strong Stundist influence after the arrival of Stundism in 1870.[35]

On August 24, 1903, in his letter to the Ministry of the Interior, the governor general of Kiev, Volynia, and Podolia praised the Ukrainian Stundo-Baptists as well. He insisted that all the Stundist peasants from Volynia could speak, read, and write not only in their native Ukrainian but also in "good literary Russian." Their talented activists composed prayers following the text of Holy Scripture, and they used the melodies of the folk songs or composed their own melodies for hymns. Some of them were musically literate and even used sheet music for their ceremonies. The governor general denied all accusations that Stundists had been involved in antigovernment activities. Moreover, he noted in his letter, "The fact that besides their prayers the Stundists read the chapters twelve and thirteen from the epistle of Paul the Apostle to the Romans proves that the first priorities in their teaching are obedience, meekness, and loyalty to the authority and the law."[36] In Volynia, the Stundists were considered "the most obedient taxpayers, sober and industrious peasants, and overall, the most peaceful and easy to get on with settlers, who did not create the problems either for the court or for the local administration."[37]

In 1877, a popular Russian newspaper presented a stereotype of Ukrainian Stundism, which was shared by the liberal portion of the Russian readership:

> Stundists are notable for their enterprise, love for work, persistence and energy in pursuit of their economic goals and tasks, as either workers or manufacturers. The Stundists respect work so much that they reject any kind of pleasure, even a slight one, which they consider a waste of time. . . . Although they reject decorations and luxury, Stundists at the same time appreciate everything beneficial to life. For instance, nearly every Stundist (even the poorest one) strives to get a watch and then, with purely German exactness, tries to plan his time and activity according to his watch. Stundists demonstrate the same attitude toward their comfortable and warm clothes. Stundists borrow their clothing styles (jackets, cloth trousers, high boots, etc.) from their teachers, Germans, and this imitating of Germans has reached a point of real pedantry.[38]

Four years later, the Orthodox Church newspaper of Kherson province expressed it more categorically: "Stundists are *those who imitate the Germans* in every manifestation of their life" (emphasis added).[39] It was remarkable that both conservative and liberal authors noted the fact of imitation among the Stundist peasants, who constructed their distinct identity based on the religious ethos of German Protestants (figures 4.1 and 4.2).[40]

The Ukrainian Stundist did not behave like a "normal" Russian Orthodox peasant. He neither drank nor smoked. He did not beat his wife and children. He read the Bible and other literature himself. His European dress and hair cut distinguished him, as his uncommon friendliness with various "religious Others," including Germans, Mennonites, and Jews. In fact, he imitated their "alien" lifestyle. In short, the Ukrainian Stundists had a completely different image, appearing more like European farmers than Russian Orthodox peasants. The Ukrainian Stundists called themselves "a brotherhood of God's friends," "evangelical Christians," or "Anabaptists," to distinguish themselves from their Orthodox opponents. "We separated from you [the Orthodox Christians]," they told the Russian priest, "because your people live very badly, drink alcohol, steal, lead a depraved life of debauchery and lust, don't follow biblical principles, and do many other sinful things. Our people lead a virtuous life.   215

Figure 4.1. A Ukrainian Stundist peasant village woman. From John Brown, *The Stundists: The Story of a Great Religious Revolt* (London, 1893), 1.

We follow what God said once to His people, 'Let My People separate from sinful people who broke My Law,' and therefore we separated ourselves from you."[41]

According to the memoirs of Tymofii Zaiats, a Stundist peasant from the village of Skibentsy, a "new believer" usually began "the construction" of his own personality by rejecting of all traditional habits and customs of peasant life. "Your first duty is to quit drinking vodka; the second duty is to give up smoking tobacco; the third duty is to stop treating each other with alcohol

Figure 4.2. A Ukrainian
Stundist peasant artisan
and his son. From John
Brown, *The Stundists: The
Story of a Great Religious
Revolt* (London, 1893), 1.

[offering vodka for any occasion]; the fourth duty is to stop swearing; the fifth
duty is to stop stealing; the sixth duty is to quit double-dealing; the seventh
duty is to stop killing and hurting people."[42] In the beginning of their search
for a true religion, Stundist peasants (like Tymofii Zaiats himself) followed
literally all the rules of the Orthodox Church and tried to excel as Orthodox

Christians in their religious piety and zeal. Only after they became personally disappointed with the "insufficiency" of the religious services and "sinful" life of Russian Orthodox communities did the Stundists reach their "highest point" of rejection. From then on, the zealous Stundists and Orthodox Christians were the worst enemies.

The Stundists peasants changed the symbolic elements of everyday life. They put their instruments and tools in the so-called red corner (the sacred, honorable position) of their house instead of Orthodox icons, and in doing so demonstrated their rationality. They placed the Bible (and a text of the New Testament, in particular) in the important central position in their home, usually on a decorated linen napkin in the center of the desk where everyone had easy access to it (figures 4.3 and 4.4). One correspondent for the Orthodox newspaper described his impressions after his first visit to Levko Lieber, the Stundist preacher in the village of Luchina in the Skvira district of Kiev province. He wrote: "On a wall where peasants usually keep the sacred icons, I saw various carpenter's tools: a saw, planes, and other instruments. Different religious books were left on the table and apparently were read with great respect." The author was surprised when he found all the pages in the Stundist's Bible covered with Levko's dense handwriting, giving comments on the content of the biblical text.[43]

Stundist communities changed the lifestyle of their villages and offered new priorities to their Orthodox neighbors. In some localities, they eradicated hard drinking and introduced a new culture of reading. Before 1878 in the village of Liubomirka (in Kherson province), a center of Ukrainian Stundism, there were two taverns (*kabak*), and the local peasants spent all their free time there drinking vodka and smoking tobacco. But after 1878, the peasants, who had joined the Stundist community ("more than a half of the village households belonged to the sect"), stopped visiting the taverns and petitioned the local administration to close them.

As a result of this initiative, the taverns were closed. After this, using the money they had saved because of the closing of the taverns, the Stundists bought a fire engine for their village. Moreover, the Stundist community collected 100 rubles every year to buy books for the local school. The Liubomirka

Figure 4.3. The interior of the house of a Ukrainian evangelical peasant. From the collection of the Dniepropetrovsk State Historical Museum, Ukraine.

Stundists sent their children to this school and supplied the school and teachers with everything they needed. According to a journalist who visited Liubomirka in 1880, the school library was one of the best he had ever seen in the Ukrainian countryside. The library's collection included not only religious literature approved by the Orthodox censorship but also books on history, nature, geography, and science. Because of the Stundists' support, the school had good, modern equipment, furniture, and maps. Indeed, the entire lifestyle of the Liubomirka peasants changed. Their behavior became more rational; they read newspapers, and they tried to introduce the innovations they had learned about into their everyday life.[44]

All observers noted the new work ethic among the dissident peasants, who were honest and kept their promises. They took fewer holidays and worked more than their Orthodox neighbors. Their achievements in agriculture were more impressive than those of their Orthodox counterparts. They became

219

Figure 4.4. The exterior of the house of an evangelical peasant in Ekaterinoslav province at the end of the nineteenth century. From the collection of the Dniepropetrovsk State Historical Museum, Ukraine.

prosperous farmers. Part of their success resulted from their temperance campaign (the normal Orthodox peasant spent more than one third of his budget on vodka).[45] During the public trial of the Kherson Stundists in 1878, all their Orthodox neighbors praised their lifestyle. One Orthodox witness told the court that the Stundist peasants "lead virtuous lives, they do not steal and do not drink alcohol." Another Orthodox peasant explained to the judge that it was impossible "to find bad people" among the Stundists. "I can say only good things about them," he continued, "There are neither thieves nor drunkards among them. Moreover, anybody who was alcoholic or criminal after joining the sect would be transformed into a virtuous person."[46]

The peasant dissidents themselves understood the social and cultural significance of their virtuous lifestyle for Russian society. In February 1886, in their petition to the governor of Kherson province, the Stundo-Baptists from the village of Ingul asked for permission to establish a meeting for worship. In a logical manner, they tried to explain their usefulness for the Russian state and society:

> We spend our free time with our families, praying for our Tsar and reading religious books. So we contribute to strong family relations, to order and discipline in the countryside. Meanwhile, our Orthodox brothers spend their free time in the bars drinking alcohol fighting each other and disturbing people. They waste their savings on vodka and tobacco and as a result are unable to pay taxes, whereas we save money and pay the state taxes on time. The majority of the Orthodox peasants are poor, and they ask for state support and assistance. We have no poor members because we support all those who need help. As a result, we do not ask for state support. Moreover, we try to strengthen the state and provide it with virtuous, literate, and loyal citizens, who will be "good family men and women," useful members of the society, true patriots of their country, and loyal subjects of the crown.[47]

Stundism had a particular appeal for women. In a conversation with an Orthodox missionary, a peasant woman who had joined the Stundist village community in the province of Kiev tried to explain how Stundism improved family life. "I don't want to quit Stundism," she said, "because the new faith led our husbands to a new life." She explained that before joining Stundism, they drank vodka and beat their wives and children. Because of such drinking problems, many peasant families lost their savings and land. "When my Alexei (husband) joined the Stunda," she continued, "we began a new life":

> Vodka, quarrels, fights, bad language, and all misery disappeared from our life. Instead of vodka, we are drinking now tea with sweets. We spend our free time reading the New Testament and praying. Our children are fond of reading the religious books. They don't go to the streets where their Orthodox classmates use bad language and smoke tobacco. In contrast to the Orthodox peasants, we and our children understand the Gospels and religious rituals. Our Orthodox peasant neighbors always drink on holidays and do not care about their families. Moreover, they were ignorant of religious theory and practice. When they visit the church, they stand like poles and do not understand either liturgy or readings from the Bible.[48]

221

These comments explain the popularity of the new dissent among Ukrainian peasant women. Stundism brought changes in the Ukrainian peasant family as well. Stundist peasants treated wives and children differently, and respect became a criterion for family relations. What struck Orthodox observers, however, was the lack of hierarchy in the Stundist family. The Stundist father behaved as equal to the women and children in his family, while in Orthodox families "the father was feared by everyone." The Stundist altered the patriarchal way of life and introduced a new, more liberal and democratic pattern into the Ukrainian village. Stundist women became active and conscious participants in local religious communities, in contrast to Orthodox women. The Stundist's wife was "his helpmate and bosom friend, with a share in his joy and trouble." One Orthodox observer gave this description of a Stundist wife and family:

> She was his sister in the assembly for worship. Her voice may be heard there in praise or prayer. She sits down with him at the same Lord's Table, and, with equal rights acknowledged before God, and the Stundist husband would never think of curtailing her rights or slighting her position in his own household. It rarely happens that a Stundist inflicts corporal punishment on his children. The law of love is the law of his home.

According to this idealized portrayal, Stundist women even organized their meetings, where they discussed problems of female members of Stundist communities.[49] According to the comments of Orthodox missionaries, the Stundist communities represented a positive example for Ukrainian and Russian peasants because "sectarians live like members of one family and in this regard they serve as an exemplary model of brotherly relations, help each other by advice and in a material way, and in their contacts they are tender and cordial."[50] The Stundists created a system of mutual peasant assistance. They supported their coreligionists and the most impoverished peasants in the village. They considered it a Christian principle of their life to help those most in need.[51]

The most important economic and cultural contribution of the Stundist religious ethos to the development of the Ukrainian countryside, however, was the spread of a new culture of the written word. The written, memorized word of Holy Scripture became the center of Stundist peasant culture. How to correctly read and comprehend the sacred word of the Bible were the main concerns of every Stundist community. As a result, the Stundists became the first peasant teachers and organizers of the new peasant schools in the Ukrainian provinces. From the very beginning of Ukrainian Stundism, the main concern of peasant dissenters was their illiteracy. Therefore, they supported existing primary schools and established their own schools. The Ukrainian Stundists became the first peasants to create their own system of religious education in the southern Russian Empire. Their schools were the first in the Ukrainian countryside to be founded by the peasants themselves.

In November 1886, responding to a complaint from the local priest, a police officer from the Chigirin district of Kiev province closed the Stundist peasant school in the village of Topilovka. As the police investigation discovered, before 1885 all the Stundist children had gone to the local Orthodox primary school and had read the Psalter and other religious books in the Church Slavonic language. But the Stundist parents were disappointed with the Orthodox school and especially with the obligatory reading in Slavonic. They considered such an education to be a waste of time. They explained to their Orthodox neighbors that teaching and reading in Russian was easier, more useful, and more intelligible for peasant children than an education based on Church Slavonic. As a result, the Stundists took their children out of the Orthodox primary school and organized their own peasant school in Topilovka. Their activists opened this school in 1885 in Nikita Dynda's big house and invited Dem'ian Nedal'chenko, a literate peasant from Topilovka and a member of the local Stundist congregation, to teach.

Over the course of a year, Nedal'chenko taught the basics of Russian by reading the Gospels to peasant children from both Stundist and Orthodox families. When the police closed the school at the end of 1886, there were nineteen students, including one Orthodox boy. The police confiscated fourteen copies of a textbook on Russian elementary grammar and copies of the Gospels in the Russian vernacular. But they were unable to open a criminal case against the Stundists, because all the confiscated books had been published with the permission of the state censor.[52]

The Stundist "reformation" was a "cultural revolution" among the Ukrainian peasants. Local Stundists took care of the schools in their villages. In the village of Karlovka in the province of Kherson, they collected money and bought new books for the local primary school. A part of this new collection was the books sent from evangelicals in Saint Petersburg and the German colonies. The local administration, however, fired the teacher of the primary school when it discovered that she had assigned the students evangelical literature as their homework. Half of the students in the Karlovka primary school were children of local Stundists. The Stundists then decided to organize their own school. They established a Sunday school and invited the children from Orthodox families to come. The local Stundist peasants taught in this school, which became popular among the peasants from neighboring villages as well.[53] But under pressure from the local Orthodox clergy, the local police raided Stundist villages and closed their schools.[54]

Stundist activists were pioneers in establishing a system of kindergarten and elementary education for poor children in the Ukrainian provinces. The first Stundist kindergarten was recorded in 1899–1903 in the city of Kiev.[55] In March 1899, Iulia Karpinskaia, the widow of a military officer, asked the city administration for permission to open "people's kindergartens, which would take care of religious, moral, and physical education of the children from the poorest families of Kiev; and for this purpose these kindergartens would use simple games and handicrafts that would be easily understood by the small children."[56] One of her ideas was that her kindergartens could protect the morality of children from poor families, saving them from the dangerous influences of city streets.

The first complaint about Iulia Karpinskaia came in September 1899 from an educational official in the city administration. He reported to his superiors that Karpinskaia had no degree in education and, therefore, was not allowed to establish elementary schools. Meanwhile, she collected money from the inhabitants in Kiev and established three kindergartens with 200 children. The main concern of this official was that, without permission from the education department, Karpinskaia had hired Jewish teachers to teach in her kindergartens. More than half of her students were Christians, and the rest were Jews.[57] This case again linked Stundists and Jews and exposed the friendly relations between them.

A more serious complaint came from the Orthodox clergy. In March 1902, the Metropolitan of Kiev and Galicia reported to the Holy Synod that Karpinskaia had joined the Stundist sect in Kiev in 1900. According to his report, she had decided to unite all evangelical groups in the province of Kiev, including the Stundists, into one movement. That was why she had opened the elementary schools in Kiev and used them as meeting places for various dissidents. The most important meeting place for Stundists was her kindergarten on Predslavinskaia Street, where she taught the Gospels and invited Stundists to instruct the children. Under pressure from the Orthodox clergy, the police closed the three kindergartens. Then Iulia Karpinskaia opened another kindergarten without permission from the authorities. She invited talented peasants from the Ukrainian countryside to teach and work as tutors in her kindergarten. The most famous peasant teacher was Valentina Kukolenko, a peasant woman who was literate enough to teach the Gospels and the Russian language in Karpinskaia's kindergarten.[58] As we can see, the Stundist schools became examples of collaboration between intellectuals and peasants, and were a foundation for an evangelical education in Kiev and other localities of Ukraine.

The local administration sent the case to the court in June 1901. The court fined Karpinskaia and ordered her to close her school. But she resisted and did not want to obey the court's decision. Notwithstanding the persecutions and heavy fines, her kindergarten stayed open until the end of 1902. A police officer reported that in 1902 there were thirty-four boys and thirty-two girls of ages seven to twelve years. He wrote:

> The majority of these children came from very poor families. The school had no established rules of admittance or education. The children of all classes were admitted free of charge there. The school has classes of divinity, where they read Holy Scripture, and classes in reading and writing, where they teach children the basics of the Russian language.

In her kindergarten, Karpinskaia taught the Gospels to children from dissident families, and another teacher supervised the reading of the Bible for

225

children from Orthodox families. Four other teachers, all of them Stundist peasant women, taught needlework and handicrafts. Most popular among the smallest children, according the police officer, were lessons in "how to make artificial flowers, baskets, rugs, and handbags from pieces of cloth."[59] The policeman emphasized the useful and practical subjects in the elementary school. Such subjects obviously corresponded to the religious ethos of Ukrainian evangelicals, with their orientation toward the rational and practical elements of education.[60]

Various educated participants in the evangelical movement also promoted educational experiments that seem to coincide with Weber's "Protestant ethic." The Russian Molokans and Dukhobors organized religious schools with their own curriculum in their settlements. Mennonites and German colonists developed Protestant principles for their schools in the German colonies. Finally, the followers of Leo Tolstoy created their own system of practical education for peasant schools.[61] The Stundo-Baptists from the southern Russian provinces collaborated with these and other educated participants in the evangelical movement. In 1883, in the province of Tavrida, Nikolai Gorinovich, a former Russian revolutionary, who had joined the evangelical circle of Colonel V. Pashkov, visited Molokan villages and Stundist communities and taught their children. At the same time V. G. Pavlov, a Russian Baptist from the Caucasus, and Zinovii Zakharov, a leader of the Neo-Molokans, joined Gorinovich and organized in one Molokan village a common meeting for worship. All the local evangelicals participated and sent their children to Gorinovich's school. [62]

As a result of such experiences, Stundist peasants contributed to the pedagogical experiments of Russian intellectuals who opposed the tsarist educational establishment. At the same time, by developing a culture of reading and practical schooling, the Stundists, who by 1900 made up a significant part of the rural population in the provinces of Kherson and Kiev, contributed to the modernization of the Ukrainian countryside and to the formation of "human capital," in the sense of skills, education, and various rational social practices.[63]

Stundist peasant activists represented a new generation of Ukrainian peasants, who through intensive reading, memorizing, and discussing of Holy Scripture developed new mental abilities. In their disputes with their religious opponents, including Orthodox missionaries and local clergy, they demonstrated not only their higher moral standards but also their natural intellectual aptitude for generating new ideas and cultural forms.[64] The peasant evangelicals (both Shalaputs and Stundists) not only tried to modernize the Russian and Ukrainian countryside; they also sought to restore respect for human dignity by forming a new mentality as literate and progressive farmers. Unfortunately, the repression initiated by the Orthodox Church prevented these popular versions of modernization from developing and flourishing.

Notes

1 On the Weberian sociology of religion and social history, see Sergei Zhuk, "Max Weber i sotsial'naia istoria," *Voprosy istorii,* nos. 2–3 (1992): 172–77; and Zhuk, "Max Weber et l'histoire des religions: 'la sociologie weberienne de la religion' est-elle productive pour l'historiographie contemporaine?" in *Etre catholique—Etre orthodoxe—Etre protestant: Confessions et identities culturelles en Europe medievale et moderne. Etudes reunites et publies par Marek Derwich et Mikhail. Dmitriev* (Wroclaw: LARHCOR, 2003), 39–64. See also the debate about Russian Old Believers and sects: Robert Crummey, "Old Belief as Popular Religion: New Approaches," *Slavic Review* 52, no. 4 (1993): 700–12; Laura Engelstein, *Castration and the Heavenly Kingdom: A Russian Folktale* (Ithaca, N.Y., 1999); Alexander Etkind, "Russian Sects Still Seem Obscure," *Kritika: Explorations in Russian and Eurasian History* 2, no. 1 (2001): 165–81; and Eugene Clay, "Review of *Khlyst* by Aleksandr Etkind (Moscow, 1998)," *Kritika: Explorations in Russian and Eurasian History* 2, no. 2 (2001): 445–50.

2 Rossiiskii gosudarstvennyi istoricheskii arkhiv (hereafter RGIA), f. 796, op. 165 (1884–85), d. 1692, l. 17, 18; f. 796, op. 168, d. 1394, l. 3, 6.

3 RGIA, f. 797, op. 51, 2 otd. 3 st., d. 81, l. 7–7ob., 10, 12–12ob.

4 Vasil'kovka was a village in the Pavlograd district of the province of Ekaterinoslav; *Ekaterinoslavkie eparkhial'nye vedomosti,* (hereafter EkEV), 1886, no. 18, 456–63.

5 *EkEV,* 1886, no. 18, 456–63. On the "Holy Fools" in Russian culture, see Ewa M. Thompson, *Understanding Russia: The Holy Fool in Russian Culture* (Lanham, Md., 1987).

6 RGIA, f. 796, op. 165 (1884–85), d. 1692, l. 8–8ob.

7 RGIA, f. 796, op. 165 (1884–85), d. 1692, l. 1–1ob., 8ob., 9–12, 14ob., 17–17ob. Due to the local priests' request, the police began their investigation in Ekaterinoslav province and seized books and other religious objects at Shalaput households. It turned out that Orthodox publishing houses had printed all these books, and all religious objects were of Orthodox origin as well. The peasant dissenters established their connections with the Orthodox monks and invited itinerant "God's fools" [*iurodivyie*], who lived at the Orthodox monasteries, to visit Shalaput communities in the province of Ekaterinoslav. The provincial administration was confused about how to tell religious peasants from sectarians. Shalaput peasants looked like overzealous Orthodox Christians, like "Orthodox Puritans,"

who wanted to restore the "purity" of original Orthodoxy. All their rituals and ideas were of Orthodox origin. On November 4, 1880, during the major trial of the Ekaterinoslav Shalaputs, the Odessa court vindicated the Novomoskovsk peasants "not finding any serious evidence of their religious dissent." See RGIA, f. 796, op. 165 (1884–85), d. 1692, l. 19–26.

8 In official documents Duplii was called either Piotr or Pavel in Russian, because the church records assigned his name to these Christian saints, his protectors; see Dniepropetrovs'kyi derzhavnyi oblasnyi arkhiv (hereafter DDOA), f. 11, op. 1, d. 61/62, l. 1–3. Varvara Iasevich-Borodaevskaia used the name Piotr; see V. Iasevich-Borodaevskaia, *Bor'ba za veru: Istoriko-bytovye ocherki i obzor zakonodatel'stva po staroobriadchestvu i sektantstvu v ego posledovatel'nom razvitii s prilozheniem statei zakona i vysochaishikh ukazov* (Saint Petersburg, 1912), 222. In 1881, the author of the first publication about Duplii used mistakenly the name Ivan; see *Zaria*, no. 13 (1881): 4. Duplii's neighbors called him Pavlo (or Petro) in Ukrainian. I will use the name Pavel, because Duplii called himself Pavlo in Ukrainian.

9 Nevertheless, the local police and clergy insisted on banning religious meetings in the houses of pious peasants such as Duplii; RGIA, f. 797, op. 37, d. 107, l. 4–7ob. During the 1860s, many pious peasants, after visiting Orthodox monasteries, tried to establish their own patterns of Orthodoxy and organize meetings for worship in their houses. E.g., in 1866 the peasant Ivan Nechai organized a group analogous to Duplii's sect in the village of Blagodatnoe in the district of Mariupol'. *EkEV*, 1886, no. 23, 593–99.

10 The following portrayal of Duplii's personality is based on the police report of March 1, 1877: DDOA, f. 11, op. 1, d. 61–62, l. 3–7.

11 Iasevich-Borodaevskaia, *Bor'ba za veru*, 181–82. The appearance of Priadivka was reminiscent of Geneva at the time of Calvin's reforms.

12 DDOA, f. 11, op. 1, d. 61/62, l. 4; Iasevich-Borodaevskaia, *Bor'ba za veru*, 185–86. Journalists wrote that Duplii was illiterate; see *Zaria*, no. 13 (1881): 4, and *Otechestvennye zapiski* (hereafter *OZ*), 1882, no. 10, 166–67. At the same time, the police officer and Iasevich-Borodaevskaia noted the Duplii's ability to make extensive precise quotations from Holy Scripture. They assumed that he could at least read the printed text.

13 Max Weber, *The Protestant Ethic and the Spirit of Capitalism* (Los Angeles, 1998), 27, 165–66, 171, 172, 180.

14 The citation is from William Penn, *Works*, 2 vols. (London, 1726), vol. 1, 295, 296. Compare this with the comments of a Quaker historian: "The Quakers adopted the New Testament ethic of the Anabaptists [who withdrew from the 'wicked world' into their own communities which were regarded as oases in the midst of the wilderness of sin], but instead of rejecting the gross world of human appetites and passions, insisted that it was the material out of which the Kingdom of God was to be fashioned. This combination of the ethical position of the Anabaptists with the Calvinist attitude towards the material world was the distinctive feature of Quaker social thought"; Frederick B. Tolles, *Meeting House and Counting House: The Quaker Merchants of Colonial Philadelphia, 1682–1763* (Chapel Hill, N.C., 1948), 53.

15 Max Weber, *The Sociology of Religion,* trans. Ephraim Fischoff, with an introduction by Talcott Parsons (London, 1965; 1st pr., 1963), 166, 167, 168, 177. He wrote about inner-worldly asceticism: "The unique concentration of human behavior on activities leading to salvation may require the participation within the world (or more precisely: within the institutions of the world but in opposition to them) of the religious individual's idiosyncratically sacred religious mood and his qualifications as the elect instrument of god. This is inner-worldly asceticism. . . . The order of the world in which the ascetic is situated becomes for him a vocation, which he must fulfill rationally. As a consequence, and although the enjoyment of wealth is forbidden to the ascetic, it becomes his vocation to engage in economic activity which is faithful to rationalized ethical requirements and which conforms to strict legality. If success supervenes upon acquisitive activity, it is regarded as the manifestation of god's blessing upon the labor of the pious man and of god's pleasure with his economic pattern of life. This type of inner-worldly asceticism included, above all, ascetic Protestantism, which taught the principle of loyal fulfillment of obligations within the framework of the world as the sole method of proving religious merit. . . . To the extent that an inner-worldly religion of salvation is determined by distinctively ascetical tendencies, the usual result is practical rationalism, in the sense of the maximization of rational action as such, the maximization of a methodical systematization of the external conduct of life, and the maximization of the rational organization and institutionalization of mundane social systems, whether monastic communities or theocracies."

16 Iasevich-Borodaevskaia, *Bor'ba za veru,* 185–86, 187; DDOA, f. 11, op. 1, d. 61/62, l. 4.

17 Iasevich-Borodaevskaia, *Bor'ba za veru,* 186.

18 DDOA, f. 11, op. 1, d. 61/62, l. 5–6, 7. Duplii was disappointed with the ingratitude of the Orthodox clergy after his community helped one of the Ekaterinoslav Orthodox cloisters financially. The peasants from Priadivka sent money and food for the local nuns. But afterward, when the cloister managed to survive using the peasants' aid, its mother superior, being afraid of Duplii's influence, accused him of dissident activities, and Duplii was arrested by the police. See also Iasevich-Borodaevskaia, *Bor'ba za veru,* 186, 188; and Ia. Abramov, "Sekta shalaputov," *OZ,* 1882, no. 9, 166–67. The local Orthodox priest, M. Zhitetskii, who reported to the police about Duplii's Shalaputstvo, was noted for his corruption and incompetence. Both the peasants and the local police complained about his cupidity and ignorance. But the diocesan administration was afraid to remove Zhitetskii from the Priadivka parish, because his son was an influential official in the Holy Synod in Saint Petersburg. See DDOA, f. 11, op. 1, d. 61/62, l. 7.

19 Weber noted, "A religious community arises in connection with a prophetic movement as a result of routinization (*Veralltaglichung*), i.e., as a result of the process whereby either the prophet himself or his disciples secure the permanence of his preaching and the congregation's distribution of grace, hence insuring the economic existence of the enterprise and those who man it, and thereby monopolizing as well the privileges reserved for those charged with religious functions"; Weber, *Sociology of Religion,* 60–61.

20 See also A. Rozhdestvenskii, *Iuzhno-russkii shtundizm* (Saint Petersburg, 1889), 72–74.   229

21 He rebuilt his new big house and he owned a big mill in the village as well. Episkop Alexii [Dorodnitsyn], *Materialy dlia istorii religiozno-ratsionalisticheskogo dvizhenia na iuge Rossii vo vtoroi polovine XIX-go veka.* (Kazan', 1908), 330–31; *Khersonskie eparkhial'nye vedomosti* (hereafter *KherEV*), 1888, no. 2, 32–35; *Chtenia v obshchestve liubitelei dukhovnogo prosveshchenia,* March 1893, 353.

22 *KherEV,* 1881, no. 8, 246–49. The revolutionary populist Lev Deich portrayed Riaboshapka in the same way. See L. G. Deich, *Za polveka* (Moscow, 1926), 170–71.

23 *Kievskie eparkhial'nye vedomosti,* (hereafter *KEV*), 1873, no. 13, 382.

24 The peasants from the village of Osnova Onishchenko and Ratushny developed their first dissident ideas and established their first relations with the Russian Shalaputs and German Pietists during their vagrancy in the southern provinces of Russia. See chapter 3.

25 To some extent, the character of Koval' fit Marxist theory of the class struggle. See such an approach in A. Klibanov, *Istoria religioznogo sektantstva v Rossii (60-e gody XIX v.— 1917 g.)* (Moscow, 1965), 216–18. For the best portrayal of Koval' in the Orthodox press and scholarship, see *KEV,* 1880, nos. 18–19, 14; A. Ushinskii, *Verouchenie malorusskikh shtundistov* (Kiev, 1883), 184–88; Rozhdestvenskii, *Iuzhno-russkii shtundizm,* 106–7. According to Russian scholars, Koval's actions looked like the "Bogomils" rebellions in mediaeval Byzantium and the Anabaptist riots in the sixteenth-century Netherlands.

26 A. Ushinskii, *O prichinakh poiavlenia ratsionalisticheskikh uchenii shtundy i nekotorykh drugikh podobnykh sekt v sel'skom pravoslavnom naselenii i o merakh protiv rasprostranenia uchenia etikh sekt* (Kiev, 1884), 32–33.

27 See John Bushnell, "Peasants in Uniform: The Tsarist Army and Peasant Society," *Journal of Social History,* 13, no. 4 (1980): 565–76.

28 RGIA, f. 797, op. 63, 2otd. 3st., d. 227, l. 13 ob.

29 These calculations are based on figures from: RGIA, f. 796, op. 174, d. 1787, l. 27–38, 59; f. 1284, op. 222 (1893), d. 41, l. 5ob.–7ob.

30 As one author noted: "If we will analyze the every day life of the Stundist households and compare their morality with the rest of peasant population, their sobriety with the prevalent alcoholism all over the countryside, and their striving for literacy, which is a necessity for them because of their religious principle to read Holy Scripture by themselves, we, of course, must admit that the Stundists are not harmful, and that they are of benefit to the country from the economic point of view; because everybody knows that hard drinking is the major evil which leads to the tremendous damage of the economic prosperity of our common folks"; *KherEV,* 1876, no. 14, 186.

31 *KEV,* 1880, no. 18–19, 12.

32 In 1880–82, the Orthodox periodical published a positive description of the local Stundists: "We see the true understanding of the main Christian rituals among the Stundists. We can find even a restoration of the ancient Christian custom of repentance among them"; *KEV,* 1880, nos. 32–33, 9; 1882, no. 16, 293.

33 A text of the report was published in: Alexii, *Materialy,* 225–37. The hierarchy of the Orthodox Church complained about such idealization of Stundism by the secular authority. See RGIA, f. 796, op. 155, d. 680, l. 12–12ob.

230

34 Alexii, *Materialy*, 260–64. He portrayed Ratushny with sympathy as "a talented and smart peasant thinker."

35 *Vera i razum*, no. 20 (1886): vol. 2, 401.

36 The governor general referred to the famous phrase of Saint Paul: "Let every soul be subject unto the higher powers. For there is no power but of God: the powers that be are ordained of God. Whosoever therefore resisteth the power, resisteth the ordinance of God: and they that resist shall receive to themselves damnation. For rulers are not a terror to good works, but to the evil" (Romans 13:1–3). The citation here is RGIA, f. 1284, op. 222, d. 29, l. 78, 96ob.–97, 99. The governor general blamed the local priests of Czech or Polish origin, who could speak neither Russian nor Ukrainian. Eventually, the Ukrainian peasants turned to the religious dissidents for the questions that these priests were unable to answer.

37 RGIA, f. 1284, op. 222, d. 29, l. 97.

38 F. A. Shcherbina, "Malorusskaya shtunda," *Nedelia*, no. 2 (1877): 58–59.

39 This is cited in Rozhdestvenskii, *Iuzhno-russkii shtundizm*, 269. John Brown, a British Congregational minister, confirmed in the 1890s this fact of imitation. "Imitating the Germans, with their flourishing little patches of fruit and flower garden," noted Brown, "he [the Ukrainian Stundist] endeavors to cleanse the yard around his cottage, to extirpate the weeds in his garden, to plant trees for shade, and use, and beauty, to rear some simple flowers that will rejoice the hearts of his children and women-folk. His standard of comparison is not his Russian neighbor, more probably he measures himself with the German colonist"; John Brown, *The Stundists: The Story of a Great Religious Revolt* (London, 1893), 66, 67.

40 The problems of the social identity of dissident peasants are discussed in chapter 6.

41 The citation is *KherEV*, 1889, nos. 14–15, 416; see also *KherEV*, 1876, no. 14, 181.

42 Skibentsy was located in the Skvira district of Kiev province. "Zapiski Timofeia Zaitsa," *Golos minuvshego*, no. 10 (1913): 149. The adherents of Leo Tolstoy, P. Biriukov, and V. Chertkov used their periodicals published abroad to promote principles of religious toleration. They published letters and other materials on the persecution of sectarians in Russia. On Chertkov, see Alexander Fodor, *A Quest for a Violent Russia: The Partnership of Leo Tolstoy and Vladimir Chertkov* (New York, 1989). The most active among Chertkov's correspondents was the Ukrainian Stundist peasant Tymofii Zaiats, who was exiled to Siberia for his non-Orthodox beliefs. In 1913, Anna Chertkova translated from Ukrainian into Russian, edited, and published the memoirs of T. Zaiats in Sytin's magazine, *Golos minuvshego*, no. 8 (1913): 152–76; no. 10 (1913): 149–74; no. 11 (1913): 162–93; and no. 12 (1913): 168–83.

43 I. Savchenkov, "Shtundisty s. Luchina, Skvirskogo uezda, Kievskoi gub.," *KEV*, 1882, no. 3, 66–67.

44 Alexei Iuzhnyi, "Na dneprovskikh porogakh i dva dnia u shtundistov," *Vestnik Evropy*, no. 7 (1881): 399–419; see especially 408–19.

45 E. R., "Russkie rathionalisty," *Vestnik Evropy*, no. 7 (1881): 318–20. The Stundists

tried to establish their own agricultural colonies with the new technology and new organization of work beginning in the 1880s. But their economic efforts were aborted by the local Orthodox clergy, who generated anti-Stundist rumors among the peasants. See about this in: *Missionerskoe obozrenie* (hereafter *MO*), 1896, March, 27–33.

46 *Golos,* no. 108 (1878); *Delo,* no. 2 (1883): 186.

47 Alexii, *Materialy,* 335–36.

48 *KEV,* 1894, no. 19, 585.

49 The citation is Brown, *Stundists,* 63–64. Brown took this description verbatim from a Russian Orthodox publication: D. Protasov, "Shtundism i razbor ego uchenia," *KherEV,* 1883, no. 22, 1016–17.

50 *MO,* July–August 1899, 103.

51 The Orthodox press interpreted cases of material assistance of the Stundists as their ideological means to attract poor peasants to Stundism. See, e.g., *KEV,* 1883, no. 6, 125–26.

52 Tsentral'nyi derzhavnyi istorychnyi arkhiv Ukrainy (hereafter TsDIAU), f. 442, op. 837, d. 24, l. 1ob.–2ob., 4ob.–50b.

53 *KherEV,* 1891, no. 18, 561–65.

54 *KherEV,* 1896, no. 17, 437. In the village of Izhitskoe in the Tiraspol' district, the police closed the Stundist primary school where the local peasant teachers taught sixteen children, including nine Orthodox and seven Stundist students.

55 TsDIAU, f. 707, op. 317, d. 77, l. 102, 103, 105, 110, 136, 143a; RGIA, f. 797, op. 72, 2otd., 3st., d. 131, l. 1–6ob.

56 RGIA, f. 797, op. 72, 2otd., 3st., d. 131, l. 5.

57 TsDIAU, f. 707, op. 317, d. 77, l. 110, 136.

58 RGIA, f. 797, op. 72, 2otd., 3st., d. 131, l. 5ob.

59 RGIA, f. 797, op. 72, 2otd., 3st., d. 131, l. 6.

60 Intellectual sympathizers tried to support the Stundist efforts in education. Evangelical intellectuals such as Karpinskaia became the organizers and the first teachers of the Stundist schools. A noble lady, a daughter of the colonel of Russian Army, Olga Zenkova, established a secret school for the children from the Stundist families in her house in Kiev in 1903. See TsDIAU, f. 442, op. 854, d. 308, l. 1–5, 8.

61 See the comments of Lev Deich, a revolutionary who lived among the Molokans, about their emphasis on practicality and usefulness in education; L. G. Deich, *Za polveka* (Moscow, 1926), 115, 118. The Pashkovites, the Russian intellectual followers of the Colonel Pashkov, tried to bring their own interpretation of practical education to the Russian countryside. On Pashkov, see S. Nesdoly, "Evangelical Sectarianism in Russia: A Study of the Stundists, Baptists, Pashkovites, and Evangelical Christians, 1855–1917" (Ph.D. dissertation, Queens University, 1971).

62 See RGIA, f. 796, op. 164, d. 1326, l. 30–31ob. The official documents recorded many cases of such a collaboration.

63 Some scholars have characterized "human capital" as "entrepreneurial ability in acquiring information and adjusting to the disequilibria inherent in the process of mod-

ernization." See Theodore W. Schultz, *Investing in People: The Economics of Population Quality* (Berkeley, Calif., 1981), 23.

64 The police reports and documents of the Orthodox Church confirmed the fact of the unique mental abilities of the Stundist peasants. See, e.g., a portrayal of the intellectual abilities and moral standards of Vasilii Orda, the Stundist activist from the province of Poltava; RGIA, f. 1284, op. 222 (1894), d. 31, l. 1ob.–4.0

Peasant Theologians and the Protestant Ethic

5 The Stundo-Shalaputs, or the Maliovantsy

The last phase in the evangelical movement began at the end of the 1880s as the Stundist peasants' reaction to the institutionalization of the Stundo-Baptist faith. The first meeting of the German Baptists and leaders of the Ukrainian Stundists took place in 1882 in the German colony of Rikenau. A year later, Colonel V. Pashkov, Baron M. Korff, and other Russian aristocrats who shared the evangelical beliefs of the Ukrainian Stundists, tried to organize a new meeting of all evangelical activists, including German and Ukrainian Stundists, in Saint Petersburg. Eventually, on April 30 and May 1, 1884, at a meeting in the village of Novo-Vasilievka in Tavrida, these efforts to unite the evangelical groups of the Russian Empire contributed to the foundation of the All-Russian Baptist Union. The unification and formalization of Stundist theology and rituals according to the German Baptist pattern followed these contacts.[1]

The radical Stundists were disappointed, however, with the new church hierarchy and the Baptist rituals. Those influenced by the Shalaput and spiritualist trend resisted Baptist institutionalization as well. The new prophets rejected Baptist preachers and promised the imminent coming of Christ's

Kingdom. The most famous prophet of the spiritualist millennial movement among the radical Stundists was Kondrat Maliovannyi, whose adherents were called Maliovantsy by their contemporaries. The Maliovantsy and similar groups of "spiritual Christians" represented a convergence of Shalaput and Stundist religious practices and theology.

Religious enthusiasm, spirit possession, a belief in the possibility of God's incarnation in any "true believer" and the notions of Christ's personification in the leaders of the religious community were distinctive features of the Shalaput tradition. This tradition did not disappear during the Stundist stage. Shalaput elements converged with Western Protestant influences during the 1860s. The result was the appearance of the so-called spiritual Christian tendency inside Ukrainian Stundism. By the end of the 1880s, the "spiritual Christians" (or Stundo-Shalaputs) had become the most active part of the oppositional movement among the evangelical Ukrainian peasants, rebelling against the institutional structures of both the Stundo-Baptist faith and Russian Orthodoxy. Chiliasm and a millennial orientation gradually became the main characteristic of the Russian Radical Reformation. All groups of "spiritual Christians" demonstrated this orientation. At the same time, the mass police persecution of peasant evangelicals and the dissidents' frustration with the new hierarchy of the Baptist congregations contributed to the spread of chiliastic ideas in Stundist communities. The desperate dissenters, tired of the struggle with authorities, turned to millennial dreams and ecstatic rituals in the hope of reaching the Heavenly Kingdom.

In August 1888, a police officer from the Anan'iev district near Kherson reported that the Stundist peasants Feodosii Gumeniuk and Dimitrii Sosin from the village of Malaia Kodymka were spreading notions reminiscent of the radical Shalaputs. In March 1887, Gumeniuk told his neighbors during their Stundist meeting that every Christian could "become Christ the Savior" if the Holy Spirit would select him and descend on him. The Stundist community from Malaia Kodymka organized enthusiastic meetings "with dances and jumps." After 1887, they completely rejected the authority of the Baptist ministers. These Stundo-Shalaputs had their own "prophetesses," who preached about the end of time.[2] It is noteworthy that in the Malaia Kodymka's Stundo-

Shalaputs stressed the authority of the individual, in contrast to the Orthodox and Baptist hierarchy. Like the first Shalaputs, the new religious enthusiasts elevated women to positions of leadership in their communities. By the late 1880s, Shalaput religious practices had emerged among the Stundists from the village of Timoshevka. In April 1891, a parish priest from that village discovered the connection between a group of twenty-five peasants, who had recently converted to the Stundo-Baptist faith, and the local Shalaputs. As it turned out, the secret Shalaput movement still existed in Timoshevka, and the new Stundist activists came from the Shalaput neighborhood in the village. Moreover, some of them belonged to famous Shalaput families.[3]

Such a convergence of Shalaput and Stundist religious practices took place all over the southern provinces at the beginning of the 1890s. In August 1895, the Holy Synod received information about an unusual Stundist sect in the village of Kebabcha in the Akkerman district of Bessarabia province. In the early 1890s, Vasilii and Feoktist Dreval', two brothers from Kebabcha, organized a Stundist meeting in their house. They told local peasants that they had been "ordained" by the Holy Spirit and that they were to represent God in their community. Vasilii explained that God ordered all angels in heaven to worship him as a Divine prophet, "as a new saint."

According to Vasilii, "the true religious meeting" was supposed to involve ecstatic prayer, singing, and dancing, after which "all believers, who would become tired from the religious exertions, would fall to the ground, and angels would guide their souls to heaven, where they would see hell and paradise." The Dreval' brothers and their preacher Dimitrii Mukhin (Rybkin) taught local peasants that "everybody who does good deeds and does not sin will become God Jesus Christ." It is noteworthy that members of the Kebabcha Stundist meeting did not separate from the Orthodox Church and read only Orthodox religious books. The police did not discover any Baptist influence among these Stundists. An Orthodox missionary, Ioann Strel'bitskii, who was called in as an expert for this case, described the Dreval' brothers and Mukhin as "sectarian-Stundists with the traces of Khlyst influence."[4] During the 1890s, Orthodox experts began using the name of "Stundo-Khlyst" (or Stundo-Shalaput) to describe the new groups of "spiritual Christians."

239

Kondrat Maliovannyi and His Movement

"Stundo-Khlyst," or "Stundo-Shalaput" sects, as we call them here, became the most typical expression of the Russian "radical reformation" during the 1890s. The best known and documented of such groups was the Maliovantsy in the province of Kiev. Iakov Koval's preaching in the Tarashcha district starting in the late 1870s prepared the ground for a more radical and spiritual interpretation of Holy Scripture among local evangelical communities. Among those who were attracted by the evangelical preaching of the radical Stundists was Kondrat (or Kondratii) Maliovannyi, a peasant wheelwright from town of Tarashcha. He joined the local Stundist community in 1884.

During the 1890s, Maliovannyi became the central figure in a new dissident movement among Ukrainian peasants in the province of Kiev. This movement, called the Maliovantsy, reflected the peasants' disappointment with the formalism and "institutionalization" of the Stundo-Baptist faith in the 1880s. The Maliovantsy also returned to the practices and ideas of the early Russian radical reformation. In its theology, rituals, and consequent effects, this movement was reminiscent of British Quakerism during the middle of the seventeenth century.[5] From his birth, Maliovannyi was doomed to suffering and humiliation.[6] He was born in 1845 in Tarashcha to Efrosinia Maliovannaya, a poor peasant widow. She had had a love affair after her husband's death, which resulted in Maliovannyi's illegitimate birth. All the neighbors despised him, and the children beat him. As a result, he lived in isolation, because as an illegitimate child he was not allowed to play with other children. His mother often went to the province of Kherson in search of work and left him with her sister in Tarashcha.

As Maliovannyi grew older, he tried to help his mother and aunt in their poor household. Each summer, he went to the forest to pick mushrooms for their family. He was so successful in his search of mushrooms that the neighbors called him a magician. Both his sympathizers and opponents noted his unusual mental abilities and kindness. He loved nature and always helped people, including those who humiliated and hurt him. When he was thirteen years of age, he began his apprenticeship at the local wheelwright shop. But his mother soon took him away and brought him to the city of Odessa. She hoped for a better life in the city with its many jobs. He became an apprentice to an Armenian barber. Instead of instructing him in the new profession, however, his new master exploited, beat, and humiliated him. He could not stand the daily beatings, and he asked his mother to take him from the Armenian household. She brought him home, and he resumed his previous apprenticeship at the wheelwright shop. He succeeded in his trade so well that by the age of twenty-two he had become a well-established craftsman with his own wheelwright shop and a good reputation in Tarashcha.

At this time, Maliovannyi began his search for Divine truth. He wanted to find the reasons for social injustice and to explain "the order of the world." In the early 1870s, he learned of new popular prophets in the province of Kherson.[7] He sought out these prophets, who were preachers of "spiritual Christianity." They advised him to repent and read the Bible. Conversations with them convinced him that he had to continue his search for Divine truth. After returning from the province of Kherson to Tarashcha, he experienced the influence of the Holy Spirit for the first time. Walking in the forest, he felt as if lightning had descended in his heart. From then on, he knew that he was the Savior and the Light. He would be resurrected again to be crucified for all the sins of humankind. He realized that he been elected by God to save "the truth which was humiliated and oppressed," and at the same time to release the human soul from the bondage of sins.

In his memoirs, Maliovannyi used various images of Ukrainian folklore, mixed with biblical symbols, to show how important the new revelations were for him. Under the influence of the Spirit, he was led to believe that God created people as free and equal human beings. Now he saw his mission as one of saving humankind and restoring Divine Truth on the Earth. But he still hesitated about his future life. He tried to find the answer in the Orthodox Church, but the local priests did not want to help him. Instead, they treated his curiosity as a sign of Stundism and suspected him of being a secret Stundist. As he became frustrated by their indifference and suspicions, he began drinking to forget his revelations.[8]

Eventually, in 1884, Maliovannyi began listening to other people's reading of the Bible. Although he told everyone that he was illiterate, contemporaries who met him were struck by his memory and by his perfect knowledge of the biblical text. The officer who interrogated Maliovannyi noted that he "tried to answer all the questions in good literary Russian, and what struck me most, regarding his illiteracy, was that he made the long and accurate quotations from the Gospels and Psalms with the exact chapter and line from the biblical text."[9] Maliovannyi stopped drinking and joined the local Stundo-Baptist congregation in 1884. As he put it in his memoirs, he "took the Old Testament man from his soul and put the New Testament man in it." He knew from then on that vice ruled the world. It resulted in wars, violence, social injustice, sin, and the exploitation of human beings. Sinful people polluted and "killed" nature by destroying forests and rivers, wasting the land and resources, and killing birds, animals, and fish. He compared the blissful sinless life of the birds and plants in the forest with the vicious corrupt existence of human civilization. He felt pity and compassion for poor suffering people. Only the spiritual rebirth of all humankind based on the comprehension of Divine Wisdom, he realized, could save the world. Only a revival of spiritual life under the guidance of the Holy Spirit could help "this rebirth to the new pure life by moral self-improvement, love, good deeds, and a search for the Divine Truth."[10]

Maliovannyi began criticizing the rigid formalities and strict discipline of the Stundo-Baptists. He became an adherent of Venedikt Dushenkovskii, the charismatic leader of the "spiritual" Stundists from the neighboring village of Skibino, who practiced the Shalaput traditions of ecstatic prayer and spirit possession. His followers considered Dushenkovskii "the living Christ" and formed a group of twelve disciples who followed him everywhere, as the apostles followed Jesus in the Gospels. Dushenkovskii's wife and disciples stayed in Maliovannyi's house. After his long conversations with Dushenkovskii and his followers, he realized that the institutionalized Stundo-Baptist faith lacked the spiritual essence of primitive Christianity. In 1888 Maliovannyi, together with other coreligionists who were disappointed in their Stundist congregation, began reading the pamphlets by Pashkov.[11]

Along with Dushenkovkii's influence, Pashkov's books changed Maliovannyi's understanding of Stundism. He believed that "because of their arrogance," the Stundo-Baptists had lost "true Christian love." As he explained during his interrogation, "they [the Stundists] seemed to speak and live according to the Gospel, but in fact, they were not meek and compassionate. As it turned out, they had more arrogance in their hearts than Orthodox Christians."[12] The evolution of Maliovannyi's beliefs stemmed from the radicalization of the evangelical movement. As we see from his testimony, on the one hand, this radicalization led to a revival of ecstatic practices among radical Stundists, such as Dushenkovskii. On the other hand, the impact of educated evangelicals such as Pashkov accentuated elements of social criticism in the theology of the radical Stundists.

During 1888, Maliovannyi experienced various hallucinations. He felt his body emitting sweet, exotic smells and losing its weight. It also seemed that his body was flying in the air. After each prayer, he experienced a terrible trembling. He explained these hallucinations by the presence of the Holy Spirit in his body. According to his testimony, he saw the skies open and heard a voice calling him from above. Afterward, he felt his head separate from his body and fly up into the open skies. His body emanated a sweet smell and an unusual light. Simultaneously, bright stars were falling from the sky straight into his yard. Maliovannyi declared that all these manifestations of the Holy Spirit were signs of the Second Coming of Christ and the approaching end of the world.[13]

A comparison of Maliovannyi's experience with analogous hallucinations among the Shalaputs and other spirit-possessed enthusiasts demonstrates similarities in their religious practices. In all the famous descriptions of "spiritual Christians," such as Anglo-American Quakers and Shakers, observers noted the same stages of the Holy Spirit's revelations: loss of the body's weight, trembling (so-called quaking of the Spirit), feelings of flying, heavenly smells, and voices. As a rule, these stages of hallucinatory activity were seen as signs of Divine revelation for every sincere believer. According to religious anthropology, each new prophet experiences these psychological stages and demonstrates the authenticity of his or her divinely inspired emotions before his or her adherents. Such demonstrations create what Weber describes as the "charisma" of religious prophets.[14]

As a result of his hallucinatory experiences, in 1889 Maliovannyi quit the Baptist congregation and established a new meeting for worship in his own house. Four families of the Tarashcha Baptists joined him, and during one ecstatic session in his house on October 15, 1889, they declared him the new Messiah, the Savior of the World, Jesus Christ.[15] As one adherent described this event in a letter to P. Biriukov, in October 1889, Maliovannyi invited to his house all those who wished to "glorify the Lord to join him in his fasting and praying:"

They prayed without a break, she wrote, for two days. Suddenly on the evening of the second day the Divine Glory arrived, and the martyr Kondrat trembled in all his body under the influence of the Holy Ghost. And then he spoke in different language and started to sing very loudly: "Do you hear the Voice of God, Who is singing in the garden, He is singing with new voice because the eternal spring is coming." After this singing, one sister, Martha, kneeled down, embraced Kondrat's legs, and cried: "Surely, you are the true Christ, the Savior of the world!" Kondrat meekly raised her from the floor and said: "Do not do this, but bow and glorify God, Who created the Heaven and the Earth." But she continued to cry louder and louder: "It is true that you are our Savior, Jesus Christ!" Then the body of another brother, Savelii, shook tremendously. Savelii trembled with great excitement because of the presence of the Holy Spirit among them and he shouted: "Yes, you are our Savior Jesus Christ!" And all who were in the house cried the same and were influenced by the descent of the Holy Ghost.[16]

This news attracted other Stundo-Baptists to Maliovannyi's house, and the number of his followers began to grow. As his adherents explained in their petition to the Russian tsar in 1901, they worshiped him from the very moment of "his Transfiguration" in October 1889 as "the Incarnation of the Word of God, which gave [them] spiritual life and served as the Living Book of the New Testament."[17] Beginning in 1890, meetings were held every day in Maliovannyi's house. Usually they began with the singing of hymns. This was followed by ecstatic prayer that reached a peak when the participants began to tremble and shake. They would then begin to cry hysterically, pronouncing a strange combination of sounds; some of them jumping, others clapping their hands and dancing. The followers of Maliovannyi explained that they were under the influence of the Holy Spirit. They interpreted their enthusiasm as spiritual preparation for the oncoming Millennium, because Jesus Christ, Kondrat Maliovannyi, had already arrived.

After 1890, this movement spread all over the province of Kiev. Hundreds of local peasants from neighboring villages came to see the new prophet. The local clergy and the Baptist ministers complained to the police about his preaching and the pilgrimage of his followers to his house in Tarashcha. After his imprisonment in February 1890, Maliovannyi was examined by a psychiatrist and diagnosed as mentally ill. Ivan Sikorskii, a professor of psychiatry at Kiev University, described Maliovannyi's disease as "mental dysfunction in the form of initial delirious madness of the religious character (Paranoia religiosa chronica)."[18] All experts in Kiev and Kazan' later confirmed this diagnosis. But even the persecution, arrest, and imprisonment of Maliovannyi from 1891 to 1905 in mental hospitals (first in Kiev, and then in Kazan') failed to stop his movement in the province of Kiev.[19] The local administration was worried by the movement's rapid growth after 1892. In Vasil'kov district all the Stundists had joined the Maliovantsy movement by 1899. The Maliovantsy stopped working and spent their time praying and preparing for the Millennium. In some localities, whole villages made collective preparations for the end of the world and the Last Judgment. On winter nights, they moved to frozen lakes, where they washed themselves and their children in the cold water. Afterward, they stayed in the snow on their knees, praying to God to save them.

In 1895, Maliovannyi was transferred from the mental asylum in Kiev to the mental hospital in Kazan' further away from his adherents. Afterward, Maliovannyi and his "prophet" Stepan Chekmariov, a Russian peasant with a Shalaput background, who was in the same mental institution in Kazan', carried on a lively correspondence with their followers in Ukraine. In May 1892, the governor of Kiev sent a special medical commission to examine the participants in this movement.[20] Sikorskii, who headed this commission, described it as a "psychotic epidemic" and singled out four distinctive features. The first was the heightened sense of smell among the active participants. At least

245

80 percent of the Maliovantsy noted a sweet smell, which they considered the sign of the Holy Spirit among them. The second was hallucinations of vision and hearing. All participants heard strange voices and sounds; they felt that they were flying in the air during their ecstatic praying. The third feature was a passivity of the will, which was related to this heightened sensibility. The Maliovantsy were easily moved, and they often cried during their meetings. Sometimes their weeping developed into hysterical sobbing. Finally, the most characteristic feature of Maliovantsy psychology was their propensity to cramp and to have convulsions. All participants in this movement experienced the trembling of their body during their meetings. When they felt the Holy Spirit, they began to shake, and sometimes someone fell to the floor and shook, rolling back and forth.[21]

It is noteworthy that Sikorskii singled out the elements of religious enthusiasm, which the majority of religious radicals shared, because such behavior was typical for radical dissidents who experienced the Inner Divine Light of the Holy Ghost, such as the Quakers and the Shakers.[22] Sikorskii tried to explain the unusual behavior of the religious radicals, their "intoxication by the Holy Spirit," as resulting from their chronic alcoholism, as did other observers of religious enthusiasm, such as the Puritan and Baptist theologians who criticized the first Quakers and Shakers.[23] Nearly all the participants in the Maliovantsy movement had long histories of alcoholism before their conversion to the Baptist faith. According to Sikorskii, the former alcoholics were more likely to feel religious ecstasy and experience hallucinations.[24] This observation could possibly explain the mass spread of ecstatic forms of religious worship in those localities of the Ukrainian provinces, where alcoholism had been a distinctive feature among the local rural population (figures 5.1 and 5.2).

The Millenarian Theology of the Maliovantsy

The entire theology of the Maliovantsy was based on the idea of the approaching end of the world and the Millennium. As the Son of God, the New Savior of the World, Maliovannyi was supposed to first ascend to heaven and then afterward return to Earth and supervise the Last Judgment for those who did

246

Figure 5.1. Chekmarev and Kondrat Maliovannyi in the Kazan' Mental Asylum. From Varvara I. Iasevich-Borodaevskaia, *Sektantstvo v Kievskoi gubernii: Baptisty i Maliovnatsy* (Saint Petersburg, 1902), picture III, between pp. 16 and 17.

not believe in him. His followers thought that Jesus Christ was not a historical character and that the Gospels were prophetic. The Gospel stories were parables that predicted the life of Kondrat Maliovannyi. He performed the miracles that had been described in the Gospels. All those who followed him became living temples, filled with the Holy Spirit. God had already chosen them for eternal life.

These elected Christians saw no need for external forms of religious organization or ritual because they had already established a direct connection to the Divine Spirit. As they explained to Iasevich-Borodaevskaia, Holy Scripture was necessary only for beginners in search of Divine Truth. The Bible was the key to Divine knowledge. But for those who had already received this knowledge through an emanation and incarnation of the Holy Spirit, the Bible was

247

Figure 5.2. The family of Kondrat Maliovannyi. From Varvara I. Iasevich-Borodaevskaia, *Sektantstvo v Kievskoi gubernii: Baptisty i Maliovnatsy* (Saint Petersburg, 1902), picture III, between pp. 16 and 17.

not so important. The Maliovantsy thought that the Holy Spirit revealed to them the true "living" law of God and not just a written one.[25] The entire theology of their movement was based on following literally the epistle of Saint Paul to the Corinthians: "You are the temple of the living God, as God hath said, I will dwell in them: and I walk in them; and I will be their God, and they shall be my people" (2 Corinthians 6:16).[26]

According to the Maliovantsy, during the Last Judgment there would be a spiritual resurrection for everyone. They understood this resurrection as a transition from the sinful life to the holy one. Sin for them was death for the soul. Without sin, the human soul could resurrect itself for eternal life. Therefore, the Maliovantsy waited for the Last Judgment and prepared themselves for eternal life. They stopped working, sold their property, and bought expensive food and clothes. The governor general of the Southwestern region gave a detailed description of the very beginning of this movement. He reported to the Ministry of the Interior on April 27, 1892, that the followers of Maliovannyi literally followed the Acts of the Apostles and denounced private property: "All that believed were together, and had all things in common; and sold their possessions and goods, and parted them to all men, as every man had need" (Acts 2:44–45).[27]

Like all other spiritual Christians, the Maliovantsy extended their notions of equality to their family relations. From then on, they avoided the traditional age hierarchy of peasant families. Spouses, parents, and their children were simply just sisters and brothers in the new Christian communities of the Maliovantsy, who "shared one Divine Body and one Divine Spirit."[28] The peasant dissenters sold all their cattle and even other food of animal origin. They believed it was a sin both to eat the meat of domestic animals and exploit them on the eve of the Millennium. All animals should be allowed to experience the coming of the New Age. All the Maliovantsy in the province of Kiev had sold their property and quit their work by March 1892 (the anticipated month of the Last Judgment). They tried to enjoy their life before the Last Judgment and live as the elect people, who deserved the happy life of the Millennium. Therefore, they ate very expensive food and wore expensive and fashionable dresses. As the governor general noted, the Maliovantsy "were dressed foppishly according to fashions of the city." He observed the reversal of the established dress code by peasant dissidents in their expectation of the decisive moment of the world to come. They had rejected their simple national dress and replaced it with the dress of the elite. The governor general wrote:

They removed their old Ukrainian national dress as the peasant symbol of their former slavery and exploitation. Their new expensive dress symbolized their expectation of freedom and their hopes of a better life and their privileged position in their Redeemer's Kingdom, which is already approaching. During the Millennium, the Earth will be cleansed of the human sins; all sinners will be purified by fire and brimstone; but everybody will be saved. After an ordeal of purification, all people will enter in the blissful and everlasting Kingdom, and the Maliovantsy, as the elected nation, will be first to get to this Kingdom of equality and prosperity.[29]

Sikorskii, who led a medical commission to study the phenomenon, confirmed this symbolic denial of the previous social status of slavery. According to his portrayal of the movement in 1892, the peasant followers of Maliovannyi stopped working and celebrated the life of leisure because Maliovannyi had led them out of the "Egypt of labor and slavery." They had changed their dress and their lifestyle to emphasize their new nonpeasant (*ne-muzhik*) identity. Their olfactory hallucinations also belonged to their new cultural identity. They denied the traditional smells of their peasant existence (e.g., the smells of sweat and cattle dung). Instead, they chose the aroma of the elite, and they associated the Holy Spirit with the perfume they smelled on their landlords. Thus, the peasant dissenters expressed symbolically their cultural protest against their social status.[30]

According to the prophecies of their leaders, the Maliovantsy expected the beginning of the Last Judgment and the end of "this sinful world" on March 25, 1892. They purified themselves both spiritually (figures 5.3, 5.4, and 5.5) and physically. The most enthusiastic and impatient washed their bodies in ice-cold water during the winter and waited for the Millennium to come, staying naked for hours in the snow. The greatest mass exodus of the naked Maliovantsy and their families in the fields took place on the freezing night of March 25, 1892.[31] Some of their leaders experienced spirit possession and "spiritual transformation." Some declared that they shared with Maliovannyi the same Divine essence of Jesus Christ. Mitrofan Mudrik, a peasant from the village of Leonovka (in the Kiev district) prophesied, calling himself "the living emanation of the Holy Spirit." The peasants who waited for the Last Judgment in March 1892 considered Mudrik a spiritual successor of Maliovannyi, "the new Savior and Redeemer of the world." A peasant couple from the village of Turbovka (Skvira district), Dementii and Agafia Rudchuk, laid the foundation for new worship inside the movement, the worship of Mitrofan Mudrik as their new "Redeemer." Sikorskii's commission sent all the spiritual successors of Maliovannyi, such as Mitrofan Mudrik, to a mental asylum in 1892.[32]

Figure 5.3. The Maliovantsy meeting for worship: singing the Psalms. From Varvara I. Iasevich-Borodaevskaia, *Sektantstvo v Kievskoi gubernii: Baptisty i Maliovnatsy* (Saint Petersburg, 1902), picture V, between pp. 30 and 31.

The Maliovantsy after Maliovannyi

After the arrest of Maliovannyi and other peasant "Redeemers," his successors changed the theology of the movement. By 1899 Ivan Lysenko, a peasant from the village Verbova (Skvira district), had become the new leader. He was another dissident with a "dislocated" identity. Since childhood, he had lived the life of a vagabond. He refused to stay at home, instead choosing to travel throughout the province of Kiev. To prevent his travels, his parents decided to force him to marry. But marriage did not stop him. In 1887 he left his wife and children and went to Siberia, where his brother was living in exile. For six years, he traveled around Siberia and the Caucasus, where he met the Shalaputs, Molokans, and exiled Stundists. He learned much from these travels and his conversations with various religious dissenters.[33]

When he returned home in 1893, Lysenko brought new religious ideas to his village. His enraged wife threw him out of their house. After this, in 1898, 251

Figure 5.4. The Maliovantsy meeting for worship: the closing prayer. From Varvara I. Iasevich-Borodaevskaia, *Sektantstvo v Kievskoi gubernii: Baptisty i Maliovnatsy* (Saint Petersburg, 1902), picture V, between pp. 30 and 31.

he settled in the neighboring village of Turbovka, where he became the new preacher for the local Maliovantsy. In his preaching about the approaching end of the world, he revived Maliovannyi's ideas about the Millennium. Moreover, his talent for preaching, his intelligence, his clean and well-made clothes, and his handsome appearance attracted many peasants (mostly young women) from the neighboring villages to his sermons. He preached that on the eve of the Millennium true Christians had to pool all their property and belongings and live as one large family.

The newborn Christians did not need laws and restrictions to regulate their personal lives. Instead of the "hypocritical" marriage laws, Lysenko offered the "free spiritual love" of the "pure souls." As a result of this preaching, Agafia Rudchuk, the most beautiful and most ecstatic prophetess among the Malio-

Figure 5.5. The Maliovantsy in Kiev province waiting for the Millennium (1901). Note the urban dresses and fashions of these Ukrainian peasants and the "nonpeasant" food they are eating—tea with lemon, sweets, and *bubliki* (bagels). From Varvara I. Iasevich-Borodaevskaia, *Sektantstvo v Kievskoi gubernii: Baptisty i Maliovnatsy* (Saint Petersburg, 1902), picture IV, between pp. 20 and 21.

vantsy from Turbovka, who was the loyal adherent of Mitrofan Mudrik (the "emanation of the Holy Spirit"), left her husband and became Lysenko's "spiritual wife." Lysenko declared Kondrat Maliovannyi to be God the Father. According to the new interpretation, Lysenko himself was called the Son of God, and his friend, the peasant Mudrik, was regarded as the Holy Spirit. Lysenko and Mudrik preached that the Millennium had already begun with the arrival of God the Father, Maliovannyi.[34]

As elected Christians, the Maliovantsy were supposed to begin a new life without property and go to the Promised Land, to Kazan', where God the Father lived. By November 1899, six families, the most zealous followers of Lysenko and Mudrik, united their households and moved all their belongings to one house in Turbovka. In that way, they tried to re-create the first Christian

253

communities described in the New Testament. The Turbovka community of the Maliovantsy organized the exodus to the Promised Land for all "reborn" Christians, who were "ready for the Millennium of their Heavenly Father and Redeemer, Kondrat Maliovannyi." Under the leadership of Lysenko, the Turbovka dissidents came to Kiev on November 6, 1899, using a cheap hotel as a place for ecstatic prayer. Their loud rituals quickly attracted the city police, and all the dissidents were arrested and sent back to their villages.[35]

Lysenko and his followers expressed in religious form the main ideas of the millennial movement, which were shared by all the religious radicals, including the Shalaputs and "spiritual Stundists." These were ideas of social protest and the notions of the reversal of traditional social and cultural roles. The dissidents' main goal was social justice on Earth. This was obvious from the police interview with Lysenko in November 1899. Responding to the police officer's question about the main reasons for the exodus, Lysenko explained that the dissident peasants were looking for more land and a better life. The peasants in the districts of Tarashcha and Skvira made up the most impoverished part of the rural population of the province of Kiev. They did not have enough land to survive. During the cold winters, they had to steal wood from the forest, which belonged to the local landlords. At the end of the interview, Lysenko asked the police officer a question, which emphasized the social background of the peasant movement. This police officer, whose parents had estates in the province of Kiev, was dressed in an expensive winter fur coat. Lysenko recognized him, and that was why he asked him the question: "Do you know, mister, the story of your fur coat?" Without waiting for an answer, he explained to the surprised officer: "My great-grandfather worked as a slave for your grandfather, who exploited and humiliated him and took the skin from my great-grandfather's body. This is how your fur coat appeared. It came from the skins of your slaves, the Ukrainian peasants."[36]

In spite of police persecutions, Lysenko's ideas spread over the province of Kiev and reached the province of Kherson by 1900. In the village of Petroostrov, a local peasant woman Marina proclaimed herself to be Christ. The local peasants came to her house to worship her. They shared the main ideas and religious practices common to all groups of the Maliovantsy. Marina offered her followers rituals of spirit possession, but also social criticism and the promise to restore social justice after the Last Judgment. In 1903, Petro-ostrov became a center of pilgrimage for the Maliovantsy from as far away as Kiev.[37] The rejection of the secular authorities and private property, the introduction of communal property, the new and more liberal sexual relations among members of the community were the elements of the movement initiated by Lysenko. Other young peasant prophets, such as Moisei Todosienko from the village of Iakhny, shared Lysenkos ideas and also combined their religious practices with social activism in the Ukrainian countryside.[38] Maliovannyi, however, worried about the radical character of Lysenko's interpretations of his ideas, and after his return to Tarashcha from the Kazan' mental hospital in 1905, he condemned Lysenko's extremism.

The theology and religious practices of the Maliovantsy, despite their varying emphasis on social criticism, remained the same from 1890 to 1905. To be saved, they taught, people should be born from Christ. Through Christ, reincarnated in the human soul, the Christian believer could receive eternal life. All true believers through their virtuous lives and ecstatic prayer could embody God in their souls by receiving the Holy Spirit. But only one man, Kondrat Maliovannyi, was able to embody the entire Divine essence and become God Himself. "The sacred theater" of the Millennium, a drama of the spiritual resurrection and personal incarnation, the elements of which had already existed in the rituals of the first Shalaputs, reached a peak of intensity in the movement of the Maliovantsy. All the participants were involved in the performances of the Holy Spirit.

If the Shalaputs and the radical Stundists expected the Millennium, the Maliovantsy performed it and created the conditions for the end of time. This was typical of all the millennial groups of the Radical Reformation in Western Europe as well as for various post-Reformation religious movements, such as the Pentecostal movement. One should note how the Maliovantsy used a system of allegories for their interpretation of Holy Scripture. They continued the old tradition of all popular radical movements in Christianity—an appropriation and elaboration of biblical images, merged with local folklore. The first Anabaptists, the early Quakers, the legendary Ranters of the English

255

Revolution, the Rogerenes in Connecticut, the first Shakers, the Russian Khlysty, and the Shalaputs all did much the same thing. One adherent of Maliovannyi told an Orthodox missionary:

> The Savior lives in sinful man, therefore He suffers inside this man, rather than on the cross. When a man learns the Divine road, Christ will be born inside this man. The Holy Virgin is Divine wisdom, and from this wisdom Christ is born in man. If somebody will feel the Spirit inside (he will feel trembling inside), this is the evidence that Christ is born. Christ was not baptized in water, because baptism is faith and repentance. The manger where Christ had been born is the human heart. Lazarus from the Gospel is an image of all people: when people sin it means that Lazarus died and stank, when the people repent, it means that Lazarus was resurrected. We will not go to heaven with our bodies. Heaven is inside of us. The body will perish, but our spirit will float in air till it will find the new shelter inside another virtuous man.[39]

One follower of Maliovannyi wrote a letter to the director of the Kazan' mental hospital and asked him to set Maliovannyi free. In this letter, he presented the same allegorical symbolism of the Maliovantsy and explained that all characters and events described in the New Testament were "the voice of God," and the "Divine sign" of Jesus Christ's arrival in Tarashcha in 1892.[40] The expectation of the Millennium explains the new and more tolerant attitudes of the Maliovantsy toward other denominations. The first followers of Maliovannyi even tried to preach to the Jews about the Millennium. Like all the groups of the Radical Reformation, they considered the conversion of the Jews to Christianity as the main condition for the beginning of the Millennium. One Maliovanets, a peasant from the district of Vasil'kovka, visited on a regular basis the synagogue in the town of Belaia Tserkva from September 1891 to March 1892. He preached to the Jews about Maliovannyi and the Millennium. But the local police stopped his proselytizing activities, and they eventually sent him to the Kiev mental asylum.[41]

The Maliovantsy considered themselves pioneers of a moral resurrection, who tried to help other people understand Divine Truth. They did not confront the Orthodox Church, as the radical Stundists had done. They explained the existence of various churches, laws, and rituals as a means of social control, which God established over sinful people. Nevertheless, in their distinction of "formal law" from "Divine grace," the followers of Maliovannyi shared the main ideas of the Radical Reformation about the priority of inner spiritual faith. "God gave all earthly laws, sacraments, Russian Orthodoxy, Roman Catholicism, and various religions to those people, who live as animals," Maliovantsy told Iasevich-Borodaevskaia:

> Such people need earthly laws and various religions as much as the wild animals need cages. As long as people will not know God, they must obey the external law, which punishes. When a man knows God, human law will be replaced in his soul by the inner, spiritual law of God. God needs neither churches, nor rituals, but He needs the sincere obedience of men in love and in truth.[42]

At the same time, like all groups of the Radical Reformation, including the Anabaptists (Mennonites) and Quakers, the Maliovantsy were pacifists and rejected violence and war. As Maliovannyi wrote to his followers, "The kings and the rulers of this world invented wars and violence." Christian teaching "denied the wars and brought peace to this world." Therefore, Christ opposed violence, and all who followed Him did the same. That was why the leaders of the Maliovantsy suffered, because they defended the principle of peace and nonviolence among the people, and the rulers of this world punished them as the opponents of their world of violence. The Shalaputs, as well as some radical Stundists, shared pacifist ideas with the Maliovantsy.[43]

In September 1901, the Ministry of the Interior received a petition signed by 500 activists demanding freedom for Maliovannyi. When he was released from the mental hospital in 1905, his movement included more than 1,000 peasants from the province of Kiev.[44] In 1909, the radical Stundists and Maliovantsy were more numerous than the Baptists there. Among 9,300 registered members of the evangelical sects, there were 3,608 Stundists, who rejected the Baptist ceremonies; 1,687 "evangelical Christians;" 1,553 Maliovantsy; and only 1,787 Baptists. By 1917, the radical evangelicals rather than the Baptists shaped the dissident movement in the province of Kiev.[45] By the end of

257

the 1890s, millennial expectations had spread all over the southern provinces of Russia. Stundo-Shalaput groups, which were similar to the Maliovantsy, appeared in the provinces of Bessarabia, Tavrida, Kherson, and Stavropol', and among them more than 5,000 members were registered by the police.[46]

By 1905, most Stundo-Shalaputs had ended their enthusiastic religious practices and turned to the practical questions of survival under the existing conditions in late imperial Russia. Some of them attempted to migrate abroad, while others tried to organize new agricultural communities inside Russia. During this adjustment, some established connections to Russian intellectuals, particularly to the followers of Leo Tolstoy and Colonel Pashkov, who shared their evangelical expectations. Under the influence of these intellectuals and socialist revolutionary propaganda, some of the most radical Stundo-Shalaputs even began engaging in social activism. Between 1900 and 1917, the Stundo-Shalaput radical version of the evangelical movement spread beyond the southern provinces and reached other provinces of Russia. Along with the Shalaput and Khlyst and the Stundo-Baptist groups, the Stundo-Shalaputs participated in the Russian "popular reformation," whose influences shaped the evangelical movement in late imperial and, to some extent, even in Soviet Russia.

Notes

1 See in Episkop Alexii [Dorodnitsyn], *Materialy dlia istorii religiozno-ratsionalistich-eskogo dvizhenia na iuge Rossii vo vtoroi polovine XIX–go veka* (Kazan', 1908), 569–84; A. Klibanov, *Istoria religioznogo sektantstva v Rossii (60-e gody XIX v.—1917 g.)* (Moscow, 1965), 209, 232–33; Edmund Heier, *Religious Schism in the Russian Aristocracy 1860–1900: Radstockism and Pashkovism* (The Hague, 1970); and Heather Coleman, "The Most Dangerous Sect: Baptists in Tsarist and Soviet Russia, 1905–1929" (Ph.D. dissertation, University of Illinois, 1998), 21–25.

2 Rossiiskii gosudarstvennyi istoricheskii arkhiv (hereafter RGIA), f. 796, op. 168, d. 1368, l. 12–13. On October 14, 1888, Nikanor, the archbishop of Kherson and Odessa, presented this information to the Holy Synod.

3 RGIA, f. 1284, op. 222 (1892), d. 24, l. 1–6, 10–11. The Stundist peasants, e.g., Vasilii Strukov and Piotr Maslov, belonged to famous Shalaput families.

4 RGIA, f. 797, op. 65, 2otd., 3st., d. 293, l. 1–4, 8ob., 10, 15ob., 20–22, 22ob.–23; f. 796, op. 176, d. 2184, l. 2–7.

5 The Anglo-American Friends saw the similarities of this movement to Quakerism. See E. J. Dillon, "The Quaker-Spiritualist Revival in Russia: A Report on Neo-Stundism. By a Russian Persecutor," *Review of Reviews* 7 (April 1893): 320–23. The author called

Maliovannyi "the Russian George Fox"; see p. 321. See also a portrayal of this movement by British author as the "spiritual evangelical revival" in Robert Sloan Latimer, *With Christ in Russia* (London, 1910), 155–64. The chapter about the movement is titled "Lo, Here Is Christ! Or There!" and it presented a a confused and mistaken picture of the Maliovantsy. The last studies of the Maliovannyi movement (both in Russian and English) presented it as a manifestation of the class struggle. See Klibanov, *Istoria religioznogo*, 218–21; G. P. Camfield, "The Pavlovtsy of Khar'kov Province, 1886–1905: Harmless Sectarians or Dangerous Rebels?" *Slavonic and East European Review* 68, no. 4 (1990): 692–717.

6 What follows is based on various versions of the recorded biography of Maliovannyi. See A. Achkasov, "Zapiski Kondrata Maliovannogo," *Kievskaia mysl'*, nos. 64, 65, 66, 67, 68, 69, 71, 72, 73, 74, 75, 76 (1913). Also see Nikolai Zhikharev, "Iskateli pravdy. Sredi 'maliovantsev,'" *Poznanie Rossii* , no. 1 (1909): 28–35; and no. 2 (1909): 1–14.

7 It is not clear who those prophets were. Maliovannyi called them "masony." But according to his description, they could be either Shalaputs or Mennonite Jumpers. See *Kievskaia mysl'*, no. 67 (1913): 2.

8 A. Yushchenko, "Kondratii Maliovannyi," *Istoricheskii vestnik*, no. 4 (1913): 239, 240.

9 Yushchenko, "Kondratii Maliovannyi," 239. It is obvious that Kondrat Maliovannyi was illiterate. At the same time, he knew the text of Holy Scripture by heart. Like many Stundists, he could learn the letters of Russian alphabet and could read with difficulties, but he could not write at all.

10 Quoted from Maliovannyi's testimony of 1901 and 1905 in: RGIA, f. 1284, op. 222, d. 51, l. 3, 17, 17ob., 18. Compare this with a refined version of Maliovannyi's letter published by Ivan Tregubov, Leo Tolstoy's follower: *Privetstvie Russkomu narodu ot Kondrata Maliovannogo* (Moscow, 1907), 18–19.

11 It seems likely that Maliovannyi could read only printed text. According to the police documents, he could not read handwriting and could not write.

12 RGIA, f. 1284, op. 222, d. 51, l. 18; *Poznanie Rossii*, no. 2 (1909): 2–3; Yushchenko, "Kondratii Maliovannyi," 240.

13 See a record of the detailed interrogation of Maliovannyi in Kazan' mental hospital, see RGIA, f. 1284, op. 222, d. 51, l. 2–3ob., 16–19.

14 Maliovannyi's hallucinatory experience is reminiscent of what "the public Friends" (the Quaker preachers) described in their memoirs as their revelations. See the most famous autobiographies of Quakers: William Edmundson, *A Journal of the Life, Travels, Sufferings, and Labor of Love* (London, 1715), 1–20ff.; Samuel Bownas, *An Account of the Life, Travels and Christian Experience* (London, 1761), 1–16ff.; John Richardson, *An Account of the Life of that Ancient Servant of Jesus Christ* (Philadelphia, 1759), 1–20ff.; Joan Vokins, *God's Mighty Power Magnified: As Manifested and Revealed in His Faithful Handmaid* (London, 1691), 1–35; and Thomas Chalkley, *A Collection of the Works* (Philadelphia, 1749), 1–21.

15 According to Maliovannyi's wife, when Dushenkovskii was arrested for his preaching and sent to the Tarashcha prison, his friends stayed at their house and talked with Maliovannyi, who then invited relatives and close friends for a meeting separately from

259

local Stundo-Baptists. At this meeting, they read and interpreted the Bible. When Malio-vannyi felt the descent of the Holy Spirit, he began to tremble and heard strange voices and smelled "Divine smells." Eventually, his friends discovered in the biblical text indica-tion that Kondrat Maliovannyi had been sent to them as the Son of God, the new Savior. Maliovannyi recalled that on October 15, 1889, his followers, who were impressed by his trembling, kneeled before him and shouted, "You are our Savior! We had crucified you and we had not believed you before. But now you are resurrected. Forgive us!" See V. Iasevich-Borodaevskaia, *Bor'ba za veru: Istoriko-bytovye ocherki i obzor zakonodatel'stva po staroobriadch-estvu i sektantstvu v ego posledovatel'nom razvitii s prilozheniem statei zakona i vysochaishikh ukazov* (Saint Petersburg, 1912), 134–35. The citation is from *Kievskaia mysl'*, no. 68 (1913): 2.

16 The citation is from P. Biriukov, *Maliovantsy. Istoria odnoi sekty,* izdanie *Svobodnogo slova* [publication of the periodical *Free Word*], ed. V. Chertkov (Christchurch, U.K., 1905), 8–9.

17 RGIA, f. 1284, op. 222, d. 115, l. 17ob. In his memoirs, Maliovannyi mistakenly gave another date, October 1889. See *Kievskaia mysl',* no. 68 (1913): 2; no. 69 (1913): 3.

18 See a description of this diagnosis in RGIA, f. 1284, op. 222 (1900), d. 115, l. 22–22ob.; op. 222 (1905), d. 51, l. 15. It is noteworthy that a doctor from a Kazan' hospital confessed that Maliovannyi was not a dangerous mental patient. But at the same time, this doctor recommended keeping him in the hospital to curtail his influence on the peasants. On Ivan Sikorskii's influence on Russian psychiatry, see Irina Sirotkina, *Diagnosing Literary Genius: A Cultural History of Psychiatry in Russia, 1880–1930* (Baltimore, 2002), especially 136–39.

19 Klibanov mistakenly gave the date of his arrest in 1892; see his *Istoria religioznogo,* 219.

20 Ivan A. Sikorskii, "Psikhopaticheskaya epidemia 1892 goda v Kievskoi gubernii," V 5-ti knigakh [in 5 vols.], in *Sbornik nauchno-literaturnykh statei* (Kiev, 1900), vol. 5, 44–103.

21 Sikorskii, "Psikhopaticheskaia epidemia," 56–60.

22 On this, see A. G. Dickens and John Tonkin, eds., *The Reformation in Historical Thought* (Cambridge, Mass., 1985), 220.

23 On the Quakers, see Increase Mather, *An Essay for the Recording of Illustrious Provi-dences: Wherein an Account Is Given of Many Remarkable and Very Memorable Events, Which Have Happened in This Last Age* (Boston, 1684), 341–47. On the rumors that the Shakers' leaders "delight themselves much in feasting and drinking spirituous liquor," see Isaac Backus, *A History of New-England, With Particular Reference to the Denomination of Christians Called Bap-tists,* 3 vols. (Boston, 1777–96), vol. 2, 297. Also see the general discussion on drunken-ness and religious enthusiasm in Clarke Garrett, *Spirit Possession and Popular Religion: From the Camisards to the Shakers* (Baltimore, 1987), 202–6.

24 Sikorskii, "Psikhopaticheskaia epidemia," 46, 92–103. The opponents of Shakers tried to explain the dissidents' rituals by their alcoholism as well; see Garrett, *Spirit Pos-session,* 208–9.

25 RGIA, f. 1284, op. 222, d. 49, l. 7–7ob. As local officials noted, the Maliovantsy

considered the Bible "the book of the prophecies," to which they had added "the teaching and letters of Maliovannyi and the revelations of other members of the sect who were inspired by the Holy Spirit."

26 "The Holy Ghost," one adherent of Maliovannyi said, "descends and lives in a man till this man is clean of sin. But when the man begins to sin, the Holy Ghost leaves him and looks for another, more virtuous man who is seeking salvation. Therefore we live a virtuous life and the Holy Spirit dwells in and directs us"; Iasevich-Borodaevskaia, *Bor'ba za veru,* 144–45. They paraphrased Saint Paul, insisting that "human body was the temple of the Holy Ghost, which was in the true believer, which he had of God" (1 Corinthians 6:19).

27 See the text of report in RGIA, f. 1284, op. 222, d. 49, l. 5–11. The governor general reported to the tsar in June 1892 that "these Stundists-mystics attempted to reproduce the basics of communism in their communitarian and every day life, by literally following the Acts of the Apostles they preached that all property, labor, food, beverages and houses should be used in common." The Maliovantsy sold their property and bought expensive dresses and food for the celebration of the coming Advent of Jesus Christ. By doing this, peasant dissidents rejected their Ukrainian peasant identity and identified themselves with the cosmopolitan community of "elect Christians."

28 RGIA, f. 1284, op. 222, d. 49, l. 5ob.–6.

29 RGIA, f. 1284, op. 222, d. 49, l. 6ob.–7.

30 Sikorskii, "Psikhopaticheskaia epidemia," 52–54; the citation is on 53.

31 N. Belogorskii, "Sekta maliovantsev," *Missionerskoe obozrenie* (hereafter *MO*), January 1908, 75.

32 RGIA, f. 796, op. 175, d. 1847, l. 1–1ob. See Sikorskii, "Psikhopaticheskaia epidemia," 44–103. See other cases of the mental treatment of the Maliovantsy in "Tsentral'nyi derzhavnyi istorychnyi arkhiv Ukrainy," f. 442, op. 691, d. 260, l. 13–14.

33 The Orthodox scholars denied direct Khlyst influences on the Ukrainian peasants, though they noted the possibility of Shalaput and Molokan influences on Lysenko during his travels. See *MO,* November 1900, 518.

34 The peasant dissenters discussed the rumors generated by the publication of the German astronomer Falk about a space catastrophe, which would affect the Earth as well. According to Falk's calculations, the disaster would take place on November 13, 1899. Lysenko and his followers used these rumors to confirm the fact of the approaching Millennium. See *MO,* September 1900, 291; October 1900, 247–48,

35 *MO,* September 1900, 291–92; October 1900, 247–48. See also RGIA, f. 1284, op. 222 (1900), d. 115, l. 1–4.

36 *MO,* September 1900, 292–93.

37 K. Sokolovskii, *Sekta maliovantsev sredi shtundistov v sele Petro-ostrove Khersonskoi gubernii, Elizavetgradskogo uezda* (Saint Petersburg, 1903).

38 *MO,* December 1901, 871–73.

39 This citation is from Savva Potekhin, "Maliovantsy," in *Russkie sektanty, ikh uchenie, kul't i sposby propagandy,* ed. M. A. Kal'nev (Odessa, 1911), 230. All observers noted the allegoric symbolism of Maliovantsy. The dissidents tried to connect the biblical images to

the simple notions of their peasant world. According to them, Maria, God's Mother, was the Divine Wisdom, Joseph was Jesus Christ Himself, Bethlehem was the town of Tarashcha, the Apostles were the predecessors of the leaders of the Maliovantsy, etc. Maliovannyi was the only One, who was predicted and described in Holy Scripture. The people expected him and painted his image in icons. That was why his last name derived from the word "one who was painted, or one who was portrayed by paint" (in Russian, *maliovannyi*). See RGIA, f. 1284, op. 222, d. 49, l. 7ob.

40 Russian State Library, Moscow, Manuscript Department (hereafter OR RGB), f. 435, k. 65, d. 45, l. 5, 8.

41 Sikorskii, "Psikhopaticheskaya epidemia," 78.

42 And they continue: "When a man comprehends the Truth, removes all the sins from his soul, and achieves spiritual re-birth, such a man will live 'not under the law, but under [Divine] grace' [Romans 6:14] and will not be able to sin any more"; Iasevich-Borodaevskaia, *Bor'ba za veru*, 148–49.

43 OR RGB, f. 435, k. 65, d. 45, l. 11.

44 RGIA, f. 1284, op. 222, d. 115, l. 6–7,14, 15; see the text of petition on l. 17–18ob. *MO* published an article or two on the Maliovantsy every year. The most interesting were S. Potekhin, "Misticheskaia shtunda: Maliovannyi i maliovannye," *MO*, 1900, no. 2, 234–49; 502–14.

45 RGIA, f. 1284, op. 241, d. 181. Calculations based on the material from: RGIA, f. 821, op. 133, d. 21, l. 275ob.–277ob. The province of Ekaterinoslav had the same proportion: 212 Stundists, 812 Evangelical Christians, and 289 Baptists.

46 In some localities, the chiliastic hysteria among the new zealots of the "spiritual Christian" sect reached the traditional communities of Old Belief and led to collective suicide among Old Believers. In 1897, near Tiraspol', twenty-five religious radical Old Believers went to a remote cave, closed themselves in, and waited for the coming end of the world. All died in the cave. See, in detail, I. A. Sikorskii, "O dvadtsati piati zazhivo pogrebionnykh v Ternovskikh khutorakh (bliz Tiraspolia) v 1896–1897 g." in *Sbornik nauchno-literaturnykh statei, V 5-ti knigakh* [in 5 vols.] (Kiev, 1900), vol. 1, 165–258.

Chapter Five

Chapter Six

6 Orthodox Peasants No More

The peasants who participated in Russia's "radical reformation" carved out new identities for themselves. They also compelled the tsarist administration, the Orthodox clergy, and the intelligentsia to question the old stereotype of the passive and loyal Orthodox believer. In contrast to the majority of Orthodox peasants—with their partly pagan, partly Christian "culture of the spoken word" and magic rituals—the peasant evangelicals from the southern provinces of the Russian Empire represented a "culture of the written word." In fact, they founded a culture in the Russian countryside on the basis of the written biblical text, and biblical images and ideas shaped their worldview and mentality. They followed biblical notions literally, especially those that fit their ideas of social justice and equality.

Therefore, the peasant dissenters attempted to "restore" equality of status and sex in their communities, which they thought had existed among the first Christians. According to contemporary observers, both the Shalaputs and Stundists put more emphasis on this phrase of Saint Paul: "There is neither Jew nor Greek, there is neither slave nor free, there is neither male nor female;

for you are all one in Christ Jesus" (Galatians 3:28). Like many Christians before them, Russian and Ukrainian dissenters interpreted this phrase as an order to put aside all divisions of status or convention arising from race, social class, or sex. Following this rule, they found both the exploitation of poor people and the subordination of women contrary to Christian belief that all persons are of equal value and dignity in the eyes of God.

They tried to alleviate the condition of women in their community and restore human dignity and social activism to their female coreligionists. The peasant evangelicals saw the disparity between the Christian ideal of equality and the reality of life, so they attempted to re-create the Christian ideal in their communities by rejecting the social divisions and sexual conventions of their Orthodox neighbors.[1] They also rejected national distinctions, developing not only non-Orthodox but also non-Russian characteristics as part of their new identity. Evangelical Christian sects everywhere have usually considered themselves "a moral minority in the body of a society in moral flux," especially during periods of transition. "The sect emerges," British sociologist, Bryan R. Wilson, wrote, "as a type of reassertion of community values in which moral consensus—albeit sometimes in totalist mould—is re-established."[2] Post-Emancipation Russian society was in flux, and traditional family and moral values were often lost among dislocated peasants. The new evangelical sects tried to create their own family values and structures in order to restore morality and order in their communities.

Radical Russian dissenters, especially members of the millennial sects, established their own rules of sexual regulation and control. In emphasizing "moral purity and exceptionalism," millennial sects with communitarian principles, such as the radical Stundists and Shalaputs, rejected conventional family organization and reversed traditional gender roles. In some groups, the rejection of traditional marital norms led to sexual experimentation and promiscuity.[3] At the same time, even those dissenters who lived in traditional families but opposed some of the conventional norms of their Orthodox neighbors became targets of various accusations of sexual misbehavior.[4] The main reason for these accusations was the unusual activism and the leading role of women among dissident groups.

The high level of women's activism was one of the most prominent features of the European Reformation. Besides the old Christian traditions of religious enthusiasm typical for all female participants of any religious movement, the Reformation created new fields of activity and self-realization.[5] With its emphasis on immediate communication with the Divine, the Radical Reformation influenced marital norms and sexual practices. Women of the Radical Reformation participated in various new religious rituals that reversed gender roles and destroyed traditional family organization.[6]

The post-Reformation movements of Christian enthusiasts attracted women as well. Scholars who have studied the millennial sects and spirit possession among religious dissenters have noted the important role of women who sometimes acted as leaders and prophetesses of sectarians. Usually, the female participants in religious movements enacted the most emotional rituals and ecstatic ceremonies, including expressions of so-called saintly hysteria.[7] Like their European and American predecessors, Russian and Ukrainian peasant dissenters expected "the end of the world and the coming of a millennial period and an earthly paradise."[8] An important part of their millennial utopia was their sexual utopian project.[9] This project attempted to replace traditional marital relations in the Orthodox peasant community, which had already been undermined by the reforms of the 1860s and 1870s and by the modernization of Russian society.

The main topics of this chapter are the new social identity of the radical evangelicals, the role of women in dissident communities, the evolution of various forms of social control over sexual urges, and sexual experimentation among religious dissidents.

The Discovery of a New Social Identity among the Dissident Peasants

According to symbolic anthropology, the disruption of "sacred symbols" and "cultural landmarks" has always resulted in cultural and ideological disorientation.[10] This happened during the spread of the "radical reformation" in the southern provinces of the Russian Empire. The new religious practices and

267

new cultural identity of the peasant dissidents disoriented not only their Orthodox neighbors but also the local administration and observant intellectuals. The traditional Orthodox peasant of Russian or Ukrainian ethnic origin disappeared in the dissident peasant communities of Shalaputs and Stundists. The image of the peasant dissenter lost the familiar features of the ignorant and obedient Orthodox believer.

The distinctive feature of traditional peasant culture was its localism. The local culture of the rural population in Russia had the character of what cultural historians describe as "vernacular culture." The vernacular culture of the peasantry in the southern provinces of the Russian Empire—which had its origins in a homeland in the central provinces of Russia and Ukraine—was structured quite differently from the "high culture" of the Russian Orthodox clergy and Russian officials. The vernacular culture of Russian peasants was diffuse. It had no single center. Whereas the high culture of the Russian intellectuals (even that of Orthodox origin) was cosmopolitan and fashion conscious, the vernacular was place bound and enduring. Much of it was carried down within what E. P. Thompson has called the "circular space" of locality, where practices and norms were "reproduced down the generations within the slowly differentiating ambience of 'custom.'"[11]

Henry Glassie, an American historian of folk culture, explains that folk material varies through space rather than time, whereas academic and popular culture operates in the reverse fashion. "The natural divisions of folk material are, then, spatial," he writes, "where the natural divisions of popular material are temporal; that is, a search for patterns in folk material yields regions, where a search for patterns in popular material yields periods."[12] Hence, the high, or academic, culture of Russian intellectuals (including Orthodox priests and police officers), which emanated from one cultural center, imparted a common appearance to the cultivated classes across all regions of the Russian Empire. Style and fashions for them changed through time in everything from clothing and hairstyles to furniture, painting, and architecture. The vernacular culture of Russian and Ukrainian peasants was slower to change through time, and it varied from region to region. The local administration and Orthodox clergy were accustomed to the varied appearance of their peasant population, and they associated the national identity of the peasants partly with these local differences in the main Russian Orthodox culture.

The new religious sects changed the appearance of local peasants. They created a universal Christian social identity that went beyond all local differences in peasant culture. Such changes first took place among the Shalaputs, who represented the popular Radical Reformation of Russian Orthodoxy. At the same time, in contrast to the Molokans and the Dukhobors, the Shalaputs tried, through their connections in southern Russia, to obliterate the theological and ritualistic differences among various dissident sects and create a common religious culture. They drew chiefly on the traditions and forms of folk culture from the central Russian provinces. As a result, from the 1840s through the 1870s the first model of dissident identity in the Russian radical reformation became associated with certain patterns of the folk culture from the provinces of Kursk and Tambov. All other local groups that joined this movement had to adjust to these prevailing patterns of folk culture.

In the Berdiansk and Melitopol districts of Tavrida, the overwhelming majority of active Shalaputs were state peasants from central Russia (mostly from provinces of Kursk and Tambov) who brought to Ukraine their old connections with the Russian non-Orthodox sects. Only a minority of the Shalaputs were local Ukrainian peasants. As the police noted, those Ukrainians who had joined the Shalaputs lost their Ukrainian cultural identity and gradually acquired the image of their Russian coreligionists from the central provinces. Another Shalaput sect, the Marianovtsy, was popular especially among the local Ukrainian peasants. In contrast to the Melitopol' and Berdiansk Shalaputs, the overwhelming majority of these Shalaputs were Ukrainian peasants. Ukrainian peasants (some of them former Cossacks) who joined the Marianovtsy also quickly lost their distinctive ethnic character and looked like their Russian coreligionists from the provinces of Kursk and Tambov, according to police reports. "The adherents of Marianna in the Dneprovskii district," one gendarme officer wrote in 1865, "were the Little Russians" who "replaced their traditional clothes with the dress from central Russia" (i.e., from the province of Kursk). These Ukrainian peasants "wear their shirts over their trousers like

Russians; and like Russians, they do not shave their beards and have the typical Russian hair style with a parting in the middle."[13]

The same loss of traditional ethnic identity occurred among the Ukrainian peasants who joined Stundist sects. Yet in this case, the prevailing model for the peasants' imitation was that of German colonists. All observers, including conservatives and liberal authors, noted the changes in the peasant sectarians' appearance, behavior, and customs by the 1880s. We have already mentioned the strong cultural impact of the German Protestants and Mennonites on the peasant Stundists. What struck contemporary observers that an overwhelming majority of all these Stundists were not Russian but Ukrainian, and mainly peasants rather than dwellers of cities and towns.[14] "Everybody knows," wrote the famous "socialist-populist" journalist Alexandr Prugavin, "that Stunda is spreading exclusively among the Little Russians [the Ukrainians]."[15] According-ing to the first serious scholar of Stundism in Russia, Arsenii Rozhdestvenskii, "Stundism was the first unsuccessful attempt by the ordinary [Ukrainian] people to create their own separate religious belief."[16] As we see, even the intel-lectual opponents of Protestantism, such as Rozhdestvenskii, had to acknowl-edge the active and independent role of ordinary Ukrainian peasants in creating their own religion while drawing on German Protestant traditions.

For their Orthodox opponents, the most striking characteristic of the first Stundists was that they were Ukrainian peasants, who created a new social iden-tity that was different from the traditional stereotype of the "Little Russian" Orthodox peasant. They spoke Ukrainian (*malorossiyskoe narechie,* in an official interpretation), and were first nicknamed "Khokhly-Shtundy" or "Nemetsko-Khokhlatskaia Shtunda" ("German-Ukrainian Stunde"). It is noteworthy that both official commentators and Russian journalists used the word Khokhol (Ukrainian) for their definition of Stundist.[17] Other observers emphasized the distinctive appearance of these Ukrainian peasants—who, unlike Russians, wore only moustaches and not beards. The Ukrainian Stundists further distinguished themselves from Russians by imitating Germans in dress and manners. Some authors stressed the special sociocultural conditions of life, which made Ukraine "susceptible to Protestant, including evangelical sectarian, propaganda." Others wrote, "One ought not to forget that each Ukrainian believes himself to be a poet and a thinker, a lawmaker, a judge, and a priest. In this unique psychological makeup we find then the origin of their flirtation with Protestantism."[18]

In 1898, the Russian émigré periodical of Leo Tolstoy's followers, the *Free Word,* published the original correspondence and journals of Tymophii Zaiats, who had become a Stundist martyr for liberal Russian intellectuals. In 1910 the Bolshevik, socialist-democrat Vladimir Bonch-Bruevich reprinted these journals in his collection of materials on the history of Russian sects. This document, which was written in Ukrainian, is a unique manifestation of the "Ukrainian nationality" of its author. In his suggestions about his future funeral, Tymophii Zaiats insists on being buried in a simple Ukrainian (Khokhol) coffin (*domovyna*) rather than in a Russian coffin (*grob*). Throughout the text, the author emphasizes his Ukrainian national identity. He opposes the Ukrainian and the Russian languages and cultures, and he links Ukrainian peasant culture to Stundism. He demonstrates the necessity of stating the "Divine truth" in the local native language, reading of the Gospels in Ukrainian, and praying in Ukrainian. He stresses the differences in appearance of Ukrainian and Russian peasants: The "Khokhol [Ukrainian] always shaves his face, while the katsap [Russian] has a beard."[19] Other Ukrainian Stundists from the provinces of Kiev and Kherson also demonstrated an awareness of their ethnic difference from the Russian nation.

In their teaching, local Stundists interpreted the Russian Orthodox Church as a political institution that exploited the Ukrainian population of southern Russia. As one Stundist activist explained, "The teaching of the Orthodox priest exists to protect those who have much money, land, property and factories, and at the same time, to keep the Ukrainian [Khokhol] under control."[20] It is noteworthy that some Ukrainian Stundists linked the questions of social justice and class exploitation with ethnicity, portraying the Ukrainian (Khokhol) as the oppressed and the Russian Orthodox priest or Russian landlord as the oppressor. Stundist activists wrote in their memoirs that "Khokhol [Ukrainian] origin" became a sign of slavery and humiliation for Ukrainian peasants, who were treated as slaves (*khlopy*) by the Russian administration. Eventually, these peasants considered their defection from the Orthodox Church as a rejection of their slavery and humiliation.[21]

These peasants brought their distinctively ethnic characteristics into the evangelical culture of southern Russia. Even the first Stundists, who followed their German "teachers," contributed their own purely Ukrainian cultural features to the evangelical teachings and rituals. They assimilated German cultural elements into their own cultural code. In 1872–73, Stundists from Kherson province still sang old Lutheran hymns in Russian translation, but as early as 1872 they also began gradually replacing German tunes and Russian lyrics with their own Ukrainian ones.[22] Contemporary scholars, such as the liberal journalist Varvara I. Iasevich-Borodaevskaia, who had studied the Ukrainian sects in the provinces of Kiev and Ekaterinoslav during the 1890s, described how the Ukrainian Stundist peasants used Ukrainian folklore and old Cossack songs and melodies for their own religious rituals. She emphasized that during the evolution of Stundism into radical spiritual sects, such as the Maliovantsy, Ukrainian sectarians gradually replaced Slavonic, Russian Orthodox, and Lutheran texts and melodies with traditional Ukrainian songs.[23]

All observers, both conservative and liberal, noted the loss of the traditional Orthodox peasant identity among religious dissidents. Russians, Ukrainians, and other ethnic groups that joined the radical evangelical sects, such as the Stundists, replaced their local cultural identity with the new international evangelical culture based on universal notions and images of Reformed Christianity. Stundist activists taught the necessity of unity for all evangelicals, regardless of different ethnic and social origins. Instead of ethnic cultural isolationism, they offered new ideas of solidarity and mutual assistance across nations based on the principle of one faith. Thus, Ivan Draganov, a Stundist peasant who was sixty-three years of age, from the province of Kherson, and a Bulgarian by ethnic origin, preached the idea of "evangelical solidarity" among Christians of all nationalities. In 1888, Draganov told his Orthodox neighbors, "Russians and Bulgarians need neither the tsar nor the government, because everybody is supposed to be the tsar in his own household."[24] Besides Germans, Ukrainians, and Russians, the local police discovered Greek, Romanian, and Jewish evangelicals, who shared similar ideas of solidarity.

As it turned out, the concrete patterns and particular ethnic forms of this evangelical culture among various dissident groups depended on cultural models of the prevailing ethnic group, which played the role of a "charter" group in a process of cultural dialogue. The charter groups of peasants from central Russia defined the character of the Shalaputs, and charter groups of German Pietists and Mennonites influenced the cultural identity of Ukrainian Stundists. In some localities, where a few German Baptists adjusted to the majority of the Ukrainian Stundists, the opposite cultural phenomenon took place. In this case, the prevailing Ukrainian peasant dissidents influenced the German cultural minority. The German evangelicals, who had become a part of the Ukrainian dissident communities, followed the cultural patterns of that charter group. As contemporary observers noted, some German evangelicals "became Russified." These Germans usually spoke Russian or Ukrainian, wore Russian dress, and built their houses according to the local architectural models.[25] Because these "Russified" (or "Ukrainified") evangelicals and Ukrainian Stundists had lost the traditional features of Orthodox peasants, they represented a new social and cultural group in the Ukrainian countryside.

The loss of a traditional Orthodox peasant identity experienced by dissenters was related, in part, to the economic problems of the post-Emancipation Russian and Ukrainian countryside. The impoverished, dispossessed peasants, who migrated to other localities in search of work, were hardly able to preserve their traditional social identity. These landless peasants lost their connections to their communities as well as to Orthodox congregations.

According to Orthodox scholars, this process of dispossession in the Ukrainian countryside was conducive to the loss of Ukrainian national identity among impoverished peasants. One of the Orthodox analysts of the new dissident movements among the Ukrainian peasants, P. Petrushevskii, noted that wealthy Ukrainian peasants with land and prosperous households were more conservative in matters of culture and language. They tried to protect their Ukrainian language and national customs from Russian cultural influences. At the same time, he wrote, the Ukrainian "landless peasant was more cosmopolitan and open to outside cultural and religious influences." He continues: "The impoverished people, such as the landless peasants, do not value their native language and native songs; they try to speak Russian [*po-moskovski*], instead of the

Ukrainian language; and they imitate all fashions and songs of their non-Ukrainian neighbors, including Russians, Germans and Jews."[26]

During the 1890s, Russian and Ukrainian journalists noted that poor Ukrainian peasants were ready to replace Ukrainian folk songs with Russian popular songs, mostly with songs about Russian soldiers. In their view, the rural Ukrainian population was losing its Ukrainian national character. The Ukrainian peasants preferred songs, manners, fashions, and diet, which came from the Russified city dwellers. Ukrainian intellectuals complained about the loss of Ukrainian identity among Ukrainian peasants and the ways in which these peasants borrowed from the cultures of Russians, Germans, and Jews.[27] Foreign cultural influences among the impoverished portion of rural population in the Ukrainian countryside had become the main topic of various reports from the local police and from Orthodox clergy as well. All these reports noted that an overwhelming majority among the first dissident activists were the poorest peasants in the Ukrainian villages.

In building their new identity, these poorest peasants (some of whom were landless) began by rejecting those cultural elements they associated with humiliation and suffering. In effect, the peasants denied their former existence. The Maliovantsy, who stopped performing their agricultural work, explained to an Orthodox missionary, "We hate our peasant work and this land because we are tired of our hard labor on it."[28] Thus, they rejected their national attire, their lifestyle, and their traditional religion. All the Stundist activists attracted the attention of observers by their urban dress. They wore the jackets of city dwellers, changing even their peasant coats according to European fashion.[29]

Eventually, the peasants realized that the roots of their misery were related to their social status as landless rural inhabitants. In searching for jobs and moving to big Russian-speaking industrial cities and German evangelical communities, such poor peasants experienced various new cultural influences. During their adjustment, they compared their earlier peasant status with the new cultural roles they encountered, and they gradually appropriated those new cultural elements, associating them with a better and more comfortable life.

274 In many cases, these peasants completely rejected the basic elements of

their traditional status, including Orthodox Christianity. They distanced themselves from their Orthodox neighbors. In fact, radical Ukrainian Stundists began publicly calling themselves "a separate nation" as early as the 1890s. In 1894, they refused to join Russian Orthodox peasants in the ceremony of an oath for loyalty of the new tsar, Nicholas II. The leader of the Stundists from the village of Pomoshnaia (in the Elizavetgrad district), Konstantin Kudelia, explained to the local administration the reason for refusing. According to him, the local Ukrainian evangelicals considered themselves a separate nation. Kudelia told the local priest that other nationalities of the Russian Empire, including the Jews, Tartars, and Poles, took the oath for loyalty according to their own religious principles, separately from the Orthodox Russians. "We do not deny the oath of loyalty," Kudelia said, "What we demand is the right to take this oath separately from the Russian Orthodox people because we constitute a separate nation, whose principle of existence is based on the Holy Gospels."[30]

It is noteworthy that other religious dissidents, such as the Molokans and Dukhobors, also requested a separate special oath according to their religious beliefs. Yet only the radical Stundists insisted on legal recognition as a "separate nation." The Ukrainian Stundists became the first Slavic evangelical group to ask the Russian administration to acknowledge their special social and religious status. In fact, the Stundist assertion about their status of a "separate nation" calls to mind the main demand of the Western Radical Reformation, whose representatives had "insisted on the separation of their own churches from the national or territorial state."[31]

The Ukrainian Stundo-Baptists considered themselves part of the European evangelical community. As members of this community, they sometimes sought protection from persecution by petitioning foreign rulers. In 1891, Stundist peasants in the Odessa district decided to write to the German emperor asking him to protect them from persecution by the Russian administration. They collected money and selected an activist to make the trip to Berlin to submit their petition.[32] All observers noted that the Stundists were different "ethnographically" from their Orthodox peasant neighbors.[33] In their cultural protest, the Stundists preferred to associate with German colonists or city dwellers rather than with their Orthodox peasant neighbors. "The German colonists live much better than the Orthodox peasants," the Stundists told the Orthodox missionary. "Therefore we prefer to live like the Germans and that is why we join the German nation."[34]

The Stundists cut off all relations with the Orthodox peasant community, which they associated with "heavy drinking, corruption, theft, violence, adultery and sloth." They used the model of the German colonists' lifestyle to construct their new social identity. A police officer from the Alexandria district (of Kherson province) noted in 1884 that, following this model, the local Ukrainian peasants, who had joined the Stundist sect eight years before, had become wealthy enough to buy a huge piece of land in the province of Stavropol' and establish their own agricultural colony there.[35] The denial of their local Ukrainian identity was so evident among the Ukrainian Stundists that some authors called them anti-Ukrainian:

> The Stundists removed all elements of Ukrainian folk culture from their life. They changed their morals, customs, character and songs. Even their language changed—it became a strange mixture of Ukrainian, German, Polish and literary Russian. The Stundists suppressed any expression of the folk culture— Ukrainian songs, dances, customs and dress. There is no sound of a folk song or sign of traditional Ukrainian folk rituals in the localities where the Stundists live. It looks as if the Stundists aspire to become a separate nation, distinct from their Orthodox peasant neighbors.[36]

The denial of their peasant past and their traditional Orthodox peasant identity became the main component of the "Stundist reformation" in the Ukrainian countryside. The Stundists changed more than just their lifestyle. They preferred any nonpeasant trade (*ne-muzhitskoe remeslo*). Stundist activists also turned to other professions. Some became craftspeople or shopkeepers. In all the localities where the Stundists played a significant role, these changes of profession were a common phenomenon. Even those Stundist peasants who stayed in their villages changed their image. To contemporaries, they looked more like European farmers than Russian Orthodox peasants.[37]

This radical denial of the Orthodox peasant identity reached a peak among the millennial zealots of Kondrat Maliovannyi during the 1890s. In their

276

expectation of the Millennium of Jesus Christ, the Maliovantsy stopped working and changed their diet, dress, and hairstyle. They replaced all peasant aspects of their everyday life with practices that they had associated with an urban middle-class existence. They wore the fashionable dress of city residence. They used decorations, perfumes, and makeup, which were unusual for Ukrainian peasants. Rather than following a peasant diet, they ate more sweets, candies, and chocolate, and they drank tea and "other nonpeasant beverages." They changed their manner of speaking, trying to avoid peasant words and imitate the language of the literate elite.[38]

Members of an investigating committee discovered in May 1892 that the followers of Maliovannyi had expensive food in their houses and were dressed in fashionable European clothes. A community of the Maliovantsy paid a large sum of 140 rubles to Jewish merchants for a set of expensive clothes for their community. As was noted by Vasilii Skvortsov, one of the members of the investigating committee, "The dissidents threw away their national costumes as peasant emblems of their former slavery and labor; their new dresses served as the symbols of their anticipated new forms of the better social life and of their expected privileged position in the kingdom of their "Redeemer," which will be established for them here on the Earth rather than in the Heaven."[39]

As we have seen, the religious radicals not only symbolically rejected their former peasant identity but also created a new evangelical identity, which played a unifying role among the different ethnic peasant groups of late imperial Russia. Thus the new evangelical culture was an agent of modernization and unification of the local cultures in the Russian countryside. To the Russian clergy and local administration, however, the evangelical culture looked like a radical threat to the Orthodox peasant tradition.

"Preparation for the Millennium": The Elimination of Gender and the Rejection of Sexuality among the Early Shalaputs

Among the Shalaputs and radical Stundists, anticipation of the Millennium changed traditional peasant attitudes toward gender roles and sexuality. As

277

millennial sects, they prepared for the Kingdom of Christ, where all social, cultural, and sexual distinctions would disappear, and where God would transform all human relations. On the one hand, in their preparation for the Millennium, some of these religious radicals tried to avoid sex and eliminate gender distinctions. On the other hand, others attempted to bring sexuality and sexual relations into the "sacred drama" of salvation and religious ecstasy.

The first form of social control over sexuality, and the first recorded sexual experiment among Russian religious dissidents, was castration. In the religious movement of "God's People," this extreme form of control over sexual urges led to mutilation and the removal of genitals among the Skoptsy.[40] According to the first investigation of "the Skopets heresy" in 1843, the castrated dissenters from the province of Kursk brought their religious practices to the southern province of Tavrida. Despite having arrested only two castrated Skoptsy in Tavrida, the police calculated that there were more than 400 "secret Skoptsy." The founding father of the Tavrida Skoptsy was the Russian soldier Login, who settled in the village of Vodianaia, in the Dneprovskii district of Tavrida. Another center of the Skoptsy's influence was the neighboring district of Melitopol'. The local Skoptsy, the police reported, annually visited "the Skopets leader Pavel Ivanovich" in the province of Kursk and usually came back "enlightened."[41]

The story of the first Shalaput communities in the provinces of Tavrida and Bessarabia, which was recorded during the 1840s and 1860s, demonstrated that the Skoptsy influenced these religious dissidents as well. In fact, the first Shalaput communities in southern Russia appeared in localities that were previously centers of Skoptsy's activity. The style and character of the Shalaput religious songs were similar to those sung among the Tavrida Skoptsy.[42] According to their theology, all Shalaput communities attempted to restore the Christian ideal of pious monastic life in the world. Carnal desires and sins, such as sexual urges and intercourse, were thought to threaten this ideal. As a result, the Shalaputs avoided sex and tried to remove any expression of sexuality from their life. The most radical dissenters physically mutilated and castrated themselves.

In 1841–42, the police discovered the first signs of castration among the most zealous activists and leaders of the Shalaputs from Bessarabia and Tavrida. Castration became an important initiation ritual for them. Those who were ready spiritually and had undergone special religious rituals were selected for castration. The special messenger of the dissident communities from central Russia visited local Shalaputs and performed castration on selected activists. All criminal cases confirmed this fact.[43] As both the police and the Orthodox clergy documents noted, until the end of the 1870s, Skopets leaders from the central Russian provinces (mainly from Kursk and Belgorod) provided guidance and performed the rituals of castration in the Shalaput communities of Tavrida and Bessarabia.

As it turned out, female Shalaputs also participated in the ceremonies of castration: They sang, danced, and prayed during the operation, and they took care of wounds.[44] The bloody baptism of castration and rejection of sex appeared to be a collective ritual, which united all male and female Shalaputs in a new antisexual identity, one that did not make a distinction between genders. As millennial Christians, they were to have neither physiological nor cultural distinctions of gender. Therefore, to prepare themselves for the Millennium, the first Shalaput zealots tried to eliminate these distinctions among both female and male dissidents.[45]

The most active Shalaput in the village of Mikhailovka (Tavrida) was Mitrofan Shakhov, a local peasant, who opened his house for secret meetings for worship. Under his direction, the Mikhailovka Shalaputs collaborated with the Shalaputs of Spasskoe, Vesioloe, and Timoshevka, all of whom were related to them. His house became the meetinghouse, where Skopets guests from central Russia performed rituals such as castration.[46] All the local Shalaput leaders had previous experience either with the Khlysty or Skoptsy. The head of the Shalaputs and the wealthiest peasant in the village of Timoshevka (Tavrida), Stepan Robotiagov, organized a special meeting for worship in his house and invited "all pious and religious people," including itinerant Orthodox monks, Khlysty, and Skoptsy. Konon Iarkin, another wealthy peasant who had been already arrested for his connections with a Skopets sect in 1854, organized a Shalaput meeting in the village of Matveevka. Iarkin continued his Skopets experiments with the children of his neighbors. He invited the most religious peasant boys, who were nine and ten years of age, to his house and performed a special medical procedure to prepare them for a happy sinless life. During

279

this operation, Iarkin pushed the boys' testicles through an inguinal hole inside the abdomen to arrest the development of their genitals. Iarkin's activities resulted in the increase of a number of Shalaputs in Matveevka.[47]

The proportion of the "castrated" female and male members among the Shalaput was different from the Skopets sects of the central Russia. Among typical Skoptsy, the castrated men prevailed over women; whereas among the early Shalaputs, female members with mutilated genitals constituted the majority.[48] The police discovered that all the castrated Shalaputs lived in large families with their "spiritual wives." Some of these women, who were presented by Skopets peasants as their wives, were not their legal spouses.[49]

Except for the few activists who were ready for the "Heavenly Kingdom," the majority of the Shalaputs controlled their sexual urges by means other than castration. They lived in closed communities and avoided sexual relations. As all contemporaries noted, a visible distinction of the Shalaputs from their Orthodox neighbors was that they avoided meat and alcoholic beverages. In other respects, they followed the rules of the Orthodox Church, regularly participated in church ceremonies, and performed all religious rituals and peasant obligations.[50]

The Shalaput movement in Tavrida did not stop with the arrest of the Skopets leaders among the local Shalaputs. In 1873, during the police interrogation, the prophet Ilya, the famous Skopets activist, told the police that the village of Bol'shoi Tokmak in the province of Tavrida was still the main center of the "Skopets sect." On July 21, 1873, a police doctor examined six peasant women, all of whom were relatives of the arrested Shalaputs. All had been "castrated" (in fact, their genitals were only mutilated with a knife), probably six or seven years earlier, when their Shalaput fathers and husbands were exiled to Siberia. The priest of the Bol'shoi Tokmak church, Apollon Shcherbakov, complained to the bishop of Tavrida about the indifference of the local police and district administration toward the Shalaputs. Though all these women from the Shalaput families visited the parish church and performed religious rituals on a regular basis, they still behaved as former Shalaputs, avoiding meat, alcohol, and sexual intercourse.[51]

The overwhelming majority of the arrested Shalaputs were women. During the trials of the 1860s and 1870s, women made up 75 percent of the most zealous Shalaputs.[52] Such involvement by women in religious dissent was a new phenomenon for peasant communities. It threatened a patriarchal system of authority in both the peasant family and community. In addition, the Shalaputs demonstrated the new identity of the peasant woman as a religious activist. From the 1860s on, such activity of peasant women became typical for the entire evangelical movement in southern Russia.

By the end of the 1870s, cases of castration had disappeared among the Tavrida and Bessarabia Shalaputs. Contemporary observers noted that evangelical influences replaced the Skoptsy practices among these dissidents. New and more "interiorized" and rational methods of sexual control became more important for peasant dissidents than physical mutilation. At the same time, a moderate "inner-worldly" asceticism, which was a typical phenomenon for Russian Skoptsy as well, began shaping the behavior and sexual practices of the Shalaputs in southern Russia. Still, the ideal of ascetic behavior among them was the monastic lifestyle, without sexual relations.[53] Even during the 1880s, Klim Malasai, a Shalaput activist from the province of Ekaterinoslav, taught local peasants that the ideal Christian would be either a castrated Skopets or a monk. According to him, any religious person could reach the Skopets level by fasting and avoiding sex and "other temptations of this world." The best way to accomplish this, he said, was to join a monastery or convent.[54]

The most widespread method of sexual control was a long fast. The Shalaputs tried to regulate the sexual energy of their coreligionists. They exhausted themselves with various ecstatic rituals, which were reminiscent of the American Shakers' religious practices. But when their coreligionists were unable to resist "the temptations of the flesh," the Shalaput leaders tried to redirect sexual urges and control sexual expression in their community.[55]

"Preparation for the Millennium" and the Elevation of Gender: "Lustful Prophets," Female Preachers, and the Restoration of Sexuality

Other Shalaputs developed quite different attitudes toward sex and sexuality. They extolled the enthusiastic women and encouraged their "sacred ecstasy" at meetings for worship. The most extreme Shalaput groups reemphasized the expression of sexuality and practiced rituals with erotic elements.

From the movement's outset, female "prophetesses" and preachers played leading roles during Shalaput meetings. In contrast to the patriarchal peasant authority with its suppression of creativity and sexuality, the dissident communities offered peasant women new opportunities to express themselves and develop their abilities for social activism.[56] According to contemporary observers, women were more likely than men to respond emotionally to the ecstatic elements of Shalaput worship. Those women who had been noted for more frequent cases of spirit possession became leaders of meetings and living incarnations of the Holy Spirit.

Following Khlyst religious practices, the Shalaputs created a dual system of power in their communities. In contrast to the traditional male-centered congregation, they introduced two interconnected centers of authority—the male type of "living Christ" and female type of "God's Mother."[57] The most ecstatic, most beautiful female members of their community played the role of God's Mother (*bogoroditsa*), or "the Virgin" of the community. Like "the Virgins" and "prophetesses" of Katasonov's sect (the "Old Israel"), the Shalaput God's Mothers ruled the dissident communities and led their meetings together with their male partners—"the living Christs."[58] Katasonov's followers from the Northern Caucasus provided the first model of such dual power for the Shalaput communities. The most famous couple of prophets for the sect of Old Israel consisted of "the living God" Porfirii (Perfil) Katasonov, who was exiled to the Caucasus in the 1870s, and God's Mother Agafia (Gania, or Gasha) Ieiskaia (Bashkatova). In 1873, after Katasonov had left for his native village in the province of Tambov, matushka (an intimate Russian word for "a mother" sometimes used for a nun or the wife of a priest) Gania Ieiskaia became the undisputed leader and arbiter of the entire Shalaput movement not only in the province of Stavropol' but also in the provinces of Ekaterinoslav, Tavrida, and Kherson.[59] Every Shalaput meeting had a final ritual of confessions and kissing the legs (or knees) of the "living Christ" and "God's Mother."[60]

In some Shalaput communities, such as the Marianovtsy, from the early beginning of their history the dual system of power was replaced by female authority. In 1864–65, a soldier's widow, Marianna Timofeieva, established a sect of 155 people in five villages in Tavrida. Before the end of the 1880s, she was the only leader of the sect.[61] At about this time, Katasonov's sect of Old Israel in the Northern Caucasus split into two factions. One was called the "Matrionovtsy" because the leader of these dissidents was "the Virgin" Matriona, a peasant girl from the village of Lezhanka in the province of Stavropol'. In this faction, the female figure of "God's Mother" eventually replaced the male prophets and "living Christs." It is noteworthy that the other faction, which was called the "Likhachiovtsy" after Roman Likhachiov, a successor of Katasonov, was also led by a woman.

The first "God's Mother" of Katasonov's sect in the province of Stavropol', Gasha Ieiskaia (Bashkatova), promoted Likhachiov's career in the Shalaput community. As an influential figure among the Shalaputs, *matushka* Gania justified Likhachiov's position as the "living God" by permitting him to marry her daughter Annushka and introducing him to other Shalaput leaders as the successor of Katasonov, who had died in 1885. Through Likhachiov, *matushka* Gasha controlled other Shalaput communities.[62] By the 1880s, in some Shalaput communities in the province of Ekaterinoslav, women had become the center of worship and discipline. According to the police from the Pavlograd district, "God's Mother" or *bogoroditsa* played a more prestigious role of the "saint" among the local Shalaputs than her male counterpart, the "prophet."[63]

Describing the Shalaputs' meetings, police officers often noted that "the young men and women (especially women) were more excited by the novelty and variety of "expressions of worship" in their secluded household life rather then by the tenets of a new faith. That was why they (mostly women) were eager to visit these newly open meetings for worship." These women visited the sect's meetings without their husbands' or families' permission, and they presented various gifts for the sect's community, "stealing something from their households."[64]

The new sects offered a cultural alternative for hundreds of peasant families who joined the Shalaputs. As the bishop of Ekaterinoslav and Taganrog reported on May 18, 1875, "The Shalaput propaganda was organized mostly among the peasant women." The Shalaputs attracted "the most zealous and

283

loyal peasants, who surpassed their surrounding peasant mass in their religious knowledge and intellect." The peasant women liked the new attitude of the Shalaputs, who respected the dignity of women and treated them as equal members of the "Christian Brotherhood and Sisterhood."[65] Even Orthodox authors who treated peasant dissidents suspiciously acknowledged that the attitudes of Shalaputs toward their female coreligionists attracted peasant women. Orthodox missionaries working in the province of Stavropol' noted that the possibility of new social activities for women in the dissident communities also attracted female believers to the Shalaputs.

Women were attracted to the new aesthetic elements—singing and dancing together with men. Peasant women who felt exploited and humiliated by men in their families and whose lives were confined to the household discovered new respect and humane attitudes in Shalaput communities. As one Orthodox author wrote, "The male and female members of the Shalaput sect called each other affectionately 'darling' or 'bread-winner' and always used pet names for each other. Such humane attitudes enticed Orthodox peasant women who were especially aware of their beauty and proud of it. It is noteworthy that the majority of women who joined the Shalaput sect were of this kind."[66]

Hence, the Shalaput community provided an obvious alternative to the lifestyle typical for Orthodox peasant women. One Dar'ia Serdiuk, a former "God's Mother" of the Shalaput community in the village of Sotnikovo in the Northern Caucasus, repented under pressure of her relatives and returned to the Orthodox Church. According to her recorded confession, "she joined the Shalaputs because she liked her growing influence among the dissidents." Dar'ia related to an Orthodox missionary how flattering it was to feel everybody worshiping her, kissing her hands and knees, and calling her "our God's Mother!" She said it was especially flattering to be the center of attention for the male members of their community.[67] We can see that peasant women discovered in the rituals of the new sect's compensation for their suppressed sexuality.

In a typical Shalaput community, a prophetess was always the center of worship. The Shalaputs explained that Jesus Christ regarded all His female followers as equal to His Mother. Likewise, they considered their female coreligionists, who were followers of the Shalaput "living God," to be their

"God's Mothers."[68] Another factor also influenced the position of women among the Shalaputs. Women who demonstrated a knowledge of herbs and the unusual abilities to cure people became Shalaput leaders as well. A peasant woman from the province of Stavropol', Glikeria Morozova, attracted her neighbors to the Shalaput sect by her ability to heal wounds and cure diseases such as rheumatism rather than by her preaching. Under her influence, 100 Orthodox peasants joined her sect and became the most zealous Shalaputs in the province of Stavropol' and the whole region of Kuban'.[69]

A majority of the Shalaputs thought that God could be reincarnated in a person who did not sin, followed biblical rules, and did only good. They believed that God made the followers of such a person worship him or her as a saint and regard his or her actions as having been directed by God Himself. According to the Shalaputs, only women were able to reach the highest level of holiness. In the village of Dobrin'kaia, the local Shalaputs worshiped their beautiful "God's Mother" Maria Lebed'. During ecstatic prayer, she cast off her robe and danced naked "under the influence of the Holy Spirit."[70] It is noteworthy that her act of undressing contributed to mass ecstasy among female participants of the ritual that combined elements of apparent eroticism (Maria's naked beautiful body), the sacred drama of resurrection (Maria imitated her death and rise from the dead), and maternal symbolism (she imitated her giving the birth to "new Jesus Christ"). Most observers of such cases of mass ecstasy noted this combination of elements. The Shalaputs, the radical Stundists (called the "spiritual Christians"), and the Maliovantsy—all shared a similar scenario of "saintly hysteria." The acts of undressing and showing a naked woman's body during the ecstatic dancing always intensified the emotions of these dissidents.[71]

The actions of the Ukrainian peasant woman Maria Lebed' in 1886 contained the basic elements (including its erotic components) of ecstatic ritual of resurrection, which were typical for all prophetesses of the radical millennial sect.[72] Scholars such as the French psychiatrist Jean-Martin Charcot and the Russian Orthodox specialist of "mystic sects" Dmitrii Konovalov have noted the pathological link between religious hysteria and eroticism in the ecstatic dancing of the religious enthusiasts.[73] Extremes of religious ecstasy

285

have always included elements of suppressed sexuality—from the earliest ecstatic Christian sects to the medieval and Renaissance "religious dance epidemics" (known as the dance of Saint Guy or of Saint Vitus). In more recent times, the American Shakers, Russian Khlysts, and Shalaputs have demonstrated this link between sexuality, a woman's body, and religious enthusiasm. The observers noted that a woman's naked body became a center of the ecstatic worship among religious radicals of imperial Russia, including the sects of Shalaputs, "spiritual" (radical) Stundists, and the Maliovantsy.

A rejection of traditional marital norms and the elevation of sexuality among religious radicals became part of their "cultural rebellion." At the same time, the replacement of castration with new methods of sexual control did not work in dissident communities, where new members were not ready for new sexual discipline. A combination of elevated sexuality and eroticism with a lack of religious indoctrination and discipline resulted in excesses of sexual permissiveness, especially after the 1870s with the disappearance of castration among the Shalaputs. In some extremist groups of Shalaputs, their leaders also offered new sexual roles and experiences to their participants. To some extent, they tried to release the suppressed sexual energy and transform the act of sexual intercourse into a "sacred drama" of transubstantiation, when the bodies of the participants became the body of Christ. Katasonov's followers from the Northern Caucasus opposed "the hypocrisy of Orthodox marriage" and insisted on a necessity of "spiritual marriages," based on "sincere love." Other Shalaputs contrasted their "sincere relations between spiritual wives and husbands" with the "sexual transgressions" of married Orthodox peasants, who tried "to hide their lewdness under their ostentatious monogamy."[74]

Some of extremist leaders presented sexual permissiveness as something inspired by God. They interpreted the Gospel story about the woman of Samaria and Jesus Christ as a description of a "Divine sexual act." According to itinerant Khlyst-Shalaput prophets—such as Fedor Lutsenko, a Ukrainian peasant from the province of Voronezh, known in Orthodox monasteries as Fedor Khokhol—the "living water" that Christ offered the woman of Samaria at the deep well was His Divine sperm. "The Savior anointed the woman of Samaria with His Divine semen," Lutsenko explained to his brother," and she accepted this anointing with love."[75] Such an extremist version of the "God's People" theology presented the Shalaput prophets as incarnations of the Holy Ghost, whose bodies emanated Divine holiness. Therefore, all their bodily functions, including ejaculation and orgasm, were also holy acts of Divine Love, which joined all true believers in Christian Brotherhood and Sisterhood. The laws and conventional rules of sexual behavior were not applicable to these "spiritual Christians:" "There is, therefore, now no condemnation of them who are in Christ Jesus, who walk not after the flesh, but after the Spirit" (Romans 8:1).[76]

Katasonov's followers explained to an Orthodox missionary that a man and woman should not resist a love generated by the Holy Spirit. Directed by such love, they said, "a man can sleep with any woman and do with her what he wants, except defiling the marital bed." Therefore, the Shalaputs justified various sexual techniques, including "coitus interruptus." Sometimes peasants who joined their sect misunderstood these new relations and interpreted them as sexual promiscuity. Some of those renegades who were disappointed with the Shalaput community always emphasized sexual permissiveness as a distinctive feature of the dissidents' lifestyle. One peasant widow, who made a pilgrimage to Katasonov in the province of Tambov, complained later to the same missionary that Katasonov raped her and "bit her hands while having sex" with her.[77] This evidence is a good illustration of how different the Shalaput communities in southern Russia were. It turned out that the widow, who claimed to have been raped, represented the mainstream of the Shalaputs who avoided sexual relations and tried to live a "monastic life." It was the scandalous behavior of the so-called Lustful Shalaput Prophets that the Orthodox clergy used in their campaign to persecute the new sects.[78]

The most scandalous figure among the "Lustful Prophets" of southern Russia and Ukraine was Fedor Lutsenko. According to his brother's memoirs, he began his religious activities as a typical Shalaput in 1872 when he was twenty years of age. He visited various Orthodox monasteries, where he met one itinerant preacher, a Shalaput who taught about Divine Love. This itinerant preacher, "Old Man" Iagor [or Egor], explained to Lutsenko that any holy man who made love to woman would transform her when "he touched her with his holy flesh." According to his explanation, Christianity denied only such "carnal love" as lacked "faith in God." After this conversation in 1872, Fedor invited Iagor to visit his village in the Ostrogozhskii district, near Voronezh. Iagor preached his teaching to Fedor's neighbors. Women confessed their sins to Iagor, who after prayers made love to each one of them. Fedor's wife was among them. She described her sexual intercourse with the Old Man as an "unearthly" experience and an act of Divine revelation. After this, Fedor followed Iagor and became his loyal adherent.

According to his brother, Fedor Lutsenko had been an activist of the Russian-Ukrainian community of Khlyst-Shalaputs for many years, and made monthly pilgrimages to different Orthodox monasteries and convents. During these pilgrimages, he attracted the attention of Orthodox nuns, especially those of peasant origin. By 1900, Old Man Fedor was the most popular pilgrim among the nuns in the province of Voronezh. He invited some of them to live with him. He dug small caves near his house for these Orthodox nuns and established a small cloister for the pious peasant women there. During the period 1898–1900, the local administration of Voronezh Diocese complained about Lutsenko's activities during his pilgrimage to monasteries. In 1898, the peasant women from his "cloister" joined the Holy Trinity nunnery, which had recently opened in the Ostrogozhskii district, and he became a regular visitor to this convent. The local clergy accused him of sexual misconduct and asked the police to arrest him and the nuns who followed him.[79]

During the investigation, Lutsenko described his theology and religious practices, which revealed the details of very unusual sexual activities of the so-called Lustful Prophets among the Shalaputs. Lutsenko taught his followers that God's Spirit dwelled in his body and generated all his thoughts and actions. Therefore, he said, all his words and acts belonged to the Holy Spirit, regardless of however strange they seemed. "My lips are just moving, but the Holy Spirit speaks," Lutsenko explained, "everything that I do is done not by me but by the Holy Spirit." In his preaching, he paraphrased the Gospels and taught his followers that "according to the Holy Scripture it is a sin to abuse the Holy Spirit and those who embody It. When the Holy Spirit dwells in me, Divine Law protects my actions."

As Lutsenko explained to his followers, the Heavenly Kingdom located in his body could be opened for others only through carnal copulation. His penis was the sacred key to the lock of the Heavenly Kingdom. Saint Peter's keys from Paradise, he said, were an allusion to the sacred flesh of the holy people. Through sexual intercourse with holy people, women received Divine grace and "sacred union with the Holy Spirit." Lutsenko called an act of sexual intercourse "an anointing by the holy people." According to his interpretation, this act had more spiritual meaning for establishing believers' intimate links with the Holy Spirit than any church ritual or ceremony.[80]

During the 1880s, Fedor Lutsenko became one of the leaders of the local Shalaput community in the Ukrainian village of Pokrovka near Voronezh. As his brother noted in his memoirs, Fedor, together with his "prophetess" Maria, organized special meetings of Divine Love in Fedor's house. After long period of fasting and long nightly praying, the holy people, Fedor and Maria, selected couples of their followers to make love under their guidance, and at the end of the meeting they picked "the most pious" coreligionists for their personal sexual intercourse as well. Usually, the majority of men had "sacred copulation" with Maria, and most of the women had sex with Fedor.

According to his brother, Fedor taught that the main element of Divine Love was an act of copulation with "a worthy believer" who was ready for union with the Holy Spirit. This act was equal to the physical purification of the body, through a spiritual link between "the believing man and woman." Fedor nevertheless preserved the same respect for asceticism followed by more traditional Shalaputs. He taught that holy people who went to monasteries and cloisters to become monks and nuns were able to avoid "the temptations of flesh" and enter the Heavenly Kingdom of the Holy Spirit without acts of carnal copulation. Those who were not strong enough to reject sex had to participate in sexual intercourse "under the guidance of the Holy Spirit." Fedor accepted only controlled acts of copulation made with Christian faith. Without strong belief, he said, sexual intercourse was sinful. But if the sexual partners made love to each other under the influence of the Holy Spirit, copulation was the most sacred ritual.[81]

According to his brother's memoirs, to avoid the pregnancy of his sexual partners, especially young and sexually inexperienced girls, Fedor used coitus interruptus during his "sessions of Divine Love." Still, there were cases when he impregnated some of his enthusiastic followers. These naturally resulted in scandal. His brother described Fedor's emotional shock, when he realized in 1882 that one of his youngest and most devoted followers, a beautiful peasant girl, had conceived his baby. The respectable leaders of the local Shalaput communities criticized his very unconventional interpretation of biblical texts and his sexual experiments.

When faced with accusations of sexual transgression, Fedor repented before *matushka,* who was the leader of the Shalaputs in Voronezh. After his confessions, she ordered him to leave the pregnant girl under her protection and sent him on a pilgrimage to Solovetskii monastery (the famous Orthodox monastery on an island in the White Sea). Before leaving, Fedor named his brother, Trofim Lutsenko, as his successor, to lead the Pokrovka' Shalaputs.

After Fedor's departure, everything changed in this community. Trofim initially performed "acts of love" with his female coreligionists, but he soon began to doubt the true nature of this sexual intercourse and felt pangs of conscience. Eventually, after the visit of the Shalaput *matushka,* who was appalled at the promiscuity of Lutsenko's followers, Trofim decided to join a new Shalaput community that avoided "the sexual excesses" of his brother. However, in spite of his criticism of his brother's "carnal sins," Trofim continued to maintain two wives. One, his old spouse, was his "worldly" wife; the other, a young and beautiful peasant woman and the wife of Trofim's neighbor, was his "spiritual" wife.

Until the end of his days, Trofim lived with both wives in one household, and they raised their children together. At the same time, he tried to influence Fedor to change his lifestyle. Trofim worried that Fedor was involved in sexual transgressions with his female "Khlyst partner." It is important that in his description of sexual sins Trofim used the word "Khlyst" as a way to distinguish him from the majority of Shalaputs. Even "the Shalaput Virgin" (*matushka*) in conversation with Trofim used this word "Khlyst" in making her accusations about Fedor's sexual excesses. As police documents revealed, the majority of the Shalaput communities avoided sexual intercourse and censured Fedor Lutsenko's experiments. At the same time, according to Trofim's mem-

290

oirs, Khlyst and Shalaput communities had a similar power structure: a male prophet, or "saint" (Fedor Lutsenko) and "a Virgin," or "God's Mother" (Fedor's partner).[82] These similarities sometimes led to all Shalaputs being accused of sexual transgressions.

Despite criticism of his transgressions, Fedor Lutsenko continued his preaching and sexual experiments. Even in his fifties and sixties, the "*starets* [sage] Fedor" was noted for his performance of "Divine Love" with his followers. His favorite locations were Orthodox convents. According to testimony from 1900, Lutsenko tried to seduce the young nuns with a variety of different methods. His usual practice was to bring his most devoted nuns at night to the cells of other more attractive, younger nuns and to lie down together with them on the floor. Then, after a long prayer, he would caress, fondle, and kiss the older nuns in front of the younger ones. Sometimes he also attracted young nuns by expressions of religiosity. As one nun explained, he bowed in prayer as fast "as a wind" and spoke eloquently like a "literate priest" rather than like an ignorant peasant. Sometimes he simply took young and inexperienced nuns by force. As a result of his scandalous activities, he was expelled from the women's convent of Holy Trinity near Voronezh, and seven nuns, including the former mother superior of this monastery, were defrocked for their participation in his "rituals."[83]

Lutsenko's punishment did not stop other Lustful Prophets. Another Shalaput, Mikhail (or Ivan) Shukin, a peasant from the province of Orenburg, a migrant to southern Russia, introduced himself to Orthodox nuns as a saint sent by God. He explained that his mission was to save ordinary people through "spiritual union," by spreading his "spiritual semen" to those who needed the guidance of the Holy Spirit. Usually, Shukin asked his female followers to fast for two or three weeks, and then afterward he invited them for a "session of Divine Love." During the meeting for worship, these fasting women prayed until exhaustion. When their emotions reached a peak of ecstasy and they felt the descent of the Holy Spirit, Shukin had sex with them. Ekaterina Savina—a nun from Pokrovskii convent ("Pokrov" in Russian refers to "the Protective Veil of the Virgin") in Voronezh—introduced him to the other nuns of her monastery. Shukin became a regular visitor there during the period

1895–99. When the police tried to arrest him, he fled to southern Ukraine and disappeared.[84]

From 1884 to 1886, in the Shalaput community of Nikolaevka (a village in the Kherson district), the local prophet Ivan Skirko also preached about Divine Love "hidden in the souls of men and women." He urged his co-religionists to release their sexual feelings that had been suppressed by the conventional norms of their peasant community. He encouraged sexual relations between "spiritual wives and husbands" in contrast to the "hypocritical marriages" of the Orthodox Church. As in other Shalaput communities, the Nikolaevka Shalaputs respected the rights of women to marry those whom they loved. Therefore, if a Shalaput woman (even a married one) were to fall in love with a Shalaput man, their leader would declare the new affair a "spiritual marriage" and recommend that they leave their former spouses.

Skirko taught that strong sexual relations were established on the "firm foundation of Christian faith," especially during ecstatic Shalaput rituals when the Holy Spirit influenced the Shalaputs. Skirko explained that the true believers did not need to hide their feelings because "hidden or suppressed desire" usually led to sin. God created men and women with genitals for procreation and joy. Therefore, Skirko said, God sanctioned the sincere sexual desire of his believers. Skirko requested all female members of his community to confess to him on a regular basis. After such confessions, two young girls conceived children by him and considered him their "spiritual husband."[85] The followers of Skirko demonstrated what radical religious dissidents had practiced to strengthen and protect their communities from outside influences. Like John Humphrey Noyes and the Oneida Community in the United States, Skirko and his Shalaputs used sexual relations inside a dissident community to create intimate ties among female and male members and to promote their spiritual unity before God.[86]

Some authors who have studied the Shalaput communities in the province of Kharkov have noted similar encouragement of sexual relations among "spiritual spouses" inside that community. In the 1890s, Vasilii Podgornyi, a leader of the Shalaputs in the Akhtyrka district, insisted on obligatory changes of sexual partners among his followers. According to his view, no woman should keep her virginity. Because of her Christian meekness, she had to let any man who desired her have sex with her. Moreover, giving her body to "any thirsty man"—especially to crippled ones (*kaleka*) or suffering coreligionists—was the "sacred" mission of a woman. Podgornyi's female adherents viewed the submissive position of woman during the sexual intercourse as an act of obedience to the Divine will.[87] Podgornyi's sect demonstrated how strong traditions of popular Orthodoxy and peasant patriarchal relations were present even among radical dissenters. Although they exploited the suppressed sexuality to strengthen their community, Podgornovtsy still saw women's sexuality as subordinate to the will of men.

Some Shalaput extremists from the province of Kherson even encouraged sex with "the Virgin" (*bogoroditsa*) of the meeting. In 1888, the police discovered the "strange sect of the Stundists with sexual promiscuity" (they apparently confused the Shalaputs and Stundists in their report) in the Anan'iev district of the same province. According to the police, the local dissident leaders, peasants Dmitrii Sosin and Feodot Gumeniuk, invited "one prophetess to their meeting for worship to have sex with their coreligionists." They organized the sexual acts with the prophetess as the special rituals of initiation for new members of their sect. It is noteworthy that the police treated such cases as exceptional. But the Orthodox clergy used the mistakenly applied name of Stundists to the communities with sexual transgressions in order to brand these dissenters as "dangerous sexual perverts" as well.[88] A majority of contemporary observers, however, emphasized that sexual promiscuity was exceptional among the Shalaputs, who tried to control and direct sexual urges through their system of "spiritual marriages." All the experts conceded that sexual promiscuity was unique to the Shalaputs—despite what the Orthodox Church claimed.[89]

Sexual rituals and experimentation were more typical of individual itinerant Shalaput "prophets" rather than of Shalaput communities as a whole. Most Shalaput communities refused to have anything to do with preachers noted for sexual transgressions. One such outcast was Ivan Naichenko, a peasant from the village of Krivoi Rog (in Kherson province). During the period 1885–91, Naichenko settled in the village of Lozovatka in Ekaterinoslav province, where

293

he preached ideas of Divine Love analogous to those of Lutsenko and Shukin. Naichenko rejected the ideas of the Shalaputs about the strict avoidance of sex in the life of Christian believers. Instead of the Shalaput rejection of sex, he made sex the primary element of his religious practices. According to the local peasants' testimony, he came to their villages as a holy prophet and asked about repentance and the confession of sins. Peasants brought money and their agricultural products to the new saint. Some of the peasant women, who visited Naichenko, confessed that they always prayed with the prophet, who asked them to undress and lie in the bed with him.

As it turned out, Naichenko had various forms of sexual relations with these women. During the police investigation, Elisaveta Dereviankina, a peasant, explained that she believed in the holiness of Naichenko. That was why she visited this "prophet" with her neighbor, Iraisa Sidorenko, to ask him to pray to God for them. These peasant women brought two large watermelons as their presents to the prophet. Naichenko met them at the entrance and smashed their melons in front of them with the words, "you will be broken like these melons." After a long prayer, the prophet brought Iraisa with him into a room, sent Elisaveta to a small antechamber, and asked Iraisa to make him a bed for the night.

Meanwhile, he went out to the antechamber and preached to Elisaveta about Divine Love. Then he put her hand on his penis, drove her into a corner, and asked her to stand with her legs apart. She was so shocked and frightened that she lost consciousness. When Naichenko returned to his room, he forced Iraisa to have sex with him. According to Iraisa's testimony, she was frightened and simultaneously attracted to him. She could not explain what kind of power made her obey his orders. [90]

During the police investigation, these peasant women described the very intimate details of the prophet's sexual rituals. Most women who had visited Naichenko tried to defend him as a "saint." Their typical response to accusations of sexual transgressions was the following: "He is not guilty, because he is a blessed person, inspired by the Holy Spirit." Even the police noted the element of fascination in these women's testimonies. Agafia Polivoda also shared her sexual experience with the police. After ecstatic praying, she said, the prophet asked her to undress and gave her a benediction. Under his spell, she suddenly realized that she was naked in his bed. She recalled that he lay with her, naked himself. As far as she could remember, it was not as unpleasant as it usually felt during sexual intercourse. Therefore, she denied that she had copulated with the prophet. Yet she admitted that later she discovered Naichenko's semen on her body.

Many women followers of such Shalaput prophets as Naichenko contrasted what they felt during "the rituals of Divine Love" with the unpleasant painful sensations of sexual intercourse in their marriages.[91] Although the police tried to emphasize the disgust and outrage of women who participated in Naichenko's sexual rituals, their reports revealed the popularity and attractiveness of Lutsenko, Naichenko, and other peasant prophets who attempted to release the suppressed sexuality of peasant women.

In addition to the perception of the sexual act as unity with a Divine Being and a means of solidarity for members of the dissident community, Naichenko's case revealed the existence of strong sexual feelings and desires among the peasant women. Feminist authors usually associate women's rights to sexual desire and the satisfaction of their sexual needs with the rise of "a modern personality" among European and American women.[92] The Ukrainian peasant women who revealed their erotic secrets to the police participated in what Michel Foucault described as a "sexual discourse."[93] Instead of confessing to Orthodox priests, whom they did not trust, these women confessed the details of their sexual adventures to the police agents. The police investigation replaced the ritual of confession as a "mode of production of truth," and it revealed the spread of sexual knowledge and erotic fantasies in the peasant society of southern Russia and Ukraine, which recent historians have portrayed as traditionalist and patriarchal.[94] In peasant families, husbands usually treated their wives cruelly, without taking into account women's individual wishes and desires. Peasant wives were subjected to cruel beatings and humiliation. Dissident "prophets" and the Shalaput communities, with their principle of "spiritual love," offered peasant women radically better treatment.

A revival of the Shalaput ideas and practices of "spiritual love" was also noted among the followers of Kondrat Maliovannyi in the provinces of Kiev

295

and Kherson during the 1890s and 1900s. One of the prophets among the Maliovantsy, Ivan Lysenko, preached about "Divine Love" and the coming Millennium to his followers in the villages of the Skvira district (in Kiev province). In 1899, his preaching attracted local peasant women, who joined his sect and participated in his rituals. Lysenko insisted that in the Kingdom of Jesus Christ there was no private property and no restrictions on "spiritual love" between men and women. According to him, the Heavenly Kingdom of Jesus Christ was coming. Therefore, he said, all true Christians should reject conventional norms and "artificial rules that predated the Millennium," including loyalty to the state and Orthodox marriages. Lysenko was a handsome and passionate preacher. Contemporary observers noted that his female adherents found him sexually attractive. One young peasant woman confessed to an Orthodox missionary, "When he breathes on me, I forget everything; I am ready to follow him as far as America."[95]

All the women who came to Lysenko to confess their sins became his lovers. A majority of them, including the beautiful Agafia Rudchuk, a niece of Kondrat Maliovannyi, were married. Eventually, they became the leading performers of spirit possession during their ecstatic rituals and played an important role in the organization of the numerically large community of the Maliovantsy in November 1899. Some of Lysenko's followers changed their sexual partners. To some extent, the experiments of Lysenko's community resembled the practices of "spiritual marriages" in the Khlyst-Shalaput communities of southern Russia. It is noteworthy that Kondrat Maliovannyi did not support Lysenko's practices of "spiritual marriage." Moreover, he condemned Lysenko's experiments as sexual transgression.[96] Despite Maliovannyi's negative reaction, Lysenko's ideas of Divine love were part of the millennial discourse initiated by Maliovannyi himself in 1889. An anticipation of the Millennium generated a negative attitude toward traditional marital norms and provoked more liberal notions about sex among all enthusiastic Christians who shared the similar ideas of the radical reformation.[97]

Contemporary observers noted that Lysenko's preaching was especially attractive in the villages of Luchina and Turbovka among communities of radical Stundists famous for their ecstatic rituals and spirit possession. That was why all local radical Stundists had converted to the Maliovantsy by 1893. The first Maliovantsy in these villages had a dual power structure. A male prophet (Ivan Mozhar) and a prophetess (Oksana) ruled their community in Turbovka in 1891–92 and they preached about Divine Love as well. As a result, the local rural population was ready for Lysenko's experiments. A majority of the local Maliovantsy supported him, despite Maliovannyi's criticism of his activities.[98]

The peak of preaching and practice of "free spiritual love" among the Maliovantsy took place when they expected the eve of the Millennium. During the first expectation of Christ's Kingdom in 1891–92, the Maliovantsy from the province of Kiev preached about the disappearance of all distinctions of social status, age, and gender among them. They rejected all former family relations and the traditional subordination of family members. They called each other "brother, or sister." The Maliovantsy considered their coreligionists to be "of one body and one spirit" without differences in age or gender. Male members of the sect explained to an Orthodox missionary, "now [on the eve of the Millennium] all women are wives of Jesus Christ." At the same time, the female members said, "for us male gender does not exist anymore; there are no gender differences in the Heavenly Kingdom."[99] On the eve of the Last Judgment, the Maliovantsy were emotionally ready to perform the acts of the sacred drama of the reincarnation.

On January 28, 1900, the family of the Stundist peasant Vasilii Avramenko, a zealous adherent of Maliovannyi in the province of Kiev, expected the end of the world. Vasilii, his wife, and daughter took their clothes off, burned them in an oven, and went naked and barefoot into their yard, which was covered by snow. Then Vasilii tried to kill his son, who resisted him, while other naked members of his family prayed in the snow. When the police arrested them, the naked dissidents denied their gender and their peasant status and called themselves "Divine creatures."[100]

During the expectation of the Millennium, according to the Maliovantsy's calculations, Christ's Kingdom would come and "the Divine universal love" would rule the world. Their activists spread the news about this not only in the province of Kiev but also in the neighboring provinces. One of their

297

prophets, Pimen Ivasiuk, visited the villages of the province of Kherson, urged his listeners to reject marriage and to accept "free sexual relations" based on "sincere love." His activities laid a foundation for new communities of the Maliovantsy in Kherson province. The visits of another coreligionist peasant from the province of Kiev, Kuz'ma Maliuk, were especially influential among the local peasant women. After Kuz'ma's passionate sermons in February 1903, Akilina Kozhukhar', a married peasant Stundist woman from the village of Petro-ostrov, left her husband and joined the Kiev prophet. Even cruel beatings by her husband did not stop her from following Kuz'ma. All observers noted the main topic of prophet's preaching, which attracted women: "free spiritual love" and the "rejection of private property."[101]

In the peasant mentality, private property was connected to the peasant household and the heavy obligations for women to work both at home and in the fields. Preparations for the Millennium, initiated by itinerant prophets of the Maliovantsy, released women from their duties in the peasant household. Moreover, the ecstatic atmosphere of expectations promoted careers of the most emotional and beautiful women in the dissident communities, and they became the leaders and inspirers of the meetings for worship.

Some of them became indisputable authorities for the Maliovantsy. Available materials make it clear that all so-called spiritual Christian groups among the Russian evangelicals—who emphasized spirit possession and the direct influence of the Holy Ghost on believers—elevated the status of woman in their communities. The Shalaputs, radical Stundists, and the Maliovantsy deified woman as God's Mother, a woman who could conceive and give birth to a "living Christ." This elevation of the social role and deification of women became the characteristic element of millennial sects such as the Maliovantsy. The predecessors of the Maliovantsy, 400 followers of the "prophet Venedikt Dushenkovskii" from the village of Skibina near Tarashcha, demonstrated the same attitude as early as 1888. They deified the young beautiful peasant widow Ganna. When the police arrested Dushenkovskii, the leader of their community, Ganna, who adored him, prayed to God for him and fasted for the entire month of December. On Christmas Eve, she had a vision: The Holy Ghost would descend on her, she would conceive a Divine baby, and then she would give birth to Jesus Christ. Through this mission, she said, she was to save humankind from Satan.

The next week, during ecstatic praying, Ganna suddenly fainted. Frightened coreligionists decided that she had died, removed her body to another room of the meetinghouse, and continued their prayer. In the middle of this prayer, Ganna was "resurrected" and cried loudly: "Christ has risen from the dead on the third day [it happened on the third day after her "divine vision"], now we have one faith, one baptism, one God Jesus Christ!" After this "miracle," Ganna prophesized and preached with long quotations from the New Testament, all of which she knew by heart. The ecstasy of prayer reached a peak, and all of Ganna's coreligionists began to worship her, embracing and kissing each other with shouts: "Christ has risen from the dead!" The local Stundists interpreted this miracle as a "visit of the Holy Spirit," accepted Ganna's "Divine authority," and called her "Divinely inspired prophetess."

One day, Ganna announced that she had had another vision about her mission. She reminded her coreligionists that she was supposed to give birth to a "new" Christ. Two peasant women confirmed this and witnessed that they had earlier seen the "beams of Divine fire" and "radiance of the Holy Spirit" on Ganna's face. The dissidents elected the most handsome man of their community to conceive a "divine baby" with Ganna. This man left his wife and stayed with "prophetess" Ganna, who later gave birth to their child. To the frustration of her adherents, this child was a girl, not a boy. Ganna then tried again. Her followers found another handsome partner for Ganna. Unfortunately, her new baby conceived by the new partner was stillborn. A majority of her adherents were disappointed in her ability to fulfill her Divine mission. Eventually they left Ganna, and in 1891 they became the most zealous followers of Kondrat Maliovannyi.[102]

All communities of the Maliovantsy had prophetesses who led ecstatic prayer and played an important role in the decision making and organization of their communities. Some of these "God's Mothers" declared themselves "Jesus Christ, the Savior" and concentrated all power in their own hands. Thus, the prophetess Marina Tikhaia, who was a center of the new millennial expectations in February and March 1903 in the village of Petro-ostrov in the

299

province of Kherson, became the "Christ" of the local community of the Maliovantsy. A majority of the dissidents had problems with this reversal of gender roles and could not accept a "female Christ." They still preferred traditional associations of the female figure with a cult of maternity and scenes of nativity. Therefore, it was declared that Marina would give birth to Kondrat Maliovannyi, "the Divine Judge and the Redeemer of all humankind."

On February 22, 1903, when Marina peeled potatoes, the entire kitchen shone with the Divine Light, and she saw a dove. This dove, she said, had asked her to open her mouth and entered in her body. Then she felt unusual anxiety and joy, and she "realized that Christ palpitated" in her breast. Thus, Marina portrayed her understanding of the sacred phenomenon of the Immaculate Conception and the Annunciation. She felt herself as both Christ and His Mother in one body. After this experience, Marina became the indisputable leader of the entire community of dissidents in Petro-ostrov.[103]

As a typical prophetess of the millennial movement, Marina incarnated simultaneously a male figure of Jesus Christ and a female figure of the Virgin who "experienced Christ's conception through the Holy Spirit." This "dual incarnation" of Christ and God's Mother in a female leader has been common to all chiliastic movements and enthusiastic sects in the history of Christianity. Both contemporaries and historians of the early Quakers and Ranters of the English Revolution, as well as of the Rogerenes and the Shakers in British North America, noted this confusion of gender roles among their enthusiastic leaders.[104]

An important theme—which all Russian peasant religious radicals used in their preaching, praying, and "sacred songs"—was the mystical union of Jesus Christ and the soul of the Christian believer. The songs of the Khlyst and Shalaputs and of the Maliovantsy especially accentuated this theme. They presented this union in terms of the marriage or even sexual encounter between bride and bridegroom. Feminist historians have noted that "this nuptial imagery, which finds much of its inspiration in the interpretation of the Song of Songs as an allegory of Christianity (Jesus as the bridegroom of the soul), has been identified as a constant category of women's—or more generally, feminine—mystical experience."[105]

The majority of Shalaput religious songs contained this nuptial imagery. The Shalaputs often sang about the intimate (almost sexual and erotically explicit) relations of the soul (in the image of the young virtuous girl) and Christ (in the image of the sexually attractive bridegroom). The beautiful girl (a soul) never betrays her bridegroom and waits loyally for the ultimate union that will bring her to the Heavenly Kingdom.[106]

Such imagery became the main component of the millennial symbolism. Both radical Stundists and Maliovantsy considered the close union of the soul and Christ as the main condition for the Millennium. Ecstatic leaders of the peasant dissidents always emphasized in their confessions that the peak of religious ecstasy was a moment of the confluence of the soul and Christ. They associated the human soul literally with the bodies of their prophetesses, such as Marianna (a leader of the Marianovtsy), Ganna, and Marina Tikhaia (from the sect of the Maliovantsy). In other words, they worshiped the women. Only ecstatic prophetesses with bodies of "the Virgin" provided the symbolic link with the collective soul of the dissident community and Jesus Christ. The more beautiful and closer to marriageable age the prophetesses were, the better they fit the nuptial imagery of the peasant mentality. Symbolically, ecstatic rituals of the millennial sects became the "wedding ceremony" of the collective soul of the dissident community, which anticipated the coming of the Heavenly Kingdom. To some extent, this symbolism explains the role of female leaders among the millennial sects, such as early Quakers and American Shakers, or Russian Shalaputs and Ukrainian Maliovantsy.

From the excesses of the Western Radical Reformation in the sixteenth century to experimentation in spirit possession of the new "charismatic" sects of our times, problems of gender and sexuality have always been present in the religious practices of the "radical revivalists." Moreover, these problems always come to the surface during cycles of religious revival in the evolution of a sect, especially a sect with millennial expectations.[107] Comparing Russian Shalaputs to groups such as early Quakers and American Shakers reveals that the more extreme these "charismatic" sects became—both in their ecstatic worship services and in their experimentation with sex—the more freedom and power they gave to women. This was obvious to outside observers, who could compare the

301

respect for and worship of women in dissident communities with the subordination and humiliation of women in the nondissident families.[108]

The experience of Russian religious radicals also showed that the dissident community tried to control expressions of sexuality and subordinated issues of gender to the general needs and goals of Christian community. The main goal of this community was not the self-indulgence of individual members or satisfaction of their erotic desires. A collective of Christian millennial "revivalists" tried to reach an ideal of the Heavenly Kingdom by desexualizing and redirecting the husband–wife relationship so that relations between the sexes became "first and foremost goal-directed." Therefore, the various experiments with sex (from celibacy to polygamy and promiscuity) of such groups can be viewed as part of the subordination of individual pleasure to "long-range group goals."[109]

As historians of ecstatic religion have noted, by means of their new belief system and communal order, both the prophets of "charismatic" sects and their followers "achieved a sense of unity and psychic wholeness which had been missing from their lives." This sense of unity and psychic wholeness became the main psychological condition for achieving the final goal of all millennial sects. The final destination of the Shalaputs, radical Stundists, and Maliovantsy was the Kingdom of Jesus Christ. In this Kingdom, there were no social, ethnic, or sexual distinctions among people who would live in "perfect harmony."[110]

This dream of the Millennium was the psychological reaction of the dispossessed and disoriented peasants of post-Emancipation Russia. As I have already shown in chapter 1, economic life was in rapid flux during the period after the Emancipation, placing special strains on relations between the sexes. The years before Emancipation marked southward expansion, as well as the first stages of industrialization, with all their attendant challenges and problems.

After Emancipation, the most important structural changes in the economy were the decline of the traditional system of peasant agriculture based on communal property and the involvement of peasant households in the market economy. Society was becoming increasingly complex. The economic activities of men and women tremendously diverged, as women were increasingly relegated to the home and men became migrant agricultural workers. The traditional stability of peasant family disappeared under these new economic and cultural circumstances. To some extent, with an intensive migration of the peasant men to the South, traditional gender roles changed in the family. During the long absence of their husbands, women played more important roles in the peasant household. Sometimes women had to perform functions of "the master of the house." The changes in economic and gender roles, together with the restructuring of peasant communes after 1861, contributed to the further disorientation of both men and women. In this situation, the radical religious community offered its own social and psychological substitutes for marital relations, eroticism, and expressions of sexuality.

Beyond the Millennium: The Stundo-Baptist Women

Among the Stundo-Baptists, the millennial trends of religious enthusiasm were obvious only at the beginning of Ukrainian Stundism in the 1860s and 1870s. Ecstatic Stundist women, like the Shalaput prophetesses, generated scenes of religious ecstasy and performed various acts of spirit possession and incarnation.[111] But after the 1870s, under the discipline of the Baptist church and its hierarchy of ministers, the conservative order and discipline suppressed the millennial trends and religious ecstasy. The prophetesses disappeared from the Baptist meetings.

Despite the conservative character of Baptist meetings, Stundo-Baptist peasant women still played a more prominent role in the life of their congregations than Orthodox peasant women did in Orthodox parishes. Contemporary observers noted that the Stundist women not only were active participants in the meetings for worship but also preached sermons and read and commented on the Bible. Sometimes not only Orthodox critics but also male Baptist ministers worried about the attempts of the Baptist women to preach and discuss the Gospels in their meetings. According to them, such women's behavior contrasted with Saint Paul's classic advice: "Let your women keep silence in the churches; for it is not permitted unto them to speak; but they are commanded to be under obedience, as also saith the law" (I Corinthians 14:34).[112]

303

Stundist peasant women represented "a culture of reading" in the Ukrainian countryside. They learned to read and write, and they spent their free time reading and discussing the Bible and other religious books in the family circle. For the first time in the history of the Ukrainian peasant households, women began to consciously opt for reading a book rather than doing regular housework. Moreover, Stundist women took pride in their ability to not only read the Bible but also understand religious rituals and ceremonies. In a conversation with an Orthodox missionary, one Stundist peasant woman from the province of Kiev tried to contrast "the positive pastime of the Stundist family;" that is, reading and no alcohol, with the lifestyle of the typical Orthodox peasant family, with a lot of drinking and no reading.[113]

The Stundist women demonstrated a different kind of behavior for peasant woman. They participated in discussions organized by Orthodox missionaries, and they answered sophisticated questions about religion and the Bible. Some of them quoted and interpreted the Bible during those discussions. They also tried to attract Orthodox neighbors to their meetings. They even organized special proselytizing campaigns among Orthodox peasant women. In one village near Kherson in 1894–95, the wife of Pavel Tsurkan, the local miller and a Stundist preacher, met their customers, the local Orthodox peasant women, at their mill, and talked with them about the Bible and how religion could help them in their lives. Eventually, she organized a separate Stundist meeting for worship for those peasant women who were attracted to her preaching at the mill. Following the local priests' complaints, the police closed this meeting in 1895, arrested all the peasant women who had participated in it, and imposed a fine on them.[114]

Stundist women actively participated in the dissemination of "a culture of reading" among peasants. They read books to their neighbors and tried to help their children learn how to read and to write. Some of them became teachers in Stundist schools. A Stundist activist, Iulia Karpinskaia, who organized a kindergarten for peasant children in Kiev, invited Stundist peasant women to teach there. In 1901, Karpinskaia hired Valentina Kukolenko, a local peasant woman, to teach the Russian language and the Holy Scripture to peasant children from the Ukrainian villages. It is noteworthy that such peasant teachers as Kukolenko taught together with female Jewish teachers from the city of Kiev.[115] It was an interesting collaboration of peasant and city women of different ethnic origins.

Moreover, the Ukrainian and Jewish women worked together with children of different ethnic origins. Officials of the Ministry of Education discovered in Karpinskaia's kindergarten Russian, Ukrainian, and Jewish students sitting and learning together in one classroom. By combining the students, the Stundist women had broken the ministry's rules. What was remarkable in this case was that the Russian, Ukrainian, and Jewish women evangelicals, who taught in the kindergarten, were also of different social origins. Iulia Karpinskaia came from a noble and wealthy Russian family, Valentina Kukolenko was a Ukrainian peasant, Anna Pushkareva was a Russian peasant, and their Jewish coreligionists came from families of city artisans and traders.

These women united their efforts in one noble cause—to educate children from impoverished families and help them to build better lives. Unfortunately, the local administration and Orthodox clergy aborted these noble efforts. One of the reasons they closed Karpinskaia's kindergarten was the unusually independent role of the women organizers and women teachers. The police discovered that no man was involved in this case. Therefore, we can view this as an example of purely feminine activity within the evangelical movement in Ukraine.

Despite the obvious opposition of conservative Baptist ministers, women became the real leaders of some Stundist communities. In 1893, Matriona Khodzitskaia, a peasant woman from the province of Kiev, organized a Stundist meeting for worship in her house and "seduced in her sect" not only members of her family but also her Orthodox neighbors. As one Orthodox missionary described her, Khodzitskaia "was a pretty woman of 46 years; she was very eccentric, with a huge energy and good skills in reading and writing."[116] The same missionary noted that Matriona had been famous before for her "depraved behavior." She had scandalous extramarital love affairs with local peasant boys and gave the birth to illegitimate children. Then, under the influence of evangelical religion, she changed her life and became an "exemplary wife and mother." She was a new type of Stundist leader. She was literate,

305

writing her own sermons to preach at the meetings and collecting her own library of religious literature.

In his report on Matriona to the Kiev governor, an Orthodox missionary noted that Matriona always carried with her religious books and used them during discussions with her neighbors. Her copy of the Gospels had her hand-written notes and comments. In her preaching, she always urged local peasants to think and act rationally. She used biblical texts to educate peasant women and showed them the example of a lifestyle that was different from the traditional patriarchal way of life in Orthodox families. In June 1894, the local police stopped her Stundist activities and exiled her to Trans-Caucasia for five years, together with other Stundist leaders.[117]

According to the police and Orthodox clergy, such female Stundist leaders as Matriona Khodzitskaia not only attracted peasant women to Stundist meetings but also spurred their husbands to use violence against them. V. Chertkov, a follower of Leo Tolstoy, published material about such abuse and persecution of dissidents in each issue of his periodical *Listki "Svobodnogo slova."*[118] On March 3, 1902, a sermon by one Orthodox missionary against the Stundists in the parish church of the town of Bogodukhov (in Kharkov province) led to the mass beating of the local dissidents by Orthodox peasants, who targeted Stundist women in the crowd. After this act of violence, all the female activists of the local Stundist community complained to the police about their wounds and bruises.[119] Afterward, the governor of Kharkov province recommended that the Holy Synod ban anti-Stundist preaching by Orthodox missionaries among local peasants so as to prevent mass violence against the Stundists, especially violence against women.[120]

The most common expression of violence of the Orthodox peasants against the female dissenters in the province of Kiev was rape. During the period 1892–96, during a surge in anti-Stundist violence, Stundist peasants from this province submitted their complaints about Orthodox fanatics' raping dissident women to the local administration. The police, however, tried to cover up such cases in their districts.[121] During September 1892, in the villages of Skibentsy and Kapustintsy (in the Skvira district), drunken peasants broke into the houses of the Stundists, pillaged them, and raped Ksenia Lisovaia and

306

Figure 6.1. Ukrainian peasant women during a break from their fieldwork, Ekaterinoslav province, at the end of the nineteenth century. From the collection of the Dniepropetrovsk State Historical Museum, Ukraine.

Akulina Pilgan[ova], two prominent Stundist activists. One of these women was pregnant, and the drunken rapists knew about this and cruelly raped her in front of her other children. The local police promised to punish the criminals but did nothing.[122] Orthodox peasants considered the active Stundist women and the new evangelical culture a threat to their traditional patriarchal authority. Therefore, they reacted violently against such attempts to reverse traditional gender roles and tried to restore male power by humiliating and raping the Stundist activists, who symbolized this threat to their peasant Orthodox community.

Despite persecution and harassment, the peasant dissenters of southern Russia created an alternative culture of sexual relations that was based on the evangelical principles of Christian love and equality of the sexes. The Shalaputs and the Stundists became "the first cultural pioneers" among the rural

307

Figure 6.2. A typical patriarchal family of Orthodox peasants in Tavrida province, 1902–3. From the collection of the Dniepropetrovsk State Historical Museum, Ukraine.

population of southern Russia.[123] They disrupted the patriarchal system of sexual relations and the organization of gender roles in the peasant community.

The most prominent figures in this process of revitalization of the peasant culture in post-Emancipation Russia were Shalaput prophetesses and female Stundist preachers, who eventually became the cultural pioneers of the feminist evangelical movement in imperial Russia. The new non-Orthodox identities and unusual female activism among the rural population of southern Russia and Ukraine symbolized the formation of a new culture, which united various local peasant cultures in a broad evangelical movement. Conversely, by rejecting the Russian Orthodox identity, this movement undermined the ideological foundations of the Russian political system and led to the spread of radical political ideas in the Russian and Ukrainian countryside (figures 6.1, 6.2, and 6.3).

Figure 6.3. A peasant woman in charge of beehives, Ekaterinoslav province, at the end of the nineteenth century. From the collection of the Dniepropetrovsk State Historical Museum, Ukraine.

Notes

1 As sociologists of religion argue, believers always judge the conventional moral rules and codes of behavior in any society "in the light of the gospel of freedom in Christ, for 'Christ is the end of the law'"; Keith Ward, *Religion and Community* (Oxford, 2000), 213.

2 Bryan R. Wilson, *The Social Dimensions of Sectarianism: Sects and New Religious Movements in Contemporary Society* (Oxford, 1990), 68. On the social control of erotic urges among religious sects, also see Rodney Stark and William S. Bainbridge, *Religion, Deviance, and Social Control* (New York, 1996), 173.

3 As Wilson noted, "Communitarian groups, in which all things are held in common, have discovered that once private property is eliminated then a major bulwark of, and perhaps even the need for, conventional family organization is removed"; *Social Dimensions of Sectarianism,* 39.

4 Like the American Mormons who practiced polygamy, or the Children of God, whose female members attracted new male members by an offer of sexual companionship, some Russian Shalaputs were noted for unusual marital behavior. See the comments of Wilson in *Social Dimensions of Sectarianism,* 39–40.

309

5 Scholars such as Natalie Davis and Keith Thomas have noted the Reformation's appeal to women, the role of women in religious change, the significance of factors such as learning and literacy, and the Reformation's effect on women's status and roles. Keith Thomas, "Women and the Civil War Sects," *Past and Present* 13 (1958): 42–62; Natalie Z. Davis, "City Women and Religious Change," in *Society and Culture in Early Modern France,* ed. Natalie Z. Davis (London, 1975), 65–95. See the comments about this literature in *The Reformation in Historical Thought,* ed. A. G. Dickens and John Tonkin (Cambridge, Mass., 1985), 308–9.

6 Among the new studies of the Radical Reformation, see Auke Jelsma, *Frontiers of the Reformation: Dissidence and Orthodoxy in Sixteenth-Century Europe* (Aldershot, U.K., 1998), especially 52–74; and Geoffrey L. Dipple, "Sebastian Franck and the Munster Anabaptist Kingdom," in *Radical Reformation Studies: Essays Presented to James M. Stayer,* ed. Werner O. Packull and Geoffrey L. Dipple (Aldershot, U.K., 1999), 91–105.

7 Clarke Garrett, *Spirit Possession and Popular Religion: From the Camisards to the Shakers* (Baltimore, 1987), 54, 56, 142, 229–30; Lawrence Foster, *Religion and Sexuality: Three American Communal Experiments of the Nineteenth Century* (New York, 1981), especially 21–22, 24–25, 228–37; Lawrence Foster, *Women, Family, and Utopia: Communal Experiments of the Shakers, the Oneida Community, and the Mormons* (Syracuse, 1991), especially 3–13, 223–38; Cristina Mazzoni, *Saint Hysteria: Neurosis, Mysticism, and Gender in European Culture* (Ithaca, N.Y., 1996); Ann Taves, *Fits, Trances, and Visions: Experiencing Religion and Explaining Experience from Wesley to James* (Princeton, N.J., 1999).

8 The citation is from Michael J. St. Clair, *Millenarian Movements in Historical Context* (New York, 1992), 7.

9 On the sexual utopia among the followers of the Free Spirit, see Robert E. Lerner, *The Heresy of the Free Spirit in the Later Middle Ages* (Berkeley, Calif., 1972); and Raoul Vaneigem, *The Movement of the Free Spirit* (New York, 1994). On sexual experiments among the early Anabaptists, see Lynda Roper, *Oedipus and the Devil: Witchcraft, Sexuality and Religion in Early Modern Europe* (London, 1994), 79–103.

10 Using Clifford Geertz's approach, we can say that the prevalent Russian ideology, based on Russian Orthodoxy, was supposed to serve as the "map of problematic social reality" and the "matrix for the creation of collective conscience." Such ideological "maps and matrices" cannot exist, however, without certain "sacred symbols" that "function to synthesize a people's ethos—the tone, character and quality of their life, its moral and aesthetic style and mood—and their worldview—the picture they have of the way things in sheer actuality are, their most comprehensive ideas of order." See Geertz, "Ideology as a Cultural System," in C. Geertz, *The Interpretation of Cultures* (New York, 1973), 220; and Geertz, "Religion as a Cultural System," in *Interpretation of Cultures,* 89. See how Geertz interpreted Max Weber's ideas of ethos and "sacred symbols" in Geertz, "Ethos, World View, and the Analysis of Sacred Symbols," in his *Interpretation of Cultures,* 126–41.

11 The citation is from: E. P. Thompson, "Eighteenth-Century English Society: Class Struggle without Class," *Social History* 3 (1978): 152–53. Here I follow American cultural historians, e.g., Henry H. Glassie and Richard L. Bushman. See Glassie, *Folk Housing in*

Middle Virginia: A Structural Analysis of Historic Artifacts (Knoxville, 1975); Glassie, *Pattern in the Material Folk Culture of the Eastern United States* (Philadelphia, 1968); Bushman, "American High-Style and Vernacular Cultures," in *Colonial British America: Essays in the New History of the Early Modern Era,* ed. Jack P. Greene and J. R. Pole (Baltimore, 1984), 345–83, especially 370; and Bushman, *The Refinement of America: Persons, Houses, Cities* (New York, 1992).

12 "In general, folk material exhibits major variations over space and minor variation through time, while the products of popular or academic culture exhibit minor variations over space and major variation through time." The citation is from Glassie, *Pattern in the Material Folk Culture,* 33.

13 Gosudarstvennyi arkhiv Rossiiskoi Federatsii (hereafter GARF), f. 109, 1 *ekspeditsia,* op. 40, part 2, d. 21, l.67–68ob; the citation is from l.67ob.

14 A. Ushinskii, *O prichinakh poiavlenia ratsionalisticheskikh uchenii shtundy i nekotorykh drugikh podobnykh sekt v sel'skom pravoslavnom naselenii i o merakh protiv rasprostranenia uchenia etikh sekt* (Kiev, 1884), 23, 24–25, 26–27.

15 A. Prugavin, *Religioznye otshchepentsy* (Saint Petersburg, 1904), 143. This author, a future Russian socialist-revolutionary, idealized the revolutionary character of the Stundist movement. Russian intellectuals, both liberals and radicals, shared this idealized vision of all Russian religious sects as predecessors of the oncoming popular revolution. The Russian psychologist Alexander M. Etkind deals with the image of Khlysty in the intellectual "discourse" of the Russian revolution. See Etkind, *Khlyst: Sekty, literatura i revoliutsia* (Moscow, 1998), 63ff.

16 A. Rozhdestvenskii, *Iuzhno-russkii shtundizm* (Saint Petersburg, 1889), 284. See also "Vopros o malorusskom narechii v otnoshenii k shtundizmu," *Kievskie eparkhial'nye vedomosti* (hereafter *KEV*), 1881, no. 4, 1–4; and "K voprosu o malorusskom slove v tserkovnoi propovedi," *KEV,* 1881, no. 13, 4–6.

17 "Khokhol" was a derogatory and insulting Russian name for Ukrainians, who neglected the Russian language and preferred to speak the "Little Russian dialect" (i.e., the Ukrainian language). The origin of this name was connected to the image of the Ukrainian Cossack who had shaved his head and left only one lock of hair on its top (this topknot was called a *khokhol* in Russian).

18 Rozhdestvenskii, *Iuzhno-russkii shtundizm,* 54; *Kievskaia starina,* no. 11 (1884): 543–44; Episkop Nikanor, "Proiskhozhdenie i znachenie Shtundy v zhizni russkago naroda," *Pravoslavnoe obozrenie,* no. 8 (1884): 605–19 (the citation is from 614). Also see *Pravoslavnoe obozrenie,* no. 4 (1876): 811; and no. 8 (1883): 709–29 (the citation is on 713).

19 *Materialy k istorii i izucheniyu russkogo sektantstva i raskola,* ed. Vladimir Bonch-Bruevich (Saint Petersburg, 1910), vol. 3, 9,12, 14, 15, 25.

20 *Materialy k istorii i izucheniyu,* vol. 3, 51. See also Otdel rukopidei: Gosudarstvennaia biblioteka Rossii, Moscow (hereafter OR GBR), f. 435, k. 67, d. 6, l.5; k. 46, d. 1, 20–22.

21 Vladimir Chertkov's periodical, *Svobodnoe slovo* [Free word], contained such descriptions in each issue.

22 The Russian priest M. Kriachkovskii noted the name of the Ukrainian composer, 311

Ivan Zaremba, who wrote the melody for Stundist religious songs; *Khersonskie eparkhial'nye vedomosti* (hereafter *KherEV*), 1873, no. 11, 327–33 and notes.

23 V. I. Iasevich-Borodaevskaia, *Bor'ba za veru: Istoriko-bytovye ocherki i obzor zakono-datel'stva po staroobriadchestvu i sektantstvu v ego posledovatel'nom razvitii s prilozheniem statei zakona i vysochaishikh ukazov* (Saint Petersburg, 1912), 164, 165–80.

24 GARF, op. 124, op. 3, d. 129, l. 9.

25 *KherEV,* 1890, no. 2, 39–45.

26 *Trudy Kievskoi dukhovnoi akademii,* no. 1 (1884): 46, 47, 49.

27 See the comments about "denationalization" of the Ukrainians in: R. L. N., "Porcha ukrainskikh narodnykh pesen," *Kievskaia starina* 41 (June 1893): 459–73.

28 *Missionerskoe obozrenie* (hereafter *MO*), November 1900, 506.

29 *KherEV,* 1891, no. 20, 619.

30 Rossiiskii gosudarstvennyi istoricheskii arkhiv (hereafter RGIA), f. 1284, op. 222 (1894), d. 114, l. 25ob.

31 See reports about other dissenters in RGIA, f. 1284, op. 222 (1894), d. 114, l. 10–24. On the refusal of the Stundists from the province of Kiev to take an oath of the loyalty, see also *KEV,* 1898, no. 16, 625. Compare with the Western religious radicals in George Williams, *The Radical Reformation* (Philadelphia, 1962), xxvi.

32 *KherEV,* 1891, no. 20, 620.

33 Episkop Alexii [Dorodnitsyn], *Materialy dlia istorii religiozno-ratsionalisticheskogo dvizhenia na iuge Rossii vo vtoroi polovine XIX-go veka* (Kazan', 1908), 69, 70; see also about the stereotypes of Stundists in GARF, f. 102, 3 d-vo, op. 88, d. 281, l. 1–2.

34 On the ethnographic differences of the Stundist peasants, see *Ekaterinoslavskie eparkhial'nye vedomosti* (hereafter *EkEV*), 1890, no. 13, 342–43.

35 Alexii, *Materialy,* 305.

36 *EkEV,* 1889, no. 23, 658–59. The observers noted that these changes took place during ten years, from 1878 to 1888.

37 RGIA, f. 1284, op. 222 (1902–4), d. 29, l. 31, 35.

38 See I. Sikorskii, "Psikhopaticheskaya epidemia 1892 goda v Kievskoi gubernii," in *Sbornik nauchno-literaturnykh statei,* V 5-ti knigakh [in 5 vols.] (Kiev, 1900), vol. 5, 52–54 (a description of 1892), and a report of the Kiev general governor (of 1895).

39 Vasilii Skvortsov, "Novoshtundism," *Moskovskie vedomosti,* no. 227 (1892).

40 From the first study of Skoptsy in 1845, Russian authors recorded all the famous cases of castration among religious dissidents. See Nikolai Nadezhdin, *Issledovanie o skopch-eskoi eresi* (Saint Petersburg, 1845); and the new studies in Russia by Alexander Etkind, "Russkie Skoptsy: Opyt istorii," *Zvezda,* no. 4 (1995): 131–63; Etkind, *Khlyst,* 82–102; and especially by Aleksandr Panchenko, *Khristovshchina,* 103–231. Compare this with the first study of the Russian Skoptsy in English by Laura Engelstein, *Castration and the Heavenly Kingdom: A Russian Folktale* (Ithaca, N.Y., 1999). On the differences of opinion about Skoptsy between Etkind and Engelstein, see Etkind, "Russian Sects Still Seem Obscure," *Kritika* 2, no. 1 (2001): 165–81.

41 Nadezhdin, *Issledovanie o skopcheskoi eresi,* 330, 335. Sometimes they brought with them the "real Skoptsy to announce the Divine Truth" for the Melitopol' Skoptsy.

42 See "The Skoptsy Songs from Tavrida" in Nadezhdin, *Issledovanie o skopcheskoi eresi,* dopolnenie [an addition], 117–20.

43 On the Tavrida Shalaputs and their case of 1841, see RGIA, f. 381, op. 1, d. 23087; on the Bessarabia Shalaputs, see RGIA, f. 381, op. 1, d. 23136 (the citation is from l. 14–14ob). Though every peasant insisted that he had performed this operation himself, without outside assistance, the doctor, comparing the similar cuts left after castration, concluded that "the same person whose name they were keeping secret performed this surgery"; RGIA, f. 381, op. 1, d. 23136, l. 18–18ob.

44 The Mikhailovka peasant Osip Bazyrev, who was then sixty years old, was one of the main activists of the Shalaputs and died of an unsuccessful castration. He was found dead in his house with an injured penis and one testicle hanging by a vein. The commission could not learn the particulars. They suspected the daughter of Osip Bazyrev, Viklitokia, a girl of twenty-five. She was the only member of the family who stayed with her father and "shared his way of life and beliefs." RGIA, f. 381, op. 1, d. 23087, l. 36.

45 See other descriptions of castration in: Engelstein, *Castration,* 84–85, 95–96.

46 RGIA, f. 381, op. 1, d. 23087, l. 3838ob.

47 RGIA, f. 381, op. 1, d. 23087, l. 38ob.–39. Under the interrogation, in the presence of Iarkin, a nine-year-old peasant boy, Timofei Krasnikov testified that Iarkin had performed the operation with testicles for him and other boys of Matveevka. In 1864, the police discovered twenty-three Shalaputs, including the recently castrated man and two boys, as well as four girls and four women with mutilated genitals.

48 See Engelstein, *Castration,* 96–97.

49 RGIA, f. 381, op. 1, d. 23087, l. 25–29ob.

50 RGIA, f. 381, op. 1, d. 23087, l. 34–35. But "they did all this," a police officer noted, "only to avoid any suspicion and persecutions." The Shalaputs avoided those neighbors who did not share their ideas, and eventually, they composed "their separate circle." They had very close friendly relations with their coreligionists; even their dwellings were located on one side of a village. Almost all of them were "wealthy, and this was a result of their eschewing vodka."

51 RGIA, f. 796, op. 154, d. 590, l. 1–2ob. The local priests asked the bishop to exile all relatives of the former Shalaputs and send their small children to Orthodox families for "their Orthodox Christian education." The bishop supported this idea. But even these cruel measures of separating the dissidents' families did not stop the Shalaput movement.

52 RGIA, f. 797, op. 45, 2 otd. 3st., d. 187, l. 3–6.

53 On this ascetic ideal among Shalaputs, see, in detail, chapters 2 and 4. Even the Orthodox opponents of the Shalaputs recognized their asceticism. Among many publications about this, see *Kavkazskie eparkhial'nye vedomosti* (hereafter *KavEV*), 1873, no. 23, 758–59; 1874, no. 2, 65, 66, 68; 1882, no. 6, 188-190 (on the Shalaputs as a preparatory

stage for Skoptsy); *EkEV,* 1884, no. 22, 425–26 (on asceticism); 1892, no. 6, 125; and *Slovo,* 1881, no. 2 (1881): 19–20.

54 RGIA, f. 796, op. 165 (1884–85), d. 1692, l. 18ob.–19.

55 *Chtenia v obshchestve liubitelei dukhovnogo prosveshchenia* (hereafter *Ch.OLDP*), March 1889, 299–300, and June 1889, 650; *Russkii vestnik,* November 1904, 128–29.

56 According to a police report, during one such meeting of the Pryguny (the Molokan version of Shalaputs) in 1863 in Novovasilievka (the province of Tavrida), Fiona Sizova, a peasant woman, the wife of a village clerk from Astrakhanka, stretched out on a bed after the common dinner, and "made herself naked up to the abdomen, showed her genitals, and said that she saw the hand of Saint Paul in the ceiling." Lisov, the local Shalaput activist, explained that she did this "because she was agitated by the Holy Spirit and had become ready to prophesy." According to rumors, Lisov was said to have unlawful relationships with another "prophetess," Avdotia Mitrofanova, the wife of another dissident. Eyewitnesses noted that "the Spirit visited her more often than others" during the meetings because she always jumped and moved around; that was why the Pryguny called her "the Old Sister" and acknowledged her as their "prophetess," and she ruled the meetings as the master of the house. RGIA, f. 797, op. 45, 2 otd. 3st., d. 187, l. 8–9ob.

57 On the Khlyst traditions of "living Gods" and *bogoroditsa,* see I. Dobrotvorskii, *Liudi bozh'i: Russkaia sekta tak nazyvaemykh dukhovnykh khristian* (Kazan', 1869), 24–26ff.

58 The first observers of the Shalaputs noted the persistence of dual power of "the living Christ" and *bogoroditsa* in dissident communities. On the Shalaput doctrine of love, see *Otechestvennye zapiski* (hereafter *OZ*), 1882, no. 10, 182–83. See also *Ch.OLDP,* March 1889, 293; *Russkii vestnik,* October 1904, 733–34.

59 *KavEV,* 1874, no. 8, 259–64. See also *KavEV,* 1874, no. 9, 289; 1881, no. 13, 455–60; RGIA, f. 796, op. 158, d. 154, l. 1–2.

60 It was also common for different groups of Shalaputs to select their most beautiful and enthusiastic young coreligionists for the role of "the Savior" and "the Virgin" for each meeting for worship. *EkEV,* 1893, no. 8, 197–214, especially 212–13; no. 19, 502–3.

61 Tsentral'nyi derzhavnyi istorychnyi arkhiv Ukrainy (hereafter TsDIAU), f. 356, op. 1, d. 60, l. 1–3.

62 *Stavropol'skie eparkhial'nye vedomosti* (hereafter *SEV*), 1891, no. 4, 119; no. 5, 141–43.

63 RGIA, f. 796, op. 165 (1884–85), d. 1692, l. 16–16ob.

64 RGIA, f. 797, op. 45, 2 otd. 3st., d. 187, l. 11. It is noteworthy that not only old dissidents, such as Molokans, but also the local Orthodox peasants, joined the Shalaput sect of Pryguny in Tavrida; at least thirteen families of them were converted (approximately 100 people) for a couple of months in 1864.

65 RGIA, f. 796, op. 165 (1884–85), d. 1692, l. 1–1ob. What attracted the local peasants to the Shalaputs was their belief in an unusually long and painless life for members of this sect. The police confirmed in 1881 that they had not found any case of sickness or death among the Shirokoe Shalaputs for the past ten years. According to the police, the sect's activists attracted peasants by promising to feed the most impoverished people and

pay a bonus of 25 silver rubles to anyone converted to the sect and 100 rubles more after three years of probation as a member of their sect.

66 *KavEV,* 1874, no. 23, 766–70; the citation is from 770.

67 *SEV,* 1891, no. 23, 613–21.

68 *KavEV,* 1881, no. 14, 499.

69 *SEV,* 1891, no. 4, 112–13.

70 RGIA, f. 796, op. 168 (1887), d. 1394, l. 1ob.–2ob. Dobrin'kaia is located in the Pavlograd district of the province of Ekaterinoslav.

71 Dmitrii G. Konovalov, *Psikhologia sektantskogo ekstaza* (Sergiev Posad, 1908), 4–12.

72 Similar behavior was portrayed at the end of the seventeenth century in colonial New England by a famous Puritan theologian and opponent of "religious enthusiasm." See Increase Mather, *An Essay for the Recording of Illustrious Providences* (Boston, 1684), 346–47. For comparative descriptions of such "enthusiastic" scenes, see Keith Thomas, *Religion and the Decline of Magic* (New York, 1971), 127, 149, 153; Christopher Hill, *The World Turned Upside Down: Radical Ideas during the English Revolution* (New York, 1972), 186–207; William G. Bittle, *James Nayler, 1618–1660: The Quaker Indicted by Parliament* (Richmond, Ind., 1986), 35 ff.; Garrett, *Spirit Possession;* and Phyllis Mack, *Visionary Women: Ecstatic Prophesy in Seventeenth-Century England* (Berkeley, Calif., 1992).

73 As a scholar has recently observed, "Through the medical model of the convulsive hysteric and the classical model of frenzied maenad, [ecstatic] dancing can be troped as a distinctively feminine activity, a way for women to discharge their excessive nervous energy, literally to let loose 'the animal' within them (the uterus as defined in antiquity)." See Mazzoni, *Saint Hysteria,* 145. See also Jean-Martin Charcot and Paul Richer, *Les demoniaques dans l'art suivi de "La foi qui gerit"* (Paris, 1984), 34, 38.

74 *OZ,* 1882, no. 10, 182–83. See also *Ch.OLDP,* March 1889, 299–300.

75 Trofym K. Lutsenko, *Spovid' virouchytelia sektanta (Istoria moei zhizni),* ed. G. Vashkevich (Kiev, 1907), 39–40, 42–43. Lutsenko referred to Saint John 4:14–15: "Whosoever drinketh of the water that I shall give him shall never thirst; but the water that I shall give him shall be in him a well of water springing up into everlasting life. The woman saith unto him, Sir, give me this water, that I thirst not, neither come hither to draw."

76 Lutsenko, *Spovid',* 32–34.

77 *KavEV,* 1875, no. 5, 170, 171.

78 See how Orthodox authors exaggerated sexual permissiveness among the Shalaputs: *KavEV,* 1875, no. 3, 98–99.

79 What follows is based on the memoirs of his brother, especially pp. 15–16, and his case from the Holy Synod's files: RGIA, f. 796, op. 181 (1900), d. 2528, l. 1ob., 3–4ob.

80 RGIA, f. 796, op. 181 (1900), d. 2528, l. 3ob.n4.

81 As Lutsenko explained, sexual intercourse made with the true belief directed all the feelings and thoughts of "true Christians" to Divine Law, fasting, and prayer, and generated in believers "brotherly love and holy tenderness of the heart with sacred tears that were the signs of soul's revival." Lutsenko, *Spovid',* 49–50.

315

82 Lutsenko, *Spovid'*, 53–55, 59–63, 72–73, 80–84, 92–94.

83 The Holy Synod and the prosecutor of Voronezh province requested that Lutsenko be exiled from the province in 1900. The court did not support this decision because of a lack of evidence. See RGIA, f. 796, op. 181 (1900), d. 2528, l. 4–4ob., 5–6, 7–7ob., 9–11, 15.

84 RGIA, f. 796, op. 181 (1900), d. 2528, l. 1–1ob.

85 TSDIAU, f. 419, op. 3, d. 60, part 1, l. 302–304ob., 318–20.

86 Foster, *Women, Family and Utopia*, 91–120.

87 *MO*, May 1901, 604–5, 606–7. For a different view of the Podgornovtsy, see J. Eugene Clay, "Orthodox Missionaries and 'Orthodox Heretics' in Russia, 1886–1917," in *Of Religion and Empire: Missions, Conversion, and Tolerance in Tsarist Russia*, ed. Robert Geraci and Michael Khodarkovsky (Ithaca, N.Y., 2001), 48–52.

88 RGIA, f. 796, op. 168, d. 1368 (1887–1903), l. 12–13.

89 See the essays by Ia. Abramov and A. Dorodnitsyn on the Shalaput communities; the latter was a famous Orthodox missionary who ended his life as a bishop of Sumy: Abramov, "Sekta shalaputov," *OZ*, 1882, no. 9, 46–55; and Dorodnitsyn, "Sekta shalaputov," *Chtenia v obshchestve liubitelei dukhovnogo prosveshchenia*, March 1889, 276–88.

90 What follows is based on the documents of the Ekaterinoslav provincial legislature, Dnipropetrovs'kyi oblasnyi derzhavnyi arkhiv (hereafter DODA), f. 20, op. 1, d. 15/316, l. 4–6.

91 DODA, f. 20, op. 1, d. 15/316, l. 3–7. See the testimony of Varvara Protsenko, who vindicated Naichenko as "the blessed person"; DODA, f. 20, op. 1, d. 15/316, l. 5.

92 On women in the West, see Joan Wallach Scott, *Gender and the Politics of History* (New York, 1988). Compare with the application of feminist theory to Russia in Linda Edmondson, "Equality and Difference in Women's History: Where Does Russia Fit In?" in *Women in Russia and Ukraine*, ed. Rosalind Marsh (Cambridge, 1996), 94–108.

93 Michel Foucault, *The History of Sexuality—Volume 1: An Introduction*, trans. Robert Hurley (New York, 1978), 59–65. I use his ideas about "sexual confessions and scientific discursivity as two modes of production of truth" about sexuality in nineteenth-century Europe.

94 Both Russian and Western historians ignore the problem of the sects and sexuality in post-Emancipation peasant society. All these authors portray peasants as traditionalist and conservative. See Natalia Pushkareva, *Women in Russian History: From the Tenth to the Twentieth Century*, trans. Eve Levin (Armonk, N.Y., 1997). Compare with the American collections of essays on Russian women: *Russia's Women: Accommodation, Resistance, Transformation*, ed. B. E. Clements, B. A. Engel, and C. D. Worobec (Berkeley, Calif., 1991), and *Russian Peasant Women*, ed. B. Farnsworth and L. Viola (New York, 1992).

95 *MO*, October 1900, 246.

96 *MO*, October 1900, 247. See the details of Lysenko's activities and the exodus of his community to Kazan' in *MO*, September 1900, 288–96; and RGIA, f. 1284, op. 222 (1900), d. 115.

97 "Lysenko's lust" and sexual promiscuity in his community were not an abnor-

mality or a purely Russian exoticism. It was a famous scenario of the Radical Reformation. The first Anabaptists in Münster introduced polygamy in the summer of 1534. According to contemporary descriptions, these German religious radicals of the sixteenth century demonstrated "excesses of sexuality" similar to the Shalaputs and radical Maliovantsy of nineteenth-century imperial Russia. In fact, 6,000 women (a majority of whom were former Catholic nuns) were eager to begin their sexual experiments with 2,000 male Anabaptists of Münster in 1534. On this, see Jelsma, *Frontiers of the Reformation*, 66–72.

98 *KEV*, 1892, no. 14, 527.

99 Vasilii Skvortsov, "Novoshtundizm," *Moskovskie vedomosti*, no. 225 (1892); no. 226 (1892).

100 TSDIAU, f. 442, op. 630, d. 2 (1900), l. 28ob.–29. The Avramenko case was a favorite one in the anti-Stundist propaganda of the Orthodox missionaries.

101 K. Sokolovskii, *Sekta maliovantsev sredi shtundistov v sele Petro-ostrove Khersonskoi gubernii, Elizavetgradskogo uezda* (Saint Petersburg, 1903), 1–2; M. Kal'nev, "Sekta maliovantsev v Khersonskoi gubernii, eia verouchenie i kul't," *MO*, November 1903, 988–90.

102 Vasilii Skvortsov, "Novoshtundizm," *Moskovskie vedomosti*, no. 224 (1892).

103 *MO*, November 1903, 992; Sokolovskii, *Sekta maliovantsev*, 3–4.

104 Among the new literature on Quakers, see Rosemary Moore, *The Light in Their Consciences: The Early Quakers in Britain 1646–1666* (University Park, Pa., 2000). On the Shakers, see Foster, *Women, Family, and Utopia*, 38–39ff. Foster followed the anthropologist I. M. Lewis, when he explained the leading role of women in ecstatic rituals and spirit possession by women's "peripheral status" outside the dominant leadership structures of the sect. See I. M. Lewis, *Ecstatic Religion: An Anthropological Study of Spirit Possession and Shamanism* (Baltimore, 1971).

105 Mazzoni, *Saint Hysteria*, 6. See also Jean-Noel Vuarnet, *Extases féminines* (Paris, 1980), 7.

106 See, e.g., a collection of the Shalaput songs about the human soul in A. Dorodnitsyn, "Sekta shalaputov," *Ch.OLDP*, June 1889, 658–59, 676–77ff.

107 See William G. McGloughlin, *Revivals, Awakenings, and Reform: An Essay on Religion and Social Change in America, 1607–1977* (Chicago, 1978).

108 Many recent studies concentrate on the role of women in the Quaker community. E.g., see Cristine Levenduski, *Peculiar Power: A Quaker Woman Preacher in Eighteenth-Century America* (Washington, D.C., 1996); Rebecca Larson, *Daughters of Light: Quaker Women Preaching and Prophesying in the Colonies and Abroad, 1700–1775* (Chapel Hill, N.C., 1999); and Julie Sievers, "Awakening the Inner Light: Elizabeth Ashbridge and the Transformation of Quaker Community, " *Early American Literature* 36, no. 2 (2001): 235–62. Compare with Jean Soderlund, "Women's Authority in Pennsylvania and New Jersey Quaker Meetings, 1680–1760," *William and Mary Quarterly* 44 (1987): 722–49. See how Foster wrote about the Shakers: "The Shakers, most extreme of the revivalistic groups, both in their ecstatic worship services and in their insistence on celibacy, were also the most extreme in giving women positions of formal equality to men at all levels of their religious structure"; Foster, *Religion and Sexuality*, 229.

317

109 Foster, *Religion and Sexuality,* 210, 212.

110 Foster, *Religion and Sexuality,* 246. Some anthropologists suggest that the process of individual psychosocial reintegration is analogous to the process by which a whole society can be revitalized by a millennial movement. See Anthony F. C. Wallace, "Revitalization Movements," *American Anthropologist* 38 (1956): 264–81.

111 Orthodox press noted the traces of Shalaput ecstatic influences in many Stundist communities. For the province of Kherson, see *KherEV,* 1884, no. 11, 352.

112 *KherEV,* 1886, no. 2, 76. Orthodox authors were especially indignant at the active role of women in the Stundo-Baptist meetings, because such women's activity contrasted to what Saint Paul said about women in the meetings for worship: "Let the woman learn in silence with all subjection. But I suffer not a woman to teach, nor to usurp authority over the man, but to be in silence" (1 Timothy 2:11–12).

113 *KEV,* 1894, no. 583–85.

114 *KherEV,* 1895, no. 15, 442.

115 RGIA, f. 797, op. 72, 2otd. 3st. (1902), d. 131, l. 5ob.; TsDIAU, f. 707, op. 317 (1899–1902), l. 105, 110. For a detailed discussion of the Stundist kindergarten, see chapter 4.

116 TsDIAU, f. 442, op. 691, d. 272 (1893–1907), l. 23, 74ob. It is noteworthy that Matriona Khodzitskaia was unusually pretty for her age and peasant status.

117 TsDIAU, f. 442, op. 691, d. 272 (1893–1907), l. 97–97ob.

118 See also material in "*fond* Chertkova" in OR GBR, f. 435, *karton* 46, 67 and others.

119 RGIA, f. 797, op. 72, 2 otd. 3st., d. 125 (1902), l. 13–14ob.

120 RGIA, f. 797, op. 72, 2 otd. 3st., d. 330 (1902), l. 1–2.

121 See the rubric "The Sufferings for the Faith" in each issue of *Svobodnoe slovo,* 1894–1900. On the humiliation of Stundist women, also see OR GBR, f. 435, *karton* 46, d. 1, l. 23–26.

122 RGIA, f. 1284, op. 222 (1892), d. 106, l. 4ob.–5, 7–9. The Stundists informed V. Chertkov in 1892 about this rape and gave his agents in Russia the copies of original police documents. But when Chertkov's friends tried to bring these documents abroad, the police confiscated them. See "Zapiski Timofeia Zaitsa," *Golos minuvshego,* no. 11 (1913): 170.

123 I refer to the famous metaphor, which was coined in 1878 by Russian liberal intellectuals: D. Kulikovskii, "Kul'turnye pionery," *Slovo,* no. 4 (1878): 95–126; and no. 12 (1880): 57–77.

Chapter Seven

7 The Religious Radicals' Rebellion

The primary concern of the Radical Reformation in Europe was the Millennium of reborn people and the establishment of Christ's Kingdom of social justice and equality on earth. The participants adopted a new identity as members of "the elect Christian nation," and they joined in utopian and "communist" projects to change society. Inspired by their millennial expectations, German peasants in the sixteenth century fought their Catholic priests and landlords and tried to restore the apostolic community of the first Christians in the German principalities.

Three hundred years later, under new historical and cultural conditions, peasant dissidents in the Russian southern provinces created their own version of the Millennium. Shalaputs, radical Stundists, and Stundo-Shalaputs shared the millennial expectations of their predecessors from the German principalities, and they also engaged in radical social and political activity. Like their German predecessors in the sixteenth century, these Russian peasant radicals struggled against both the official church and the local administration. Unlike the German reformists, however, these Russian peasants became involved in the tangled web of relations with radical intellectuals and disaffected nationalities, such as Germans and Jews. Sometimes they appropriated the radical political ideas of the Russian socialists, and in some cases the professional revolutionaries tried to use the religious radicalism of the peasant sects. As a result, the peasant religious dissenters became participants in a broad oppositional movement, occasionally becoming leaders of the peasant riots in southern Russia.

The Millennial Discourse and "The German-Stundist Threat" in Orthodox Propaganda

The social radicalism of the peasant dissidents was evident from the beginning of the evangelical movement in southern Russia. The first Shalaput communities in the 1860s and 1870s demonstrated a social activism unusual for Orthodox peasants. To stop the Shalaputs' activities and provoke their legal persecution, the Stavropol' Orthodox clergy tried to attract the attention of the police to the new sect. The local bishop reported that in 1872 one of the Shalaput leaders, Vlas Shilov, a Cossack from the settlement of Zakan-Yurtovskaya in the Terek region, said in public: "The tsar-emperor is not the anointed sovereign and head of the state, because the real anointed sovereign for us is only Jesus Christ, who made all secular authorities, laws, state institutions and establishment illegal, and military service sinful." Another Shalaput, Pavel Makukha, tried to reassure the peasants, who were afraid that police would confiscate their property because of their membership in the sect, by proclaiming:

> Let the police rob us! Let them confiscate oxen and other property as they wish, but soon they will return all our things that the police have stolen from us. The Emperor himself, Alexander, will protect us, our entire brotherhood. He knows everybody and he follows the same path of salvation. Now our Majesty waits only for a time when we will be more numerous than the infidels. Now we have one hundred and forty thousand adherents, including generals and colonels. The whole Stavropol' province follows us. On the border with the Terek region, all the priests [popy] have locked up their meetinghouses for worship and observed our growth. But soon, our Tsar will stand up for us, then we shall

revenge ourselves: nowadays we are hiding from the infidels, but afterwards these infidels will be hiding from us.[1]

This statement reflects the typical idealization of the tsar. The overwhelming majority of the peasant dissidents shared this idealization of the tsar and tsar's family. The Shalaputs, Molokans, Dukhobors, and later Stundists and Baptists told the peasants that the his family belonged to their sects. Among the millenarian dissidents, the idealization of the tsar had the eschatological character. The Russian millenarians saw the tsar as the fulfillment of the biblical prophecy of the great emperor who in the Last Days would lead all "suffering Christians from the slavery to the Promised Land."[2] But the political police (gendarmes) interpreted all such rumors about the tsar's membership in the dissident sects and his leadership in the peasant millennial movement as antistate activity and persecuted sectarians for the dissemination of these rumors.

If the first Shalaputs and Stundists idealized the tsar and demonstrated their loyalty to him, the radical Stundists of the 1870s publicly rejected the tsar's authority and declared their opposition to "this sinful world." Both the police and the Orthodox clergy identified the strong radical current in the peasant evangelical movement. The radical religious activists criticized in public all Russian authorities, including the tsar. In most cases the police associated the revolutionary activities among peasants with the radical Stundists who symbolized for the Russian administration the "dangerous cultural aliens" in the Ukrainian countryside.

The first interpreters of Stundism treated the movement suspiciously, given the fact that Russian socialist intellectuals were active among the peasants during the same period. One of the most famous descriptions of Stundists described them in 1867 as communists.[3] As early as March 1868, the archbishop of Kherson reported to the Holy Synod about "the communist goals" of the Stundist sect. According to his report, the dissidents disseminated the antistate and communist notions among the local peasants. He wrote:

According to Stundists, the Orthodox clergy and Russian government used unnecessary and invented church rituals to control ordinary people and to keep them in ignorance, working like cattle on the farms. [They assert] that true Christians do not need any ruler but Jesus Christ, and that the contemporary social and political order, based on the slave relations of exploitation by the upper classes, is outdated and has to be replaced with relations based on social justice and equality. Such relations, which exist only in the Stundist sect, are protected by the Holy Spirit.[4]

In 1873, the police officers of the Third Department likewise confirmed that Ukrainian Stundism had exhibited radical communist trends in its development. According to one officer's report, the Stundists preached "that all belongings should be divided equally among all people." By such propaganda, these dissidents attracted followers among the peasants who were dissatisfied with their small plots of land and who sought a just land redistribution. At the same time, in their report of 1873, the police noted that the majority of Stundists opposed violence and bloodshed. Only a few radicals among them insisted on revolutionary measures for political solutions.[5]

Fear of social radicalism was one reason why the Orthodox Church perceived Stundism to be so dangerous. For Orthodox officials, the Stundists' public rejection of icons and other sacred church symbols, their new pro-Western lifestyle, their reading of books, and their public criticism of the Orthodox clergy were signs of social recalcitrance and disrespect. In 1884, the Reverend Nikanor, the bishop of Kherson and Odessa, warned the Kherson governor that Stundism was "a dangerous political doctrine." He wrote in his letter: "Isn't it well known that the Stunde is disseminated everywhere in our motherland and supported not only by noble and affluent people of high rank, but also by foreign activists, who have a huge amount of money, activists, who, being the enemies of Orthodox Church, are hostile to the Russian state as well? . . . the Stunde, in the basic principle of its teaching, is undermining the foundations not only of the Church, but also of the social order and state system!" [6]

Conversely, the liberal and socialist press praised and admired "the sects' idea of liberation," because "in practice," the Stundists' "slogans easily turned into socialist ones. The denial of mundane goods in Christ's community, which has been emancipated according to the evangelical rule, usually created the foundation for the sectarians' practical or theoretical communism."[7] In 1883,

Gleb Uspenskii, a famous Russian writer close to the revolutionary Populists, described his meeting with Baptist sectarians, the successors of the Stundists, in the Caucasus. He noted that he "felt very comfortable with them, as with people who aspire to a conscious life and wish to give meaning to their existence on Earth."[8] Another famous Populist writer, Sergei Stepniak-Kravchinskii, devoted one of his novels, *Stundist Pavel Rudenko,* to the story of relations between the Ukrainian Stundist peasantry and "leftist" Russian intellectuals. In another book, one about Russian peasants that he published in English in 1888, he expressed his admiration for the Stundists:

> This movement is so sprightly and fresh, so full of young reformatory zeal, that it is not easy to determine its precise formulation; but its novelty affords us a precious opportunity for feeling the very palpitation of the popular heart, which seeks in religion a solace for its pains and the satisfaction of its yearnings.[9]

At the same time, Kravchinskii acknowledged the German cultural influence on Stundist peasants, which he interpreted as progressively "structuring" the Russian peasant's new modern calling as a builder of a future agricultural society, educated and refined.[10]

Although the Orthodox clergy blamed all evangelicals and accused them of "communist heresy," the police treated various groups of the peasant dissidents differently. Police officers usually separated the radical Stundists from the Baptists. In their reports, they praised the Baptists as loyal, thrifty, and industrious peasants. At the same time, they criticized the "rebellious and unruly" Stundists and their "theories of social justice and leveling of property."[11]

The anti-Stundist hysteria culminated in the 1890s, when some authors declared that "the propagation of Stundism in the south of Russia was a result of aggressive German policies."[12] V. M. Skvortsov, the editor-in-chief of the main Russian Orthodox Church periodical, the *Missionary Review,* warned the Russian government not to tolerate the Stundists' activities because "being separated from the unity of the Church and based on the liberty of thought, our sectarianism is inflammable material." He further warned that "it would be able, in the course of time, to burst into a terrible political conflagration anywhere and ruin the fresh 'spiritual-political world view' of our Orthodox population and, therefore, serve the purpose of the enemies of our Church and state."[13]

Local Orthodox priests organized the persecution of "revolutionary" Stundists, and the Synod and central church authorities coordinated anti-Stundist activity. After 1881, the year of Alexander II's assassination by Populist revolutionaries, a new reactionary period began, leading to a surge in anti-Stundist activity. Fears of the socialist revolutionary movement and its connections with "German Stundism" were intense. The Russian Church formed a chain of anti-Stundist missionary organizations all over southern Ukraine and Russia and sponsored "annual missionaries congresses" in an attempt to limit Stundist influence among the Russian Orthodox population.[14]

According to Orthodox authors, the dissemination of Stundist ideas threatened to destroy the foundation of the Russian peasant identity (literally "to obliterate the *image* [*obraz*] of the Russian peasant") by replacing Russian Orthodox values and images with German ones and by mixing Slavic ethnic elements with hostile German, Dutch or even Jewish components![15] Although the Russian government still seemed inclined to indulge German colonists and Stundists, conservatives asked for severe measures against the "German-Stundist threat." During sessions of the Missionary Congress in the Tavrida region, Skvortsov warned the Russian administration not to allow Stundists to build their meetinghouses according the rules of German church architecture.

Such a "construction" in a Russian or Ukrainian village would inevitably ruin the "sacred landscape of the Russian countryside" by replacing the usual "Byzantine style" roof of Russian churches with alien "Gothic style" architecture. Skvortsov then asked the tsarist authorities to cancel the German Lutherans' official permission to print religious books for Russian audiences. He explained that publication of German Lutheran religious literature in the Russian language would distort the perceptions of Christianity among Russian peasants and replace Orthodox ideas with German cultural notions. Only state restrictions on German landownership in southern Russia would stop the German-Stundist expansion. Unfortunately, he felt, Russian intellectuals,

326

poisoned with the spirit of Western nihilism, welcomed the Stundist experiments with "common Russian people." They viewed any pro-German act of the Stundists as an expression of modern progress. But this "progress" was destroying traditional habits and ways of life.[16] Such speeches and publications during the 1880s and 1890s signaled to the Russian administration that the Orthodox clergy had already become aware of the danger Stundists posed to traditional Orthodox culture in the Russian and Ukrainian countryside.

The outward appearance of the Russian Stundist-peasant represented an obvious visual rejection of important features of the traditional Russian self-image. To betray this self-image meant symbolically to deny the essence of Russian nationality itself! According to the Orthodox clergy, this was equal to the betrayal of cultural and political loyalty. During the 1880s, Bishop Nikanor complained that instead of learning from the economic improvements and achievements of German colonists, Russian and Ukrainian peasants imitated blindly German hair styles, clothing fashions, and the like: "After such imitation it's difficult to distinguish a Russian from a German." Moreover, the style of church building changed from the habitual ancient Byzantine to that of the modernist German *Kirche*. He called on Russian patriots to unite against "such an invasion of Western influence:" "Do not retreat, do not give up before the corrupting impact of the European culture that is hostile to us, do not worship the ideal of the cosmopolitan European."[17]

The Russian Orthodox clergy clearly understood that when foreigners (including Germans) attempted to change and substitute their own symbols for traditional cultural and economic landscapes in Ukrainian Orthodox villages, the result would be cultural disorientation. Bishop Alexii tried to attract the attention of the higher Russian bureaucracy to the dangerous cultural situation in southern Ukraine:

Merely the fact that there are the German *Kirche*, or the Polish *kostiol*, or the Jewish synagogue, or at last, the Sectarian meeting house near the Orthodox Church building, harms the religiosity of the people, developing in it, so to say, religious cosmopolitanism. Having met with adherents of different creeds and become acquainted through this with their religious beliefs, ordinary people are loosing the purity and strength of their own religious feelings.[18]

327

Both Bishop Nikanor and Bishop Alexii pointed to German landownership in the South of the Russian Empire as the main material "source" of the plurality of religious beliefs and ways of life among local peasants, "who imitated Germans."[19]

The worst result of the "imitation of Germans" was to create and maintain, in Ukraine among Ukrainian-speaking peasants, a new cultural identity of "non-Russianness," which contradicted the myth of the so-called Little Russian (Orthodox) religious identity of the Ukrainian population. The "Stundo-Baptists try to imitate Germans not only in faith, but also in dress, in outward appearance, and in the education of their children," wrote N. Kutepov, one of the missionary Russian Orthodox priests.[20] The Ukrainian Stundists themselves described in a humorous light the typical image of the Ukrainian peasant, preferable for the Orthodox priest:

> A priest is satisfied if a peasant regularly visits the alehouse; and according to the Russian priest, the real Russian Orthodox Christian needs to get drunk with wine and vodka, and to smoke a pipe or take a snuff of tobacco. The real Russian Christian should be reeling, intoxicated with alcohol, although with a holy cross on his breast and a tobacco pipe between his teeth. This Christian must swear every moment, cheat somebody and steal something when it is possible.[21]

Orthodox missionaries usually blamed the German colonists for the spread of anti-Orthodox sects in Ukraine. They always complained about German cultural influence, which they linked to the material prosperity of Germans.[22]

The Orthodox professor Alexei Voronov questioned the usefulness of the German colonists as agents of economic and cultural progress. He stressed the danger of "cultural denial" by local Ukrainian peasants, who replaced Russian cultural symbols with alien ones. The Germans, he wrote, especially influenced seasonal agricultural workers, who were dislocated poor peasants from northern Ukraine. Another negative fact was the Russian clergy's poverty, which contrasted with the prosperous German Protestant ministers. He argued that to preserve "sacred symbols" in the countryside the Russian government had to forcibly curtail the economic activities and prosperity of the German colonists and their Jewish and Polish "agents."[23]

Figure 7.1. In the left-hand illustration, an old Russian peasant, hero of an "anti-Stundist" chapbook titled *How Grandfather Pakhom Disgraced the Stundists,* admonishes a young Ukrainian blacksmith, Vakulenko, who had joined the Stundists: "You, Stundists, now follow not Christ but German teachers, who left Christ's Church and distorted Holy Scripture at their own sweet will. . . . You were born of Orthodox parents, raised in the Orthodox faith; but you were seduced by Germans, started to dance to German tunes, and even came to look more like a German than a Russian in outward appearance. Of course [as the right-hand illustration shows], the young Ukrainian smith soon quit his sect and returned to his 'native Russian Orthodox Church.'" From P. P. Skubachevskii, *Kak dedushka Pakhom posramil shtundistov* (Kharkov, 1913), 13.

The amount of anti-German and anti-Stundist propaganda produced by Orthodox clergy and missionaries grew during the 1890s and the first decade of the twentieth century (figure 7.1). They used popular booklets, lampoons, even chap books to portray the Stundist as a "cultural enemy." The authors of such books emphasized features of the German style of life, appearance, hair style and fashion, which were alien to Russian peasants and subversive of Russian Orthodoxy. They leveled curses on Stundists for betraying their people and country for "the prosperous well-to-do life provided by German money." All of these antisectarian authors warned Russian peasants: "to beware of the *German* Stunde!"[24]

Russian intellectuals, even patriotic Pan-Slavists and Slavophiles, felt that such an intensive anti-Stundist and anti-German ideological campaign would encourage the Russian government to mistreat peaceful God-seeking Ukrainian peasants and industrious German colonists. I. Aksakov, V. Soloviev, and others tried to discredit the testimonies of the official Church against Stundists.[25] But their efforts were in vain. The Russian administration used official and unofficial complaints from the local Russian clergy as a pretext to attack sectarians and Germans as "instigators" of Stundism.

Although in 1879 the Russian government permitted the activities of foreign Baptists in Russia, it did not include Russian sects with Baptist theology. The rejection of icons and other sacred symbols, the denial of Orthodox religious rituals, unauthorized reading and interpreting the Bible at home (common for all evangelicals, including Stundists) was considered criminal activity for "Russians." The Russian administration was especially frightened by the attempt of different Russian evangelical groups (including Ukrainian Stundists, Saint Petersburg Pashkovites, and Transcaucasian Baptists and Molokans) to unite and meet in Saint Petersburg in 1884. The participants of that meeting were persecuted, and under the influence of the anti-Stundist campaign in southern Russia, the Russian government banned Stundist activities as "illegal and subversive."[26]

On July 4, 1894, and September 3, 1894, new laws approved by the Russian Committee of Ministers and a special rule of the Ministry of Internal Affairs declared "the Stunde to be . . . [the] most dangerous sect." They prohibited all Stundist meetings. The justification was that "by rejecting all Church rites and sacraments, the Stundists not only deny any [state] power and rebel against oaths and military service, equate loyal defendants of the throne and motherland with robbers, but they also preach socialist principles, i.e., general equality, partition of property, and their teaching radically undermines the basic foundations *of the Orthodox faith and Russian nationality.*"[27] If we compare the text of this law and the main accusations and complaints of the Orthodox

330

opponents of Russian Stundism, we shall see obvious similarities. Those accusations were included verbatim in the tsar's law.

"The Chigirin Affair" and Radical Stundists: The Criminal Case of Feodosii Chepurnoi and Stepan Shutenko, 1877–1895

This new anti-dissident legislation outlawed the entire mass evangelical movement among the Ukrainian peasants. Much has been written about this legislation and the mistreatment of the first Russian evangelicals, by both Russian and Western historians.[28] But these historians missed the police materials, which related the discovery of the close ties between the Ukrainian peasant dissidents and Russian and Jewish revolutionaries in the 1870s and 1890s. This discovery not only convinced the tsar to support the anti-Stundist legislation in 1894, but it also contributed to the negative attitude of the Russian police to all Russian evangelicals before 1905.

The "socialist" ideas of the radical Stundists were not merely an invention of the Russian police or a utopian dream of Russian revolutionaries who sought a peasant revolution in the Russian countryside. Police documents reveal the participation of Stundist peasants in revolutionary politics. Moreover, these documents undermine the historiographical tradition in which peasants of the Russian Empire appear obsessed with the tsarist illusions.[29] Although traditionally both the Russian administration and Russian revolutionaries associated peasants' behavior with "tsarist loyalism," the radical Stundists demonstrated anti-tsarist and antistate attitudes. The most striking case of such social activism was that of Chepurnoi and Shutenko, two peasants from the village of Mordva (Chigirin district).[30]

In the 1880s and 1890s, this case became a central moment in the anti-Stundist campaign unleashed by the Russian police. During the period 1881–83, in his recommendations to the governors of the southern provinces, the minister of the interior paid special attention to the new "dangerous trends" among peasant Stundists from the Chigirin district. As he wrote to the Kherson governor, "the dissident peasants from Chigirin district disseminated socialist

331

ideas, which not only undermined the traditional Orthodox faith, but also discredited the Russian government and incited the peasants against the local administration." The minister especially noted that the village of Mordva was a center of the "socialist movement among Stundists." In 1882, the Russian emperor read the Orthodox clergy's reports about the "socialist Stundists" from Mordva and ordered the police to take special measures to prevent "the spread of these sects" among peasants. As a result of the tsar's attention, the case of the Mordva "socialist Stundists" provoked mass persecutions of Stundist peasants during the 1880s, which partly resulted in the anti-Stundist legislation of 1894.[31]

The famous "Chigirin affair" of 1877 involved Ukrainian peasants from the Chigirin district of Kiev province in an insurrectionary conspiracy organized by the revolutionary populist Iakov Stefanovich. Every historian in the Soviet Union and the United States who has studied this event, however, has ignored the link between the peasants' radical religious beliefs and their social activism.[32] At the same time, the traditions of such activism among these Chigirin peasants influenced their version of Stundism and prepared their Stundist leaders for a cultural dialogue with representatives of other radical groups in Russia, from revolutionary populists to New Testament Jews.

Historically, the Ukrainian rural population of the Chigirin district was noted for various acts of social protest, including the land riots of 1875 and the conspiracy of 1877. Having become dissatisfied with land reform, impoverished peasants from twenty-five local villages refused to obey the new rules for land redistribution. These peasants demanded redistribution according to the number of family members ("souls") rather than the number of households. More than 40,000 local peasants participated in the riots of 1875. At least 336 peasants were arrested, and 74 were sentenced to various terms of imprisonment. The police discovered that religious dissenters had participated in the riots of 1875.

The most active participant in these events was Anastasia Likhosherstaia, a Stundist peasant woman from the village of Tiun'ki.[33] Being a pious Stundist, she interpreted the peasant riots as the beginning of the Millennium and the coming of the Last Judgment. On August 24, 1875, she began to preach publicly about the Millennium, and she called on her Stundist and Orthodox neighbors to join the peasants from the villages of Shabel'niki and Adamovka (the centers of the riots) in their struggle for social justice. On August 29, she visited the local priests from the villages of Tiun'ki and Adamovka and criticized them for betraying the peasants. She went from one peasant house to another, reading the Gospels loudly and calling on the peasants to revolt "because the happy days of social justice were approaching."

On the evening of August 29, a crowd of peasants followed Anastasia and called her the Divine Prophetess. She explained to the peasants that she had been sent by God to organize the redistribution of land according to principles of social justice. The village steward and the local priest tried to arrest her and have her sent to the Chigirin prison, but the enraged peasants released "the rebellious Stundist" and brought her to the village of Tiun'ki. Eventually, the village administration managed to distract her peasant followers and re-arrest her. The police sent her to the Chigirin prison, where she was diagnosed as being mentally ill and sent to the Kiev mental institution.[34] Thus in 1875, for the first time, the police noted the involvement of Stundist activists in the peasant movement in the Chigirin district, and later the police discovered connections between the Stundist peasants and the socialist revolutionaries in the same localities.

As it turned out, the Russian revolutionary populists were ready to use the Chigirin peasants' antigovernment activities as a model for their own conspiracy. In 1876, a leader of the Kiev populist circle, V. Debagorii-Mokrievich, planned to organize a rebellion of these frustrated peasants against the local administration, using the false tsarist documents "about liberty and land" for all people. His friends I. Stefanovich, L. Deich, I. Bokhanovskii, and S. Chubarev followed his plan, and by the middle of 1877 had accepted more than 2,000 peasants of the Chigirin district into the secret organization. They introduced themselves to these peasants as the tsar's "commissars," and they explained that the local administration had hidden the real tsarist plans for the peasants' liberation. Stefanovich composed a false "imperial secret charter." In the name of the Russian emperor, he wrote that the tsar "freed all peasants from servile dependency" and granted them all the land without requiring any

333

payment. But the noble landlords prevented the fulfillment of these orders and "by cunning and deception they kept for themselves the better and greater portion of the land, and assigned only the lesser and poorer portion to peasants, and burdened this land with excessive redemption and quitrent payments." In his charter, the tsar had supposedly issued a special order for all his loyal peasants to "unite in secret societies called 'Secret Druzhina' [people's militia], in order to prepare a rebellion against the nobles, officials, and all the higher estates of the realm."[35]

The populists used this fabricated document to organize a peasant rebellion against the local officials and landlords "in the name of the tsar." Unfortunately for the rebels, the police discovered this secret organization in June 1877. Stefanovich, Bokhanovskii, Deich, and more than 1,000 peasants from twenty villages in the Chigirin district were arrested by December 1877. When the populist leaders escaped from prison in 1878, 55 peasants, members of "the Secret Druzhina," were still under arrest in the Kiev prison. Twenty-two of them were found guilty and given prison terms. Liberal lawyers blamed the revolutionary intellectuals for deceiving "the gullible peasants." Therefore, during the summer of 1879, the local court sentenced only 6 peasants and acquitted the rest.[36]

The former members of the "Secret Druzhina" later joined local Stundist groups in the province of Kiev. Two of the sentenced peasants—Timofei (Feodosii) Anisimovich Chepurnoi from the village of Mordva, and Stepan Karpovich Shutenko from the village of Pogorel'tsy (both in Chigirin district)— converted to the evangelical faith. After their return from the jail, these peasants became the center of a new police investigation in the Chigirin district. In June 1881, a local police officer reported to his superiors about the complaint of Piotr Shutenko, a peasant from the village of Pogorel'tsy, the inhabitants of which had participated in the events of 1877. Piotr had complained that his distant relative Stepan Shutenko [fifty years old] and Chepurnoi [forty-eight years old] had disseminated rumors that "in the future all the land would be distributed equally among all peasants, and that the government and clergy would cease to exist."

The police investigation revealed that Chepurnoi and Shutenko had told

334

the peasants about the existence of a country where all the land was distributed equally among everyone and that they wished that such economic order would be introduced in Russia as well. Shutenko confessed that in a conversation with local peasants he had reproduced a story he had heard in the Kiev prison from revolutionary populists who had been imprisoned for terrorist activity. Shutenko and Chepurnoi assumed that "the criminals, who assassinated the late tsar (Alexander II), planned to establish similar social rules in Russia."[37]

After considering the case of Chepurnoi and Shutenko, who were accused of "high treason," the Kiev court did not find any evidence of their crime and acquitted them on August 17, 1881. The public prosecutor of Kiev province ordered the police to stop the investigation on August 25, 1881, and the Ministry of Justice affirmed this decision on December 5, 1881.[38]

After interrogating these peasants, the local police officer sensed something suspicious in their behavior. He was surprised that all the other peasants unanimously supported their testimony and denied even those facts that the defendants themselves had confessed. The officer suspected that local peasants had tried to cover up for Chepurnoi and Shutenko, who were noted for their role in the "Chigirin affair" and were respected by all their neighbors. That was why the local police and Kiev provincial gendarme department objected to the court's decision to acquit Chepurnoi and Shutenko. The head of the provincial gendarmes even sent a special letter to the Kiev prosecutor, asking him to reconsider the court decision.

In this letter, the head of the gendarmes noted that the defendants had been the most zealous participants in the Chigirin conspiracy of 1877. He mentioned that both Chepurnoi and Shutenko had been elected elders of the secret peasant society and that they had used their houses for "the ceremony of the holy oath" for those who joined "the Secret Druzhina." The defendants were the conspiracy's most active propagandists among the peasants and had copies of the secret organization's Code, Charter, and "Holy Oath." As elders of the Secret Druzhina, they had contacts with "the commissars" (the revolutionary populists, the real organizers of the conspiracy). The Senate and Russian central authorities had already acquitted almost all the participants in the Chigirin

335

conspiracy (including Chepurnoi and Shutenko) as "traditionally naïve and backward rural dwellers," deceived by the socialists with the "false tsar's documents." But the police insisted that Chepurnoi and Shutenko, as the main leaders of the secret peasant society, should be punished for their criminal activities.[39]

It turned out that the police were right. New rumors about antigovernment activities among Chigirin peasants began circulating again in the spring of 1882. In March and April of that year, the police officers Vybodovskii and Kotliarov organized an investigation of those rumors and discovered that Chepurnoi and Shutenko had "tried to undermine their neighbors' religious feelings and incite them to resist" the tsarist administration. Moreover, on April 15, the local priest, Mikhail Tregubov, submitted a report to the police about the plans of Chepurnoi and Shutenko to blow up the village church and the administrative buildings in Mordva and Pogorel'tsy.[40] Although the police found neither explosives nor weapons, they still arrested Feodosii Chepurnoi and Stepan Shutenko.

Chepurnoi and Shutenko were kept under arrest from March 25 to May 9, 1882, in the district prison of Chigirin. According to the investigation, they had established a "new religious faith" with its center in the village of Topilovka. The members of this religious group did not visit the Orthodox Church; "they met at home for reading the Gospels and other holy books, and promised to be diligent workers, live without alcohol and tobacco." The Pogorel'tsy elder (*starosta*) praised them as industrious and sober peasants who always paid their taxes on time.[41]

The most striking testimony, however, demonstrated the anti-tsarist, pro-socialist notions among the members of "the new faith." At the end of March 1881, as one witness testified, Chepurnoi and Shutenko told the peasants "don't worry about the assassinated tsar, because we have only one tsar in heaven, who is the only Lord for us." Chepurnoi explained that the new emperor would be killed as well. Soon the entire tsar's family would be exterminated, and new rules and a new social order would be established in Russia; all people would be equal, living happily without taxes in one brotherhood. In 1882, Shutenko refused to send his cart to help the village church; and he said in public, "we need neither churches, nor priests." In a confidential conversation with his neighbor, Chepurnoi mentioned that the main source of his and Shutenko's information about a new social order came from the "commissars" (the revolutionary populists) who were prisoners in the same jail where he was incarcerated in 1879–80.[42]

The socialist ideas of Russian revolutionaries influenced Chepurnoi and Shutenko's religious activities. Using images from the Book of Revelation, the peasant radicals called the tsar a beast and the policemen scorpions, and they predicted their coming overthrow. According to them, all state passports and official papers were "the Devil's signs" because the state was a creation of Satan. They explained to their neighbors that God created all people equal, and that at the act of creation there were no tsars, nor government, nor clergy, and that land belonged to all people without any taxes. Under the influence of the populists, Chepurnoi and Shutenko added a communist perspective to their interpretation. Their adherents repeated their ideas about the future of a "commissars' Russia without tsars," when all people would be equal again and work together and receive all they needed from the community.

Chepurnoi and Shutenko, together with other Stundists, rejected the holy icons and sacraments of the Orthodox Church as fake objects that were used by the clergy to exploit the peasants. Using the language of the Gospels, they criticized the priests as Pharisees who betrayed Jesus Christ. They used to say, "we do not need any superiors, all people should be equal; we don't need churches because where people are reading the Bible together, there is a church." They used revolutionary images in their theological interpretations. Thus, they employed the description from Revelation (12:1)—"And there appeared a great wonder in heaven: a woman clothed with the sun, and the moon under her feet, and upon her head a crown of twelve stars"—as a prophesy about a female terrorist who waved her kerchief before the assassination of Alexander II on March 1, 1881. Shutenko emphasized that tsar's kingdom came from the Devil and that the Russian terrorists had just followed the divine prophecy about destroying the Devil's kingdom.[43]

The defendants asserted that all accusations were the slander of the local priest, who hated Stundists. Notwithstanding this, in his decision of June 6,

1882, the Kiev prosecutor recommended exiling Chepurnoi and Shutenko to Eastern Siberia. In his official decision, he noted that the defendants were members of a sect "similar to the Stunda, which rejected all the Orthodox Church rituals and the worship of icons." At the same time, under the influence of "intellectual propagandists who had organized the secret peasant society," Chepurnoi and Shutenko added antigovernment aspects to their religion and preached this "radical faith" among their neighbors.[44]

The origin and theology of the sect, "implanted in Topilovka" by Chepurnoi and Shutenko, demonstrated its radical Protestant character. As the local priest noted, during the 1860s and 1870s, peasants from the Chigirin district showed the first signs of their interest in learning more about the Christian faith.[45] This interest in Bible studies and Christian theology intensified after the failure of the Chigirin conspiracy. After their intensive study of Holy Scripture, they decided that they would not need any kind of mediator between themselves and God—neither a priest nor an Orthodox saint. Therefore, like Western Protestants, they refused to worship icons and other visible symbols of Orthodox Christianity, such as the cross. "Sincere Christians," they said, "were supposed to carry the inner cross inside their souls as a reminder of God's sufferings and human sins."

The Topilovka Stundists preached that they had only one "Shepherd," Jesus Christ, whose teachings they followed, and they became His equal brothers and sisters. By denying social rank and differences, they rejected the institution of the Orthodox clergy as well. The Topilovka peasants considered priests to be impostors, who, in pursuing their own profit, invented methods to call people to church for prayer. These peasants taught their neighbors that they did not need churches for their prayers, because every Christian could pray at any place at any moment of his life without the assistance of a priest. Human beings were created in God's own image. Therefore, their souls, if they would not pollute them with sins, were like living churches in which God Himself dwelled. The Topilovka Stundists insisted on inner, spiritual, and individual prayer to God rather than the external and "hypocritical" prayers of the Orthodox Christians inside the church.

The Topilovka peasants criticized the Orthodox calendar of fasting, instead stressing the individual and spiritual character of fasts as an important means for the soul's cleansing. Emphasizing the importance of good acts and individual dialogue with God, they rejected all the external rituals of the Orthodox Church, such as the rite of confession. According to them, the Holy Spirit "lived only in a good heart" and could guarantee salvation only for those who performed good acts, rather than those who sinned and visited the church on a regular basis. Faith in Christ and good deeds made all Christian believers equal in God's eyes.

Therefore, Christians should accept only God's authority to rule the society and deny any temporal authority. The Stundist activists interpreted the phrase from the Gospels "render therefore unto Caesar the things which are Caesar's; and unto God the things that are God's" (Matthew 22:21) as a recommendation to struggle against all secular authority. For them, Caesar and all secular authorities were an embodiment of evil. The Stundist radicals considered the tsarist administration to be Satan's servant and called on Christians to resist it. Thus, they told their neighbors: "Put on the whole armor of God, that ye may be able to stand against the wiles of the devil. For we wrestle not against flesh and blood, but against principalities, against powers, against the rulers of the darkness of this world, against spiritual wickedness in high places" (Ephesians 6:11–12).

The leaders of these radical Stundists, including Chepurnoi and Shutenko, were former participants in the Chigirin conspiracy. Witnesses testified that these radical dissidents were highly critical of the existing social and political order and advocated redistributing the land among all peasants according to the principle of social justice. Chepurnoi and Shutenko told their coreligionists, the Topilovka Stundists, that the Stundist sect was "just a game, or a disguise to conceal an existence of the antigovernment notions among poor peasants." According to their interpretation, in reality, the Stundist peasants had to combine their efforts with "the oppositional revolutionary party and act together with it against the government."[46]

The Ministry of the Interior supported the recommendations of the Kiev prosecutor to punish Chepurnoi and Shutenko as the most dangerous of the Topilovka Stundists. According to the ministry's decision, they were charged

339

"with dissemination of false rumors of a dangerous political character, for an incorrect interpretation of Holy Scripture as socialist propaganda, and for public criticism of the political system in Russia."[47] The police and local administration—worried about their antigovernment activities in a locality noted for the peasant riots—unanimously supported the decision to prosecute Chepurnoi and Shutenko on charges of state treason. On September 17, 1882, they were exiled to Eastern Siberia for five years under police supervision.[48]

In 1888, Chepurnoi and Shutenko returned from exile to the Chigirin district. Under their influence, according to police information, the number of the local Stundists grew from fewer than 400 to 670 members in Topilovka, Mordva, Pogorel'tsy, and other neighboring villages by the end of 1890.[49] After the return of Chepurnoi and Shutenko, the Topilovka Stundists moved further in the direction of radical social activism. Information as to the situation with local Stundists remained rather unclear. In December 1889, the police received the first signals about antigovernment propaganda and the dissemination of dangerous "socialist" rumors by only one of those two persecuted Stundists, Shutenko. According to the new police investigation, Chepurnoi had quit the Stundist sect and rejoined the Orthodox Church.

But Shutenko persisted in his dissent, explaining to his fellow Stundists, and to the Orthodox peasants, that the Gospels were "invented by the first Christians" according to their own historical imagination and their limited knowledge of the world. Therefore, the new Christians should be careful with their acceptance of everything written in the old Christian texts. If the Gospels were merely an invention of the human mind, even if inspired by the Holy Spirit, the new Christians should not believe in the Gospel's insistence on veneration of the tsar and obedience to secular authorities. Shutenko explained in Stundist meetings that "the wealthy people unjustly had more property than poor people." That is why all the peasants should unite in one peasant society against the rich landlords and establish only one form of landownership—common peasant property, with communal houses and mills. With the peasants' control over landed property, the tsarist administration would be liquidated. "Therefore all the peasants will unite their efforts and 'exterminate' all the noble landlords, their administration, and the 'main enemy of all the peasants—the Tsar.'"[50]

The police discovered that Shutenko had intensified his proselytizing efforts among local Orthodox peasants. Shutenko became the most active figure in the Russian evangelical movement, and he contacted other Stundists from various provinces of southern Russia. The Kiev governor, worried about Shutenko's dissident activity, requested that the governor general of the South-Western Region order a new exile for Shutenko. Paradoxically, Shutenko changed his views at the end of 1889. He became more involved in the religious activities of local evangelicals and began preaching about Christian meekness and loyalty to the secular authority. By the beginning of 1890, he had stopped criticizing the tsarist administration. Notwithstanding this, in January 1890, he was arrested and exiled to Elizavetgrad, where he had worked before and had a place to stay. He left a family with four small children behind in Pogorel'tsy without material support.[51] Eventually, the Elizavetgrad Stundists provided the Shutenko family with money and helped to bring his oldest son to Elizavetgrad for his education.

The turmoil among the Chigirin Stundists did not end with the exile of Shutenko. In June 1893, the local priest, Grigorii Grushevskii, reported that Chepurnoi had become a leader of the new oppositional movement among the peasants of the Chigirin district. A rich peasant from the village of Pogorel'tsy, Ivan Yeremenko, whose threshing machine was destroyed by participants in the movement, complained to the priest. As it turned out, a Stundist peasant, Teet Shutenko, had confessed to him that radical Stundists had destroyed Yeremenko's threshing machine with only one goal in mind: to teach the rich peasants a lesson and to show them the possibility of the future expropriation of their property for the needs of the whole peasant society. Only one peasant testified against Chepurnoi and Shutenko in 1893—Teet Shutenko, a relative of the evicted Stundist radical Stepan Shutenko. After six years in the Stundist sect, Teet left Stundism for the Orthodox Church. According to him, the radicalism of Chepurnoi's ideas divided the local Stundist community into two groups: one group sharing this radicalism, the other rejecting it. A majority of the Stundist and Orthodox peasants still covered up for him because they respected him as a defender of their interests. During the investigation, all the peasants called Chepurnoi and Shutenko "apostles of Christian faith and benefactors of the peasant community."

341

During his Siberian exile, Chepurnoi saved some money. He returned to his native village relatively well off. In contrast to other rich peasants, he was ready to help his neighbors financially, and he loaned them money whenever they asked for it. He used to say when he loaned money to poor neighbors: "Don't worry. You can pay me back when you are rich. I can wait." Moreover, being a good carpenter, Chepurnoi assisted in building houses and flourmills for local peasants, and he never rejected their appeals for help. Therefore, none of these peasants testified against him. Only the newcomers, retired soldiers who had settled in the village recently, and renegades, former Stundists, such as Teet Shutenko, who envied Chepurnoi's influence, denounced him to the police.[52]

The police immediately reacted to the reports of the Orthodox clergy about the new activities of Chepurnoi and began a new investigation on February 6, 1894. The police discovered the real role of Chepurnoi, who had become a more important figure for radical Stundists in the Chigirin district than the evicted Stepan Shutenko. From the first days of his return to the village in 1888, Chepurnoi told the local Stundists to "go further" than "the text of the Gospels recommended." The Stundists, as the most intelligent peasants, he said, should organize a secret peasant society, the main goal of which would be mutual assistance and preparation for the future struggle with *nachal'stvo* (government) for social justice. He announced that the struggle of all the united peasants would be possible when they "liquidated the head of the government." When the peasants removed "the head," "it would be easy for them to cope with the government; and then all the land will be allotted equally among all peasants, and judges and courts will be composed of the peasants' representatives and will serve the needs of the common folk."[53]

Chepurnoi taught the peasants that they had to establish communal property and common rule so that they could distribute all goods on an equal basis. There was only one obstacle to accomplishing this plan—the tsar and his government, the peasants' main enemies. According to Chepurnoi, even some noble gentlemen who occupied influential positions in the army and courts shared these ideas and created an antigovernment organization. When these noblemen took control of the crucial political positions in the empire, it would be the right time for a coup d'état to overthrow the tsarist regime. As it turned out, Chepurnoi found support among radical Stundists who shared his ideas. Thus, Chepurnoi's preaching reflected that by 1894 the radical Stundist peasants from the Chigirin district had replaced the myth of a good and benevolent tsar with radical social criticism.

Chepurnoi, who was influenced by his long conversations with revolutionary populists in the Kiev prison and in Siberian exile, tried to apply the socialist ideas of revolutionary intellectuals to the reality of peasant life. He even had plans to organize a new kind of Gaidamatchina. It was noteworthy that he used the name of the famous Ukrainian peasant movement of 1768 against the Polish noble landlords and their Jewish tenants who exploited the rural population of the Ukrainian countryside. This event became part of Ukrainian folklore, and it played an important role in the historical memory of Ukrainian peasants. Chepurnoi, who tried to provoke a radical movement among local Stundists, called them the Gaidamaki in a way of justifying their oppositional behavior. In his propaganda, the tsar, the tsarist administration, the judges, and the Orthodox clergy played the same role of "cultural aliens" as the Polish landlords and their Jewish tenants in Ukrainian folklore's interpretation of the Gaidamatchina movement.

Chepurnoi's sons and other young peasants from Mordva and Pogorel'tsy, some of whom were active Stundists, followed Chepurnoi in his attempt to recreate the spirit of Gaidamaki. At the same time, all observers noted that there was no anti-Semitism in "Chepurnoi's movement."[54] The Stundist radicals even tried to restore social justice in their own villages according to traditional ideas of the Cossacks and Gaidamaki. The police discovered some cases of theft in these villages, which were committed by young enthusiasts influenced by the tradition of Gaidamatchina. The followers of Chepurnoi stole beehives, horses, and bags of corn from the richest and wealthiest peasants and distributed them among the most impoverished peasants. When these Stundist Gaidamaki destroyed the threshing machine of the rich peasant Ivan Yeremenko, they told him that it was unfair for him to own more property than other peasants.

The enraged Yeremenko pointed out to these rebels that they should begin with the famous capitalist Tereshchenko, whose factories and plantations were located not far from the village of Mordva, and who had much more property than wealthy industrious peasants, such as himself. Chepurnoi's followers responded that it was their "first experience with a small action against rich people" and in the future they would try more serious actions against "the wealthy parasites."[55]

After his return in 1888, Chepurnoi, who called himself "the Orthodox Ukrainian [Maloross]" in all official papers, continued to visit Stundist meetings. He explained to the Stundists that he did this on purpose. Chepurnoi planned to transform their Stundist group into a radical peasant organization, which would unite with other oppositional forces in the Russian Empire in their struggle against the tsarist administration. That was why he recommended that his coreligionists officially join the Orthodox Church but retain their Stundism in secret. This would make their lives easier and save them from police persecution. Under Orthodox cover, the Stundists could safely continue their secret oppositional activities.

In a Stundist meeting, Chepurnoi insisted that the Stundists unite with the political revolutionary party because they had a common goal—the future happiness of all suffering and poor people. In Russia, the main source of all secular authority and social injustice was the tsar. Therefore, the Stundists and "political activists" had to unite their efforts and overthrow him. Only after this could they destroy all the officials and landlords and establish public property and social justice all over the country. Under the new social order, after the tsar's overthrow, life would be better, and the common folk would work only three hours a day, "as the Americans work in the United States."[56]

It is important to note that Feodosii Chepurnoi, in elaborating on his revolutionary ideas, combined traditional populist propaganda, which could be traced back to "the Chigirin conspiracy" and the "going to the people" campaign of the 1870s, with the old Ukrainian Cossack myth of the Gaidamatchina. Preaching among the Stundists, he presented the future socialist society as the fulfillment of Saint John's prophesy from the Book of Revelation and connected Christian images to the historical memory of the Ukrainian peasants about their resistance movement. At the same time, Chepurnoi promoted the cooperative ideal of the Russian populists. According to his propaganda, the Stundist community should demonstrate the practical patterns of a new, better, and prosperous life for the peasants. Only material success and prosperity could attract the Orthodox peasants. Local Stundists had to organize a profitable agricultural community with new advanced agricultural technology and cooperative principles of organization.

Chepurnoi invited his coreligionists to invest money in new land, mills, and agricultural machines for their community. He also planned to use property, "expropriated from the rich people" for the needs of the Stundist community. According to his interpretation, Christian, communal, property would guarantee the "harmonious" economic prosperity of all members. At the same time, Chepurnoi was very critical about any attempt of separate individuals to improve their own households or use machinery or other agricultural innovations only for their own profits without benefiting the peasant society. That was why he approved the punishing of the rich peasant Yeremenko, when the young Stundist Gaidamaki destroyed his threshing machine.[57]

After the special trial on May 25, 1894, the court of the Kiev province unanimously convicted Feodosii Chepurnoi and Stepan Shutenko for "committing the acts of treason." The Kiev prosecutor sentenced Chepurnoi to exile for five years in East Siberia, and Shutenko to a five-year restriction to the central Russian province of Vologda. The provincial court considered Chepurnoi more dangerous than Shutenko, the latter of whom later repented and devoted himself to religious activities. The official indictment noted:

Chepurnoi became a close friend of political criminals during his imprisonment and exile and adopted their harmful antigovernment and socialist ideas. After his return to his village, he became the mouthpiece for the new harmful current in Stundism, which rejected not only the main principles of its faith, but also all religiosity and the existence of God. During 1888–93, among the peasants of the villages of Mordva and Pogorel'tsy in Chigirin district, he circulated the dangerous ideas of disrespect for the principles of private property and urged the peasants to resist and fight the authorities. Having malicious intentions, he preached antigovernment sermons and disseminated false rumors, which had the politically pernicious goals and were insulting to the government.[58]

In May 1894, the Kiev prosecutor recommended reconsidering the criminal charges against Shutenko because the police had not found any connection between him and Chepurnoi after 1890. The minister of justice approved the recommendation of the Kiev persecutor, and Shutenko was acquitted in December 1894 due to a lack of evidence. But the gendarme officer who was in charge of the police investigation opposed this decision and submitted new evidence of Shutenko's involvement in antigovernment activities.

As it turned out, Stepan Shutenko, who proudly called himself "a Ukrainian Stundist," had never cut his connections to the radical Stundists from the Chigirin district. Together with Chepurnoi, he was considered their main leader, even after his exile in 1890. Moreover, he also became an influential leader of the Elizavetgrad Stundists, and he served as their minister during his exile in the 1890s. He established connections between the Topilovka Stundists and other centers of the evangelical movement and provided his fellow countrymen with new religious literature. According to the police, the peasants from the Chigirin district visited his meetings for worship in Elizavetgrad and participated in Stundist ceremonies there. Because of Shutenko's connections, his Topilovka coreligionists became active participants in the evangelical network of communication, and these peasants were important agents in the Stundist "secret mailing system" during the period 1894–1905, the years of Stundist persecution in Russia. Shutenko always sent the necessary information for the Topilovka Stundists in time, and his fellow-countrymen were ready to help anybody in need. They always provided their coreligionists who had been convicted and deported with accommodations and food when they were near their villages. What struck the police was that the Stundist peasants were always notified about those movements of prisoners well in advance.[59]

Some of the Stundists from the Kherson province considered Shutenko too radical. In fact, Shutenko's activities demonstrated an obvious division within the Ukrainian evangelical movement into radicals, who expressed notions similar to Shutenko, and moderates, who emphasized only the religious side of their social activism. As one of these moderates noted, in Shutenko's preaching there was "some of the tension and passion of a man embittered against everything, especially against wealthy people and the authorities." According to this testimony, "under the disguise of preaching evangelic love and brotherhood," Shutenko "concealed propaganda, which was far from peace and Christianity." The same critic continued: "According to his preaching during the meetings for worship," it was evident that he was "a fervent socialist-rebel" who led "the criminal propaganda" of Stundism "in the direction of socialism."[60]

Shutenko was noted also for his itinerant preaching. He learned the cooper's handicraft, and he began to travel throughout southern Russia, selling his products at provincial markets. At the same time, he preached his evangelical sermons to peasants in local pubs. As police agents reported, during his preaching Shutenko, criticized the Orthodox clergy and the social order, and he promised his listeners that a war between Russia and Germany would result in the lifting of sanctions against the Russian evangelicals. Shutenko was a close friend of various people suspected by the police of revolutionary activities. Two of them were noblemen connected to populist organizations: A. Zagurskii, a landlord from the province of Kherson, and A. Shimanskii, a landlord from the province of Kiev, tried to establish relations between Stundist peasants and revolutionary intellectuals.

After summarizing all this information, the police arrested Shutenko and reported to the governor of Kiev about his subversive activities. The enraged governor asked the Ministry of the Interior to reconsider Shutenko's case. This ministry's special meeting changed the Kiev court's decision about Shutenko. On December 28, 1894, Shutenko was indicted for "high treason" and sentenced to a five-year exile in the province of Souvalki. The ministry approved the notes of Kiev governor about the radical character of Stundism in the Chigirin district. These notes were included in the official verdict. According to this verdict, "the entire Chigirin Stunda" in nine neighboring villages was "imbued with the harmful antigovernment notions of Chepurnoi and Shutenko." This Stunda had "a character which was similar to a political organization rather than to the religious sect."[61] Other radical Stundists in the Chigirin district shared the revolutionary ideas of Chepurnoi and Shutenko. In 1893–94, a leader of the Stundists from the village of Zhuravki, the local peasant Serbovets, preached among his neighbors that landlords controlled all

347

landed property and perpetuated social injustice. After his sermons, local peasants (together with Stundists) demanded that the land be redistributed and that rich landowners' property be expropriated.[62]

Socialist Revolutionaries and Jews in the Evangelical Movement of Southern Russia

The most striking aspect of the Chepurnoi and Shutenko case was the police's discovery of the stable and well-established relations between Ukrainian peasants and radical Russian and Jewish intellectuals. The spread of the radical evangelical movement in the Ukrainian countryside by the 1880s coincided with the activities of revolutionary intellectuals, who tried to exploit the anti-state feelings of persecuted dissidents. Some of these revolutionaries were Jews. The involvement of Jewish intellectuals in revolutionary activities provoked anti–Semitic pogroms in 1881 in the southern Russian provinces. As a result, many Jews tried to emigrate, while others tried to survive by converting to Christianity. This movement of New Testament Jews converged with the evangelical movement in the Ukrainian provinces of Kiev, Kherson, and Tavrida and influenced peasant dissidents as well.

The police knew about the unsuccessful attempts of the Russian revolutionaries to establish their connections with various sects of religious dissidents, and especially with Stundists. In 1884, a police officer reported that Stundist peasants from the village of Troitskoe in Kherson province, Nikita Poukhovoi, Trofim Gouz', and Nikita Vsevolodovskii, read and discussed not only Holy Scripture but also revolutionary pamphlets. During his interrogation, Poukhovoi recalled that in 1880 Vsevolodovskii gave him a small book containing a popular explanation of Marxist political economy and socialist ideas.

Influenced by this book, Poukhovoi began preaching his new interpretation of the Bible. He preached to his neighbors that there would be no "autocratic tsars" in the future. All people would elect their rulers; everybody would be equal. People in future societies would experience no poverty or misery, and they would hold all property in common.[63] Although the police did not find illegal books in Poukhovoi's possession, his Orthodox neighbors accused him of disseminating revolutionary literature. In 1886, a police officer from the Elizavetgrad district, who reported to the Kherson governor about local Stundist activists, assumed that Poukhovoi had burned the revolutionary books before his arrest.[64] Another Stundist activist, a peasant from the province of Tavrida, Alexei Klimenko, not only disseminated revolutionary literature but also participated in the meetings of local revolutionary intellectuals.[65]

Famous revolutionary populists such as L. Deich, I. Fesenko, and E. Breshko-Breshkovskaia tried to organize revolutionary propaganda among sectarians, but their efforts came to nothing. In February 1888, Lazarev and Drovogub, two revolutionary populists, tried to settle among the Stundists from Zvenigorodka district and propagate socialist ideas among them. They were unable, however, to influence the peasant radicals because the police arrested them immediately after their arrival in the Ukrainian village.[66]

The case of the Topilovka Stundists (1877–95) was different. It demonstrated the real danger for the secular and religious authorities of the possible union of revolutionaries with Stundist peasants, who had been influenced by socialist propaganda and were ready to resist the authorities. The leaders of the Topilovka Stundists, Chepurnoi and Shutenko, had had contacts with revolutionary intellectuals not only in prison but also during their Siberian exile. Their Stundist organization became a place for strengthening old connections and establishing new ones. In the Stundist meeting in Elizavetgrad, Shutenko met Evgenii Gar, a local doctor, who played a prominent role among the liberal intellectuals in the province of Kherson. Gar liked this "wise old Ukrainian peasant" (Shutenko was sixty years old in 1890). He invited Shutenko to work as his *prikazchik* (steward) in his estate near the village of Bezvodnaia (in the Elizavetgrad district), after the police expelled him from the Chigirin district.

Gar attracted the attention of the police because he involved his friends, the Elizavetgrad Jews, in Stundist activities as well. He was a Russian Orthodox nobleman by origin, and he married Rosa Fainzilberg, a Jewish obstetrician who had converted to Orthodoxy and changed her name to Raisa. Doctor Gar became an active member of the Jewish-Christian society, "The Spiritual Biblical Brotherhood." He invited Ukrainian and Russian peasants to join this

349

"Brotherhood." Eventually he staged a special wedding ceremony for himself and his Jewish bride, according to the rules of this society, which followed the biblical customs of the Old Testament. The police began secretly surveying Gar and his Jewish wife and discovered their close connections to Russian and Jewish populists.

As it turned out, Gar and his Jewish friends visited Stundist peasant communities all over the province of Kherson. On the pretext of medical and obstetrical assistance, they came to various centers of the evangelical movement in the Ukrainian countryside and linked the evangelical peasants to other oppositional groups of the southern Russian Empire, including "the Spiritual Biblical Brotherhood" and the New Testament Jews as well.[67] Both the police and the Orthodox clergy reacted negatively to these connections.

In the police materials, Jews were linked to conspiratorial activities involving religious dissidents in other cases as well. In 1875, the Jewish populist Lev Deich lived with Tavrida Molokans and unsuccessfully tried to propagate socialist ideas among the members of this sect.[68] Other revolutionary Jews attempted to do this among the Kherson and Kiev Stundist peasants during the period 1874–75. The most alarming case of Jewish involvement was the Chigirin conspiracy of 1877, when at least three Jewish intellectuals—Lev Deich, Anna Rozenshtein, and Mark Natanson—took part in an organization of the peasant movement in the province of Kiev.[69] The Russian police discovered these connections first, but the Orthodox clergy and Russian conservative press used this information about the collaboration of Jews and Stundists for their ideological campaign against the evangelical peasants. The Jewish theme contributed to the construction of the anti-Russian image of the first Russian Stundists, who were Ukrainian peasants by origin.

Russian Jews participated in the widespread evangelical movement from the early days of Stundism. A police officer from the Odessa district reported to the Kherson governor that in 1870 he discovered in the village of Adamovka a Jewish woman who had converted to Stundism.[70] As early as 1875, the Orthodox press noted the unusual activities of the Jews among the Kherson and Kiev Stundists. These Jews were attracted to Stundism "because of its Protestant character," the journalist wrote, and "its stress on the inner spirituality which had disappeared from the Jewish religion long ago." Therefore, along with the Ukrainian peasants, Jews from the southern provinces of Russia became active members of Stundist communities.[71]

The first records of Kherson Stundists mention a seventeen-year-old Jewish boy named Israel who "had been baptized into the new faith" and followed "loyally everywhere" a leader of the Ukrainian Stundo-Baptists, Ivan Riaboshapka. Riaboshapka baptized this Jewish boy, who became one of the first Jews converted to the Russian Baptist faith.[72] Another Jew, Joseph (Ios'ka) Zeeserman, a pub owner in the village of Chaplinka (in the province of Kiev) assisted another leader of the Ukrainian Stundists, Gerasim Balaban. The local Stundists and their coreligionists from neighboring villages used Zeeserman's tavern for "Stundist agitation" among peasants who visited it.[73]

The Orthodox missionary organization of Kherson diocese in its report for 1887–88 described the proselytizing activities of converted Jews, who became "zealot Stundist preachers." The Orthodox missionaries complained about "one unknown Jew who was preaching Stundism" in the village of Izhitskoe (iu the Tiraspol' district) in March 1888. According to another report, "in the small village [khutor in Ukrainian] of Soldatskoie in the Novoukrainskii district, a Jewish preacher, who had been converted from Judaism to Orthodox Christianity before joining the 'Stunda,' delivered purely Stundist sermons for local peasants."[74]

The Russian secret police traced the dangerous relationship between Jews and Ukrainian peasants from the first Stundist meetings in the 1860s and 1870s. Because of the Jewish revolutionaries' involvement in socialist propaganda among Stundist peasants, the police were very suspicious of any contact between them and religious dissidents. Sometimes local literate Jews composed letters for Stundist peasants who had problems with grammatically correct writing. Despite the fact that such Jews were not engaged in socialist activism, the police still persecuted them. In March 1891, the administration of Kiev province submitted a request for the exile of Leiba Itskov Portnoy from the Vasil'kov district.

The story of Portnoy's exile begins with the local Stundists (who called themselves "evangelical Baptists") from the villages of Romashki, Ol'shanitsa,   351 and Teleshovka (in the Vasil'kov district), who sent letters to the Russian minister of the interior asking that they be allowed to hold their meetings for worship. When the police checked these letters, it turned out that the "Stundist petition" and letters had been composed and hand written by the local Jewish "resident" Portnoy and his twenty-one-year-old son Nekheim. On March 29, 1891, Portnoy was exiled by the police to Radomysl' in the western part of the Russian Empire. According to the police papers, Portnoy was punished "because Jews writing for Stundists was considered very undesirable, especially since an unemployed Jewish person [without certain profession] composed various petitions and documents for [the ignorant local peasants]."[75]

The police records from the 1870s until the February Revolution of 1917 show the unusually tolerant attitudes of Stundists toward Jews. Whereas the Orthodox Ukrainian peasants participated in the infamous anti-Semitic "pogroms" of 1881 and 1905, the Stundist peasants not only avoided any violence against their Jewish neighbors but also tried to help them and invited them to their meetings for worship. Jewish intellectuals, especially those who were connected to "underground" revolutionary groups, tried to maintain good relations with Stundist peasants. Usually, the evangelical peasants—especially the moderate Stundo-Baptists—rejected any kind of proposal for collaboration with revolutionaries, especially those who propagated violence and "individual terror."

It is noteworthy that in his correspondence, a Stundist peasant Tymophii Zaiats, who was an opponent of violence, urged Christians to follow the politics of "reformist" liberalism and the religious tolerance of the governments of Britain, France, and the United States rather than the revolutionary activities of Russian socialists (populists and social-democrats).[76] But the radical Stundists, as the case of Chepurnoi and Shutenko demonstrates, were ready to respond to socialist propaganda and contribute to antigovernment activities in the Ukrainian countryside.

Adherents of Count Leo Tolstoy and Colonel V. Pashkov also participated in the evangelical movement of Ukrainian peasants. Prince Dmitrii Khilkov and members of the Chertkov family preached among these peasants. In contrast to the revolutionary populists, they brought a peaceful version of social activism to the Ukrainian countryside. Tolstoy's followers rejected violence and insisted on a "rational" interpretation of the Gospels. The Pashkovites and Tolstoyans preached about the reformation of the entire social order in Russia on evangelical principles and struggled to restore Christian principles of social justice among the rural population. Local Stundists regarded them as "evangelical Christian brothers and sisters" who were persecuted for their faith. According to police records, Jewish activists played a prominent role among these intellectuals as well.

Eventually, all the oppositional groups of southern Russia—liberals, revolutionaries, and various religious dissenters—were linked to each other, and the Jewish participants in these groups played an active role in establishing the connections and creating the infrastructures of the new oppositional subculture in southern Russia during the 1870s and 1890s. Jews and Ukrainian Stundist peasants were the most active agents in the creation of this subculture, which laid the foundation for the conscious organized resistance to the secular authorities in the southern Ukrainian countryside.[77]

At the end of 1888, the Russian secret police submitted their report with an analysis of the issues of the local periodical of the Russian Orthodox Church, published in Kherson. The police paid special attention to information regarding the antisectarian Saint Andrew Brotherhood of the Orthodox Church. The Orthodox correspondent complained of the activities of the Jewish "Spiritual-Biblical Brotherhood," which involved Orthodox Christians and Stundist peasants. In the debates of the Orthodox missionaries with Stundists, he wrote, "those Jews took the Stundist side and supported the sectarians in everything." A police agent noted in his report a fragment from the Orthodox publication about the active participation of Jews in the Stundist meetings in Elisavetgrad area. He cited a sentence in this publication describing how "during a meeting one pale Jew solemnly argued that the present-day Orthodox Christian Church did not resemble the original Christ's Church of the first century A.D. and that Jesus Christ would drive out the Russian people from their new churches as he had done before with the Jews in Jerusalem."[78]

In response to requests from the administration of the Orthodox Church, the police began their own investigation. In December 1881, the head of the local police in Kherson noted the activities of Iakov (Iankel') Mikhelev Gordin, a Jewish resident from Vitebsk (Belarus), who had organized "the Spiritual Biblical Brotherhood" in Elisavetgrad. In fact, Gordin pioneered the efforts of liberal Jewish intellectuals to create organizations for a cultural dialogue with Christian dissidents of the southern Russian Empire. His society particularly targeted the Stundist peasants.

Gordin is an interesting figure in the history of Russian and American Jewry. He was born on May 1, 1853, in Mirgorod in the Ukrainian province of Poltava to a poor Jewish family. Although he did not receive a formal college education, he was a talented student of both Jewish and Russian literature. Since 1870, he had been contributing essays and articles to various Russian periodicals. During the 1870s, he worked as a farm laborer, longshoreman, traveling actor, teacher, and journalist. He became a permanent author for such periodicals as *Zaria, Nedelia,* and *Elizavetgradskii vestnik,* where he worked as an editor as well, and *Odesskie novosti,* in which he published under the pseudonym "Ivan Koliuchii" (Ivan the Sting). During his travels, he met different people and visited Stundist meetings in the Ukrainian countryside. The police noted that Gordin was a close friend of the revolutionary populists who visited Elizavetgrad where he had lived since the late 1870s. He even published a novel "Liberal-Narodnik," in which he described his personal experience and his meetings with religious dissidents and populists.[79]

In 1877, Gordin invited all the progressively minded Jews of Elizavetgrad to establish a Jewish Bible society in the city. This society would unite those who "denied all religious dogmas and ceremonies and acknowledged only the moral doctrines of the Bible." Its members rejected "all mercantile pursuits, and endeavored to live by physical labor, primarily by agriculture."[80] The main goals of this society were the religious education of Jews, the transformation of Jews into farmers living on land, and the prevention of their further practice of usury and financial speculation.

Under pressure from the Orthodox clergy, the police reported on Gordin's old connections in Elizavetgrad to the revolutionary circle of the "People's Will" (a populist organization involved in the assassination of the tsar in 1881). The police also confirmed Gordin's connections to the Ukrainian Stundists, who often visited his "Spiritual Biblical Brotherhood." Moreover, the police learned that he lectured to Stundists on the political economy of Karl Marx. In May 1890, a Kherson police officer tracked down revolutionaries, such as Galushkin (Teraspol'sky), Gaevsky, Afanasii Mikhalevich, and Ivan Basovsky, "who came to Elisavetgrad, in particular, to propagate revolutionary ideas among Stundists." All these Populists were Jews!

According to the police reports, "all revolutionary efforts to collaborate with Stundist peasants turned out to be a failure." That was why the disappointed Populists decided to combine their propagandist efforts among Stundists with their activities among local Jews, who in 1877 founded "an organization for Jewish artisans" (the above-mentioned "Brotherhood," with Gordin, Zlatopol'sky, and Portnoy as its leaders). The populists even used the meetings of the "Spiritual Biblical Brotherhood" for their readings of Marx, Ferdinand Lassale, and other Western socialists. They sent their own agents— Vasilii Gorbunov, Vladimir Tsenkovsky, and Pavel Levandovsky—to the Stundist meetings and "by presenting Jesus Christ as the first socialist in world history, they tried to persuade the Stundists to quit the sect and join the revolutionary movement."

But the religious Jewish "Brotherhood" and its leader Gordin did not approve of these populist efforts. Members of the organization moved to the countryside and organized their own community on communist principles, following the example of the Tolstoyans. Gordin's supporters rejected the violence and terrorism of the Populists and distanced themselves from revolutionary radicalism. The activists of the society, including Gordin himself, visited cities with a significant Jewish population, such as Odessa. They promoted ideas of cultural dialogue between Jews and Christians, and, for the Jewish community, agricultural activity and nonviolence in politics.[81]

The Jewish members of the "Spiritual Biblical Brotherhood" also distanced themselves from the local traditionalist Jewish community. As the governor of Kherson province reported in January 1885, the local administration had already permitted this society to establish its own separate synagogue and elect its own rabbi in July 1884. The Ministry of the Interior initially supported this society because it rejected "Jewish nationalism and fanatical religiosity,"[82] and on December 8, 1888, the Ministry of Justice agreed to the request of the "Biblical Brotherhood" to establish a register of births, separate from other Elizavetgrad Jews. This organization also demonstrated its nontraditional Jewish character by attempting to appear more "civilized" and "Russified."[83]

In 1888, they elected the founder of their "Brotherhood," Gordin, as their new rabbi. They asked the local administration for special privileges for their agricultural community and demonstrated their innovative practices in the distribution of goods, mutual assistance, rejection of traditional circumcision, and permission for marriage between Christians and Jews according to the ancient Hebrew rituals described in the Old Testament. Kalenik Kozhemiachenko and Larion Dragulenko, two Ukrainian Stundists, both former Orthodox peasants, participated in the meetings and followed the rules and rituals established by the Brotherhood. The marriage of Evgenii Gar, the Russian Orthodox doctor, and Rosa Fainzilberg, the Jewish obstetrician, according to the rituals of Brotherhood demonstrated the ideal of this society—the rapprochement of Christians and Jews. Members of the Brotherhood declared that their main goal was "the spiritual and moral renovation of the Jewish religion, and introducing Jews to Christian teaching."[84]

At first, the Russian police permitted the activities of the Jewish Brotherhood because it did not appear to be a dangerous organization, especially after its conflict with the Jewish revolutionaries and its opposition to terrorism. According to police reports, the Brotherhood tried to create a version of Christian Tolstoyanism among Elisavetgrad Jews and brought the pacifist evangelical groups, such as Stundists, into their improvised Judeo-Christian community. Only the persistent demands of the administration of the Russian Orthodox Church and conservative leaders of the Jewish community provoked police persecutions of the new Jewish agricultural community in the Elisavetgrad district. Police agents reported that the Jewish members of the Brotherhood settled in the Ukrainian countryside and tried to establish contacts with local Stundist peasants "without any terrorist goals." But new cases of socialist propaganda among the Ukrainian Stundists of Kherson and Kiev provinces during the period 1888–91, and the disclosed connections of Gar and Gordin to peasant radicals such as Stepan Shutenko, changed the police's attitude.

356

A police detective noted in 1890 the unusual popularity of Stundist ideas among young radical Jewish intellectuals such as Gordin, who visited numerous dissident meetings in Kherson province. According to the police, these young Jews were influenced by populist ideas of socialism. As a result, they decided to combine the evangelical ideas of social justice with a communist utopia, but without political violence. Therefore, they tried to organize communist agricultural colonies in localities with a strong Stundist influence. On June 18, 1890, a police officer informed his superiors that in November 1889, "prominent members" of the "Spiritual Biblical Brotherhood" established an "agricultural colony on communist principles in Glodossy (a famous center of Ukrainian Stundism), got acquainted with local peasants, invited these peasants to their houses, and read them the Gospels with their own Jewish interpretation."[85]

The members of the "Spiritual Biblical Brotherhood" followed Leo Tolstoy's interpretation of Christianity as well. Along with the Bible and socialist literature, they began to read and discuss Tolstoy's work. They even tried to put Tolstoy's ideas into practice in their colony. In 1889, they opened a building for the distribution of agricultural products among members who were in need and among local peasants. Simultaneously, the "Brothers-Biblists" used this building for reading and discussions with the peasants about the Bible and Tolstoy's books. The Glodossy Stundists became active participants in these discussions. As the police officer noted, the practical peasants liked their new neighbors because the Jewish colonists helped them with medication and with "various advice of a medical and agricultural character." At the same time, the colonists disseminated the evangelical literature and tried to influence the Stundist peasants, as one officer noted, in "a direction that was unreliable from the political point of view."[86]

In August 1891, after a special investigation, the Department of the Police came to a final conclusion about the negative results of the activity of the "Brothers-Biblists" among the Stundists. The police had confirmed the spread of the socialist ideas among the religious radicals. As a result, they closed the "Spiritual Biblical Brotherhood" on October 7, 1891, and canceled the election of a new rabbi for a new synagogue established by Gordin's adherents.

Moreover, the police agents began a secret surveillance of Gordin and ordered his arrest in January 1892. But the police missed their chance. Gordin and his sixty followers had migrated to the United States a year earlier and had become American citizens. Nevertheless, the secret police ordered frontier-guards all along the Russian border to arrest Gordin as "a dangerous criminal" if he appeared, even if he was carrying a U.S. passport.[87]

As far as we know, however, Gordin never returned to Russia. As one who was convinced that "the only remedy for Jewish persecution was economic reconstruction," he tried to establish a Tolstoyan agricultural colony in America for Russian Jews. But his attempts failed. Eventually he settled in New York City and became a famous Yiddish playwright and writer for the local radical press. Until his last days, he played an important role among New York's socialists and kept the old traditions of his "Spiritual Biblical Brotherhood" alive among Russian-speaking Jews. In his written works and lectures, he resisted any kind of nationalism, including Zionism. He also rejected political violence (even in the name of socialism). He remained convinced that the Judeo-Christian ideal of the Bible pointed to the friendship of all nations rather than to the superior position of one particular ethnic group.[88]

In 1882, the young Jewish intellectuals in Odessa made another attempt to establish a cultural dialogue between Jews and Christians. Iakov Priluker, a Jewish teacher from Odessa, followed Gordin's example and organized the group of "New Israel," which was open to both Christians and Jews. As Semion Dubnow has noted, "New Israel" followed only the teachings of Moses "and rejects the Talmud, the dietary laws, the rite of circumcision, and traditional forms of worship; the day of rest is transferred from Saturday to Sunday; the Russian language is declared to be the 'native' tongue of the Jews and made obligatory in everyday life; usury and similar distasteful pursuits are forbidden."[89]

As with Gordin's group, a majority of the Jews did not support the idea of cultural dialogue. According to contemporaries as well as historians, Russian Jews opposed Gordin's and Priluker's experiments. They accused Gordin and Priluker of "seeking to win from the Russian government those equal rights denied to the Jews collectively." As conservative critics in the Jewish community argued, the "reform of Jewish religious practice would be accepted by the masses [of Jews] only if based on the Talmud and sanctioned by established rabbis."[90] After the pogroms of the 1880s, Russian Jews became occupied with the problems of physical survival. A mass emigration from Russia was a more realistic solution for the majority than the utopian projects of Jewish-Christian communities. Only a radical minority of Jewish intellectuals, who had been involved already in the revolutionary activities of Russian intellectuals, joined Gordin's and Priluker's organizations. When the police stopped the activities of the "New Israel" in Odessa at the end of the 1880s, Priluker migrated to England, joined one of the local Protestant congregations, and devoted his life to Christian missionary activities among the Jews.

Attempts to establish new relations between Jews and evangelical peasants resulted in the conversion of some of these Jews to Christianity. As a result of this cultural dialogue with Russian evangelicals, a new movement began among young Jewish intellectuals, whom Russian contemporaries called "New Testament Jews." This movement converged with the evangelical movement of Ukrainian peasants and demonstrated again the international character of the religious revival, which only confused its outside observers. The participation of the Jews in the evangelical movement also influenced the peasant dissidents, who developed more tolerant and more cosmopolitan attitudes.

The most important representatives of the New Testament Jews were the members of the group established by Iosif Rabinovich in 1884 in Kishinev (Bessarabia). As the governor of Bessarabia reported to the Ministry of the Interior on November 3, 1884, eleven Jews from Kishinev requested permission to establish a community separate from the Old Testament Jews. Their community included the Jews who believed in Jesus Christ and the New Testament. Their leader, Iosif Rabinovich, entered a special Protestant theological seminary in Berlin, converted to Christianity, and was ordained as a Congregationalist minister in March 1885. In Russia, he prepared for the publication of four books about the Christian Jews and submitted the manuscripts of these books to a censor. At the same time, he established connections between his "New Testament Israelites" and local evangelicals and Orthodox Christians. The governor of Bessarabia supported his activities among Bessarabian Jews and asked his superior in Saint Petersburg to satisfy Rabinovich's request for the official registration of his "sect" and publication of his books. Rabinovich planned to expand the activities of the New Testament Jews to other provinces of the Russian Empire and to attract young Jews to Christianity. Therefore, he planned for a propagandist "literature and special schools for Jews who would join Christianity."[91]

The Ministry of the Interior consulted the Holy Synod about Rabinovich's "New Testament Israelites." Meanwhile, the local Orthodox clergy and Kishinev landlords submitted their complaints about Rabinovich's activities among the peasant population of the province. According to these complaints, the movement of New Testament Jews "recast all Christian principles in their own Jewish fashion" and brought "obvious German influences to the Russian countryside," confusing the local Orthodox population. In their letters to the Holy Synod, Russian conservatives, who knew about his graduation from a German theological institution, treated Rabinovich as a German spy and portrayed him as "the secret agent of German imperialism and the German Protestant Church." The Holy Synod asked the police to stop the anti-Russian activities of Rabinovich and his Jewish adherents.

In 1886, the secret police began a special investigation of the case of the "New Testament Israelites" but found nothing criminal in Rabinovich's activities. Nevertheless, K. Pobedonostsev, the ober-procurator of the Holy Synod, insisted on banning the New Testament Jews' movement in southern Russia. Pobedonostsev explained to the officials of the Ministry of the Interior that it was pointless to officially permit "the activities of Rabinovich sect in the localities noted for the mass spread of Baptism and various rationalist sects like the Stundists." According to Pobedonostsev, "this sect promoted a new religious dissent among Russian citizens and their defection from the Orthodoxy." Therefore, he recommended that Rabinovich join the officially permitted Protestant church in Russia rather than establish a new sect.

On August 4, 1886, the Holy Synod refused to grant Rabinovich's request and banned all his publications. Nevertheless, Rabinovich tried to persuade the local administration that his activities were legal. He stopped his contacts with the Stundist peasants, and in December 1888, he wrote to the minister of the interior with an explanation of his intention to promote a rapprochement of Jews and Christians. He even agreed to register his sect with the police and to follow the rules and requirements of the Orthodox Church. But the Ministry of the Interior and the Department of Police did not want to contradict the Holy Synod. The police were influenced by the scandalous rumors about Gordin and Priluker's Jewish organizations, and they feared new socialist and German propaganda among the peasants.[92]

Yet, the police could not sever the ties of the New Israel sect of Rabinovich with the Stundists in Kishinev. During the 1890s, the Christian Jews and Russian and Ukrainian evangelicals received religious literature through the German coreligionists of Rabinovich. The Stundist peasants regularly visited meetings for worship in Rabinovich's house in Kishinev. Nikita Sharakhovich, one of the Russian followers of Rabinovich, played a prominent role in maintaining contacts with dissident peasants. In 1895, the local clergy complained to the governor of Bessarabia about new cases of the defection from the Orthodox Church under the influence of the "New Israel" and the Kishinev Stundists. As it turned out, all suspected Stundists, including Sharakhovich, were using the meetinghouse of Rabinovich for "Stundist" propaganda among the local Orthodox peasants. In December 1895, the district court of Kishinev sentenced Sharakhovich and his coreligionists to imprisonment for their Stundist propaganda among Orthodox Christians. As we see, during the 1890s, Kishinev, along with Odessa, became an important center in the expansion of the evangelical movement among the rural population of southern Russia.[93]

This movement connected the New Testament Jews, radical intellectuals, and peasant religious radicals in one mainstream of opposition to Russian Orthodoxy and to the tsarist administration as well. As it turned out, all these groups participated in the same "eschatological" discourse, and they shared the same belief concerning the end of "this sinful world of social injustice" and the ultimate destiny of mankind. Socialists, radical evangelicals, and New Testament Jews alike believed in the possibility of "a new human Paradise on the Earth" without exploitation and humiliation. At the same time, all these radicals viewed the future society as a congregation of individuals, based on principles of moral purity and human dignity. According to their eschatological dreams, such a society would have no racial or ethnic hatred. This ideal

361

attracted intellectual radical Jews who took part in the Russian revolutionary movement and collaborated with peasant evangelicals as well.

All over the southern Russian Empire, Jewish Christian Baptists became a common phenomenon. Under the influence of different Western Christian missionary organizations, some Russian Jews converted to Christianity. During the 1880s, these Christian Jews even tried to establish a Baptist colony in the Crimea.[94] But the Russian administration did not like the missionary activities of the British and German Protestant preachers. The police worried about cases of Jewish conversion to Stundism and the Baptist faith. They followed closely the formation of the Jewish evangelical organization in Odessa. Its agents analyzed publications of the Jewish newspaper *Zions Freunde*, which concerned the activities of Jews who preached for the evangelical Christians. They found out that Isaac-Leon Rosenberg, an Odessa Jew, regularly preached evangelical sermons at the Stundist meetings for worship every Tuesday and Friday evening. During these meetings in 1908–9, the police counted forty Stundists who usually visited the "meeting house with the Jewish preacher" on 23 Kouznechnaya Street in downtown Odessa.[95]

The police documented the convergence of New Testament Jews and Baptists. One police agent reported that the Jewish Baptist Christian community in Odessa had a "Jewish priest Rosenfeld who was preaching Christian sermons exclusively in Hebrew." The Russian administration worried about this Jewish involvement in the Christian sectarian movement, because "given the Jewish inclination to political intrigues, the Jewish intrusion in the Russian sectarian movement could turn these sectarians in an undesirable anti-Russian political direction." The administration of the Russian Orthodox Church informed the police about four Jewish Baptist ministers in the southern Russia, but the police found only three—Vladimir I. Melamed, Barukh N. Shapiro, and Leon Rosenberg—who all served as Baptist preachers for local Stundo-Baptist communities. In addition, the police discovered that Rosenberg, a Jewish shopkeeper from Odessa, corresponded with another Christian Jew, Samuil Vilshenzon, an agent of the London Biblical Society, who sent money and literature to Jews and Stundists in the Odessa district.[96]

362   In November 1902, in the village of Snegourovka (in the Vasil'kovka dis-

trict of Kiev province), the police agents arrested a group of "enthusiastic" Stundist peasants who were waiting for "the works and performance of the Holy Spirit." Among the 126 spectators of this "performance," at least two were Jewish. One of them was "a Jewish resident of town Korsun' (in the Kanev district of Kiev province), Berko Ievsei Gershkov Ostrovsky, who called himself a Stundist and who had been arrested as a Stundist on April 10 [of 1902];" the other was "a subject of the Austrian crown, a baptized Jew, Piotr Kramar', who had converted to Greek Roman Christianity from Judaism." As it turned out, these Jews were connected to the New Testament Jewish movement, and they brought new religious literature and money to local Stundists. The police agents who reported on them shared the prevailing anti-Semitic stereotypes. In short, they warned of the "Jewish exploitation of ignorant Ukrainian peasants and of the subjugation of the Ukrainian population by Jewish entrepreneurs."[97]

The Orthodox press shared this fear. The authors who wrote for the Kiev Orthodox Church Academy pointed to "the Jews who exploited our countryside and our peasants in particular."[98] But police documents show a different picture of the relations between Stundist peasants and the New Testament Jews, that of friendship and mutual assistance. Educated Jewish intellectuals tried to help the Russian and Ukrainian peasants in their search for a better life and social justice. Evangelical religion and the dissident movement created common ground between Jews and poor Ukrainian peasants—the two groups of outsiders in Russian society.

Radical Stundists, the Maliovantsy, and Tolstoyans in Search of the Millennium, 1894–1905

The legislation of 1894 did not halt the radical trends in the peasant dissident movement. Police documents and reports of Orthodox missionaries demonstrated their further development. Moreover, during the 1890s the evangelical movement underwent a new radicalization. Orthodox missionaries noted "the penetration of socialist and communist ideas," the influence of Tolstoy's teachings, "the intensive contact of peasant dissident leaders with other Russian and foreign sects," and the support of the religious radicals by revolutionary intellectuals.[99] The radicalization of the popular evangelical movement provoked a counterreaction among the Orthodox clergy and Orthodox missionaries, including the publication of new periodicals, such as the *Missionary Review*, the establishment of Orthodox libraries, and the formation of clubs for discussion. But neither missionary activities nor police persecutions could stop the spread of the radical dissident movement.

All religious radicals, including Shalaputs and Stundists, identified social justice with the ownership of land.[100] They thought that the unjust distribution of land resulted in the exploitation and humiliation of the peasants. In a conversation with a police officer, one of the Uman' Stundists (in the province of Kiev) explained that the dissidents did not care about icons, but he added jokingly, "If the Russian government gives me land, I would hang the icons again in my house."[101] Later on, in 1899, radical Stundists from the Uman' district insisted in a discussion with an Orthodox missionary that all land be held in common: "Everybody should take as much land as he or she needs and can cultivate." One Stundist activist explained that with social equality being based on economic equality, everybody would have access to power and could be elected "to serve as an administrator or a priest."[102]

Another Stundist peasant, Ivan Draganov, a Bulgarian by origin, expressed obvious social criticism in a conversation with his neighbors. He said that "everything that is bad—theft, corruption, violence, and misery—came from the Orthodox Church, or the Orthodox tsar, or from the Orthodox government, or the Orthodox administration. Like the robbers, the tsar and his Orthodox officers take away the property of the poor peasants and send their children to the army to be killed." Therefore, he taught his listeners, the main source of evil was the Russian Orthodox authorities. Without them—without the Orthodox Church and tsarist administration—ordinary people would live much better.[103]

This opposition to the Orthodox Church as an institution of oppression was typical of all Stundists. In 1900, Ivan Kravets, a peasant activist associated with the Stundists from the village of Pereshchepino in the province of Ekaterinoslav, explained to an Orthodox missionary that the dissident peasants believed in Jesus Christ, a fighter for the rights of all oppressed and exploited people, rather than in the Jesus of the Orthodox Church. "We do not like your Jesus Christ, " he told to the Orthodox priest, "You, together with your Christ, traded people for dogs before Emancipation; we, with our Jesus Christ, want to be liberated from your oppression now."[104]

The criticism of the existing political system in Russia and the anti-tsarist feelings among the radical Stundists were frequently the subject of police reports from the Ukrainian provinces. Before the Revolution of 1905, Stundist peasant radicals demonstrated their rejection of the tsar's authority and disrespect for the most sacred aspect of the Russian political culture—the tsar. On April 17, 1902 (the Orthodox Easter), Nikifor Iazev, the Stundist itinerant preacher, a peasant by origin, told the peasants from the village of Novo-Troitskoe in Ekaterinoslav province that the Russian tsar was not worthy to be ruler of the Russian people. Iazev tried to explain his own vision of the tsar's sins. According to him, the emperor had bought all free land in Russia and now he established high prices for this land instead of redistributing it equally among his subjects. With equal distribution of land, there would be no need for authorities, criminal courts, prisons, or thieves. Using the Gospels as a "textbook for everyday life," Iazev taught that economic and social inequality generated social turmoil, and soon there would be a riot in Ekaterinoslav. "The tsar will be killed," Iazev said, "and afterwards life will be much better."[105]

The police discovered that anti-tsarist attitudes among the dissident peasants stemmed from the strange combination of the millennial ideas of religious radicals and the socialist propaganda of revolutionary intellectuals. According to the police, the main source of eschatological expectations among Ukrainian peasants was the Stundist-Shalaput movement of Maliovantsy from the Tarashcha district in the province of Kiev. The major source of antistate ideas was, as it turned out, the propaganda of various liberal and socialist theories by local landowners such as Prince Khilkov, who spread Leo Tolstoy's ideas among the peasants of the Sumy district in the province of Kharkov. The villages, which had belonged to these liberal landlords before 1861, became centers of peasant protest in the 1890s and 1900s. According to the police, most

365

of the antistate activities of the dissident peasants arose in such village dissident centers in the province of Kharkov.

According to police reports in the 1890s, the most famous center of antigovernment criticism among the religious radicals was the former Khilkov's property, the village of Pavlovki (Pavlovka in Russian) in the Sumy district. As early as 1892, the police discovered a connection between the anti-tsarist preaching of the Ukrainian Stundists and the socialist and Tolstoyan ideas of Pavlovki's inhabitants. In 1892, the local priest informed the police that two Stundist activists from the village of Alekseievka in the province of Kharkov, Philip and Lev Tkachiov, who were father and son, disseminated "dangerous political ideas." As it turned out, these Stundist peasants preached to their neighbors that the time was close when everybody would be equal and would live without tsars, landlords, and priests.[106] Lev Tkachiov explained to his listeners that for future progress it was necessary to hang and execute all authorities, including the tsar. Divine justice would not tolerate the sinful state administration. When their neighbors asked how to live without the tsar and authorities, the Tkachiovs responded: "We will elect our own tsars and authorities from the ordinary people, as we elect the village administration." According to his explanation, only after the tsar's execution and the punishment of all who had power in Russia, could citizens acquire the political rights that the Western Europeans had already.[107]

In one conversation, Philip Tkachiov noted that it would be better for Russia to live under the "foreign tsars." And he explained that European rulers spared their subjects, took care of the prosperity of ordinary people, distributed all land equally, and removed the heaviest taxes. During one discussion in May 1892, Philip Tkachiov announced in the street to a crowd of peasants: "Our tsar is a son of the bitch; he gave unlimited rights and privileges to the clergy and the nobility; we will have no order in the country until we punish all our priests, landlords and the tsars."

During 1892 and 1893, Lev and Philip Tkachiov preached the Gospels to their neighbors and used Holy Scripture for their criticism of the Orthodox clergy and tsarist authorities. They interpreted the Pharisees as symbols of the hypocritical and oppressive authority of the Russian Orthodox Church and the local administration. During a police interrogation, Lev and Phillip Tkachiov confessed that in their preaching they repeated the ideas of Prince Khilkov and followed the interpretation of Holy Scripture by Khilkov's followers from the village of Pavlovki. As it turned out, the Tkachiovs had a relative from Pavlovki, Daniil Vernidub. Through Vernidub, the defendants knew that prince Khilkov had distributed all his land among his peasants and taught them not to visit the Orthodox Church and not to respect the authorities. According to the testimony of Vernidub, Khilkov told the Pavlovki peasants to be ready for the oncoming revolution and explained to them that religion was not necessary for survival. The local priests reported that Khilkov insisted that everyone in Russia, including the local Stundists, should not study the new religion but try instead to change the state system of their country.

Both the Orthodox Church and the police organized a special investigation of Khilkov's activities. The police identified his teaching with radical Stundism. The Orthodox clergy went further, and portrayed his adherents as "followers of anarchism and socialism, because they rejected the authorities, the oath of loyalty, compulsory military service, and taxes; and because they expected a restructuring of the state on the basis of the general equality of the people and leveling of property."[108] Local priests reported in the 1890s that peasants from Pavlovki refused to baptize their infant children in the Orthodox Church. As one peasant, Fedot Stryzhak, explained, "A child should grow up and be baptized when he will understand the ritual of baptism." And he reminded the priest, "Do you remember how John the Baptist taught that before baptism a person had to repent his sins and understand Christian teaching?" The peasants who refused to follow Orthodox rituals considered Prince Khilkov their teacher. They spoke about him with great respect and sympathy.[109]

In November 1890, the archbishop of Kharkov sent Timofei Butkevich, an intelligent Kharkov priest who was well known for his missionary activity among the dissident peasants, to Pavlovki to meet Prince Khilkov and collect information about him (figure 7.2). Butkevich spent a week in Pavlovki and had long conversations with the prince over three days. His report contained detailed information about the prince and his influence on local peasants.[110]

Prince Dmitrii Aleksandrovich Khilkov (1858–1914) was an interesting

367

person. Before 1877, he led the typical life of a Russian aristocrat. He drank, chased women, and fought with his rivals. But during the Russo-Turkish War of 1877–78, Khilkov, a military officer, had an experience that changed his outlook on life. He killed a Turkish soldier in combat, and the very act of killing shocked him very much. After this, he fell under the influence of a Dukhobor peasant. As he told the Reverend Timofei Butkevich, by this time he had already become disappointed with Russian aristocratic society and the elite military Guards in which he served as an officer. He remembered only orgies, hard drinking, and numerous adulterous affairs with women. The psychological shock during the war changed his life. He resigned from the army, and in 1885 he went to his estate near Pavlovki, where he studied religion and tried to find his own path to Divine Truth.[111]

At the same time, Khilkov decided to help his peasants find God as well. His first move was to ask the local Orthodox clergy about helping with the religious education of the peasants. After efforts to attract the local clergy to his project, the prince decided that "the Orthodox priests had betrayed their Christian mission, and become state officials protecting the interests of the nobles and wealthy people."[112] In his search for truth, Khilkov read many books, but a story by Leo Tolstoy shaped his understanding of the Christian religion. This was the short story, "Krestnik" (Godson), in which Tolstoy portrayed his vision of a good Christian life.

After reading the story, Khilkov visited Tolstoy. And after his conversation with the great writer, he decided to follow Tolstoy's principles in his own life. As he told Butkevich, Tolstoy showed him that "Divine Truth and peace of mind can be found in the peasant's hut and in manual labor rather than in Saint Petersburg or the Orthodox Church." In 1886, the prince gave 400 *desiatin* of his land to his peasants from Pavlovki. He settled with his wife and a son among them as an ordinary farmer on a small farm of 3 *desiatin,* where he worked on the field doing all his work by himself.[113]

The prince taught his peasants to follow the Gospels in their lives and rejected the Orthodox Church because of "its subjection to the earthly authorities." As a follower of Tolstoy, Khilkov considered the main principle of the Christian life to be the law of Jesus Christ: "nonresistance to evil by force." According to Khilkov, the root of all evil was in any association or union of different people. As he explained, such "an association" necessarily led to the social and political institutions, which controlled, directed, and eventually exploited the people. Therefore "any kind of institution—state, or church—was evil." Khilkov taught his peasant neighbors that if all people in the world followed the Gospels and the Christian principle of nonresistance, then the Kingdom of God appear on Earth. There would be no "bloodshed, and all nations would live in brotherhood, equality and freedom." In this future society, based on Christian principles, there would be no need for "the state, or the church, or army, or police."[114]

At the same time, Khilkov was opposed to socialism and violence. He stressed the differences between Christian teaching and revolutionary communist ideology. Nevertheless, the police and Orthodox clergy worried about his influence on Kharkov peasants. Hundreds of peasants from various districts of Kharkov province went on a pilgrimage to Pavlovki to visit "the saintly prince Dmitrii." The local clergy complained that Khilkov's ideas had spread to other villages all over the province by 1890.[115]

The Pavlovki peasants declared themselves "true Christians" and stopped visiting the church. Some ceased paying state and church taxes. The most radical of Khilkov's peasant followers refused to take oaths and enter military service. These "dangerous practices" spread to other localities of the Ukrainian provinces during the 1890s.[116] Responding to the clergy's complaints, the governor of Kharkov province interfered and ordered Khilkov to stop his "propaganda" among local peasants. Under the pressure of the hierarchy of the Russian Orthodox Church, the police arrested the prince in February 1891 and exiled him to Transcaucasia. At the same time, they established strict police control over the Pavlovki peasants and prevented their "suspicious activities." In fact, in 1892 the local administration introduced severe repressive measures against all the rural population in the vicinity of Pavlovki.[117]

It is noteworthy that the dissident peasants who were already influenced by the radical Stundists and various Shalaput sects appropriated the Tolstoyan teaching of prince Khilkov. Those who had suffered from severe persecution or serious economic problems emphasized particularly millennial ideas when they appropriated the abstract theories of Russian intellectuals such as Khilkov. During the 1890s, dissident Ukrainian peasants developed their own version of the Millennium. The most radical and most famous form of their millennial movement was the Maliovantsy. That was why the radical activists of this movement became new prophets for such dissidents as the Pavlovki peasants.

Social criticism and eschatological expectations played an important role in Kondrat Maliovannyi's preaching from the outset. The Maliovantsy interpreted Christianity as religious teaching for oppressed and suffering people. They believed that only poor common folk could understand Jesus Christ's suffering and lead other people, including "wealthy noble landlords," on the road

Chapter Seven

to Divine Truth.[118] Wealthy people were not ready to carry the cross of truth and suffering. As one follower explained, "Only poor people, not the rich nobility, have been prepared by their miserable life for suffering in the name of Jesus Christ; the beaten and humiliated common folks are ready to carry the cross of Christ and suffer for a true religion."[119]

In one of his epistles, Maliovannyi wrote to his followers about the necessity to suffer and fight "spiritually" for true religion: "Put on the Armour of Divine Truth on and take up the arms of God, be ready to withstand His enemies, be brave and kind as the warriors of your invincible Christ and Savior." Making allusions to Slavic mythology and Russian folklore, Maliovannyi compared true Christians to the legendary Ilia Muromets, who fought the Nightingale Highwayman (Solovei-Razboinik), killed him in combat, and liberated the inhabitants of Kiev from the oppression of this brigand. He contrasted the "purity" of true Christianity with the "hypocritical theology" of the Orthodox Church and the "falsehood" of the Russian mass media and education.

According to Maliovannyi, his followers and all true Christians should resist the temptations of popular culture and the social norms inculcated in Russian society by the ruling classes through education, newspapers, and literature. In a letter, edited by a follower of Tolstoy, Maliovannyi portrayed his dreams of a future Russia that would be transformed by evangelical Christianity and the oncoming Millennium. He foresaw a world in which all people would live in one brotherhood without private property, without exploitation, war, or violence. Maliovannyi taught his followers: "We will beat swords, rifles and guns into ploughshares, sickles, and other tools necessary for the household and we will live happily in an earthly paradise." He condemned "all bars, inns, theatres, circuses and other brothels, which enrich the wealthy people and make the poor people poorer." When people have stopped sinning and imitating the sinful lifestyle of the rich, he believed, they will be ready for the Kingdom of Christ. He expected this kingdom to come on Earth for his generation, which would live "in equality, without authorities and administration, in happiness and peace."[120]

Preaching the oncoming Millennium of Jesus Christ, Maliovannyi invoked images of Armageddon and the Last Judgment, which he expected to resolve all earthly problems, including the disparity between poverty and wealth. "Rich people with their wealth," Maliovannyi taught his adherents, "are the main evil on the Earth." He warned his followers "not to be corrupted by examples of the sinful life of well-to-do people." He compared the wealthy to the ancient bandits who robbed, raped, and killed for money, and he promised that they would be in the Last Judgment. Only the long-suffering poor, God's elect, would be saved. All observers noted that equality and brotherhood without private property and exploitation were the essence of Maliovannyi's teaching.[121]

The Maliovantsy interpreted the Last Judgment as a sacred act of social justice under God's guidance. Like the radical Stundists, the Maliovantsy sought to reward the poor and punish the wealthy. Yet Maliovannyi's followers went further than the radical Stundists (the so-called Neo-Stundists, or "young" Stundists) in anticipating social justice, because they emphasized the millennial drama of social revenge of poor over rich. During a police investigation in 1892, one peasant follower of Maliovannyi told a police officer, "Now the authorities [nacahl'stvo] accuse us. Soon everything will change," he said, "all the authorities and nobility will jump like goats because the Holy Spirit will descend on them, and all the wealthy people except those who refused to repent will join us." It is noteworthy that the dissident peasants accepted some violence in their portrayal of their future revenge. The same peasant told the police, "When our faith celebrates a victory, you (the authorities) will be sent to prison and punished [for all that you have done to us]."[122]

According to the dissident peasants, the logic of social revenge required the redistribution of property and the punishment of those who abused poor people and exploited them. Although Maliovannyi rejected violence and insisted on nonresistance, his radical followers demonstrated disrespect of all authority except the Bible and their "Heavenly Father," and they criticized the Russian social and political order. As was mentioned above, in Kiev on November 4, 1899, the police arrested 70 peasants who stopped there on a trip to Kazan'. During the police interrogation, Orthodox missionaries were invited to help the police determine the sect to which the arrested peasants belonged. When a missionary asked the peasants the reason for their stop in Kiev, their leader,

Ivan Lysenko, answered that they wished to meet the leading officials of the Orthodox Church and tell them about problems of peasant life. During his conversation with the Orthodox clergy, Lysenko described how economic and social problems in the Ukrainian countryside gave rise to millennial expectations among peasant dissenters:

The noble landlords [*pany-pomeshchiki*] took all the land, enclosed it with high fences and left only the smallest parcels of land for us, the peasants. We have small children, one horse, one cow, and a couple of chickens per household— but with little land to feed them all. Whereas the landlords have too much land and too many pastures with good grass. If our cattle by chance stray to their pastures, they catch our animals and fine us, poor peasants. But if a peasant has no money to pay the fine, the landlord will send him to prison. The police officers and judges are good friends of the landlord. Therefore they will drink and eat together and afterward indict the poor peasant for theft. There is no truth on the Earth, and there is no life for the peasant [*muzhik*] here. That is why we leave our huts and go to meet the Heavenly Father, whom you call Kondrat Maliovannyi.[123]

The radical Maliovantsy were ready for the oncoming millennial paradise, when there would be no need of courts or police, when all property would be in common use, and "a brother will not tell his own brother, 'this property is mine,' and the police will not torture and torment the poor peasant to make him to take his last shirt off and give it to the wealthy man."[124] They refused to follow the civil laws of the Russian Empire because they felt that these laws subjugated the peasants to police, priests, and landlords. As one of the prophetesses of the movement, the peasant woman Agafia Rudchuk, declared to an Orthodox missionary, "We have no need of your tsar, or your laws— we have our own tsar already." According to the Maliovantsy, the oncoming Millennium would liberate them from the tsarist laws, the army, the police, and all conventional rules of conduct.[125]

In contrast to the radical Stundists, the Maliovantsy were more radical in their approach to problems of their peasant life. The most radical Stundists, with all their criticism of the Russian social system and their involvement in revolutionary activity, were still members of "this sinful world." They tried to

373

change their life and "the world" for the better, but they perceived their existence as a prelude to the future coming of Jesus Christ. Therefore, they did not reject "this world" completely. The Maliovantsy had already witnessed the arrival of their Christ, Maliovannyi, and all the promises of biblical prophets were fulfilled for them. To some extent, they had already entered the Millennium. That was why their rejection of "this world" was so total and so complete.

The oppositional discourse of the Maliovantsy spread over the Ukrainian provinces of the Russian Empire during the late 1890s and early 1900s. It was attractive to persecuted peasant dissidents who struggled to survive emotionally and physically. This was the experience of Khilkov's followers in the village of Pavlovki in Kharkov province. The most radical follower of Maliovannyi, Moisei Todosienko, a peasant from the village of Iakhny, linked Khilkov's Pavlovki dissidents to the radical Maliovantsy from the province of Kiev.

The village of Iakhny in the Vasil'kov district became a center of mass spirit possession as early as 1890. All the members of the local Stundo-Baptist congregation became Maliovantsy. Convulsions and body trembling were part of their daily meetings. The leader of the Iakhny Maliovantsy was Moisei Todosienko, a peasant twenty-seven years of age, who became the new prophet Moses of the Maliovannyi movement. He experienced his first hallucinations in October 1890. He saw a strange light in the sky. Then in the middle of the light, the skies were opened, and he saw the Orthodox Saint Tikhon Zadonskii kneeling at the Divine Throne. Then Todosienko heard a voice from the sky, asking people to repent. After this experience, he went to Tarashcha and met Kondrat Maliovannyi personally.

At the beginning of 1891, Todosienko proclaimed himself the prophet Moses, the representative of Maliovannyi in Iakhny. After this, he changed his image. Instead of peasant dress, he bought a fashionable hat, an expensive umbrella, and a new suit in Kiev. When Todosienko announced to his coreligionists the oncoming Last Judgment in May 1892, he was already a famous young leader of the movement. He organized the procession of the local Maliovantsy to the place where he expected the Advent of their Savior, Kondrat Maliovannyi. Todosienko and his adherents dressed in white robes, spread out pieces of decorated fabric and expensive coats on the road to that place, and

374

began praying ecstatically, waiting for the miracle. The local police arrested the dissidents. Todosienko cried that he was not only the biblical Moses but also the Messiah, "the Redeemer of Humankind." He tried to explain to the police that his first name in Russian should be spelled as "Messiia" (Messiah). The police sent Todosienko to a mental asylum. In 1892, he became one of Ivan A. Sikorskii's new patients.[126]

In late 1892, after his release from the Kiev mental hospital, Todosienko resumed his dissident activities. He presented himself as a representative of both the Maliovannyi and the tsar who supposedly sent him to the peasants to prepare them for the oncoming Millennium. Despite the anti-tsarist criticism of the radical Stundists, a majority of the Orthodox Ukrainian peasants still shared tsarist illusions. Todosienko understood this. The major component of the millennial scenario, according to Todosienko's interpretation of Maliovannyi's epistles, was the redistribution of land as property, including the landlords' estates. Moisei Todosienko changed his peasant dress into a special uniform, which symbolized his new status as an important messenger and emphasized the significance of his mission. He visited landlords' estates and peasant households, and he dressed in a Cossack costume—including trousers with military stripes on them and a military hat with cockade. He showed the peasants that he had surveyed the land for future redistribution.

Since 1892, Todosienko had visited the Pashkovites in Saint Petersburg each year and participated in their evangelical meetings in the house of Princess Lieven on the Nevsky prospekt (near the Cathedral of Saint Isaac) and in the house of Princess Chertkova on Vasiliev Island. According to his testimony, at one of the evangelical meetings in Saint Petersburg on May 1, 1900, he met a person who introduced himself as Tsar Nikolai Aleksandrovich. After a long conversation with this man, who asked him to help his Christian brothers in the Ukrainian provinces, Todosienko believed that his mission was to fulfill wishes of the "evangelical tsar." In March 1901, he brought "the tsar" from Saint Petersburg to his peasant coreligionists in the villages of Iakhny and Malo-Polovetskoe, where they read the New Testament and prayed together about the approaching Kingdom of God, the kingdom of social justice and equality.[127]

375

At the same time, Todosienko urged his coreligionists—the radical Stundists and Maliovantsy—to move from "the Egyptian land" (i.e., Russia) to "Canaan." With his Cossack uniform and stories based on the Bible and Ukrainian folklore, he evoked among the Ukrainian peasants familiar images of the legendary Gaidamaki, who had promised to liberate them from the landlords' rule.[128] He interpreted his first name, Moisei, as a symbol of the Ukrainian peasants' "Exodus" from slavery to freedom. As the biblical Moses led the Jews from "Egyptian slavery" to the Promised land of Canaan, following God's order, so Todosienko would lead the suffering peasants to freedom following the teaching of Kondrat Maliovannyi. Todosienko told his followers to go to the village of Snegourovka near a railway station of Fastov to wait for a special train, supposedly sent by the tsar for their trip to the Promised Land. It seems as if Todosienko planned to stop the railway train at the large station of Fastov, occupy it, and then direct it to Kazan', where Maliovannyi would meet them. Hundreds of peasants followed Todosienko to Fastov, but their leader was not able to stop the train at this station. Disappointed, Todosienko blamed the police and the Orthodox Church for what happened.

After this failure, on December 18, 1900, Todosienko led forty dissident peasants to the parish church in his native village of Iakhny, where he presented a new millennial scenario. Instead of organizing an Exodus, he decided to prepare the ground for oncoming Kingdom of God in his native land and purge the churches of "idolatry and Pharisees." Following this new plan, he came to Iakhny to occupy the parish church and oust the Orthodox priests from the church building. When, on the morning of December 18, the crowd of excited dissidents broke into the church building, Todosienko declared to the local priest that the church belonged to the ordinary people, who would cleanse it of all signs of idolatry. But the local Orthodox peasants expelled Todosienko's followers from the church building and almost beat them to death.[129]

After this second failure, Todosienko traveled widely searching for reborn Christians ready for his eschatological plans. He visited the meetinghouses of the aristocratic evangelicals in Saint Petersburg and Moscow, where he participated in the meetings for worship organized by the followers of Pashkov. At the same time, he went to the southern provinces of Kherson and Tavrida, where he communicated with other religious radicals among peasant dissidents. During one of his trips to Saint Petersburg, he learned about the evangelical peasants from the village of Pavlovki. On August 10, 1901, together with his friend, another follower of Maliovannyi, Ipatii Litvin, a peasant from Kiev province, Todosienko visited Pavlovki, where he met peasants who eagerly responded to his preaching about the oncoming Millennium and the necessity to prepare for the Kingdom of God.[130] As it turned out, both the evangelical and Orthodox peasants had reasons for discontent.

The peasant dissenters of Pavlovki were mistreated and cruelly persecuted by the police both as Stundists and Tolstoyans because the local clergy presented them as "the Stundist followers of Leo Tolstoy." Following the anti-Stundist legislation of 1894 and the Holy Synod's recommendations of 1897 about the treatment of Tolstoyans as dangerous sectarians, the local police tried to stop any social activity by the Pavlovki dissidents. They were not allowed to work outside their village, and "any gathering of two or more was likely to be broken by police and the participants subjected to a fine." Because of the continual harassment by police and numerous restrictions on their economic activities, the life of the Pavlovki peasants became unbearable. In January 1899, thirty-eight families (comprising 216 peasants) of the local dissidents petitioned Kharkov administration for permission to emigrate. These peasants began their preparation for their "Exodus from the Egyptian slavery" in the spring of 1900 and sold their land and possessions. But the administration of Kharkov province granted passports only for those who were not eligible for military service. The majority of the male dissidents, who planned to emigrate, were supposed to stay in Russia until they were forty-two years old and had served in the army. Therefore, all petitioners were forced to stay and live under the strict police regime in Pavlovki.[131]

Orthodox peasants expressed dissatisfaction as well. The exile of Prince Khilkov, who gave the peasants land and treated them better than other landlords, generated animosity among Pavlovki's inhabitants toward the church and local administration. Two of the most detested local landowners, a husband and wife, Fedor and Glafira Ivanitskii, known for their cruel mistreatment of peasants as well as their alcoholism and dissolute life, granted money

377

for the building of an Orthodox church school and requested that their names be attached to it. Every local peasant, including the Orthodox ones, protested. Moreover, the new school was built on land where a bar and brothel once stood. The landlord, Ivanitskii, had purchased this land illegally twenty-five years earlier. There were also rumors about Ivanitskii's "worship of Satan." The local peasants considered the location of the new school "a cursed place."

By 1901, the new church school of the "saints Fedor and Glafira" had become the most hateful place in the village. Many Orthodox peasants refused to send their children to this school, because in their minds it symbolized the rule of corrupt and dissolute landlords. The corruption of the local Orthodox clergy was another reason for the peasants' discontent. Indeed, the local police reported numerous cases of the cupidity of Pavlovki's priest, who charged high fees for religious services and even delayed a burial ritual if peasants lacked the money to pay. The deacon of the local church was known for his hard drinking and for dancing with women at peasants' weddings.[132] The strict police regime against the Pavlovki dissenters affected Orthodox peasants as well. Because it was difficult to distinguish the Orthodox from the dissidents, the police often mistreated the Orthodox peasants as well.

When Todosienko brought the ideas of Kondrat Maliovannyi about social justice and the revenge of the Millennium to Pavlovki, he attracted peasants from both dissident and Orthodox households who were ready to explode in anger. On August 10 and 11, 1901, Moisei Todosienko and Ipatii Litvin preached about Maliovannyi and the Last Judgment. According to them, in the Kingdom of God all land was to be taken from the landlords and distributed equally among the peasants. "To continue working for the masters was sinful," they told the peasants who came to the house of Timofei Nikitenko, where "the prophets" stayed. To prepare for the Millennium, the prophets urged the peasants to cleanse the churches of "the filth of corruption." At the same time, both Todosienko and Litvin presented themselves as agents of the tsar. "I am sent by Tsar Nicholas to enlighten you and to prepare for the new laws," Todosienko said, "the Tsar has sent out many of ours; your Khilkov has been sent to people of another land, and I to you."[133] Local peasants helped the prophets with money and food, and Todosienko and Litvin safely left for Saint Petersburg.

By the time of Todosienko's next visit on September 10, all the registered peasant dissidents from the fifty households in Pavlovki who called themselves "Christians defected from the Orthodoxy" had converted to the Maliovantsy.[134] Now Todosienko came without his friend, and his preaching became more radical. The major topic of his sermons was the need to release the Divine Truth that was imprisoned in the Orthodox churches. This topic attracted many peasants from the neighboring villages, who were discontented with the building of the new church school near Pavlovki. Some of the guests considered the very existence of this school dedicated to the infamous sinners, the landlords Ivanitskii, sacrilegious. A local police officer visited the meetings organized by Todosienko in Pavlovki and arrested him for "the absence of an identification document."

When the police escorted Todosienko to the district town of Sumy, the Pavlovki dissidents accompanied them, and insisted that they knew him. After a brief interrogation, the police released him, and he returned to Pavlovki as a hero. The enthusiastic meetings reminiscent of the Kiev Maliovantsy now resumed in Pavlovki. Todosienko invited representatives of Pavlovki's dissidents to go with him to the province of Kiev and establish relations with the Maliovantsy there. According to Todosienko, the unity of all "true Christians" was a necessary condition for the Millennium. On September 13, 1901, the Pavlovki peasants collected money, bought new clothes for Todosienko, and sent their representative, Piotr Kovalenko, with the prophet "Moses" to the province of Kiev.[135]

When Moisei Todosienko left Pavlovki, the former followers of Khilkov, who now became adherents of "the Heavenly Father" Maliovannyi and his "prophet Moses," began their ecstatic praying, which lasted for two days and nights (September 14–15) without interruption. By the end of the second day's praying in the house of Timofei Nikitenko, one of the youngest participants of the meeting, a twenty-five-year-old peasant, Grigorii Pavlenko, declared that he felt the descent of the Holy Spirit on him and the Divine Power inside his soul. Pavlenko revealed to his coreligionists that the prophet Moses "gave him the ability to receive the Divine Power" and become a new incarnation of God. Following Todosienko's preaching about the necessity of cleansing the churches on the eve of the Millennium, Pavlenko called on those "who waited for the Holy Ghost" to go to the Pavlovki church and transform it into the Divine throne of God.

When one peasant lost consciousness and fell "dead" on the floor, Pavlenko demonstrated his Divine abilities and "raised him from the dead." All the peasants called him Jesus Christ and confessed their sins before him. Pavlenko, who believed in his Divine mission and the coming of the Last Judgment, called on his coreligionists "to destroy the pagan temples and punish the Pharisees, the Orthodox priests who spread lies among the people." He asked his followers to help him to occupy the Divine throne in the church. Meanwhile, the dissidents, who expected the millennial kingdom of equality and social justice, destroyed their property and threw away their belongings and money. According to their eschatological dreams, they would not need them in the future.[136]

On the morning of September 16, the crowd of excited dissidents marched through the village, shouting, "Truth is coming, Christ is risen." At the head of the peasant procession there was a wagon, in which Pavlenko's wife sat, holding her infant baby in her arms. "Believe in this baby. This is Christ," she shouted. It was Sunday of the Christian holiday known as Exaltation of the Cross. Many peasants, including the Orthodox ones who joined Pavlenko, had fasted for a week, and they were ready emotionally for the religious ecstasy of the millennial preaching of Todosienko and Pavlenko.

The local police officers, who had heard rumors about Pavlenko's plans, closed the church school and put guards near it and near the church of Saint Michael in Pavlovki. Meanwhile, the procession of 20 dissenters had become a crowd of 500 peasants who moved toward the church school. The police officers tried to stop the crowd. One of them on a horse rode into a crowd to disperse "rebellious peasants." The largely Orthodox crowd of peasants, whose majority hated "the cursed school," rushed to fight with the police officers, beat them, and broke their swords. After this fight with the police, 200 peasants broke into the school, destroyed the icons and crosses, and damaged the central doors of the iconostasis, the shrine, and other objects in sanctuary of the church. According to the police reports, the dissident peasants were the most active participants in this vandalism in the church school. But the dissidents noted that Orthodox peasants joined them in ransacking the interior of the school. All the Pavlovki peasants disliked "the cursed place" dedicated to "most hated Fedor and Glafira."

According to the testimony of the Pavlovki evangelicals, when they marched to the church of Saint Michael to "clean it of pagan filth," the Orthodox peasants from Pavlovki who had participated in the attack on the church school joined the police and other Orthodox peasants from the neighboring villages in their fight against ecstatic dissidents. The priest locked the church door before the arrival of the crowd of dissidents, while Orthodox peasants who were summoned by the clergy and police prepared cudgels and sticks for beating the "Stunda." Anticipating the beginning of the Millennium, the Maliovantsy from Pavlovki rushed to the church. When the police tried to stop them, they assaulted the district police officer, two of his colleagues, and two soldiers near the church gates. When the dissident leaders began to break the church locks and disassemble the fence, the crowd of Orthodox surrounded the "crazy Stundists."

After a long fistfight, the Orthodox peasants, affected by vodka and anti-Stundist sermons, began beating the retreating dissidents. Even official police documents did not conceal the mass beating. According to medical investigation, thirty-five dissident peasants were cruelly beaten and one of them died. By November 1901, sixty-seven peasants from Pavlovki had been arrested, and the Sumy district court recommended a court trial for "their attack." Moisei Todosienko was also indicted, along with Pavlovki dissident peasants (figure 7.3).[137]

Eventually, fifty-three peasants were acquitted, and fifteen, including Todosienko, were sentenced to the hard-labor prisons of Nerchinsk and Sakhalin in February 1902.[138] It is noteworthy that the secret police agents from the gendarme department also accused the Orthodox peasants of Pavlovki. According to the reports of the secret agents, the slogans of social justice and social revenge were what attracted the mass of the Orthodox peasants to the dissidents' meetings. Therefore, the majority of the Orthodox population in Pavlovki supported the local Maliovantsy. As one agent noted, the Orthodox

381

Figure 7.3. The Pavlovtsy, who were convicted and sentenced to 515 years of hard labor. From *Delo pavlovskikh krest'an (ofitsial'nye dokumenty)*, ed. V. Bonch-Bruevich (London, 1902), 13.

crowd "felt compassion for the dissidents who called for redistribution of land and punishment of landlords." Especially impressive for Orthodox peasants was a scene on September 16, 1901, when the marching dissidents threw away their money and trampled it under their feet. "That was why," wrote the agent, "the Orthodox peasants did not interfere when the dissidents were beating the police officer."

Only the arrival of Orthodox peasants from other villages changed the situation. These peasants did not know the dissidents who were introduced by the clergy and the police as the worst enemies of the Orthodox population. Nevertheless, the secret police suspected that many Orthodox peasants in the crowd near the church were "secret friends" of the Pavlovki dissidents. As it turned out, the dissident peasants from Pavlovki articulated and expressed in their radical acts of social vengeance on September 16, 1901, the deepest and the most cherished notions of the peasant mass. The secret police agents noted that the most popular ideas of the local peasants were the redistribution of land, the equalizing of property, and the punishment of corrupt priests.[139] The riot at Pavlovki in 1901 was the last known act in the drama of the Millennium for the radical Maliovantsy. It was the end of millennial dreams for both the radical Stundists and the Maliovantsy. Moreover, the scandal in Pavlovki resulted in more police restrictions for the Russian evangelicals. Orthodox missionaries increasingly used tactics of provocation and incited the Orthodox peasants against dissidents. Sometimes, the provocative preaching by Orthodox missionaries generated real pogroms, such as those in 1902–3 against evangelical peasants.[140]

Despite the strong pagan and magical (occult) influences in peasant religion, millennial expectations of social justice and social revenge have always existed among the most oppressed and humiliated parts of the rural population in the Russian countryside. Religious dissidents, such as Neo-Stundists and Maliovantsy, simply expressed and articulated these widely shared expectations, using biblical language and images. Paradoxically, the conflicts and debates between dissidents and their Orthodox neighbors led the nondissident peasants to make an unusual religious justification for what they dreamed about—social justice and revenge. The explosions of hatred against Shalaputs and Stundists in Russian and Ukrainian villages could not hide the peasants' secret compassion for millennial ideas.

Therefore, encounters between dissident and Orthodox peasants, who lived side by side, contributed to the spread of the millennial discourse among the rural population of those localities where the millennial preaching and practices of the dissidents were most effective. As a result, millennial expectations shaped the worldview, mentality, and behavior of all peasants, including nondissidents. In employing the millennial discourse of the religious radicals, the rebellious and angry peasants replaced their traditional identity with the cosmopolitan nonpeasant identity of the true Christian. The Ukrainian dissidents rejected both their peasant and Ukrainian identities because they were associated with exploitation and humiliation. In denying the national principle in the construction of their identity, they admitted Jews into their community. By doing so, they invoked one of the conditions for the Advent of Jesus Christ—the conversion of Jews to Christianity. Some Jewish intellectuals responded to the invitation of the Ukrainian evangelicals and joined their Christian movement.

At the same time, peasant dissenters used the familiar elements of their

383

national folklore and traditions in their construction of the millennial drama of social justice. The radical Stundists Chepurnoi and Shutenko from the Chigirin district and radical followers of Kondrat Maliovannyi, such as Moisei Todosienko, invoked images of Gaidamaki and Ukrainian Cossacks in their millennial discourse and dreams of social vengeance. The social radicalism of the peasant dissidents attracted Russian and Jewish revolutionaries, who tried to secularize their millennial discourse for political purposes. Although only a minority of the evangelicals responded to "socialist propaganda," the Orthodox ideologists used the cases of "communist activism" among dissidents for antisectarian pogroms, such as the riot in Pavlovki, and for their ideological campaign in the mass media. The radical evangelicals did in fact contribute to the oppositional discourse and the social practices of resistance that became part of peasant culture in the Ukrainian countryside on the eve of Revolution of 1905.

Although the evangelical peasants did not participate in the political struggle during the Revolutions of 1905 and 1917, they contributed to shaping millennial expectations among the mass of the oppressed and exploited rural population.[141] Even those Orthodox peasants who actively participated in the anti-Stundist pogroms initiated by the Orthodox clergy were eventually exposed to the millennial ideas and images of the radical evangelicals.[142] One can say that the various millennial discourses and social practices of the peasant dissenters prepared the ground for future political and social reform based on radical Christian eschatology. Moreover, the shaping of a new nonethnic, international evangelical identity among the rural population of the southern Russian Empire contributed to both the modernization and the "Bolshevization" of the southern provinces of Russia.

Notes

1 Rossiiskii gosudarstvennyi istoricheskii arkhiv (hereafter RGIA), f. 796, op. 154, d. 582, l. 1b–2. This idealization of the tsar as the millenarian leader is similar to what Norman Cohn found among the medieval millenarians. See Norman Cohn, *The Pursuit of the Millennium* (New York, 1961), 71–74.

2 Episkop Alexii [Dorodnitsyn], *Materialy dlia istorii religiozno-ratsionalisticheskogo dvizhenia na iuge Rossii vo vtoroi polovine XIX–go veka* (Kazan', 1908), 202–3. Sometimes the

Stundists described members of the tsar's family as their coreligionists. See Gosudarstvennyi arkhiv Rossiiskoi Federatsii (hereafter GARF), f. 102, op. 226, d. 12, part 5, l. 46. Some radical Stundists demonstrated their loyalty to the tsar and simultaneously their opposition to the local administration. See RGIA, f. 1574, op. 2, d. 62, l. 10. More loyal were the Baptists who also disseminated rumors about Baptist members of the tsar's family. See GARF, f. 124, op. 5 (1896), d. 269, l. 10–10ob.

3 "Communism is a hook by which the Stundists [in the text, "Shtundovye"] catch their neophytes. Here is how the Stundists explain communism. They say that Jesus Christ suffered for entire human race, and therefore his love is equal for everyone; and if Jesus Christ's love is the same, then possessions all over the world should be divided equally among all human beings. By expressing such notions, Stundists attract a multitude of adherents among Russian peasants [who want] to get more land through a common redistribution of the state's and noblemen's lots of land. Communism is a magnet, which draws new followers to them and keeps old adherents; take away their communist ideas, and the Stundist sect would disintegrate." See Alexii, *Materialy,* 63. Another representative of the Russian nobility discovered "the origins of socialism" in the Stundist movement; *Materialy,* 191.

4 RGIA, f. 796, op. 149, d. 448, l. 4.

5 RGIA, f. 797, op. 43, 2otd. 3 st., d. 43, l. 8ob.–9.

6 Alexii, *Materialy,* 321. Episkop Nikanor, "Proiskhozhdenie i znachenie Shtundy v zhizni russkago naroda," *Pravoslavnoe obozrenie,* no. 8 (1884): 605–19. During the 1880s, Bishop Nikanor started preaching a special series of public sermons all over Southern Russia warning of the dangers that Stundism posed for Orthodoxy. The Orthodox Faith "was the core of Russian personality" from the first pages of Russian and Ukrainian history, beginning with the Orthodox Cossacks who had defended and protected the Orthodox Christian Church against Muslim Turks, Catholic Poles, Germans, and Jews in Southern Ukraine and Russia.

7 A. M. Bobrishchev-Pushkin, *Sud i raskol'niki-sektanty* (Saint Petersburg, 1910), 23, 28.

8 Gleb Uspenskii, "Melochi putevykh vospominanii," *Polnoe sobranie sochinenii* (Moscow, 1947), vol. 8, 209.

9 S. M. Stepniak-Kravchinskii, *The Russian Peasantry: Their Agrarian Condition, Social Life and Religion* (Westport, Conn., 1977; 1st pr., 1888), 341; see his novel "Stundist Paul Rudenko" in his *Sochineniia* (Moscow, 1958), vol. 2, 5–194.

10 In his novel, the priest Paisii, who had arrested the Stundist minister Luk'ian says: "You (Luk'ian) borrowed everything from Germans. How dare you to betray your Mother, the Orthodox Church!" In his response, Luk'ian agreed that Stundists imitated Germans: "For an ordinary peasant the Orthodox Church is a stepmother rather than a loving mother. Why shouldn't we learn from Germans? Germans didn't invent all their truths, they found out them in Holy Scripture!" Stepniak-Kravchinskii, *Sochineniia,* 92.

11 Among many police reports during the 1870s and 1880s, see Alexii, *Materialy,* 288–89. Responding to the clergy's complaints, the police were not able to find any signs

385

of socialism among the Baptist communities in the Ukrainian countryside. See Alexii, *Materialy,* 284, 285, 287, 291, 294.

12 One of these authors explained to his readers that a distinctive feature of Stundism, besides its obvious Protestant character, was its own "secret sociopolitical nature." From this vantage point, he argued that "it was religious teaching in a form that hid the real political aspirations of the Stundist propagandists. The dogmatic assertions of the Stundists were only a cover, hiding the underhanded plotting of German activists. And the brotherhood of the Stunde should be considered as the expression of a secret German policy to Germanize the Russian nation." I. Strel'bitskii, *Kratkii ocherk shtundizma i svod tekstov, napravlennykh k ego oblicheniyu* (Odessa, 1893),17, 22, 198; Bobrishchev-Pushkin, *Sud i raskol'niki-sektanty,* 23, 28; Compare with other publications on subversive pro-German and procommunist character of Russian Stundism: "Kommunisticheskaya propaganda v Rossii," *Moskovskie vedomosti,* no. 106 (1890): 2; "Sotsialisticheskaya propaganda shtundizma," *Moskovskie vedomosti,* no. 183 (1890): 2; "Stunda i eya protivogosudarstvennyi kharakter," *Russkoe slovo,* no. 107 (1895): 1–2.

13 Bobrishchev-Pushkin, *Sud i raskol'niki-sektanty,* 63–64. Skvortsov criticized "the new methods of propaganda of Stundism and socialist free thought among the people of Little Russia" during the 1880s and 1890s; *Missionerskoe obozrenie* (hereafter *MO*), January 1898, 371–85. See also Alexii Dorodnitsyn's essay in *MO,* October 1896, 221–30.

14 Besides the traditional *Pravoslavnoe obozrenie* [The Orthodox Review], a new central periodical of the Russian Orthodox Church, *Missionerskoe obozrenie* [Missionary Review], intensively covered the antisectarian activities of those missionary congresses during the 1890s.

15 Some authors pointed to the role of Polish and Jewish elements in encouraging Stundism in Ukraine; *Kievskaya starina,* no. 10 (1884): 305–20, and no. 11(1884): 499–506.

16 *MO,* October 1899, 304–7.

17 And he commented, "The ancient Russian spirit did not tolerate the anarchy of intellect, especially the anarchy of faith; such intolerance excluded any anarchy from Russian life. The anarchy of intellect would . . . result in an anarchy of beliefs, then in an anarchy of social foundations etc." Episkop Nikanor, "Proiskhozhdenie i znachenie Shtundy," 614, 615, 617, 616.

18 Episkop Alexii, *Religiozno-ratsionalisticheskoe dvizhenie na Iuge Rossii vo vtoroi polovine XIX veka* (Kazan', 1909), 196.

19 So, according to them, to lessen the cultural influence of German colonists on the Ukrainian population would mean automatically to limit German property in the South of Russia. See Alexii, *Religiozno-ratsionalisticheskoe dvizhenie,* 178–90.

20 And he explained, "Instead of the Russian *chuyka* (special peasant jacket), hat, unshaved beard, and hair cut in a fringe, the Stundo-Baptist, for the most part, put on a German jacket, hat, and cap, and has a shaved chin and short haircut. As a matter of fact, instead of choosing a Russian school, the Stundo-Baptist sends his child to the school of German colonists." N. Kutepov, *Kratkaya istoria i verouchenie russkikh ratsionalisticheskikh i misticheskikh eresei: doukhobortsev, Molokans, desnago bratstva, shtundy, tolstovtsev, khlystov i skoptsov* (Novocherkassk, 1907; 1st pr., 1891), 57.

21 Citation from "the manuscript, written by Timofei A. Zaiats" published in *Materialy k istorii i izucheniyu russkogo sektantstva i raskola,* ed. Vladimir Bonch-Bruevich (Saint Petersburg, 1910), vol. 3, 15, 16. Russian priests worried about the positive example Stundist communities represented for Ukrainian and Russian peasants because "sectarians live like members of one family and in this regard they serve as an exemplary model of brotherly relations, help each other by advice and in a material way, and in their contacts they are tender and cordial." *MO,* July–August 1899, 103.

22 They complained of the economic threat from "the German colonists, who in numbers of many thousands, settled" in southern Ukraine and "captured the best of the best lands; and therefore, in this region they represent a real economic power that enslaves the Russian people, whom they harmed spiritually corrupting the ancient religious and moral outlook of the Orthodox believers." *MO,* July–August 1899, 105–6.

23 See *Otechestvennye zapiski,* 1878, no. 5, 206–30. Russian clerical critics found the same "German poison" even in the newly born sect of Adventists, which during the 1880s came to the Tavrida region in Southern Russia from the United States rather than Germany. Therefore, they reported to Russian authorities that the newborn sect of the Seventh-Day Adventism was also a "creation" of the German colonists from Russia, who, as it turned out, had emigrated to America and established their "new" religion there. See RGIA, f. 1284, op. 222 (1891), d. 49, l. 1–2, 7–9; and S. D. Bondar', *Adventizm 7–go dnia* (Saint Petersburg, 1911), 28.

24 Citation from: N. Griniakin, *Beregis' Shtundy!* (Saint Petersburg, 1912), 8; emphasis added. See also popular booklets: X. Korchinskii, *Kievskaia sekta Shtundizm ili Baptizm?* (Kiev, 1899); P. Beliaev, *O Baptizme* (Saratov, 1910); and a big missionary compendium: M. Kal'nev, *Oblichenie lzheucheniia russkikh sektantov-ratsionalistov (shtundobaptistov, adventistov, "evangel'skikh khristian," Molokans, dukhoborov i dr.)* (Odessa, 1913). Some of these titles are missing in a bibliography, *Evangelical Sectarianism in the Russian Empire and the USSR: A Bibliographic Guide,* collected and edited by Albert W. Wardin Jr. (Lanham, Md., 1995); see especially 82–100.

25 On the reaction of Russian intellectuals, including L. Tolstoy and F. Dostoevsky, to the evangelical movement, see E. Heier, *Religious Schism in the Russian Aristocracy, 1860–1900: Radstockism and Pashkovitism* (The Hague, 1970). Compare with V. Soloviev, "Russkaia ideia," in *O Khristianskom edinstve* (Moscow, 1994), 171.

26 Rozhdestvenskii, *Iuzhno-russkii shtundizm* (Saint Petersburg, 1889), 139–44; V. I. Iasevich-Borodaevskaia, *Bor'ba za veru: Istoriko-bytovye ocherki i obzor zakonodatel'stva po staroobriadchestvu i sektantstvu v ego posledovatel'nom razvitii s prilozheniem statei zakona i vysochaishikh ukazov* (Saint Petersburg, 1912), 286, 289, 577; A. Vvedenskii, *Bor'ba s sektantstvom* (Odessa, 1914); Vvedenskii, *Deistvuiushchie zakonopolozheniia kasatel'no staroobriadtsev i sektantov* (Odessa, 1912).

27 The citation is from the text of the law published in Iasevich-Borodaevskaia, *Bor'ba za veru,* 560; emphasis added.

28 See, e.g., Andrew Q. Blane, "The Relations between the Russian Protestant Sects and the State, 1900–1921" (Ph.D. dissertation, Duke University, 1964); M. Klimenko,

387

"Die Anfaenge des Baptismus in Suederussland nach officiellen Documenten" (Ph.D. dissertation, Erlangen, 1957); S. Nesdoly, "Evangelical Sectarianism in Russia: A Study of the Stundists, Baptists, Pashkovites, and Evangelical Christians, 1855–1917" (Ph.D. dissertation, Queens University, 1971).

29 On this, in English, see Daniel Field, *Rebels in the Name of the Tsar* (Boston, 1989), and Maureen Perrie, "Popular Monarchism: The Myth of the Ruler from Ivan the Terrible to Stalin," in *Reinterpreting Russia,* ed. G. Hosking and R. Service (New York, 1999), 156–69.

30 This case attracted an attention of the Orthodox press and the Ukrainian intellectuals as well. See P. Kozitskii, "Shtundistskaia obshchina na poberezh'i Dnepra v Chigirinskom i Cherkasskom uezdakh, Kiev. gub.," *Kievskie eparkhial'nye vedomosti* (hereafter *KEV*), 1890, no. 6, 215–17; *MO,* July 1897, 642–44; V. L. Val'kevich, *Zapiska o propagande protestantskikh sect v Rossii i, v osobennosti, na Kavkaze* (Tiflis, 1900), 317; Trokhym Zin'kivskyi, "Shtunda, ukrains'ka ratsionalistychna sekta," in *Pysannia Trokhyma Zin'kivs'kogo,* ed. Leonid Smolens'ky and Trokhym Zin'kivs'kyi, 2 vols. (L'viv, 1906), vol. 2, 272. Soviet Ukrainian historian Dmitrii Poida mentioned this case as well. But given the ideological restrictions of the Soviet historiography, he was afraid to show any connections to religious dissent in his book. See D. P. Poida, *Krest'ianskoe dvizhenie na Pravoberezhnoi Ukraine v poreformennyi period (1866–1900)* (Dnepropetrovsk, 1960), 232–33, 439–40.

31 Alexii, *Materialy,* 280–81.

32 Field, *Rebels,* 113–202. He based all of his story of the Chigirin affair on the Russian published collections of documents and on the book by Dmitrii Poida. See Poida, *Krest'ianskoe dvizhenie,* 209–15, 220–34. But Field ignored a large amount of Ukrainian literature devoted to the "Chigirin conspiracy." See the most important studies about this, which Field had missed: V. S. Zhuchenko, *Sotsial'no-ekonomichna programa revoliutsiinogo narodnytstva na Ukraini* (Kiev, 1969), 91–95; A. N. Katrenko, "Revoliutsionnoe narodnichestvo kontsa 70-x—nach. 80–x gg. XIX v" (Ph.D. dissertation, Kiev State University, 1969); M. P. Rud'ko, *Revoliutsiini narodnyky na Ukraini (70-ti roky XIX st.)* (Kiev, 1973), 120–37; M. T. Loboda, "Krest'ianskoe obshchestvo 'Tainaia druzhina' (t.n. 'Chigirinskii zagovor')" (Ph.D. dissertation, Kiev State University, 1974); S. A. Sosnovchik, "Revoliutsionnaia propaganda narodnikov na Ukraine (70–80-e gg. XIX v.)" (Ph.D. dissertation, L'vov State University, 1974); S. Svetlenko, *Revoliutsionno-narodnicheskoe dvizhenie 70–kh godov XIX veka na Ukraine v vosponinaniiakh sovremennikov* (Dnepropetrovsk, 1990). Sergei Svetlenko of Dniepropetrovsk University is now finishing a book on the revolutionary populists in Ukraine. He presents a revised story of the Chigirin conspiracy based on archival documents. See also, in English, Erich Haberer, *Jews and Revolution in Nineteenth-Century Russia* (Cambridge, 1995), 138–41.

33 What follows is based on *Kievlianin,* nos. 36 and 47 (1876) and no. 97 (1879); and *Delo,* no. 1 (1883): 220–23.

34 *Delo,* no. 1 (1883): 222–23.

35 Cited from the text published in "Dokumenty k Chigirinskomu delu," *Byloe,* no. 12 (1906): 257–61. Compare with the English translation in Field, *Rebels,* 172–74.

36 See, in English, Field, *Rebels,* 113–202. More information about these events is in

memoirs and monographs: Ia. S. [Stefanovich], "Chigirinskoe delo," in *Chiornyi peredel* (Moscow, 1923), nos. 1–2; L. G. Deich, *Za polveka* (Moscow, 1926), 198–246; V. K. Debagorii-Mokrievich, *Ot buntarstva k terrorizmu* (Moscow, 1930), book 1, 143–47, 238–58; Poida, *Krest'ianskoe dvizhenie*, 220–34; Zhuchenko, *Sotsial'no-ekonomichna programa*, 91–95; and Rud'ko, *Revoliutsiini narodnyky*, 120–37. The first serious study of the Chigirin conspiracy was the Soviet Ph.D. dissertation by the Ukrainian historian Mikhailo Loboda, defended in 1974; see Loboda, "Krest'ianskoe Obshchestvo," 14, 20, 22.

37 RGIA, f. 1405, op. 80, d. 8561, l. 6–6ob.

38 RGIA, f. 1405, op. 80, d. 8561, l. 6ob., 7, 8.

39 Tsentral'nyi derzhavnyi istorychnyi arkhiv Ukrainy (hereafter TsDIAU), f. 317, op. 1, d. 44, l. 5–7, 8, 9, 11–30, 32–33ob.

40 TsDIAU, f. 442, op. 832, d. 122, l. 1–2.

41 RGIA, f. 1405, op. 86, d. 9284, l. 2, 4ob–5; f. 1405, op. 521, d. 409, l. 463–64.

42 RGIA, f. 1405, op. 86, d. 9284, l. 2ob.–3ob; f. 1405, op. 521, d. 409, l. 464–65.

43 RGIA, f. 1405, op. 86, d. 9284, l. 4, 5; f. 1405, op. 521, d. 409, l. 466, 467.

44 RGIA, f. 1405, op. 86, d. 9284, l. 7–7ob.

45 This description of Topilovka Stundists' theology is based on the summary of the reports from the criminal case of Chepurnoi and Shutenko (January 11–July 6, 1882). See RGIA, f. 1405, op. 86, d. 9284, l. 10–13.

46 GARF, f. 124, op. 3, d. 131, l. 13ob.

47 RGIA, f. 1405, op. 521, d. 409, l. 469.

48 RGIA, f. 1405, op. 86, d. 9284, l. 12ob.–13, 21, 23–24ob.; f. 1405, op. 521, d. 409, l. 470–70ob.

49 These figures are from the police report: TsDIAU, f. 317, op. 1, d. 936, l. 41.

50 GARF, f. 124, op. 3, d. 131, l. 12ob.–13; TsDIAU, f. 442, op. 618, d. 109, l. 5–5ob.

51 GARF, f. 124, op. 3, d.131, l. 9-9ob., 13–13ob., 14.

52 GARF, f. 124, op. 3, d.131, l. 14ob.–16; TsDIAU, f.317, op. 1, d. 936, l. 34–35.

53 TsDIAU, f. 317, op. 1, d. 936, l. 1–1ob. Once Chepurnoi said to his neighbors: "We need, brothers, to liquidate the tsar, first of all; then we need to exterminate all the government; and only after this will all the land be ours and we will judge by ourselves."

54 In Ukrainian folklore, the legendary Gaidamaki represented a Ukrainian version of the English Robin Hood. These peasant rebels took the property of the rich Poles and Jews and distributed it among the poor Ukrainian peasants.

55 GARF, f. 124, op. 3, d. 131, l. 17; TsDIAU, f. 317, op. 1, d. 936, l. 29–29ob.

56 TsDIAU, f. 317, op. 1, d. 936, l. 35ob.–36.

57 TsDIAU, f. 317, op. 1, d. 936, l. 36ob., 29–29ob.; f. 442, op. 618, d. 109, l. 26.

58 The citation is from GARF, f. 124, op. 3, d. 131, l. 19.

59 TsDIAU, f. 442, op. 618, d. 109, l. 25–25ob.

60 TsDIAU, f. 442, op. 618, d. 109, l.28–28ob.

61 TsDIAU, f. 442, op. 618, d. 109, l. 28ob., 40ob.–41.

62 *KEV*, 1895, no. 12, 425, 541.

389

63 Alexii, *Materialy,* 298–303.

64 Alexii, *Materialy,* 333–34. At the same time, this police officer noted that other Stundists did not support Puokhovoi's activities in the village.

65 *Khersonskie eparkhial'nye vedomosti* (hereafter *KherEV*), 1890, no. 21, 579–82.

66 GARF, f. 102, op. 88 (1890), l. 1ob.

67 TsDIAU, f. 317, op. 1, d. 936, l. 36ob.–37.

68 Deich, *Za poveka,* 60, 66–67, 110–31, 134–35.

69 Haberer, *Jews and Revolution,* 139.

70 Alexii, *Materialy,* 174.

71 "Izvestia o shtundizme," *Pravoslavnoe obozrenie,* no. 1 (1876): 810–11.

72 *Kievskaya starina,* no. 10 (1884): 316–17.

73 *Trudy Kievskoi dukhovnoi akademii,* no. 1 (1884): 192.

74 *KherEV,* 1889, no. 4, 115.

75 TsDIAU, f. 442, op. 620, d. 22, 1–3ob.

76 *Materialy k istorii i izucheniyu russkogo sektantstva i raskola,* 50. About pogroms in Ekaterinoslav, revolutionary activities, and anti-Jewish feelings among Russian and Ukrainian residents of the Ekaterinoslav region in 1905, see Dniepropetrovs'kyi derzhavnyi oblasnyi arkhiv, f. 20, op. 1, d. 24/394; f. 20, op. 1, d. 23/371, d. 11/506, d. 16, d.33/955, d. 36/456.

77 These traditions and patterns of repression and resistance contributed to the Russian Revolution of 1917, the Civil War of 1918–21, the tragedy of Stalinist collectivization in Ukraine, and to the rise of a new Evangelical movement in Soviet Ukraine after World War II. On the Civil War and the Makhno movement in southern Ukraine, see Paul Avrich, *The Russian Anarchists* (New York, 1967), 209ff. About the evangelical movement in the Soviet Ukraine, see Walter Sawatsky, *Soviet Evangelicals since World War II* (Scottdale, Pa., 1981), 43–44, 62, 67, 86, 90ff.

78 *KherEV,* 1888, no. 21, 315–16; A report of the Spiritual Affairs Department to the Police Department authorized an investigation about Jewish involvement in Stundist activities; see GARF, f. 102, op. 84 (1888), d. 454, l. 2–2 ob.; and RGIA, f. 821, op. 8, d. 345 (1884), l. 97.

79 See *The Jewish Encyclopedia,* ed. Isidor Singer (New York, 1904), vol. 6, 46; S. M. Dubnow, *History of the Jews in Russia and Poland from the Earliest Times until the Present Day,* trans. I. Friedlaender (Philadelphia, 1918), vol. 2, 333–35; Kalman Marmor, *Yaakov Gordin* (New York, 1953); Nora Levin, *While Messiah Tarried: Jewish Socialist Movements, 1871–1917* (New York, 1977), 143–46; and Jonathan Frankel, *Prophesy and Politics: Socialism, Nationalism, and the Russian Jews, 1862–1917* (Cambridge, Mass., 1981), 56–57; John Klier, "From Elisavetgrad to Broadway: The Strange Odyssey of Iakov Gordon," in *Extending the Borders of Russian History: Essays in Honor of Alfred J. Rieber,* ed. Marsha Siefert (Budapest, 2003), 113–25.

80 Quoted in Dubnow, *History of the Jews,* vol. 2, 333.

81 RGIA, f. 821, op. 8, d. 345 (1884), l. 36, 38ob.

82 The Russian administration praised the goals of the new society, which "attempted

to eradicate the coarse fanaticism and religious delusions in the Jewish masses." RGIA, f. 821, op. 8, d. 345 (1884), l. 3–4ob.

83 Jewish members of this society kept all their records "exclusively" in the Russian language, and they rejected circumcision, prenuptial agreements and other old Jewish traditions as "barbarous customs." RGIA, f. 1405, op. 89, d. 2269, l. 1–1ob., 3–3ob.

84 GARF, f.102, op. 87 (1889), d. 606, l. 20, 61ob., 65ob., 71ob.

85 GARF, f. 102, op. 87 (1889), d. 606, l. 4, 11, 19–20, 21, 23, 24, 57–57ob. In his report, this officer noted, "In November 1889 Isaac Finerman, a prominent member of the Jewish society, bought two peasant houses, rented 20 *desiatin* of the land in the village of Glodossy in Elisavetgrad district, settled there with like-minded Jews having in mind the propagation of their religious antigovernment notions among the adherents of the Stundist persuasion who densely inhabit this area. Finerman's wife, Khana Liubarskaia, Antolii Butkevich, Mark Goldfeld, Kelman Galitsky and his wife Roza Kogan, Izik Ostry, and Isaia Burshtein, who followed after Isaac Finerman, were the most active propagandists among the settlers of this Jewish colony."

86 RGIA, f. 821, op. 8, d. 345 (1884), l. 118–119ob.

87 GARF, f. 102, op. 87 (1889), d. 606, l. 60, 61, 65, 66, 71, 73, 90–91.

88 See Ezekiel Lifschutz, "Jacob Gordin's Proposal to Establish an Agricultural Colony," in *The Jewish Experience in America,* ed. Abraham J. Karp (New York, 1969), vol. 4, 253–64; Levin, *While Messiah Tarried,* 143–45.

89 Dubnow, *History of the Jews,* vol. 2, 334.

90 The quotations are from M. [M. I. Rabinovich], "Talmud li, ili zhizn' prepiatstvuet evreiam zanimatsia proizvoditel'nym trudom?" *Vol'noe slovo,* August 15, 1882, no. 43, 11, and Frankel, *Prophesy and Politics,* 57. See Priluker's memoirs in English: Jaakoff Prelooker, *Under the Tsar and Queen Victoria: The Experiences of a Russian Reformer* (London, 1895); on the close connections of Gordin and Priluker to peasant Stundists and on their meeting with Balaban, see pp. 109–11.

91 RGIA, f. 821, op. 8, d. 345 (1884), l. 1, 11–11ob., 14–15, 16, 17, 22–23. The detailed description of Rabinovich's plans are presented in a special police report, "The Religious Movement among the Jews in the South of Russia"; RGIA, f. 821, op. 8, d. 345 (1884), l. 45–83.

92 RGIA, f. 821, op. 8, d. 345 (1884), l. 24, 34, 41–44, 47, 102–7ob. See also a biographical study of Rabinovich in English: Steven J. Zipperstein, "Heresy, Apostasy, and the Transformation of Joseph Rabinovich," in *Jewish Apostasy in the Modern World,* ed. Todd M. Endelman (New York, 1987), 206–31; Kai Kjaer-Hansen, *Joseph Rabinowitz and the Messianic Movement* (Edinburgh, 1995).

93 RGIA, f. 796, op. 176, d. 2145, l. 1–8, 10–14.

94 Christopher M. Clark, *The Politics of Conversion: Missionary Protestantism and the Jews in Prussia 1728–1941* (Oxford, 1995), 246.

95 Rosenberg was a respected bookseller in Odessa. According to his announcement, he exclusively sold "Biblical spiritual-moral" books. See TsDIAU, f. 268, op. 1, d. 448 (March 19–November 3, 1909), l. 14, 16.

96 TsDIAU, f. 268, op. 1, d. 448 (March 19–November 3, 1909), l. 17, 18, 19, 20–23ob.

97 GARF, f. 102, op. 226, d. 12, part 5, p. 35; TsDIAU, f. 275, op. 1, d. 1 (1902), l. 89–89ob.; TsDIAU, f. 1597, op. 1, d. 7, l.8–8ob.

98 P. Petrushevsky, "O shtundizme: Usloviya ego proiskhozhdenia i razvitiya, i mery potrebnyya pravoslavnoi Tserkvi dlya bor'by s nim," *Trudy Kievskoi dukhovnoi akademii,* no. 2 (1884): 187.

99 *KEV,* 1898, no. 16, 621–22.

100 TsDIAU, f. 301, op. 1, d. 132 (1885), l. 28, 41. During the 1880s, the police in the provinces of Poltava and Kharkov stopped the activities of the strange sects, which spread ideas about common property and the equality of all people.

101 RGIA, f. 1574, op. 2, d. 62, l. 53.

102 *KEV,* 1899, no. 13, 488, 490, 491, 498. Sometimes the Stundists defended their notions of the social equality in fistfights with their Orthodox neighbors. See TsDIAU, f. 442, op. 834, d. 16 (1884), l. 5–8.

103 Ivan Draganov explained to his neighbors: "If people had not harmed each other, had not stolen and robbed from each other, they would live without the authorities, who rule the people." Because of the crimes committed by the people and because of their sins, God established government, a tsar, and other authorities to keep the people under control. According to Draganov, some of these authorities could turn evil and "ungodly." Draganov told the local peasants that the political order in the Russian Empire had stopped serving God and the people. Moreover, the Russian system of power generated only evil and "bad things." TsDIAU, f. 442, op. 834, d. 16 (1884), l. 9ob.–10. In July 1894, Draganov was sentenced to three months in prison and five years of the exile to Transcaucasia. See l. 5–8, 13–14; and RGIA, f.1405, op. 521, d. 439, part 1, l. 408–11.

104 RGIA, f. 1284, op. 222 (1901), d. 47, l. 2–2ob.

105 GARF, f. 124, op. 11 (1902), d. 1602, l. 11–12.

106 What follows is based on the criminal case of 1894–95: GARF, f. 124, op. 3, d. 130, l. 1–1ob., 9–11.

107 In the Russian original, Tkachiov said, "there are no political rights for ordinary people in Russia"; GARF, f. 124, op. 3, d. 130, l. 1–1ob.

108 GARF, f. 124, op. 3, d. 130, l. 10, 11ob.

109 RGIA, f. 796, op. 174, d. 1673A, l. 1–1ob.

110 What follows is based on RGIA, f. 796, op. 172, d. 1619, l. 1–22ob. On Khilkov and the Pavlovki peasants, see also, in English, G. P. Camfield, "The Pavlovtsy of Khar'kov Province, 1886–1905: Harmless Sectarians or Dangerous Rebels?" *Slavonic and East European Review* 68, no. 4 (1990): 692–717. This is the best essay about the riot in Pavlovki in English.

111 RGIA, f. 796, op. 172, d. 1619, l. 2–4. See the biographical details in D. Khilkov, "Zapiski," *Svobodnoe slovo,* no. 1 (1898): 79–125; and notes to "Nachalo zhizni khristian i stradanie ikh v sele Pavlovkakh," *Materialy k istorii i izucheniiu russkogo sektantstva i raskola,* ed. V. Bonch-Bruevich (Saint Petersburg, 1908), vol. 1, 187–89. See also, in English, Jonas

Stadling and Will Reason, *In the Land of Tolstoy: Experiences of Famine and Misrule in Russia* (London, 1897), 169–82.

112 RGIA, f. 796, op. 172, d. 1619, l. 5–6.

113 RGIA, f. 796, op. 172, d. 1619, l. 6ob.–7ob. Compare with Camfield, "Pavlovtsy," 696–97. The story "Krestnik" is published in all main editions of Leo Tolstoy's works. See L. N. Tolstoy, *Sobranie sochinenii v 20–ti tomakh* (Moscow, 1963), vol. 10, 397–413.

114 RGIA, f. 796, op. 172, d. 1619, l. 8–9ob., 16–16ob. See, in English, Khilkov's confession of his newfound faith: Stadling and Reason, *In the Land of Tolstoy*, 180–82.

115 RGIA, f. 796, op. 172, d. 1619, l. 17–18, 20–22.

116 Orthodox missionaries noted the new, Tolstoyan influences among the Ukrainian Stundists. See *KEV,* 1899, no. 13, 487–503; and TsDIAU, f. 317, op. 1, d. 1967, l. 24–25, 31–34, 36ob.

117 Camfield, "Pavlovtsy," 699–702. On the beating, humiliation, and insulting of Pavlovki peasants by the police and their Orthodox neighbors, see "Nachalo zhizni khristian . . . ," 186–92, and N. N. Gusev, "Pavlovtsy," part 1, *Russkaia mysl',* no. 7 (1907): 40–71.

118 See *Kievskaia mysl',* no. 67 (1913): 2. Compare with Maliovannyi's class interpretation of Jesus Christ's teaching in Nikolai Zhikharev, "Iskateli pravdy (Sredi 'maliovantsev')," *Poznanie Rossii,* no. 2 (1909): 11–13.

119 Iasevich-Borodaevskaia, *Bor'ba za veru,* 143.

120 *Privetstvie Russkomu narodu ot Kondrata Maliovannogo* (Moscow, 1907), 10, 11–12. Maliovannyi criticized Russian society for "pogroms" and intolerance as well. Compare these with similar ideas in Vasilii Skvortsov, "Novoshtundism," *Moskovskie vedomosti,* no. 227 (1892).

121 He wrote, "Wealthy people seduce themselves and other people by their financial capital and they request obedience and respect from poor people." Iasevich-Borodaevskaia, *Bor'ba za veru,* 154–57; I. Sikorskii, "Psikhopaticheskaia epidemia 1892 goda v Kievskoi gubernii," in *Sbornik nauchno-literaturnykh statei,* V 5-ti knigakh [in 5 volumes] (Kiev, 1900), vol. 5, 53. See also the memoirs of a social-democrat about his meeting with Maliovannyi in the mental hospital: A. P. Raevskii, "Svidanie s Kondratom Maliovannym," *Razsvet: Sotsial-demokraticheskii listok dlia sektantov* (Zheneva, 1904), vol. 1, 21. P. Biriukov, *Maliovantsy: Istoria odnoi sekty,* izdanie "Svobodnogo slova" [publication of the Periodical "Free Word"], ed. V. Chertkov (Christchurch, U.K., 1905), 16–18. Biriukov and other authors used mainly the material of Iasevich-Borodaevskaia. See also an essay by the famous Ukrainian writer and a study by the Ukrainian historian Ivan Franko, "Baptysty i Maliovantsi Kyivs'koi gubernii," *Literaturno-naukovyi visnyk* 19, no. 9 (1902): 157–60; Mykhailo Hrushevs'ky, *Z istorii religiinoi dumky na Ukraini* (Lviv, 1925), 139–45.

122 Sikorskii, "Psikhopaticheskaia epidemia," 80.

123 Lysenko stressed the desperate position of the arrested peasant's family: "So the peasant will be in prison, his household will be ruined and his wife and children will become homeless tramps. There are many trees in the landlord's property and there are

none in the poor peasant's household. But if this peasant will cut small branches from the landlord's trees for heating the peasant's hut or cooking the borsch, the landlord again will send poor peasants to jail. Where are the woods which God has grown for the peasants' share?" And he used the symbolism of both the Exodus and Revelation: "We are the falling star rain . . . and the main star will fall on November 13 [i.e., Maliovannyi will open his kingdom on this day]. We are going to meet this star, which will lead us to the Promised Land, where there will be no landlords, no policemen, no judges; where all people will be equal and live in one brotherhood." See *MO,* January 1908, 78–79.

124 *MO,* November 1900, 504.

125 *MO,* November 1900, 510. See also about anti-tsarist and antistate declaration of the Maliovantsy in *MO,* November 1903, 1002–4.

126 Sikorskii, "Psikhopaticheskaia epidemia," 83–84; *MO,* December 1901, 870–71.

127 RGIA, f. 797, op. 71, 2otd., 3st., d. 319, l. 2ob.–3.

128 The reports of provincial administration from all Ukrainian provinces noted a persistence of the Cossacks' ideas of freedom and social justice among Ukrainian peasants, who "still remembered the times of Cossack freedoms." Citation from the report of Ekaterinoslav governor: RGIA, f. 1276, op. 17, d. 189, l. 98ob.

129 *MO,* December 1901, 872–74. See Todosienko's explanation of his mission of Moses in Exodus in his criminal case: RGIA, f. 1405, op. 530, d. 990, l. 98ob.; f. 797, op. 71, 2otd., 3st., d. 319, l. 2ob. About an incident in December of 1900, see *Delo pavlovskikh krest'an (ofitsial'nye dokumenty),* ed. V. Bonch-Bruevich (London, 1902), 49.

130 See a description of the events in *Delo pavlovskikh krest'an,* 45; and "Nachalo zhizni khristian . . . ," 194.

131 The best summary of a story of this in English is Camfield, "Pavlovtsy," 704–5. For a detailed description of the police harassment see "Nachalo zhizni khristian . . . ," 186–94, and *Russkaia mysl',* no. 7 (1907): 70.

132 See the details about the new church school in: "Nachalo zhizni khristian . . . ," 203–4. About corruption of the clergy in Pavlovki see RGIA, f. 797, op. 71, 2otd., 3st., d. 319, l. 8–8ob. Orthodox missionaries avoided Pavlovki, which was noted for its dissidents.

133 The quotation in English is from Camfield, "Pavlovtsy," 707. This is an English translation from *Delo pavlovskikh krest'ian,* 45. It is noteworthy that neither the Pavlovki dissidents nor Todosienko mentioned any preaching of social revenge. See "Nachalo zhizni khristian . . . ," 194; and RGIA, f. 797, op. 71, 2otd., 3st., d. 319, l. 3ob. Todosienko promised the oncoming Millennium next year, "with the coming of the new year the new order will come, when and then there will be no more masters and authorities."

134 RGIA, f. 1405, op. 530, d. 990, l. 98ob.

135 What follows is based on material from the collections of V. Bonch-Bruevich and the Kharkov Court documents in RGIA, f. 1405, op. 530, d. 990, l. 98ob.–104. In my interpretation, I correct some mistakes made by G. P. Camfield in his description of the events on pp. 707–8.

136 TsDIAU, f. 336, op. 1, d. 79 (1901), l. 10–11.

137 RGIA, f. 1405, op. 530, d. 990, l. 102ob.–104. The district court incriminated the Pavlovki dissidents with "their attack on the church building, their committing an act of sacrilege, and their resistance to the authorities."

138 See the sentence in RGIA, f. 797, op. 71, 2otd. 3st., d. 319, 10–12ob. About the court trial, see V. A. Maklakov, *Iz vospominanii* (New York, 1954), 254, and Camfield, "Pavlovtsy," 709.

139 TsDIAU, f. 336, op. 1, d. 79 (1901), 9–11, 18–19.

140 Even the police accused Orthodox clergy and missionaries of provoking anti-Stundist pogroms. On the anti-Stundist pogrom in the town of Bogodukhov in Kharkov province, see GARF, f. 102, op. 226, d. 12, part 5, l. 20–27; and RGIA, f. 797, op. 72, 2otd. 3st., d. 125 (1902). In Kupianskoe in the same province, see RGIA, f. 797, op. 72, 2otd. 3st., d. 330 (1902).

141 Robert Edelman noted that during the Revolution of 1905, peasants of the southwest Ukrainian provinces "rarely expressed traditional and millenarian goals (total repartition in particular). Instead, they came to concentrate on the more immediately realizable." At the same time, according to his material, all the major cases of peasants' movement took place in the localities (e.g., the Chigirin district) under the strong influence of radical peasant sects. See Robert Edelman, *Proletarian Peasants: The Revolution of 1905 in Russia's Southwest* (Ithaca, N.Y., 1987), 122, 156, 157.

142 On Russia as a "multireligious society" where "various religions" influenced political behavior of the peasants, see Simon Dixon, "How Holy Was Holy Russia? Rediscovering Russian Religion," in *Reinterpreting Russia,* ed. Geoffrey Hosking and Robert Service (New York, 1999), 22–39.

Epilogue: From Christian Millennium to Bolshevik Utopia

The southern European provinces of imperial Russia became a unique social and cultural laboratory in which various patterns of colonization, including the military expedition, the moral economy, and the "charismatic" model, collided with the cultural influences of German colonists, Mennonites, and Jews. This commingling of actors and traditions contributed to the rise of a broad evangelical movement similar to the Radical Reformation in Western Europe. The region of southern Russia and Ukraine, the territory of the Dnieper and Black Sea's confluence, became a meeting place for peoples and empires. This region was defined not only geographically by the confluence of the great river and the old "inner" Eurasian sea but also culturally by a confluence of different human traditions. On the one hand, the Turkish nomads, Ukrainian and Russian peasants and Cossacks, Polish and Jewish settlers, and German and Mennonite colonists with their different religions met each other and developed various patterns of intercultural relations. On the other hand, this area was influenced by rivalries among the three major Eurasian powers, Russia, Turkey, and Poland. By the end of the eighteenth century, Russia had displaced its imperial rivals on the northern Black Sea coast, incorporated the Ukrainian borderlands, and tried to dominate this area politically and culturally.[1]

Despite the prevailing model of military expedition at the beginning of Russian colonization, the "charter groups" of settlement in this region, such as Russian and Ukrainian peasants and Cossacks, and Germans and Mennonites, shaped the main cultural patterns and regional identities. A combination of these patterns and the post-Emancipation transformation of Russian society—the rise of a more commercial agrarian economy and the increased migration of the rural population—created conditions for the spread of radical evangelical religion among the majority of the rural population in southern Russia.

This Russian "radical reformation" began during the 1830s and 1840s in the small communities of Russian migrant peasants from the central provinces of Tambov and Kursk, who brought the traditions of the old Russian dissent, "the Christ-Faith," to the provinces of Tavrida and Bessarabia in the South. Different versions of this movement, including the Molokan, Dukhobor, and Khlyst and Skopets traditions, were incorporated into the new religious practices of the Shalaputs, the successors of the Christ-Faith tradition there. These old traditions also converged with new Western Protestant influences, including Lutheran Pietism and the Mennonite Jumpers movement. During this cultural dialogue between the Russian Shalaputs and their Protestant coreligionists from the German colonies, all participants contributed equally to the new phenomenon in the evangelical movement—Ukrainian Stundism, which appropriated various Russian and Western European traditions of religious dissent.

Later on, after 1884, Ukrainian Stundism—together with the Pashkovites, the intellectual evangelicals from the Russian aristocracy, and the evangelical movement among the Molokans from the Caucasus—laid the foundation for the Russian Baptist Union. The institutionalization of the evangelical movement and the spread of the Baptist faith led to the division of the Stundist movement into Stundo-Baptists and the radical "spiritual" version of Stundism. The new stage of the Russian "radical reformation" began among the radical Stundists and the Maliovantsy, who rejected human authorities and church rituals. During the 1890s, the radical reformation demonstrated the revitalization of the ecstatic and millennial elements of the Shalaputs within the context of the Stundist movement in the South. As a result, after 1900, these three phases of the evangelical movement—Shalaput, Stundist, and Stundo-Shalaput—determined the main framework of the entire popular Reformation not only on the southern frontier but also in other provinces of Russian Empire. The Shalaput, Stundist, and Stundo-Shalaput movements became the main versions of evangelical dissent, which differed from the traditional dissent of the Russian Old Believers who had been shaping a religious opposition in Russia since the late seventeenth century.

Starting in the 1860s, it was not the Old Believers but the Shalaputs, radical Stundists, and Maliovantsy who structured the popular oppositional discourse in imperial Russia. They developed theologies and religious practices equivalent to those of the Western Radical Reformation. Russian religious evangelical dissent was not an aberration in the cultural development of the Russian countryside. This movement was an integral part of the universal development of the Reformation, which had begun in the sixteenth century in Western Europe and reached the southern provinces of the Russian Empire only in the nineteenth century.

The most important element of the Russian "radical reformation" was its "spiritualist" trend, which included practices of spirit possession and the sacred theatre of the Millennium. In the 1860s, the Russian radical reformation continued with the Shalaputs' attempts to reform popular Orthodoxy with Anabaptist influences. But eventually, in the struggle with the formalism of the German Baptist faith, the Russian radical reformers reemphasized the practices of spirit possession and stressed the work of the Holy Spirit in the souls of the believers. In this respect, the Russian radical reformation was close to the theology and practices of the Quakers and the Shakers. The overwhelming majority of the groups of the Russian radical reformation shared the theology and practices of their Western counterparts. These groups should, therefore, be treated as a part of one international Christian movement rather than as exotic characters in Russian religious history. The Russian dissenters not only rejected their former peasant identity, but they created a new evangelical identity, which played a unifying role among the different ethnic peasant groups of late imperial Russia. They represented both "the Protestant ethic" and a "culture of the written word" because biblical images and ideas shaped their worldview and mentality. As a result, their evangelical culture became an agent of modernization and unification of the local cultures in the Russian countryside.

In addition, the new sects among the peasants of southern Russia created an alternative culture of sexual relations, based on the evangelical principles of Christian love and the equality of the sexes. The Shalaputs and the Stundists disrupted the patriarchal system of sexual relations and the organization of gender roles in the peasant community. The most prominent figures in this process of the revitalization of peasant culture in post-Emancipation Russia were female leaders, who, acting as Shalaput prophetesses or Stundist preachers, inspired this process and eventually became the cultural pioneers of the feminist evangelical movement in imperial Russia. The new non-Orthodox identities and unusual female activism among the rural population of southern Russia and Ukraine symbolized the formation of the new culture, which united various local peasant cultures in a broad evangelical movement. Conversely, by rejecting the Russian Orthodox identity, this movement undermined the ideological foundations of the Russian political system and led to the spread of radical political ideas in the Russian and Ukrainian countryside.

The distinctive feature of the peasant evangelical movement in imperial Russia was its relatively weak intellectual base. Despite the participation of few Russian aristocrats in this movement, a genuine high (or magisterial) reformation like that in Western Europe was absent in Russia. An overwhelming majority of Russian and Ukrainian dissenters came from the most oppressed, suffering, and mainly uneducated part of rural population. This largely explains why they brought their millennial expectations of social justice and social revenge into their sects. They expressed these expectations very emotionally, in ecstatic and mystic rituals, but without a systematic theological explanation that was typical for the Western Reformation. The Protestant ethic of some successful dissident farmers did not replace the millenarianism of the entire movement. Constant police harassment not only prevented the normal economic activity of the dissidents but also pushed even the moderates among them in the direction of radical millenarianism. Religious radicals, such as the Neo-Stundists and the Maliovantsy, simply expressed and articulated the widely shared (by all peasants) expectations of social justice and social revenge, using biblical language and images.

Paradoxically, the conflicts and debates between dissenters and their Orthodox neighbors exposed the non-dissident peasants to an unusual religious justification for what they dreamed about—social justice and revenge. The explosions of hatred against Shalaputs and Stundists in Russian and Ukrainian villages could not hide the peasants' secret compassion for millennial ideas. Therefore, encounters of dissident and Orthodox peasants, who lived side by side, contributed to the spread of the millennial discourse among the rural population of those localities where millennial preaching and the practices of the dissidents were most effective.[2]

A series of "acts of toleration" between 1903 and 1905, especially the legislation on "religious freedoms" during the Russian Revolution of 1905–7, lifted the most onerous restrictions for religious dissenters in the Russian Empire. After 1905, anyone could leave the Russian Orthodox Church and join the religious confession of one's preference. But despite these acts of toleration, the Russian administration still tried to control the evangelical movement using various police restrictions and interfering in the affairs of evangelical congregations. According to a circular, "On the Order for Sectarian Meetings," that was issued on October 4, 1910, the authorities treated the non-Orthodox religious groups of Russians as "sectarian ones," with presumably dangerous anti-state intentions.[3] In 1910 and 1912, under pressure from Orthodox critics, the Russian government attempted to limit activities of the Protestant sects and to deprive them and "colonists of German origin of the right to buy or rent landed property" in the Ukrainian provinces.

In their rhetoric, new Russian politicians usually lumped German colonists and Russian sects such as Stundists and Baptists together. During the war with Germany, the anti-dissident and anti-German campaigns converged and reached a peak in the laws of February 2 and December 13, 1915, restricting German landholding in Russia and providing for "the liquidation of landownership and land tenure of Russian subjects of Austrian, Hungarian, or German descent." Between 1914 and 1917, the Stundists and other Russian evangelicals were harassed as "potential traitors because their faith was of German Protestant origin."[4]

Only the Revolution of 1917 removed all restrictions for the Russian religious dissidents, including 150,000 registered members of evangelical congregations. In January 1918, the famous decree on the separation of church and state declared that "every citizen may confess any religion or profess none at all. Every legal restriction connected with the profession of certain faiths or with the profession of no faith is now revoked."[5] Moreover, until 1924 the Bolshevik state tried to use the radical evangelical sects for promoting communist ideas among the rural population. Communist ideologists praised Russian evangelicals as representatives of the Radical Reformation and idealized their contribution in the history of the world communist movement.[6] But gradually, with strong atheist propaganda, the official attitude toward sects changed for the worse.

The antireligious politics of the Soviet state reached a peak in April 1929 with the promulgation of the law on religious cults. Following this legislation, all activities of the Soviet evangelicals were persecuted, more than 60 percent of religious congregations were closed, and their activists were arrested, sent to labor camps, or executed. It was the end of collaboration between religious and political radicals in Russian history.[7] Afterward, Soviet ideologists forgot about this collaboration. Moreover, they later tried to erase the story of religious radicals from historical memory. As a result of their efforts, the history of the Russian peasant millenarian movements, the story of the Russian "radical reformation," disappeared completely from the official historiography.

Notes

1 See also the recent study on national and imperial identities on another southeastern frontier of the Russian Empire—in the Volga region, in "Tataria"—Robert P. Geraci, *Window on the East: National and Imperial Identities in Late Tsarist Russia* (Ithaca, N.Y., 2001).

2 It was a long historiographical tradition, which emphasized the millenarians' contribution to "Marxist revolutionism." Some suggested a theory of "socioreligious chain" that "stretched from the Reformation to Marx." See, especially, Henri Desroche, *The American Shakers: From Neo-Christianity to Presocialism* (Amherst, Mass., 1971); and J. A. G. Roberts, "'Golden Bricks and Golden Houses Await You': Prophesy and Millenarianism in the Taiping Rebellion," in *Prophesy: The Power of Inspired Language in History 1300–2000,* ed.

Bertrand Taithe and Tim Thornton (Phoenix Mill, U.K., 1997), 158. On religion and political activism among Russian industrial workers, see Reginald Zelnik, "'To the Unaccustomed Eye': Religion and Irreligion in the Experience of St. Petersburg Workers in the 1870s," *Russian History* 16, nos. 2–4 (1989): 297–326. On the influence of the peasant religious dissent on the official politics of the last Romanovs through the figure of Rasputin, see Edvard Radzinsky, *The Rasputin File,* trans. Judson Rosengrant (New York, 2000), esp. 39–45 on Khlysty.

3 Only regular meetings of the sects registered by the police were allowed. As Walter Sawatsky noted, "All additional meetings outside of the registered building required two weeks' advance notice to the police with a request for permission. The evangelization and teaching of minors was prohibited as were also various special gatherings for reading and discussion. A representative of the police was to attend every prayer meeting. See Walter Sawatsky, *Soviet Evangelicals since World War II* (Scottdale, Pa., 1981), 36. For the best coverage of legal relationships between the Russian state and the sects, see Andrew Blane, "The Relations between the Russian Protestant Sects and the State, 1900–1921" (Ph.D. dissertation, Duke University, 1964), 31, 46–47, 80–82.

4 K. E. Lindeman, *Zakony 2–go fevral'a i 13–go dekabr'a 1915 g. (ob ogranichenii nemetskogo zemlevladenia v Rossii) i ikx vliianie na ekonomicheskoe sostoianie iuzhnoi Rossii* (Moscow, 1916). The rules of 1916–17 actually meant the elimination of all German property in Russian empire. During World War I, 1914–18, the Russian administration practically treated the evangelicals as non-Russians. According to the law of 1915 on the compulsory expropriation of the German colonists, only Russian citizens with characteristics of Russian national identity were exempt from the enforcement of this law. The new law defined as Russian those who "(1) were of *Greek Orthodox faith* by birth or have embraced it prior to January 1, 1914; (2) belonged to the *Slavic race;* (3) had personally *participated* as an *officer* or as a *volunteer* in some actual action of the *Russian army* against an external enemy, or were able to point to such participation by a male ancestor or descendant; (4) had received a *personal decoration,* or (5) had a male ancestor or descendant who had obtained such for bravery in war, or have lost a father, husband or son (though only as officer or volunteer) on the battlefield." Therefore, the Stundists were considered to be non-Russians. See V. S. Diakin, "Pervaia mirovaia voina i meropriiatia po likvidatsii tak nazyvaemogo nemetskogo zasil'ia," in *Pervaia mirovaia voina,* ed. A. L. Sidorov (Moscow, 1968), 227–38.

5 V. Kuroedov and A. Pankratov, eds., *Zakonodatel'stvo o religioznykh kul'takh* (Moscow, 1971), 53. See also Sawatsky, *Soviet Evangelicals,* 39, 36–37.

6 On this, see A. Etkind, "Russkie sekty i sovetskii kommunizm: proekt Vladimira Bonch-Bruevicha," *Minuvshee,* 1996, 19, 275–319.

7 On the relationship among Orthodox clergy and laity and Communist Party "activists" during the establishment of Soviet power in the Russian countryside (1921–28), see Glennys Young, *Power and the Sacred in Revolutionary Russia: Religious Activists in the Village* (University Park, Pa., 1997). For the best coverage for this in Russian, see S. N. Savinskii, *Istoria evangel'skikh khristian-baptistov Ukrainy, Rossii, Belorussii, Chast' II {part 2} (1917–1967)* (Saint Petersburg, 2001), esp. 13–148.

Appendix A: Population of Southern Russian and Ukrainian Provinces, 1861–1900, according to the Governors' Reports

Reports for 1861	Province of Kherson	Province of Kiev	Province of Tavrida	Province of Ekaterinoslav	Province of Bessarabia	Province of Stavropol	Province of Kharkov
Total population	1,035,038	1,997,683	527,431	1,115,046	1,014,207	353,174	1,599,682
State peasants and Cossacks (or military settlers)	106,255 +270,604 military settlers	243,501 +69,081 Freemen, Odnodvorets, et al.	320,933	533,615	69,876 +505,772 Tsarans +36,030 Cossacks, et al.	206,419 (including 191,797 peasants +14,622 Cossacks)	743,703
Former serfs	323,868	1,161,380	34,733	355,322	6,381	19,269	467,608
Foreign colonists and Mennonites	59,558 +19,918 Jews	282 Mennonites +12,122 Jews	51,544	33,908 +36,053 Greek +8,838 Armenian Settlers	93,072 (54,129 Danube settlers, 26,607 Germans, 10,092 Jews)	1,515	2 colonists +4,749 settlers +8,018 Cantonists
Russian Orthodox	909,147	1,161,380	375,154	1,066,620	881,771	250,630	1,595,421
Armenians	927		3,210	8,838	2,328	15,726	
Roman Catholics	26,000	89,170	7,141	2,384	4,751	955	1,311
Lutherans and Reformed	28,421	1,851	18,668 +1,981 Pietists	1,648	26,094	1,513	1,198
Jews	62,272	247,740	9,477	18,983	90,358	42	

Karaites	283		3,476	64		
Muslims	53		80,926			7,012
Pagans						
Old Believers	7,923			5,895 13 Skoptsy	8,203 1 Skopers	75,643
Mystical sects: Shalaputs, Khlysty, Skoptsy, et al.	5,552 1 Skopets					1,565 7 Skoptsy +82 Molokans
Rationalist sects: Molokans, Dukhobors, Stundists, et al.	5 Molokans		4,598 Molokans +22,800 Mennonites	24 Molokans and Dukhobors +10,525 Mennonites	651 Molokans and Dukhobors	1,651 6 Skoptsy
Judaizers and Sabbatarians			52	52	50	95 Molokans

Appendix A

Reports for 1865–66	Province of Kherson	Province of Kiev	Province of Tavrida	Province of Ekaterinoslav	Province of Bessarabia	Province of Stavropol	Province of Kharkov
Total population	1,200,562		625,360	1,220,176	1,099,700		
State peasants and Cossacks	105,611 peasants + 306,121 settlers		370,692	952,993	80,251 peasants + 551,209 Tsarans + 28,164 Cossacks, et al.		
Former serfs	380,600		35,496	52,772	109,558 (including 64,308 settlers, 31,665 Germans, 13,587 Jews)		
Foreign colonists and Mennonites	65,881 colonists + 11,448 Jews		88,227 Colonists	46,022			
Russian Orthodox	1,038,677		433,047	1,129,105	937,314		
Armenians	2,187		4,586	21,162	3,107		
Roman Catholics	42,028		10,449	9,026	4,935		
Lutherans and Reformed	35,693		23,024	11,273	35,355		
Jews	63,316		10,851	28,272	114,110		

Karaites	520	3,214	15	15
Muslims	8,327	107,944	6,212	9,177
Old Believers				
Mystical sects: Shalaputs, Khlysty, Skoptsy, et al.		225 Shalaputs (in 1865); 432 (in 1866)		1 Skopets
Rationalist sects: Molokans, Dukhobors, Stundists, et al.		5,587 Molokans + 24,215 Mennonites + 2,215 Pietists	13,978 Mennonites	562 Molokans
Judaizers and Sabbatarians	9,814	3		59

Reports for 1870	Province of Kherson	Province of Kiev	Province of Tavrida	Province of Ekaterinoslav	Province of Bessarabia	Province of Stavropol	Province of Kharkov
Total population	1,383,283	2,175,132	682,310	1,304,264	1,078,932	439,278	1,726,849
State peasants and Cossacks	512,337	1,587,562 (including former serfs)	454,102 (including former serfs)			[for 1871]	
Former serfs	303,318		88,742				
Foreign Colonists	94,174 +25,960 Jews	12,888					
Russian Orthodox	1,160,755	1,813,382		1,199,619	925,639		
Armenians	2,587	4		20,137	3,327		
Roman Catholics	41,613	73,570		12,470	5,500		
Lutherans and Reformed	55,557	3,334		29,539	36,805		
Jews	108,137	277,479		35,185	98,114		
Karaites	591						
Muslims	101	117		210	10		
Old Believers	12,724	8,246		6,886	9,188	1,540	
Mystical sects: Shalaputs, Khlysty, Skoptsy, et al.	98	All dissidents were included		18		439 Shalaputs	

Appendix A

Rationalist sects: Molokans, Dukhobors, Stundists, et al.	26 Molokans + 547 Stundists	280	18 Molokans
Judaizers and Sabbatarians		69	252

Reports for 1875	Province of Kherson	Province of Kiev	Province of Tavrida	Province of Ekaterinoslav	Province of Bessarabia	Province of Stavropol	Province of Kharkov
Total population			735,208	1,454,691	1,138,905	500,580	
State peasants and Cossacks					790,996, including all peasants		
Foreign colonists					10,496		
Russian Orthodox					948,917		
Armenians					3,410		
Roman Catholics					5,958		
Lutherans and Reformed					42,159		
Jews					127,448		
Karaites							
Muslims					24		
Old Believers		5,140, for 1873 [892 Strundists in 1876]		5,965	9,797		
Mystical sects: Shalaputs, Khlysty, Skoptsy, et al.				All together, including Shalaputs		488 Shalaputs	

Appendix A

Rationalist sects: Molokans, Dukhobors, Stundists, et al.	350 "open" and 100 "secretive" Stundists	1,128
Judaizers and Sabbatarians		64

414

Reports for 1880	Province of Kherson	Province of Kiev	Province of Tavrida	Province of Ekaterinoslav	Province of Bessarabia	Province of Stavropol	Province of Kharkov
Total population	1,434,427		861,662	1,497,160			
State peasants and Cossacks	1,023,638 rural population			1,272,822 (85 percent) rural population			
Foreign colonists							
Russian Orthodox				90 percent			
Armenians				2 percent			
Roman Catholics				1 percent			
Lutherans and Reformed				3 percent			
Jews				3 percent			
Karaites				0.5 percent			
Muslims							
Pagans							
Old Believers		6,834		7,641 All sects, with 95 percent of Old Believers			5,333 Including all sects
Mystical sects: Shalaputs, Khlysty, Skoptsy, et al.							

Appendix A

Rationalist sects: Molokans, Dukhobors, Stundists, et al. Judaizers and Sabbatarians	1,480 Stundists	9,895, with over-whelming majority of Molokans

Reports for 1885	Province of Kherson	Province of Kiev	Province of Tavrida	Province of Ekaterinoslav	Province of Bessarabia	Province of Stavropol	Province of Kharkov
Total population	1,697,584		992,125	1,707,578			2,230,111
State peasants and Cossacks	1,234,133 rural population		768,687 rural population	1,482,248 rural population			
Foreign colonists							
Russian Orthodox	1,450,260		704,719				
Armenians	813		7,099				
Roman Catholics	51,857		21,338				
Lutherans and Reformed	40,151 Lutherans + 3,095 Reformed		53,548				
Jews	121,418		30,265				
Karaites	733		5,002				
Muslims	249		157,074				
Old Believers	19,668 "of all sects," including 14,213 Old Believers		13,066 all together	10,698 all together			5,574

Mystical sects: Shalaputs, Khlysty, Skoptsy, et al.			430 Shalaputs in 1883	124 Shalaputs
Rationalist sects: Molokans, Dukhobors, Stundists, et al.	3,049 Stundists, 2,328 Baptists, 3,885 Mennonites, 78 Molokans	3,085 Stundists	200 Stundists in 1883	
Judaizers and Sabbatarians				

Reports for 1890	Province of Kherson	Province of Kiev	Province of Tavrida	Province of Ekaterinoslav	Province of Bessarabia	Province of Stavropol	Province of Kharkov
Total population	1,868,448 (without Odessa)		1,119,266	1,627,425	1,690,776	688,006	2,465,668
State peasants and Cossacks			845,891 all peasants		1,039,165 all peasants		
Foreign colonists					105,930 colonists		
Russian Orthodox			814,774	1,572,000	1,213,001		
Armenians			7,052		829		
Roman Catholics			20,817		5,382		
Lutherans and Reformed			57,249		45,696		
Jews	155,865		35,166		86,580		
Karaites			6,270				
Muslims			159,709		5		
Old Believers		10,192	2,358	7,701	9,581		6,176, including sects
Mystical sects: Shalaputs, Khlysty, Skoptsy, et al.				361 Shalaputs	45		240, all sects together

| Rationalist sects: Molokans, Dukhobors, Stundists, et al. | 4,648 Stundists | 5,002 Stundists | 12,880 | 267 Stundists (352 Stundists in 1891) | 1,546 |
| Judaizers and Sabbatarians | | | 88 | | 12,117 |

Appendix A

Reports for 1895	Province of Kherson	Province of Kiev	Province of Tavrida	Province of Ekaterinoslav	Province of Bessarabia	Province of Stavropol	Province of Kharkov
Total population	2,127,566	3,500,000	1,273,816	2,009,899	1,823,651		2,621,595 (for 1896)
State peasants and Cossacks	1,195,029 peasants with land + 151,922 landless peasants + 73,484 Cossacks		961,842, all peasants				
Foreign colonists	20,625 Bulgarians + 98,391 Germans + 26,087 Jews		6,161 settlers + 5,756 colonists				
Russian Orthodox	1,797,945		922,537				
Armenians	669		8,314				
Roman Catholics	61,271		23,301				
Lutherans and Reformed	42,886 Lutherans + 3,540 Reformed		60,890				

Jews	178,442		41,575		
Karaites	800		7,275		
Muslims	1,280		176,942		
Old Believers	29,312	11,743	1,324	8,840	
Mystical sects: Shalaputs, Khlysty, Skoptsy, et al.				84 Shalaputs (381 for 1894)	
Rationalist sects: Molokans, Dukhobors, Stundists, et al.	4,514 Mennonites + 6,869 Stundists	4,494 Stundists (in 1893, 4,955 Stundists)	15,829	317 Stundists (320 for 1894) + 188 Baptists	526 Stundists
Judaizers and Sabbatarians			2,305		

Reports for 1897–1900	Province of Kherson	Province of Kiev	Province of Tavrida	Province of Ekaterinoslav	Province of Bessarabia	Province of Stavropol	Province of Kharkov
Total population			1,388,427 (1,434,270 in 1900)	2,113,674 (for 1897); 2,458,750 (for 1900)	2,101,489	962,317	2,757,568
State peasants and Cossacks			1,038,045, all peasants	87.40 percent		861,842 rural population 46,453 nomadic population	
Foreign Colonists			10,181 settlers + 9,537 colonists				
Russian Orthodox			1,000,276	90.05 percent			
Armenians			7,647				
Roman Catholics			25,217	1.52 percent			
Lutherans and Reformed			79,854	39,530 Lutherans + 157 Reformed (3.06 percent)			
Jews			33,415	4.80 percent			
Karaites			7,268				
Muslims			197,548				

Old Believers	2,930	0.44 percent; in 1900—9,000 586 Shalaputs in 1900;
Mystic sects: Shalaputs, Khlysty, Skoptsy, et al.		
Rationalist sects: Molokans, Dukhobors, Stundists, et al.	18,098 Molokans	23,922 Mennonites; 1,150 Baptists + 874 Stundists in 1900
Judaizers and Sabbatarians		

Sources: The governors', police, and clergy reports are the main sources for all tables: Rossiiskii gosudarstvennyi istoricheskii arkhiv, "Otchety gubernatorov," and *fond* 1263 for 1861–1906; *fond* 1284, *opis'* 241, delo 181 (1901); *fond* 821, *opis'* 133, *delo* 21 (1909–10).

Appendix A

Appendix B: Sects in the Southern European
Provinces of the Russian Empire, according
to the Census of 1897

Province	Provincial population	Mystical sects: Shalaputs, Khlysty, Skoptsy, et al.			Rationalist sects: Molokans, Dukhobors, Stundists, et al.			Total of all sects in the South, 1897
		Male	Female	Total	Male	Female	Total	
Astrakhan	1,936,392				4,525	4,544	9,069	9,069
Bessarabia	2,989,482	2	1	3	660	673	1,333	1,336
Volynia					8	9	17	17
Voronezh	2,564,238	1	4	5	1,524	1,451	2,975	2,980
Don Army	2,113,674	55	52	107	1,734	1,744	3,478	3,585
Ekaterinoslav	3,559,229	4	3	7	95	100	195	212
Kiev	3,018,299	30	30	60	1,600	1,690	3,290	3,350
Podolia	2,778,151				89	85	174	174
Poltava	1,447,790				39	32	71	71
Tavrida	(1,388,427)	35	38	73	4,805	4,729	9,534	9,607
					(9,039)	(9,059)	(18,098)	(21,028)
Kherson	2,733,612	1			1,909	1,777	3,686	3,687
Kharkov	2,492,316				418	366	784	784
Chernigov	2,297,854				12	5	17	17
Total population in the South	93,442,864			255			34,623	34,878
Total in Russian Empire	125,668,190							

Sources: The governors', police, and clergy reports are the main sources: Rossiiskii gosudarstvennyi istoricheskii arkhiv, "Otchety gubernatorov," and *fond* 1263 for 1861–1906; *fond* 1284, *opis'* 241, *delo* 181 (1901); *fond* 821, *opis'* 133, *delo* 21 (1909–10).

Appendix C: The Registered Sects in the Southern European Provinces of the Russian Empire, according to the Census of 1909–10

Province	Khlysty	New Israel	Molokans + Dukhbors	Stundists + Maliovantsy	Baptists	Evangelical Christians	Adventists and Sabbatarians	Total of all registered sects for 1909–10
Astrakhan			4,553				3,150	9,637
Bessarabia			2,000					2,000
Volynia				506	13,366	668	23	14,000
Voronezh			3,876	147	100	844		7,259
Don Army			1,000	520	1,077	320	1,300	3,697
Ekaterinoslav		600		212	1,300	877	13	1,463
Kiev	132	85	127	3,608+ 1,553	1,787 (total Stundo-Baptists 9,300)	1,687	955	12,067
Podolia								1,000
Poltava				547	17		2	566
Stavropol	2,240	1,793	1,338	36	5,866		4,492	11,762
Tavrida			14,985 in 1911				205 in 1911	20,238 (20,355 in 1911)
Kherson					3,251	3,419		6,670
Kharkov				5,000				4,325
Chernigov				30	540			570
Total sects in the South								95,254
Total sects in the Russian Empire								262,966

Sources: The governors', police, and clergy reports are the main sources: Rossiiskii gosudarstvennyi istoricheskii arkhiv, "Otchety gubernatorov," and *fond* 1263 for 1861–1906; *fond* 1284, *opis'* 241, *delo* 181 (1901); *fond* 821, *opis'* 133, *delo* 21 (1909–10).

Selected Bibliography

Archival Sources

Dniepropetrovs'kyi derzhavnyi oblasnyi arkhiv, Dniepropetrovsk, Ukraine
    Fond 11, Kantseliaria Ekaterinoslavskogo gubernatora
    Fond 20, Ekaterinoslavskoe gubernskoe pravlenie
    Fond 106, Ekaterinoslavskaia dukhovnaia konsistoria
    Fond 134, Innostrannykh kolonistov
    Fond 177, Ekaterinoslavskii okruzhnoi sud
Gosudarstvennaia biblioteka Rossii, Otdel rukopisei, Moscow
    Fond 369, Arkhiv Vladimira Dm. Bonch-Bruevicha
    Fond 435, Arkhiv Vladimira Gr. Chertkova
    Fond 648, Arkhiv Aleksandra Il. Klibanova
Gosudarstvennyi arkhiv Rossiiskoi Federatsii, Moscow
    Fond 102, Departament politsii. Osobyi otdel
    Fond 109, Tretie Otdelenie. Pervaia ekspeditsia
    Fond 124, Vremennaia kantseliaria po proizvodstvu osobykh ugolovnykh del pri Ministerstve iustitsii
Library of Congress, Washington, D.C.
    Plumer Papers
Rossiiskii gosudarstvennyi arkhiv drevnikh aktov i rukopisei, Moscow
    Fond 16, Kollegia inostrannykh del. Ob inostrannykh poselentsakh.

Rossiiskii gosudarstvennyi istoricheskii arkhiv, Saint Petersburg

Biblioteka chital'nogo zala, Otchety gubernatorov za 1861–1905.

Fond 379, Departament gosudarstvennykh imushchestv ministerstva finansov

Fond 381, Kantseliariia ministra ministerstva gosudarstvennykh imushchestv

Fond 383, Pervyi departament ministerstva gosudarstvennykh imushchestv

Fond 384, Vtoroi departament ministerstva gosudarstvennykh imushchestv

Fond 391, Pereselencheskoe upravlenie

Fond 396, Departament gosudarstvennykh zemel'nykh imushchestv ministerstva gosudarstvennykh imushchestv

Fond 398, Departament zemledeliia ministerstva gosudarstvennykh imushchestv

Fond 560, Obshchaia kantseliariia ministra finansov

Fond 565, Departament gosudarstvennogo kaznacheistva ministerstva finansov

Fond 573, Departament okladnykh sborov ministerstva finansov

Fond 733, Departament narodnogo prosveshcheniia

Fond 796, Kantseliariia Sinoda

Fond 797, Kantseliariia ober-prokurora Sinoda

Fond 821, Departament dukhovnykh del inostrannykh ispovedanii (MVD)

Fond 1263, Komitet ministrov

Fond 1282, Kantseliariia ministra ministerstva vnutrennikh del

Fond 1284, Departament obshchikh del ministerstva vnutrennikh del

Fond 1287, Khoziaistvennyi departament ministerstva vnutrennikh del

Fond 1291, Zemskii otdel ministerstva vnutrennikh del

Fond 1354, Obshchie sobraniia i soedinennye prisutstviia kassatsionnykh departamentov senata

Fond 1405, Ministerstvo iustitsii

Fond 1473, Sekretnyi komitet po delam raskola

Fond 1574, K. P. Pobedonostsev

Tsentral'nyi derzhavnyi istorychnyi arkhiv Ukrainy, Kiev

Fond 127, Kievskaia dukhovnaia konsistoria

Fond 268, Yuzhnoe raionnoe okhrannoe otdelenie

Fond 274, Kievskoe gubernskoe zhandarmskie upravlenie

Fond 275, Kievskoe okhrannoe otdelenie raionnoe okhrannoe otdelenie

Fond 276, Yugo-Zapadnoe raionnoe okhrannoe otdelenie

Fond 301, Podol'skoe gubernskoe zhandarmskie upravlenie

Fond 313, Ekaterinoslavskoe gubernskoe zhandarmskie upravlenie

Fond 317, Prokuror Kievskoi sudebnoi palaty

Fond 320, Poltavskoe gubernskoe zhandarmskie upravlenie

Fond 336, Kharkovskoe gubernskoe zhandarmskie upravlenie

Fond 355, Pomoshchnik nachal'nika Khersonskogo gubernskogo zhandarmskogo upravlenia v Anan'ievskom i Tiraspol'skom uezdakh

Fond 356, Kantseliaria Nikolaevskogo voennogo gubernatora

Fond 385, Odesskoe zhandarmskie upravlenie

Fond 419, Prokuror Odesskoi sudebnoi palaty
Fond 442, Kantseliaria Kievskogo, Podol'skogo i Volynskogo General-Gubernatora
Fond 705, Yugo-Vostochnoe raionnoe okhrannoe otdelenie
Fond 707, Upravlenie popechitelei Kievskogo uchebnogo okruga
Fond 711, Kievskaia dukhovnaia akademia
Fond 1335, Volynskoe gubernskoe zhandarmskie upravlenie
Fond 1439, Chernigovskoe gubernskoe zhandarmskie upravlenie
Fond 1597, Ekaterinoslavskoe okhrannoe otdelenie

Contemporary Newspapers and Journals

Baptist
Byloe
Chtenia v Obshchestve liubitelei dukhovnogo prosveshchenia
Delo
Ekaterinoslavskie eparkhial'nye vedomosti
Etnograficheskii obzor
Golos
Golos minuvshego
Istoricheskii vestnik
Kavkaz
Kavkazskie (Stavropol'skie) eparkhial'nye vedomosti
Khersonskie eparkhial'nye vedomosti
Khristianskoe chtenie
Kievlianin
Kievskaya starina
Kievskie eparkhial'nye vedomosti
Kievskii telegraf
Listki "Svobodnogo slova"
Literaturno-naukovyi visnyk
Missionary Review of the World
Missionerskoe obozrenie
Moskovskie vedomosti
Nedelia
Odesskii vestnik
Otechestvennye zapiski
Poznanie Rossii
Pravoslavnoe obozrenie
Pravoslavnyi sobesednik
Razsvet. Sotsial-demokraticheskii listok dlia sektantov
The Review of Reviews
Russkaya mysl'

431

Russkii vestnik
Russkoe slovo
Slovo
Strannik
Svobodnoe slovo
Tavricheskie eparkhial'nye vedomosti
Trudy Kievskoi dukhovnoi akademii
Tserkovnyi vestnik
Vera i razum
Vestnik Evropy
Virginia Gazette
Vol'noe slovo
Zaria
Zhurnal Ministerstva gosudarstvennykh imushchestv
Zhurnal sel'skogo khoziaistva i ovtsevodstva

Printed Sources

Bekker, Jacob P. *Origin of the Mennonite Brethren Church: Previously Unpublished Manuscript by One of the Eighteen Founders,* trans. by D. E. Pauls and A. E. Janzen. Hillsboro, Kans., 1973.

Biriukov, P. *Maliovantsy: Istoria odnoi sekty.* Izdanie "Svobodnogo slova" [publication of the periodical *Free Word*], ed. V. Chertkova. Christchurch, U.K., 1905.

Bonch-Bruevich, Vladimir D., ed. *Delo pavlovskikh krest'an (ofitsial'nye dokumenty).* London, 1902.

———. *Materialy k istorii i izucheniiu russkogo sektantstva i raskola.* Saint Petersburg, 1908–10.

———. *Materialy k istorii i izucheniiu sovremennogo sektantstva i staroobriadchestva.* Saint Petersburg, 1911.

Bondar', S. D. *Sekty khlystov, shelaputov, dukhovnykh khristian, Staryi i Novyi Izrail', subbotnikov i iudeistvuiushchikh.* Petrograd, 1916.

Brown, John. *The Stundists: The Story of a Great Religious Revolt.* London, 1893.

Charcot, Jean-Martin, and Paul Richer. *Les demoniaques dans l'art suivi de "La foi qui gerit."* Paris, 1984.

Cherniaev, V. *Sel'skokhoziaistvennoe mashinostroenie: Istorichesko-statisticheskii obzor promyshlennosti Rossii.* Saint Petersburg, 1883.

Chto podgotovilo pochvu dlia shtundizma? Kiev, 1875.

Dalton, H. *Der Stundismus in Russland: Studie und Erinnerungen.* Guetersloh, 1896.

Debagorii-Mokrievich, Vladimir. *Ot buntarstva k terrorizmu.* Moscow, 1930.

Deich, Lev G. *Za polveka.* Moscow, 1926.

Dobrotvorskii, I. *Liudi bozh'i: Russkaia sekta tak nazyvaemykh dukhovnykh khristian.* Kazan', 1869.

[Dorodnitsyn], Episkop Alexii. *Materialy dlia istorii religiozno-ratsionalisticheskogo dvizhenia na iuge Rossii vo vtoroi polovine XIX-go veka.* Kazan', 1908.

————. *Religiozno-ratsionalisticheskoe dvizhenie na Iuge Rossii vo vtoroi polovine XIX veka.* Kazan', 1909.

————. *Shelaputskaia obshchina.* Kazan', 1906.

————. *Yuzhno-Russkii Neobaptism, izvestnyi pod imenem shtundy. Po offitsial'nym dokumentam.* Stavropol, 1903.

Dostoevsky, Fedor M. *The Diary of a Writer,* trans. B. Brasol. New York, 1954.

Drahomanov, Mykhailo. *Novi ukrainski pis'ni pro gromadski spravy (1764–1880).* Geneva, 1880.

————. *Pro Bratstvo Khrestyteliv abo Baptystiv na Ukraini.* Kolomiya, 1892.

Edmundson, William. *A Journal of the Life, Travels, Sufferings, and Labor of Love.* London, 1715.

Friesen, Peter M. *The Mennonite Brotherhood in Russia (1789–1910),* trans. J. B. Towes, A. Friesen et al. Fresno, Calif., 1978 (1st pr. in German in Russia, 1911).

Hrushevs'kyi, Mykhailo. *Z istorii religiinoi dumky na Ukraini.* L'viv, 1914.

Iasevich-Borodaevskaia, Varvara I. *Bor'ba za veru: Istoriko-bytovye ocherki i obzor zakonodatel'stva po staroobriadchestvu i sektantstvu v ego posledovatel'nom razvitii s prilozheniem statei zakona i vysochaishikh ukazov.* Saint Petersburg, 1912.

————. *Sektantstvo v Kievskoi guvernii: Baptisty i Maliovantsy.* Saint Petersburg, 1902.

Kal'nev, M.A., ed. *Russkie sektanty, ikh uchenie, kul't i sposby propagandy.* Odessa, 1911.

Klaus, A. *Nashi kolonii. Opyty i materialy po istorii i statistike inostrannoi kolonizatsii v Rossii.* Saint Petersburg, 1869.

Konovalov, Dmitrii G. *Psikhologia sektantskogo ekstaza (Rech' pred zashchitoi magisterskoi dissertatsii: "Religioznyi ekstaz v russkom misticheskom sektantstve").* Sergiev Posad, 1908.

————. *Vozniknovenie entuziasticheskikh sekt.* Moscow, 1912.

Kozitskii, Piotr. *Vopros o proiskhozhdenii yuzhno-russkago Shtundizma v nashei literature.* Saint Petersburg, 1908.

Kutepov, K. *Sekta khlystov i skoptsov.* Kazan', 1882.

Latimer, Robert Sloan. *With Christ in Russia.* London, 1910.

Leatherbarrow, W. J., and D. C. Offord, eds. *A Documentary History of Russian Thought: From the Enlightenment to Marxism.* Ann Arbor, Mich., 1987.

Life of William Allen with Selections from His Correspondence. In 2 vols. Philadelphia, 1847.

Livanov, F. *Raskol'niki i ostrozhniki.* Saint Petersburg, 1872.

Lutsenko, Trofym K. *Spovid' virouchytelia sektanta (Istoria moei zhizni),* ed. G. Vashkevich. Kiev, 1907.

Maklakov, V. A. *Iz vospominanii.* New York, 1954.

Materialy dlia geografii i statistiki Rosii: Khersonskaia gubernia. Sostavil general'nogo shtaba podpolkovnik A. Schmidt [compiled by A. Schmidt, an officer of the General Headquarters]. Saint Petersburg, 1863.

Materialy dlia geografii i statistiki Rossii, sobrannye ofitserami General'nogo Shtaba. Ekaterinoslavskaia gubernia. Sostavil general'nogo shtaba kapitan V. Pavlovich [compiled by captain V. Pavlovich, an officer of the General Headquarters]. Saint Petersburg, 1862.

Mather, Increase. *An Essay for the Recording of Illustrious Providences: Wherein an Account Is*

433

Given of Many Remarkable and Very Memorable Events, Which Have Happened in This Last Age. Boston, 1684.

Nadezhdin, Nikolai. *Issledovanie o skopcheskoi eresi.* Saint Petersburg, 1845.

Nedzel'nitskii, Ioann. *Shtundizm, prichiny poiavlenia i razbor ucenia ego.* Elisavetgrad, 1893.

Penn, William. *The Papers of William Penn,* ed. M. Dunn and R.Dunn. In 5 vols. Philadelphia, 1981–86).

———. *Works.* In 2 vols. London, 1726.

Plett, Delbert F., ed. *The Golden Years: The Mennonite Kleine Gemeinde in Russia (1812–1849).* Steinbach, Manitoba, 1985.

———. *History and Events: Writings and Maps Pertaining to the History of the Mennonite Kleine Gemeinde from 1866 to 1876.* Steinbach, Manitoba, 1982.

———. *Leaders of the Mennonite Kleine Gemeinde in Russia, 1812 to 1874, Volume Six: The Mennonite Kleine Gemeinde Historical Series.* Steinbach, Manitoba, 1993.

Polnoe sobranie zakonov Rossiiskoi imperii s 1649 goda. In 45 vols. Saint Petersburg, 1830–75.

Prelooker, Jaakoff. *Under the Tsar and Queen Victoria: The Experiences of a Russian Reformer.* London, 1895.

Privetstvie Russkomu narodu ot Kondrata Maliovannogo. Moscow, 1907.

Rathbun, Valentine. *Some Brief Hints of a Religious Scheme.* Boston, 1782.

Reutskii, N. *Liudi bozh'i i skoptsy.* Moscow, 1872.

Riker, James, Jr. *The Annals of Newtown, in Queens County, New York: Containing Its History from Its First Settlement.* New York, 1852.

Rozhdestvenskii, A. *Iuzhno-russkii shtundism.* Saint Petersburg, 1889.

———. *Khlystovshchina i skopchestvo v Rossii.* Moscow, 1882.

Shelukhin, S. P. *Nemetskaia kolonizatsia na iuge Rossii.* Odessa, 1915.

Shtakh, Ia. *Ocherki iz istorii i sovremennoi zhizni juzhno-russkikh kolonistov.* Moscow, 1916.

Sikorskii, I. A. *Sbornik nauchno-literaturnykh statei.* V 5-ti knigakh [in 5 vols.]. Kiev, 1900.

Skubachevskii, P. P. *Kak dedushka Pakhom posramil shtundistov.* Kharkov, 1913.

Sokolovskii, K. *Sekta maliovantsev sredi shtundistov v sele Petrosotrove Khersonskoi gubernii, Elizavetgradskogo uezda.* Saint Petersburg, 1903.

Stadling, Jonas. *In the Land of Tolstoy: Experiences of Famine and Misrule in Russia.* London, 1897.

Stepniak-Kravchinskii, Sergei M. *The Russian Peasantry: Their Agrarian Condition, Social Life and Religion.* Westport, Conn., 1977 (1st pr., 1888).

Story, Thomas. *A Journal of the Life of Thomas Story.* Newcastle upon Tyne, 1747.

Strel'bitskii, I. *Kratkii ocherk shtundizma i svod tekstov, napravlennykh k ego oblicheniyu.* Odessa, 1893.

T. G. Shevchenko v dokumentakh i materialakh. Kiev, 1950.

Umissa, A. I. *Sovremennoie polozhenie zemledeliia na iuge Rossii.* Kherson, 1874.

Ushinskii, Alexander. *O prichinakh poiavlenia ratsionalisticheskikh uchenii shtundy i nekotorykh drugikh podobnykh sekt v sel'skom pravoslavnom naselenii i o merakh protiv rasprostranenia uchenia etikh sekt.* Kiev, 1884.

———. *Verouchenie malorusskikh shtundistov, razobrannoe na osnovanii Sviashchennogo pisania v besedakh pravoslavnogo mirianina s sektantami.* Kiev, 1883.

Val'kevich, V. L. *Zapiska o propagande protestantskikh sect v Rossii i v osobennosti, na Kavkaze.* Tiflis, 1900.

Varadinov, N. *Istoria ministerstva vnutrennikh del,* vol. 8. Saint Petersburg, 1863.

Velitsyn, A. A. *Nemtsy v Rossii: Ocherki istoricheskogo razvitia i nastoiashchego polozhenia nemetskikx kolonii na Iuge i Vostoke Rossii.* Saint Petersburg, 1893.

Vsia Rossia: Russkaia kniga promyshlennosti, torgovli, sel'skogo khoziajstva i administratsii.Torgovopromyshlennyi kalendar' Rossiiskoj imperii. Saint Petersburg, 1895.

Zin'kivs'kyi, Trokhym. "Shtunda, ukrains'ka ratsionalistychna sekta." In *Pisannya Trokhyma Zin'kivs'kogo,* ed. Leonid Smolens'ky and Trokhym Zin'kivs'kyi. In 2 vols. L'viv, 1906, vol. 2, 121–287.

Secondary Sources

Avramenko, An. M. "Evoliutsia zemel'nykh otnoshenii na Levoberezhnoi Ukraine v kontse XIX–XX veka." Ph.D. dissertation, Khar'kov State University, 1985.

Bagaley, D. *Kolonizatsia Novorossiiskogo kraia i pervye shagi ego na puti kul'tury.* Kiev, 1889.

Bartlett, Roger P. *Human Capital: The Settlement of Foreigners in Russia, 1762–1804.* Cambridge, 1804.

Barrett, Thomas M. *At the Edge of Empire: The Terek Cossacks and the North Caucasus Frontier, 1700–1860.* Boulder, Colo., 1999.

Bell, Catherine. *Ritual: Perspectives and Dimensions.* Oxford, 1997.

Beznosova (Kudinova), Oksana V. "Pozdnee protestantskoe sektantstvo Iuga Ukrainy (1850–1905)." Ph.D. dissertation, Dniepropetrovsk University, 1998.

Billington, James H. *The Icon and the Axe: An Interpretive History of Russian Culture.* New York, 1966.

Blane, Andrew Q. "The Relations between the Russian Protestant Sects and the State, 1900–1921." Ph.D. dissertation, Duke University, 1964.

Bogdanov, K. A., and A. A. Panchenko, eds. *Mifologiia i povsednevnost'.* Saint Petersburg, 1998.

Bolshakoff, Serge. *Russian Nonconformity: The Story of "Unofficial" Religion in Russia.* New York, 1950.

Brandenburg, Hans. *The Meek and the Mighty: The Emergence of the Evangelical Movement in Russia.* New York, 1977.

Breyfogle, Nicholas B. "Heretics and Colonizers: Religious Dissent and Russian Colonization of Transcaucasia, 1830–1890." Ph.D. dissertation, University of Pennsylvania, 1998.

Brooks, Jeffrey. *When Russia Learned to Read: Literacy and Popular Literature, 1861–1917.* Princeton, N.J., 1985.

Brower, Daniel R., and Edward J. Lazzerini, eds. *Russia's Orient. Imperial Borderlands and Peoples, 1700–1917.* Bloomington, Ind., 1997.

Bushnell, John, "Peasants in Uniform: The Tsarist Army and Peasant Society." *Journal of Social History* 13, no. 4 (1980): 565–76.

435

Camfield, G. P. "The Pavlovtsy of Khar'kov Province, 1886-1905: Harmless Sectarians or Dangerous Rebels?" *Slavonic and East European Review* 68, no. 4 (1990): 692–717.

Carroll, Kenneth. "Singing in the Spirit of Early Quakerism." *Quaker History* 73 (1984): 1–13.

Chistovich, I. A. *Istoria perevoda Biblii na russkii iazyk.* Saint Petersburg, 1899.

Chulos, Chris J. *Converging Worlds: Religion and Community in Peasant Russia, 1861–1917.* DeKalb: Northern Illinois University Press, 2003.

———. "Peasant Religion in Post-Emancipation Russia: Voronezh Province, 1880–1917." Ph.D. dissertation, University of Chicago, 1994.

Clay, John Eugene, "Orthodox Missionaries and 'Orthodox Heretics' in Russia, 1886–1917," *Of Religion and Empire: Missions, Conversion, and Tolerance in Tsarist Russia,* ed. Robert Geraci and Michael Khodarkovsky. Ithaca, N.Y., 2001, 48–52.

———. "Russian Peasant Religion and Its Repression: The Christ-Faith (Khritovshchina) and the Origins of the 'Flagellant' Myth, 1666–1837." Ph.D. dissertation, University of Chicago, 1989.

Clowes, E. W., S. D. Kassow, and J. L. West, eds. *Between Tsar and People: Educated Society and the Quest for Public Identity in Late Imperial Russia.* Princeton, N.J., 1991.

Cohn, Norman. *The Pursuit of the Millennium.* New York, 1961.

Coleman, Heather. "The Most Dangerous Sect: Baptists in Tsarist and Soviet Russia, 1905–1929." Ph.D. dissertation, University of Illinois, 1998.

Conybeare, Frederic C. *Russian Dissenters.* Harvard Theological Studies 10. Cambridge, Mass., 1962.

Croatto, J. Severino. *Exodus: A Hermeneutics of Freedom,* trans. Salvator Attanasio. Maryknoll, N.Y., 1981.

Crummey, Robert. "Old Belief as Popular Religion: New Approaches." *Slavic Review* 52, no. 4 (1993): 700–12.

Dickens, A. G., and John Tonkin, eds. *The Reformation in Historical Thought.* Cambridge, Mass., 1985.

Dmitriev, Mikhail V. "Nauchnoe nasledie A. I. Klibanova i perspektivy sravnitel'no-istoricheskogo izucheniia istorii khristianstva v Rossii." *Otechestvennaia istoria,* no. 1 (1997): 77–93.

Druzhinina, Elena I. *Iuzhnaia Ukraina v period krizisa feodalizma, 1800–1825 gg.* Moscow, 1970.

———. *Severnoe Prichernomorie v 1775–1800 g.* Moscow, 1959.

Dubnow, Simon. *History of the Jews in Russia and Poland, from the Earliest Times until the Present Day.* In 3 vols. Philadelphia, 1916.

Edelman, Robert. *Proletarian Peasants: The Revolution of 1905 in Russia's Southwest.* Ithaca, N.Y., 1987.

Eklof, Ben. *Russian Peasant Schools: Officialdom, Village Culture, and Popular Pedagogy, 1861–1914.* Berkeley, Calif., 1986.

Eklof, Ben, and Stephen Frank, eds. *The World of the Russian Peasant: Post-Emancipation Culture and Society.* Boston, 1990.

436

Eldridge, J. E. T., ed. *Max Weber: The Interpretation of Social Reality.* London, 1971.

Engelstein, Laura. *Castration and the Heavenly Kingdom: A Russian Folktale.* Ithaca, N.Y., 1999.

Etkind, Alexander. *Khlyst. Sekty, literatura i revoliutsia.* Moscow, 1998.

———. "Russian Sects Still Seem Obscure." *Kritika: Explorations in Russian and Eurasian History* 2, no. 1 (2001): 165–81.

Farnsworth, Beatrice, and Lynne Viola, eds. *Russian Peasant Women.* New York, 1992.

Field, Daniel. *Rebels in the Name of the Tsar.* Boston, 1989.

Fodor, Alexander. *A Quest for a Violent Russia. The Partnership of Leo Tolstoy and Vladimir Chertkov.* New York, 1989.

Foster, Lawrence. *Religion and Sexuality: Three American Communal Experiments of the Nineteenth Century.* New York, 1981.

———. *Women, Family, and Utopia: Communal Experiments of the Shakers, the Oneida Community, and the Mormons.* Syracuse, 1991.

Foucault, Michel. *The History of Sexuality. Volume 1: An Introduction,* trans. Robert Hurley. New York, 1978.

Frank, Stephen, and M. D. Steinberg, eds. *Cultures in Flux: Lower-Class Values, Practices, and Resistance in Late Imperial Russia.* Princeton, N.J., 1994.

Frankel, Jonathan. *Prophesy and Politics: Socialism, Nationalism, and the Russian Jews, 1862–1917* Cambridge, Mass., 1981.

Freeze, Gregory L. *The Parish Clergy in Nineteenth-Century Russia: Crisis, Reform, Counter-Reform.* Princeton, N.J., 1983.

Friesen, John, ed. *Mennonites in Russia, 1788–1988: Essays in Honour of Gerhard Lohrenz.* Winnipeg, 1989.

Garrett, Clarke. *Spirit Possession and Popular Religion: From the Camisards to the Shakers.* Baltimore, 1987.

Geertz, Clifford. *The Interpretation of Cultures.* New York, 1973.

Gingerich, Owen. "Relations between the Russian Mennonites and the Friends during the Nineteenth Century." *Mennonite Quarterly Review* 25 (1951): 283–95.

Glassie, Henry H. *Pattern in the Material Folk Culture of the Eastern United States.* Philadelphia, 1968.

Greene, Jack P. *Pursuits of Happiness: The Social Development of Early Modern British Colonies and the Formation of American Culture.* Chapel Hill, N.C., 1988.

Greene, Jack P., and J. R. Pole, eds. *Colonial British America: Essays in the New History of the Early Modern Era.* Baltimore, 1984.

Gutsche, W. *Westliche Quellen des russischen Stundismus. Anfaenge der evangelischen Bewegung in Russland.* Kassel, 1956.

Haberer, Erich. *Jews and Revolution in Nineteenth-Century Russia.* Cambridge, 1995.

Heier, Edmund. *Religious Schism in the Russian Aristocracy 1860-1900: Radstockism and Pashkovism.* The Hague, 1970.

Hempton, David. *The Religion of the People: Methodism and Popular Religion c.1750–1900.* London, 1996.

Herlihy, Patricia. "The South Ukraine as an Economic Region in the Nineteenth Century." In *Ukrainian Economic History: Interpretive Essays,* ed. I. S. Koropeckyj. Cambridge, Mass., 1991.

Hill, Christopher. *The World Turned Upside Down: Radical Ideas during the English Revolution.* New York, 1972.

Istoria evangel'skikh khristian-baptistov v SSSR. Moscow, 1989.

Jelsma, Auke. *Frontiers of the Reformation: Dissidence and Orthodoxy in Sixteenth-Century Europe.* Aldershot, U.K., 1998.

Kabuzan, V. M. *Zaselenie Novorossii (Ekaterinoslavskoi i Khersonskoi goubernii) v 18—pervoi polovine 19 veka (1719–1858 gg.).* Moscow, 1976.

Keller, P. Conrad. *The German Colonies in South Russia, 1804–1904.* In 2 vols. Saskatoon, 1968–72.

Kingston-Mann, Esther, Timothy Mixter, and Jeffrey Burds, eds. *Peasant Economy, Culture, and Politics of European Russia, 1800–1921.* Princeton, N.J., 1991.

Kjaer-Hansen, Kai. *Joseph Rabinowitz and the Messianic Movement.* Edinburgh, 1995.

Klibanov, Alexandr I. *Istoria religioznogo sektantstva v Rossii (60-e gody XIX v.—1917 g.).* Moscow, 1965.

———. *Reformatsionnye dvizhenia v Rossii v XIV—pervoi polovine XVI vv.* Moscow, 1960.

Klier, John. "From Elisavetgrad to Broadway: The Strange Odyssey of Iakov Gordon," in *Extending the Borders of Russian History: Essays in Honor of Alfred J. Rieber,* ed. Marsha Siefert, 113–25. Budapest, 2003.

———. *Imperial Russia's Jewish Question, 1855–1881.* New York, 1995.

———. *Russia Gathers Her Jews: The Origins of the Jewish Question in Russia, 1772–1825.* DeKalb, Ill., 1986.

Klimenko, Mikhail. *Die Anfaenge des Baptismus in Suederussland nach officiellen Documenten.* Erlangen, 1957.

Klippenstein, L. "Religion and Dissent in the Era of Reform: The Russian Stundobaptists, 1858-1884." M.A. thesis, University of Minnesota, 1971.

Knox, Ronald. *Enthusiasm: A Chapter in the History of Religion.* Oxford, 1950.

Kolarz, Walter. *Russia and Her Colonies.* London, 1952.

Kreider, Robert. "The Anabaptist Conception of the Church in the Russian Mennonite Environment, 1789–1870." *Mennonite Quarterly Review* 25 (1951): 5–16.

Kulynych, I. M., and N. V. Kryvets'. *Narysy z istorii nimetskikh kolonii v Ukraini.* Kiev, 1995.

Leshchenko, M. N. *Klasova borot'ba v ukrains'komu seli v epokhu domonopolistychnogo kapitalizmu (60–90–ti rr. XIX st.).* Kiev, 1970.

Levin, Nora. *While Messiah Tarried: Jewish Socialist Movements, 1871–1917.* New York, 1977.

Lincoln, W. Bruce. *The Great Reforms: Autocracy, Bureaucracy, and the Politics of Change in Imperial Russia.* DeKalb, Ill., 1990.

Loboda, M. T. "Krest'ianskoe obshchestvo 'Tainaia druzhina' (t.n. 'Chigirinskii zagovor')." Ph.D. dissertation, Kiev State University, 1974.

Löwe, Heinz-Dietrich. *The Tsars and the Jews: Reform, Reaction, and Anti-Semitism in Imperial Russia, 1772–1917.* New York, 1993.

Luckey, H. *Johann Gerhard Oncken und die Anfaenge des deutschen Baptismus.* Kassel, 1958.

Mack, Phyllis. *Visionary Women: Ecstatic Prophesy in Seventeenth-Century England.* Berkeley, Calif., 1992.

McLoughlin, William G. *Revivals, Awakenings, and Reform: An Essay on Religion and Social Change in America, 1607–1977.* Chicago, 1978.

Marini, Stephen A. *Radical Sects in Revolutionary New England.* Cambridge, Mass., 1982.

Marsh, Rosalind, ed. *Women in Russia and Ukraine.* Cambridge, 1996.

Mazzoni, Cristina. *Saint Hysteria: Neurosis, Mysticism, and Gender in European Culture.* Ithaca, N.Y., 1996.

Miliukov, Pavel. *Ocherki po istorii russkoi kul'tury.* In 4 vols. Paris, 1931.

Mironov, Boris, with Ben Eklof. *A Social History of Imperial Russia, 1700–1917.* Boulder, Colo., 2000.

Moore, Rosemary. *The Light in Their Consciences: The Early Quakers in Britain 1646–1666.* University Park, Pa., 2000.

Narayan, Uma. *Dis-Locating Cultures: Identities, Traditions, and Third-World Feminism.* New York, 1997.

Nesdoly, S. "Evangelical Sectarianism in Russia: A Study of the Stundists, Baptists, Pashkovites, and Evangelical Christians, 1855–1917." Ph.D. dissertation, Queens University, 1971.

Newman, Lois Israel. *Jewish Influence on Christian Reform Movements.* New York, 1925.

Panchenko, Aleksandr A. *Khristovshchina i skopchestvo: fol'klor i traditsionnaia kul'tura russkikh misticheskikh sekt.* Moscow, 2002.

Plokhy, Serhii. *The Cossacks and Religion in Early Modern Ukraine.* New York, 2001.

Poida, Dmitrii P. *Krest'ianskoe dvizhenie na Pravoberezhnoi Ukraine v poreformennyi period (1866–1900 gg.).* Dnepropetrovsk, 1960.

Porter, John. *The Vertical Mosaic: An Analysis of Social Class and Power in Canada.* Toronto, 1965.

Pushkareva, Natalia. *Women in Russian History: From the Tenth to the Twentieth Century,* trans. Eve Levin. Armonk, N.Y., 1997.

Radzinsky, Edvard. *The Rasputin File,* trans. Judson Rosengrant. New York, 2000.

Rempel, David. "The Expropriation of the German Colonists in South Russia during the Great War." *Journal of Modern History* 4 (1932): 49–67.

———. "The Mennonite Colonies in New Russia: A Study of Their Settlement and Economic Development from 1789 to 1914." Ph.D. dissertation, Stanford University, 1933.

———. "The Mennonite Commonwealth in Russia: A Sketch of Its Founding and Endurance, 1789–1919." *Mennonite Quarterly Review* 47 (1973): 259-308, and 48 (1974): 5–54.

Sarychev, Vasilii V. "Sotsial'no-ekonomicheskie i politicheskie aspekty rasprostranenia baptizma v Rossii (evropeiskaia chast', 1860–e–1917 gg.)." Ph.D. dissertation, Iaroslavl' University, 1989.

Savinskii, Sergei N. *Istoria evangel'skikh khristian-baptistov Ukrainy, Rossii, Belarussii (1867–1917).* Saint Petersburg, 1999.

439

——. *Istoria evangel'skikh khristian-baptistov Ukrainy, Rossii, Belorussii. Chast' II {part 2} (1917–1967).* Saint Petersburg, 2001.

——. *Istoria russko-ukrainskogo baptizma: Uchebnoe posobie.* Odessa, 1995.

Sawatsky, Walter. *Soviet Evangelicals since World War II.* Scottdale, Pa., 1981.

Schultz, Theodore W. *Investing in People. The Economics of Population Quality.* Berkeley, Calif., 1981.

Scott, James C. *Domination and the Arts of Resistance: Hidden Transcripts.* New Haven, 1990.

——. *The Moral Economy of the Peasant: Rebellion and Subsistence in Southeast Asia.* New Haven, Conn., 1976.

Scott, Joan Wallach. *Gender and the Politics of History.* New York, 1988.

Shevzov, Vera. "Popular Orthodoxy in Late Imperial Russia." Ph.D. dissertation, Yale University, 1994.

Sirotkina, Irina. *Diagnosing Literary Genius: A Cultural History of Psychiatry in Russia, 1880–1930.* Baltimore, 2002.

Solzhenitsyn, Alexander I. *Dvesti let vmeste (1795–1995): Part 1.* Moscow, 2001.

Spufford, Margaret, ed. *The World of the Rural Dissenters, 1520–1725.* Cambridge, Mass., 1995.

Steffens, Lincoln. *Moses in Red: The Revolt of Israel as a Typical Revolution.* Philadelphia, 1926.

Stein, Stephen J. *The Shaker Experience in America: A History of the United Society of Believers.* New Haven, Conn., 1992.

Stumpp, K. *The Emigration from Germany to Russia in the Years 1763 to 1862.* Lincoln, Neb., 1973.

Suydam, Mary A., and Joanna E. Ziegler, eds. *Performance and Transformation: New Approaches to Late Medieval Spirituality.* New York, 1999.

Svetlenko, Sergei I. *Revoliutsionno-narodnicheskoe dvizhenie 70-kh godov XIX veka na Ukraine v vosponinaniiakh sovremennikov.* Dnepropetrovsk, 1990.

Taves, Ann. *Fits, Trances, and Visions: Experiencing Religion and Explaining Experience from Wesley to James.* Princeton, N.J., 1999.

Thomas, Keith. *Religion and the Decline of Magic.* New York, 1971.

Thompson, E. P. *The Making of the English Working Class.* London, 1963.

——. "The Moral Economy of the English Crowd in the Eighteenth Century." *Past and Present,* no. 50 (1971): 76–136.

Thompson, Ewa M. *Understanding Russia: The Holy Fool in Russian Culture.* Lanham, Md., 1987.

Tolles, Frederick B. *Meeting House and Counting House: The Quaker Merchants of Colonial Philadelphia, 1682–1763.* Chapel Hill, N.C., 1948.

Troeltsch, Ernst. *The Social Teaching of the Christian Churches,* trans. Olive Wyon. In 2 vols. New York, 1931.

Turner, Frederick Jackson. *The Frontier in American History,* ed. Wilbur R. Jacobs. Tucson, 1986.

Turner, Victor W. *Process, Performance and Pilgrimage. A Study in Comparative Symbology.* New Delhi, 1979.

——. *The Ritual Process: Structure and Anti-Structure.* Chicago, 1969.

Urry, James. *None but Saints: Transformation of Mennonite Life in Russia, 1789–1889.* Winnipeg, 1989.

———. "'Servants from Far': Mennonites and the Pan-Evangelical Impulse in Early Nineteenth-Century Russia." *Mennonite Quarterly Review* 67 (April 1987): 213–27.

Vasianovich, V. F. "Sel'skokhoziaistvennyi proletariat Iuzhnoi Ukrainy nakanune i v perios pervoi russkoi burzhuazno-demokraticheskoi revoliutsia." Ph.D. dissertation, Dnepropetrovsk University, 1975.

Versluis, Arthur. *Wisdom's Children: A Christian Esoteric Tradition.* Albany, N.Y., 1999.

Vsesoiuznyi Sovet Evangel'skikh Khristian-Baptistov. *Istoria evangel'skikh khristian-baptistov v SSSR.* Moscow, 1989.

Wagner, William L. *New Move Forward in Europe: Growth Patterns of German Speaking Baptists in Europe.* South Pasadena, Calif., 1978.

Wallace, Anthony F. C. "Revitalization Movements." *American Anthropologist* 38 (April 1956): 264–81.

Wallerstein, Immanuel. *The Modern World-System: Capitalist Agriculture and the Origin of the European World-Economy in the 16th Century.* New York, 1974.

———. *The Modern World-System: Mercantilism and the Consolidation of the European World-Economy, 1600–1750.* New York, 1980.

———. *The Modern World-System: The Second Era of Great Expansion of the Capitalist World-Economy, 1730–1840s.* San Diego, Calif., 1989.

Walzer, Michael. *Exodus and Revolution.* New York, 1985.

Ward, Keith. *Religion and Community.* Oxford, 2000.

Wardin, Albert W., Jr., ed. *Evangelical Sectarianism in the Russian Empire and the USSR: A Bibliographic Guide.* Lanham, Md., 1995.

Wcislo, Frank W. *Reforming Rural Russia: State, Local Society, and National Politics, 1855–1914.* Princeton, N.J., 1990.

Weber, Max. *The Protestant Ethic and the Spirit of Capitalism,* trans. Talcott Parsons. New York, 1930.

———. *The Sociology of Religion,* trans. Ephraim Fischoff, with an introduction by Talcott Parsons. London, 1965 (1st pr., 1963).

Williams, George Huntston. *The Radical Reformation.* Philadelphia, 1962.

Wilson, Bryan R. *The Social Dimensions of Sectarianism: Sects and New Religious Movements in Contemporary Society.* Oxford, 1990.

Wortman, Richard. *Scenarios of Power: Myth and Ceremony in Russian Monarchy—Volume 1: From Peter the Great to the Death of Nicholas I.* Princeton, N.J., 1995.

Zhuk, Sergei I. "'La tradition hebraique': les Puritans, les Calvinistes hollandiase et le debut de l'ambivalence des Juifs dans l'Amerique britannique coloniale." *Les Chretiens et les Juifs dans les societes de rites grec et latin. Approche comparative. Textes reunis M. Dmitriev, D. Tollet et E. Teiro.* Paris: Honore Champion, 2003, 123–64.

———. "Leveling of the Extremes: Soviet and Post-Soviet Historiography of Early American History." In *Images of America: Through the European Looking-Glass,* ed. William L. Chew III. Brussels, 1997, 63–78.

———. "Max Weber et l'histoire des religions: 'la sociologie weberienne de la religion' est-elle productive pour l'historiographie contemporaine?" *Etre catholique—Etre orthodoxe—Etre protestant: Confessions et identities culturelles en Europe medievale et moderne. Etudes reunites et publies par Marek Derwich et Mikhail. Dmitriev.* Wroclaw: LARHCOR, 2003, 39–64.

———. "Nemetskaia diaspora 18 veka i kolonizatsia Dneprovskogo regiona Ukrainy: Theoreticheskie aspecty sotsiokul'turnoi istorii." In *Voprosy germanskoi istorii,* ed. S. I. Bobyliova. Dniepropetrovsk, 1995, 16–29.

———. "Rannia Amerika: Sotsiokul'turnaia preemstvennost' i 'proryv v Utopiiu.'" In *Annual Studies of America 1992.* Moscow, 1993, 16–31.

Zhuk, Sergei I., and Jeffrey Brooks. "Sovremennaia amerikanskaia istoriografia o krest'ianstve poreformennoi Rossii." *Voprosy istorii,* no. 1 (2001): 151–59.

Zipperstein, Steven J. "Heresy, Apostasy, and the Transformation of Joseph Rabinovich." *Jewish Apostasy in the Modern World,* ed. Todd M. Endelman. New York, 1987.

Index

443

Index

Chernosvistova, Tatiana Markarovna (Remizova), 2
Chertkov, V., 306
Chigirin Affair, 331–48, 350
children and castration, 279–80
"chiliasm of the defeated and hopeless," 63, 80
"chiliastic optimism of oppressed," 63
Christ, reincarnation of. *See* reincarnation of Christ
"Christ-Faith" tradition: and first studies in religious historiography, 14–15; liturgy of, 128; and millenarianism, 106; and Molokans, 107; oral tradition in, 107; outlawing of, 101; Shalaputs as combination of Christ-Faith with other elements, 123–29; successors of, 398. *See also* Khlysty (Khristovshchina)
Christian Millennium to Bolshevik Utopia, 397–403
Chubarev, S., 333
churches, architectural style of, 326
church hierarchy: challenges by religious radicals to, 184; contrasted with authority of individual, 239; dual system of power in communities, 282, 297; and female authority, 282–83; rejection of, 9, 186–87; among Shalaputs, 123
Church of Apostle Agreement, 116
"circular space" of locality, 268
clergy: alienation from Russian-speaking, 59; and bribery, 65–66; corrupt clergy and conflicts between peasants and priests, 64–75; inadequacy of Orthodox, 4; minister's role in Baptist rules and rituals, 174; minister's role in Stundo-Baptist movement, 180; rejection of hierarchy of, 186–87; rejection of rituals of, 104; and Ukrainian peasants, 57
clothing and peasant identity, 276–77, 327
Cohn, Norman, 18
coitus interruptus, 287, 289–90
collectivism, 5, 54
colonization, emancipation, and religious radicalism on Southern Russian frontier, 33–96; corrupt clergy and conflicts between peasants and priests, 64–75; economic, social, and cultural causes of religious awakening, 75–80; economic instability and dispossession of peasants, 59–64; ethnicity and demography, 36–40, 405–23; German colonization, 40–52; models and theories of colonization, 33–36; Ukrainian

(Little Russian) peasant as distinctive cultural type, 52–59
Communal (Obshchaia) sect, 108
communal village system in Ukraine, 54, 62
communion rituals, 128
Communism, 324–25, 384, 402
Cossacks: and colonization of Southern Russian frontier, 42, 79, 397, 398; and demography of Southern Russian frontier, 37; and Gaidamatchina, 343, 344, 376, 384; and military expedition model of colonization, 35; and pluralistic society of Southern Russian frontier, 34; population data of, 405–28; removal of Ukrainian, 40; and sects, 102, 109; tradition of freedom of, 53, 58
Creole cultures, 35–36, 45
criminal case of Feodosii Chepurnoi and Stepan Shutenko, 331–48
cults, laws on religious, 402
cultural aliens, 63, 343
"cultural configurations" for future colonial society, 34
"cultural landmarks," disruption of, 267
cultural war against religious dissenters, 3
"culture of written word," 399–400

Dakhnova, Maria, 102, 104
dancing in religious services: and Khlysty and Skoptsy, 15; and Maliovannyi, 244–45; and Marianovtsy, 127; and Mennonite revivalists, 158; religious dance epidemics, 286; and Shakers, 135; and Shalaputs, 16, 125, 128, 135, 285; and spiritual ecstasy, 15, 285–86; and Stundists, 238; and Ukrainian Stundists, 184. *See also* ecstatic practices; religious enthusiasm; spirit possession
Debagorii-Mokrievich, Vladimir, 57, 333
Deich, Lev, 333, 334, 349, 350
demons, struggling with, 118
Dereviankina, Elisaveta, 294
Descent of Holy Spirit, 184–85
dislocated identity, 60, 62–63
dissent. *See* religious dissent
dissidents: anti-dissident campaigns and practices, 5, 401–2; and anti-Orthodox peasants, 165; asceticism and sexual practices, 15, 16;

Index

448

Index

449

Maliovantsy (*continued*): social justice, 400–401; free spiritual love, 296–98; as group of religious dissenters, 16; and millenarianism, 12, 245, 246–50, 252, 253, 254, 265, 276–77, 296–98; and peasant identity, 274, 276–77; and popular oppositional discourse, 80, 399; population of, 256–57; and prophetesses, 299–300; radical Stundists, Maliovantsy, and Tolstoyans in search of Millennium, 363–84; revival spiritualist mystical trend, 169–70; and Russian radical reformation, 12, 398; and sexuality, 124, 286, 296–302; and Shalaputs, 139; and spiritual love, 295–97; women as leaders, 298, 301–2

Maliuk, Kuz'ma, 298

Mannheim, Karl, 63

map of South Provinces of Russian Empire, *xiii*

Marianovtsy: Duplii description of, 138; female authority in, 282–83; and imminence of divine presence, 99; origin of, 115–16; and peasant identity, 269–70; and sacred performances, 132; and Shalaputs, 16; theology and rituals of, 126–28. *See also* Timofeieva, Marianna (Mariamna) Stepanovna

Marina, a prophetess, 254–55

marriage: rejection and experimentation, 266, 267; and women, 292. *See also* sexuality; women

Marx, Karl, 355

maternity, cult of, 300

Mather, Increase, 133–34

Matrionovtsy, 283

meetinghouses, 326

Melamed, Vladimir I., 362

Mel'nikov, Pavel, 124

Mennonite Brethren Church, 159, 160, 161, 162, 163, 178–79

Mennonites, 54; and colonization, 35, 41, 42, 45–50, 80, 397, 398; and demography of Southern Russian frontier, 38; dialogue with Russian religious dissidents, 37; evangelical awakening among colonies, 155–60; honesty and work ethic of, 48–49; Jumpers, 135, 159–60, 161, 162, 398; Mennonite-Shalaput Revival and beginning of Ukrainian Stundism, 160–63; as pacifists, 257; population data on, 405–28; Pryguny and Molokan Phase of Shala-

puts movement and collaboration with, 107–17; and Radical Reformation, 11; relationship to Stundism, 8; role in modernization of frontier, 46–47; and schools, 226; and Shakers, 135; and Shalaputs, 100, 101, 139; and Stundists, 9, 273

mental institutions, incarceration of spirit-possessed, 130, 131, 245–46, 256

Methodists, 99, 113, 128, 133, 134, 136, 181

Mikhalevich, Afanasii, 355

military expedition model of colonization, 34–35, 398

millenarianism, 363–84; and castration, 106; and charismatic model of colonization, 35; and dissident Ukrainian peasants, 370; as dream of dispossessed peasants, 12–13, 302; and Likhosherstaia, 332–33; and Lutheran Pietists, 156; and Maliovantsy, 12, 245, 246–50, 252, 253, 254, 265, 276–77, 296–98; and Mennonites, 156, 158; and negative attitude toward traditional married norms, 296; nuptial imagery, 300–301; peasants' dream of social justice and equality, 5; primary concern of, 321; among radical Molokans, 114; and radical social transition, 18; sacred theater of, 255; and Shalaputs, 118, 124, 265–66, 277–81; spirit possession and divine reincarnation in anticipation of Millennium, 129–36; and spiritualist trend of Russian radical reformation, 399; and Ukrainian Stundism, 178

Milukov, Pavel N., 7

minister, role of, 180

Missionary Review, 325, 364

Mokshin, Vasilii Fedorovich, *141*

Molchanovskii, Vasilii, 66

Moldavskii, Victor, 66

Molokans: and castration, 106; and charismatic model of colonization, 35; and communal property, 107; and demography of Southern Russian frontier, 37; and enthusiastic Mennonites, 161; idealization of tsar by, 323; and loyalty oath, 275; meeting in St. Petersburg, 330; and millenarianism, 114; population data of, 405–28; and Pryguny Phase of Shalaput movement and collaboration with Mennonites, 107–17; rejection of sacraments and ceremonies by, 175, 176;

Index

454

Index

455

Stundists (*continued*): categories of, 212; and "Chigirin Affair," 331–48; derivation of name of, 4; development of, 11–12, 17, 164–71, 398, 399; evangelical awakening among German and Mennonite colonies, 155–60; "German-Stundist threat" in Orthodox propaganda, 322–31; guidance of Holy Ghost and rejection of Church institutions by, 178–79; hatred against, 401; institutionalization of Stundo-Baptist movement, 180–81; and Jews, 350–53; and Kherson province, 164–71; and Khilkov, 367; and land ownership, 364; lifestyle of, 214–22; meetinghouses of, 326; and millenarianism, 321, 363–84; as new oppositional religious movement, 80; opposition to Orthodox Church, 364–65; and peasants, 14, 64, 210–27, 276, 370; and popular oppositional discourse, 399; population data of, 6, 7, 177–78, 405–28; and present day evangelicals, 5–6; and radicalism of "Chaplinka Creed," 181–87; as rationalist sect, 16; and rejection of conventional family norms and gender roles, 266; rejection of tsar, 323; religious influence of, 117; religious practices of "radical Stundists," 181–87; rituals of, 59; role of minister, 174, 186–87; role of retired soldiers in, 213; and sexuality, 293, 400; and Shalaputs, 139; and Southern Russian frontier, 34; and Topilovka, 338–40, 349; use of term, 169–70; and women, 305–6, 308. *See also* Ukrainian Stundists

Stundo-Baptists, *186, 187;* development of, 172–78, 398, 399; and education, 226; institutionalization of movement, 180–81; lifestyle of, 221–22; and peasant identity, 275–76; praise for, 214; and revolutionaries, 352; women, 303–8

Stundo-Khlysty, 12, 16. *See also* Maliovantsy

Stundo-Shalaputs, 237–62, 321, 399. *See also* Maliovantsy

"subsistence ethic," 19–20

symbols, 18

Syrokvasha, Filimon, 130–31

systematic theology and Western Reformation, 400

Tambov Postniks, 2

technology and Mennonites, 46, 47

Tereshchuk, Kliment, 172

Thompson, E. P., 50, 63, 268

Tikhaia, Marina, 299–300, 301

Timofeieva, Marianna (Mariamna) Stepanovna, 115–16, 126, 283, 301

Tkachiov, Lev, 366–67

Tkachiov, Philip, 366–67

Todosienko, Moisei, 255, 374–79, 381, 384

Tolstoy, Leo, 14, 357, 363–64, 365, 369

Tolstoyans: agricultural community in New York, 358; and communist principles, 355; and evangelical movement of Ukrainian peasants, 352; and exposure of persecution, 306; periodical of, 271; and schools, 226; in search of Millennium, 363–84; and Stundo-Baptists, 258

transubstantiation, sacred drama of, 286

Tregubov, Mikhail, 336

tsar: anti-tsarist attitudes, 365–66; idealization of, 323; loyalty to, 331; peasant rebellion in name of, 331–48

Tsenkovsky, Vladmir, 355

Tsyba, Sergiy, 118

Tsybul'skii, Pavel, 172

Tsymbal, Efim, 173

Turner, Frederick Jackson, 34

Turner, Victor, 18–19, 123

Tyshkevich, Iosif, 172

Ukrainian (Little Russian) peasants, *60;* and colonization of Southern Russian frontier, 398; discovery of new social identity among, 267–77; as distinctive cultural type, 52–59, *60;* and pluralistic society of Southern Russian frontier, 34. *See also* peasants

Ukrainian Orthodox Church, 13

Ukrainian Stundists, *216, 217;* anti-tsarist attitudes, 366; and classification of dissenter groups, 17; development of, 9, 11, 155–56, 160–63, 170–71, 398; discovery of new social identity among, 267–77; German influence on, 17, 328; and Gordin, 354–55; leaders of, 171; meeting in St. Petersburg, 330; and Millenarianism, 12; new center of, 168; population of, 8, 169, 177; as positive movement, 213, 215–16; propaganda among, 356; and Protestant ethic, 12;